EXCEPTIONAL INDIVIDUALS IN FOCUS

SEVENTH EDITION

J. M. BLACKBOURN
The University of Mississippi

JAMES R. PATTON
Austin, Texas

AUDREY TRAINOR
Austin, Texas

PEARSON

Merrill
Prentice Hall

Upper Saddle River, New Jersey
Columbus, Ohio

Library of Congress Cataloging-in-Publication Data

Blackbourn, J. M.
  Exceptional individuals in focus / J. M. Blackbourn, James R. Patton, Audrey Trainor.—
7th ed.
    p. cm.
  Previous edition lists James R. Patton as first author.
  ISBN 0-13-113491-4
  1. Special education—United States.   2. Children with disabilities—Education—
United States.   I. Patton, James R.   II. Trainor, Audrey.   III. Title.
    LC3981.P38 2004
    371.9′0973—dc21

                                                                    2003013920

Vice President and Publisher: Jeffery W. Johnston
Editor: Allyson P. Sharp
Editorial Assistant: Kathleen S. Burk
Production Editor: Sheryl Glicker Langner
Production Coordinator: Karen Ettinger,
   The GTS Companies/York, PA Campus
Design Coordinator: Diane C. Lorenzo

Photo Coordinator: Sandy Schaefer
Cover Designer: Jeff Vanik
Cover art: Superstock
Production Manager: Laura Messerly
Director of Marketing: Ann Castel Davis
Marketing Manager: Amy June
Marketing Coordinator: Tyra Poole

This book was set in ITC Bookman by The GTS Companies/York, PA Campus. It was
printed and bound by R. R. Donnelley & Sons Company. The cover was printed by The
Lehigh Press, Inc.

Photo Credits: Tom Watson/Merrill, pp. 2, 138; Todd Yarrington/Merrill, pp. 24, 100;
Anthony Magnacca/Merrill, pp. 46, 66; Scott Cunningham/Merrill, pp. 82, 180, 290; David
Grossman/PH College, p. 120; Rhoda Sidney/PH College, p. 162; Laima Druskis/PH
College, pp. 196, 238; Barbara Schwartz/Merrill, p. 212; Anne Vega/Merrill, p. 256.

Pearson Education Ltd.
Pearson Education Singapore Pte. Ltd.
Pearson Education Canada, Ltd.
Pearson Education—Japan

Pearson Education Australia Pty. Limited
Pearson Education North Asia Ltd.
Pearson Educación de Mexico, S.A. de C.V.
Pearson Education Malaysia Pte. Ltd.

PEARSON
Merrill
Prentice Hall

10 9 8 7 6 5 4 3 2
ISBN: 0-13-113491-4

To Dr. Donald M. Baer (1931–2002)
Roy A. Roberts Distinguished Professor of Psychology
Department of Human Development and Family Life
University of Kansas

Psychologist, Philosopher, Scientist, Writer, Teacher,
Colleague, Role Model, and Friend

To Dr. Virgil S. Ward
Professor Emeritus
University of Virginia
A Gifted Friend and Supporter

Educator Learning Center: An Invaluable Online Resource

Merrill Education and the Association for Supervision and Curriculum Development (ASCD) invite you to take advantage of a new online resource, one that provides access to the top research and proven strategies associated with ASCD and Merrill—the Educator Learning Center. At **www.EducatorLearningCenter.com** you will find resources that will enhance your students' understanding of course topics and of current educational issues, in addition to being invaluable for further research.

How the Educator Learning Center will help your students become better teachers

With the combined resources of Merrill Education and ASCD, you and your students will find a wealth of tools and materials to better prepare them for the classroom.

Research
- More than 600 articles from the ASCD journal *Educational Leadership* discuss everyday issues faced by practicing teachers.
- A direct link on the site to Research Navigator™ gives students access to many of the leading education journals, as well as extensive content detailing the research process.
- Excerpts from Merrill Education texts give your students insights on important topics of instructional methods, diverse populations, assessment, classroom management, technology, and refining classroom practice.

Classroom Practice
- Hundreds of lesson plans and teaching strategies are categorized by content area and age range.
- Case studies and classroom video footage provide virtual field experience for student reflection.
- Computer simulations and other electronic tools keep your students abreast of today's classrooms and current technologies.

Look into the value of Educator Learning Center yourself

Preview the value of this educational environment by visiting **www.EducatorLearningCenter.com** and clicking on "Demo." For a free 4-month subscription to the Educator Learning Center in conjunction with this text, simply contact your Merrill/Prentice Hall sales representative.

Preface

People who work with exceptional individuals sometimes convey the impression that life is always serious and tragic. Stressing the sorrows that arise for individuals with disabilities, these people tend to overlook the joys and rewards in the fields of human services and education. Moreover, professors in teacher training institutions so often preoccupy themselves with statistical data and basic facts that they neglect to give students a "feel" for exceptional people and what it is like to work with them. Thus, the unknowing may get the erroneous impression that working in these fields will be dry and tedious or, even worse, full of sadness.

We have found that working with exceptional children, youth, and adults is exciting, engaging, and uniquely rewarding. Despite occasional "down" moments, it is a world of joy and delightful communication. When working with exceptional persons, one's perspective becomes very important. We can mourn because a rosebush has thorns or rejoice because a thornbush has roses. Those who cannot see the joy and humor in life's struggles will soon find that the thorns drain their enthusiasm and strength to endure the difficult periods.

Shortly after undertaking the writing of this book, we looked up from our professional journals full of confusing definitions, elaborate theories, conflicting results, and current controversies. We suddenly realized we had fallen into the same trap as many others in attempting to teach students about exceptional individuals. We had blindly missed the essence of our field. Our preoccupation with academic analysis had distracted us from viewing the emotional side of our work. We had forgotten the joy of watching a child with a physical disability take her first steps, an adolescent with mental retardation get his first job, or a child with a behavior disorder bring his temper under control. We had even forgotten about the bad times—our disappointment when an elementary student with a learning disability returned from summer vacation having lost much that he had worked so hard to learn; our agony when we held down a self-destructive child with emotional disturbance; and our anxiety as we told desperate parents about the lack of local adult services for their daughter who was about to finish school.

If we, as professionals in special education and human services, do not project the joys as well as the pains of working with exceptional people, we are not projecting reality. If students enroll in an introductory course about exceptional people and they only learn how many times a child with Down's syndrome rocks during lunchtime, the frequency of thumb sucks of a student with a severe disability, or the number of head bangs exhibited by a child with serious emotional disturbance, then it is no wonder that individuals with disabilities are thought to be odd. And it is no wonder that those of us working with people with disabilities are also considered a little crazy. It is imperative that we stress that exceptional individuals are just like the rest of us and should be included in ongoing events of everyday life—whether that be in a school setting, the workplace, or community.

Our message is simple: The fields of human services and education are exciting and vibrantly alive. Rather than permitting dry academic commentary, nit-picking detail, and only sorrowful emotional experiences to dominate introductions to exceptionality, basic courses should impart a flavor of the personal joy of dealing with exceptional people.

However, we are worried about misinformation and misconceptions concerning exceptional individuals. Please note that we consider exceptionality to apply to people whose physical traits, mental characteristics, psychological abilities, and/or observable behaviors are significantly different from the majority of any given population. This deviation can be in either direction and includes giftedness. Our concern derives from the fact that misinformation and misconceptions can have a profound effect on the attitudes of the general public and therefore influence interpersonal relations and public policy.

With these ideas in mind, we have pushed aside traditional academic format and customary formalities in an attempt to provide you with a light, enjoyable reading experience. You need not take copious notes or scrutinize the print; just sit back, gather some basic information, and share with us the joys of working with exceptional people.

ACKNOWLEDGMENTS

We are extremely grateful to our colleagues who have been part of the "Focus" family since the first edition and whose contributions have made this book so very special. Former coauthors include Jim Payne, Jim Kauffman, Gweneth Brown, Richard DeMott, Ruth Ann Payne, and Kathleen S. Fad. We are particularly thankful to Jim Payne (teacher, scholar, writer, entertainer, consultant . . . car salesman) for being instrumental in getting this family project going from the beginning.

We also want to thank Dr. Virgil S. Ward, who gave us helpful comments regarding giftedness, and Ed Polloway and Dave Smith, who shared some of their experiences with us. We are very appreciative of those reviewers who validated the goals we set for this edition: Manuel Barrera, University of Minnesota, Duluth; Donald R. Clerico, Charleston Southern University; Nancy Mamlin, Appalachian State University; and Joyce Strand, University of Minnesota, Duluth. Also, a special thanks to Peggy Sneed and Mary Kellum for their logistical support with the final steps in the development process for the seventh edition. We are also very fortunate to be working with some wonderful folks at Merrill/Prentice Hall Education. We appreciate the support, assistance, and patience (as usual) that Allyson Sharp and Kathy Burk showed us during the development of this book. We are also grateful for the assistance provided by Karen Ettinger at The GTS Companies in guiding this manuscript through the production process.

A final acknowledgement must be given to the individual to whom the seventh edition of *Exceptional Individuals in Focus* is dedicated. Our collective experience with Dr. Don Baer extends over 25+ years. Don was an inspiration to several generations of special educators, developmental psychologists, and behavior analysts. The extent (which was prodigious) and quality (which was exemplary) of his professional work set him far apart from others in our field. Don was the consummate professional, balancing the three components of professional life (research, teaching, and service) in an elegant manner. His leadership in establishing a philosophical foundation for the field of behavior analysis, his emphasis on a research agenda emphasizing functional application of behavioral principles and developing a technology of behavior, his demand for strong empirical proof, his undying defense of academic freedom, and the generosity and kindness he showed to students and colleagues alike will remain as the legacy he has bequeathed to us.

J. M. B.

J. R. P.

A. T.

Discover the Companion Website Accompanying This Book

THE PRENTICE HALL COMPANION WEBSITE: A VIRTUAL LEARNING ENVIRONMENT

Technology is a constantly growing and changing aspect of our field that is creating a need for content and resources. To address this emerging need, Prentice Hall has developed an online learning environment for students and professors alike—Companion Websites—to support our textbooks.

In creating a Companion Website, our goal is to build on and enhance what the textbook already offers. For this reason, the content for each user-friendly website is organized by topic and provides the professor and student with a variety of meaningful resources. Common features of a Companion Website include:

For the Professor—

Every Companion Website integrates **Syllabus Manager™**, an online syllabus creation and management utility.

- **Syllabus Manager™** provides you, the instructor, with an easy, step-by-step process to create and revise syllabi, with direct links into Companion Website and other online content without having to learn HTML.
- Students may logon to your syllabus during any study session. All they need to know is the web address for the Companion Website and the password you've assigned to your syllabus.
- After you have created a syllabus using **Syllabus Manager™**, students may enter the syllabus for their course section from any point in the Companion Website.
- Clicking on a date, the student is shown the list of activities for the assignment. The activities for each assignment are linked directly to actual content, saving time for students.
- Adding assignments consists of clicking on the desired due date, then filling in the details of the assignment—name of the assignment, instructions, and whether or not it is a one-time or repeating assignment.

- In addition, links to other activities can be created easily. If the activity is online, a URL can be entered in the space provided, and it will be linked automatically in the final syllabus.
- Your completed syllabus is hosted on our servers, allowing convenient updates from any computer on the Internet. Changes you make to your syllabus are immediately available to your students at their next logon.

For the Student—

- **Overview** and **General Information**—General information about the topic and how it will be covered in the website.
- **Web Links**—A variety of websites related to topic areas.
- **Content Methods and Strategies**—Resources that help to put theories into practice in the special education classroom.
- **Reflective Questions** and **Case-Based Activities**—Put concepts into action, participate in activities, examine strategies, and more.
- **National and State Laws**—An online guide to how federal and state laws affect your special education classroom.
- **Behavior Management**—An online guide to help you manage behaviors in the special education classroom.
- **Message Board**—Virtual bulletin board to post and respond to questions and comments from a national audience.

To take advantage of these and other resources, please visit the *Exceptional Individuals in Focus,* Seventh Edition, Companion Website at

www.prenhall.com/blackbourn

Brief Contents

Contents

PART ONE
LEARNING AND BEHAVIORAL DISORDERS   45

CHAPTER 3
Learning Disabilities   46

CHAPTER 4
Attention Deficit/Hyperactivity Disorder   66

CHAPTER 5
Emotional/Behavioral Disorders   *82*

CHAPTER 6
Mental Retardation   *100*

CHAPTER 9
Blindness and Low Vision

PART THREE

CHAPTER 1

Introduction to Exceptionality

A citizen advocate captured the essence of the paradox that many individuals with disabilities struggle against on a daily basis:

> It seems funny and ironic . . . that most people spend an exorbitant amount of time trying to distinguish themselves as unique and different while all that a person with a disability wants is to be just like everyone else.

The other day the little 4-year-old girl from next door came over and watched me rake leaves. For over 30 minutes she watched and then, out of the blue, said, "My daddy has a glass eye."

Well, how do you respond to that? Since I didn't know what to say or do, I just kept on raking the leaves and said, "Oh."

She continued, "Yeah, he really does, but I don't understand it. He can't see any better with it in than he can with it out."

Most people would agree that there's humor in the innocence of that 4-year-old's statement. It's funny to me, it's probably funny to you, and it was certainly funny to my one-eyed neighbor. Thank goodness we can occasionally share a laugh about a circumstance that involves an unfortunate condition.

DEFINITIONAL PERSPECTIVE

The title of this book and the table of contents indicate that we will be examining certain types of exceptionality. In so doing, two problems arise: First, what exactly makes one exceptional; and second, how does one select only a few topics from a potential vast array of choices? This chapter is designed to answer these two questions as well as provide a backdrop for approaching all of the other chapters in the book.

As the citizen advocate's statement suggests, individuals who are different in some way often have to struggle to be treated like others. This is not to say that persons who are exceptional in some way do not want to have an individuality of their own. The message is that for too long *difference* has meant different treatment rather than understanding, acceptance, and inclusion. What is desirable is a scenario in which we can celebrate difference in a context of acceptance and support.

Nature of Exceptionality

A generally accepted international, federal, provincial, or state definition of *exceptionality* does not exist. The notion of exceptionality suggests something that is noticeably different. Sometimes, the term is misinterpreted to mean above average only, as reflected in the Dear Abby letter in Figure 1.1. In addition to reprimanding the letter writer, Abby's response addresses the narrow definition of exceptionality that is often associated with the term *exceptionality*.

Dear Abby

Reader Takes Exception To Use of 'Exceptional'

By Abigail Van Buren

DEAR ABBY: You recently published a letter from the mother of a Mongoloid child in which she refers to him as "exceptional" and "special." I must thank you for printing such letters, since they always give me a good laugh.

Imagine having the gall to use words describing excellence, superiority and noteworthiness in reference to people with mental and physical deficiencies.

I can hardly wait for a SWAT team to discover that their "special weapons" are slingshots, or to hear of the shock of a teacher who has been refused tenure as a result of his or her "exceptional" work in the field of education.

—WILLIAM G. ANDERSON JR.

DEAR MR. ANDERSON: My Webster's New Collegiate Dictionary defines "exceptional" as "forming an exception: rare." Also "better than average" and "BELOW average."

And "special" is defined as "that which is distinguished by some unusual quality; being other than usual; unique."

I am always pleased when a reader "gets a good laugh" from something in my column, but the letter I published about the Down Syndrome (please, not "Mongoloid") child was not meant to be amusing. Furthermore, what gives you a good laugh strikes me as being FUNNY—meaning "different from the ordinary." And more than a little cruel.

Figure 1.1
Source: Taken from the DEAR ABBY column by Abigail Van Buren. © UNIVERSAL PRESS SYNDICATE. Reprinted with permission. All rights reserved.

The concept of exceptionality, as used in this book, includes the ideas expressed in the Dear Abby response and adds some additional features that relate to diversity in general.

Exceptionality refers to individuals, including children, youth, and adults, whose behaviors, features, and/or situations deviate from the norm to such an extent that special needs are present and certain services and/or supports may be warranted.

Although this perspective provides a guide for understanding exceptionality, it also has some inherent problems. First, how does one determine what the norm is in a society where normal is hard to define? Norms are influenced significantly by factors such as culture and context. This is an obvious problem with a condition like behavior disorders where culture and context are key defining factors. Second, how much deviation is needed to make one exceptional? For many conditions addressed in this book, arbitrary criteria have been developed for eligibility purposes. Third, must one require services to be considered exceptional? It is very possible for a person to have special needs but not require services or supports or only require such interventions for a limited amount of time. These are legitimate concerns and, unfortunately, they do not lead to easy solutions. However, if the above definition can be considered a general guide that does not lead immediately to eligibility criteria, then it can serve as a global way of considering those individuals who fit the concept of exceptionality.

Terminology

This section on terminology addresses four major topics. First, an attempt to clarify the difference between the terms *disability* and *handicap* is undertaken. Second, a discussion of "person-first" language is presented. Third, we provide a brief discussion of what is meant by the term *at risk*. Lastly, a primer on frequently used acronyms and initialisms is provided.

A considerable amount of confusion and misapplication continues regarding the use of the terms *disability* and *handicap*. Currently, the term *disability* is the preferred terminology, and most professional and advocacy groups support its usage. However, use of the term *handicap* is still quite prevalent in the popular media (e.g., headlines using the term *handicap*), professional literature (e.g., visual handicap), and public policies (e.g., signage for handicapped parking).

The two terms do have different meanings. *Disability* is a general term that describes any temporary or long-term reduction of a person's activity or ability as a result of an acute or chronic condition. *Handicap* refers to the additional negative burden placed by society on an individual through barriers affecting areas such as access, transportation, and attitude. Ramsey (cited in Orlansky & Heward, 1981) provides a good example of how this plays out in reality:

> Take a man who has been a carpenter for twenty years. He's skilled. He belongs to a union. One day on the job, he hacks off several fingers on his right hand. At that point, he has a disability, because everyone else has ten fingers and he doesn't. Now he probably would still be able to do carpentry work. He may have to do it a little bit different from before. It becomes a handicapping condition when, let's say, the labor union to which he belongs says, "Hey, man, we can't keep you on any more because the insurance will not cover you, and you are a risk. We feel like you can't do the work any more, because you don't have all ten fingers." At that point in time, his disability has become a handicapping condition. (p. 166)

New contemporary terminology has emerged in recent times. Phrasing such as *physically challenged* or *mentally challenged* is being used much more frequently. Other terms such as *differently abled* are becoming more commonplace in the professional literature and popular media. The general feeling is that these terms are more acceptable (i.e., less offensive) than the other options.

The current convention when referring to individuals with disabilities is to use *person-first language*. Although this notion definitely falls under the category of political correctness, the value of doing so supersedes any seeming awkwardness that might arise. This stylistic convention stresses that, for an individual with a disability, attention should be directed first to the person him- or herself and second to the disabling condition. Therefore, the phrase "student with a mental retardation" is preferred over "mentally retarded student." As can be seen in the latter expression, emphasis is on the condition rather than the person. Note that even knowledgeable people will lapse back into the older convention from time to time, and the older phrasing will appear in materials that were published before a few years ago. Furthermore, the use of the term *handicap* will occur when referring to various historical print resources or events such as early legislation. Nevertheless, person-first language should be used at all times in all current contexts.

In an effort to expand our coverage of the concept of exceptionality, we have introduced a new chapter (Chapter 13) on individuals who are "at risk" in this edition of the book. The discussion of individuals who are at risk focuses most directly on children and youth; however, many of the identified issues apply to adults as well. It is important to provide a general sense of what is meant by the term *at risk* to demonstrate how it relates to the notion of exceptionality. The concept presented in Chapter 13 espouses the idea that children and youth are *placed at risk*. This definitional perspective stresses that the source of ongoing problems/ issues is more situational rather than a result of factors *within* the student. Children and youth placed at risk can be considered individuals who are in situations that can lead to academic and behavioral problems that could limit their success in school and later in life. The principal feature implied by this description, as it relates to exceptionality, is that these individuals are in circumstances that deviate from the norm in some significant way and that may require certain services or supports.

The field of human services, including special education, rehabilitation, and social work, is prone to use shortcuts regarding commonly used terms, resulting in a plethora of acronyms and initialisms that only insiders might recognize. To assist the person new to the field of human services, a list of common acronyms and initialisms is provided in Table 1.1. This particular list is not exhaustive but does include many of the most frequently used expressions.

Exceptionality in the Context of Diversity

A discussion about the merits or problems of specifically identifying individuals as having some type of exceptionality continues. Without question, strong arguments for and against labeling can be made. Nevertheless, most systems in operation today that involve individuals who are exceptional rely on the use of different categories of disability or superior abilities.

It is possible, however, to conceptualize exceptionality in the context of a more general notion of diversity. Although diversity includes areas such as culture, ethnicity, religion, gender, and sexual orientation, the notion of diversity also relates closely to all of areas of exceptionality, as defined previously. Figure 1.2 depicts the different areas of diversity, along with the ones that receive the most attention in this book.

On a day-to-day basis, categorical systems are used in regard to individuals who differ in some noticeable way from the norm. Disabling conditions and their

Table 1.1

Commonly Used Acronyms and Initialisms

Term	Meaning	Term	Meaning
AAC	alternative and augmentative communication	LD	learning disability
ADA	Americans with Disabilities Act	LDA	Learning Disabilities Association
ADHD	attention deficit/hyperactivity disorder	LEA	local education agency
ADL	activities of daily living	LEP	limited English proficiency
ASL	American Sign Language	LRE	least restrictive environment
AT	assistive technology	MR	mental retardation
BD	behavior disorder	NCD	National Council on Disability
CA	chronological age	O&M	orientation & mobility
CAPD	central auditory processing disorder	OHI	other health impairment
CBI	community-based instruction	OI	orthopedic impairment
CCTV	closed-circuit television	OSERS	Office of Special Education and Rehabilitative Services
CEC	Council for Exceptional Children		
CNS	central nervous system	OT	occupational therapist
DD	developmental disability/developmental disorder/developmental delay	PBS	positive behavioral supports
		PD	physical disability
DOE	Department of Education	PDD	pervasive developmental disorder
DSM	Diagnostic and Statistical Manual of Mental Disorders	PHI	physical and health impairments
		PL	public law
ED	emotional disturbance	PT	physical therapist
EHA	Education of the Handicapped Act	RID	Registry of Interpreters of the Deaf
EI	early intervention	RS	related services
ESL	English as a Second Language	SCI	spinal cord injury
FAPE	free, appropriate public education	SEA	state education agency
FBA	functional behavior assessment	SES	socioeconomic status
GT	gifted and talented	SLI	speech/language impairment
HH	hard of hearing	SLP	speech/language pathologist
HI	hearing impairment	SPED	special education
IDEA	Individuals with Disabilities Education Act	TBI	traumatic brain injury
IEP	individualized education program	TDD	telecommunication device for the deaf
IFSP	individualized family service plan	VI	visual impairment
IPE	individual plan for employment	VR	vocational rehabilitation
ITP	individual transition plan		

resulting nomenclature used in schools are based on federal or state statutes. The terminology used to describe disabling conditions in adult settings may change, depending on locale and agency involvement. Various ways to subcategorize giftedness are discussed in Chapter 12.

A way to organize the areas of diversity covered in Chapters 3 to 12 of this book is based on the areas of functioning that are the primary areas affected (see Figure 1.3). One must not overlook the fact that a person may have secondary problems in other areas as well and that some individuals (e.g., those with various pervasive developmental disorders) have needs of such scope that they cut across all areas of functioning. Children and youth placed at risk may, and often do, have problems and challenges in these areas of functioning, as will be discussed in Chapter 13.

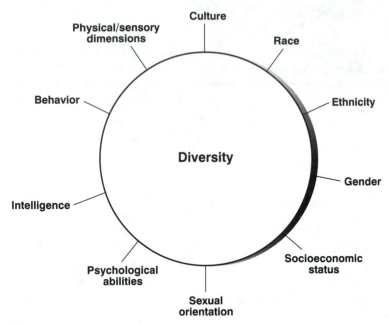

Figure 1.2
Dimensions of Diversity

	Areas of Functioning		
Learning	**Socioemotional**	**Communication**	**Physical (Motor, Vision, Health)**
mental retardation	emotional/behavior disorders	speech/language disorders	orthopedic/physical impairments
learning disabilities	social maladjustment	hearing impairments	health impairments
attention deficit/ hyperactivity disorder			traumatic brain injury
			visual impairments
← autism, pervasive developmental disorders →			
← gifted →			

Figure 1.3
Categorical Distinctions by Area of Functioning

It is also noteworthy to point out that each area of exceptionality covered in this book represents a heterogeneous group of individuals. Within any of the areas, much variation exists. With this in mind, caution must be exercised in discussing characteristics of a general nature; that is, one must not overgeneralize a set of characteristics to everyone within a given category.

Disability Statistics

Quantifying the extent of exceptionality is not an easy task. In discussing the number of individuals with various types of disabilities, we must examine two different data sources: school-based data and adult data. In regard to individuals who are placed at risk, many different sources must be consulted. In this section, we focus only on the data available for individuals with disabilities.

School-Age Statistics.   The most complete source of data on students with disabilities is the *Annual Report of Congress* published by the Department of Education (2001). The 23rd Annual Report published in 2001 provided the statistics shown in Table 1.2 on students ages 6 to 21 identified as needing special and/or related services for the school year 1999–2000. The third column indicates the percentage of change in these numbers since the 1990–1991 school year—these values reflect positive increases for all relevant categories. The extraordinary increase in numbers for the category of "other health impaired" is due in great part to the inclusion of students with attention deficit/hyperactivity disorder in this category, a

Table 1.2

Categories of Disability (IDEA) and Corresponding Numbers of Students for Students Ages 6–21 Served in the 1999–2000 School Year and Percentage Change Since 1990–1991

Specific learning disabilities	2,871,966	34.0%
Speech or language impairments	1,089,964	10.3
Mental retardation	614,433	11.4
Emotional disturbance	470,111	20.3
Other health impairments	254,110	351.0
Multiple disabilities	112,993	15.7
Hearing impairments	71,671	21.0
Orthopedic impairments	71,422	44.8
Autism	65,424	*
Visual impairments	26,590	12.3
Developmental delay	19,304	*
Traumatic brain injury	13,874	*
Deaf–blindness	1,845	21.1
TOTAL	**5,638,707**	**30.3**

*Data did not exist at an earlier point.
Source: From *To Assure the Free Appropriate Public Education of All Children with Disabilities: Twenty-Third Annual Report to Congress on the Implementation of the Individuals with Disabilities Act* (p. II-23), by U.S. Department of Education, 2001, Washington, DC: Author.

change that occurred in the early 1990s. When the ages 0 to 2 and 3 to 5 groups of children with special needs are added to this figure, the number of children and youth served is 6,477,776. The figures presented for students ages 6 through 21 represent approximately 8.3 percent of the population of all children and youth in this age group.

Adult Statistics.   Although the school-based figures are subject to error for a variety of reasons (e.g., interstate variation for determining eligibility), it is even more difficult to determine the number of adults who have disabilities. It is an obvious fact that, as people age, the reality of disability becomes an inevitability for most people.

One useful resource for getting a picture of disability in adulthood is the findings of the "Survey of Income and Program Participation (SIPP)" sponsored by the U.S. Bureau of Census. The data were analyzed by the Bureau of Census and the Centers for Disease Control and Prevention and published in the *Morbidity and Mortality Weekly Report* (McNeil & Bineete, 2001). The findings indicate that in 1999, 41 million adults reported having a disability (22 percent of the adults age 18 and older who were surveyed). Table 1.3 shows selected conditions that were identified as the main cause of the disability.

A number of observations can be made based on the two data sets presented in Tables 1.2 and 1.3. First, it is obvious that the adult data reflect the reality that as people get older, they acquire any number of physical and/or heath conditions that require services or supports. Second, the data do not represent an upward extension of the school-identified population. It is safe to say that many individuals with learning disabilities or emotional/behavior disorders are not being picked up in the adult studies of disability. Third, the disability statistics for adults must be examined with caution given the nature of disability in adulthood. In other words, some conditions that lead to recognition during school become more difficult to detect in adulthood settings, even though their impact on a person's life may be significant. It might be suggested that the categorical distortions between the school data and adult data are very much a function of the nature of adult services that determine eligibility as well as the ways the data are collected.

Disablism

Many people in our society, who are exceptional in some way, are treated differently by members of the community. This results most frequently by being perceived in a less than favorable way. All of the categories of exceptionality covered in this book are vulnerable to devalued treatment.

A concept that provides a framework for measuring mistreatment is *disablism.* The original term, *handicapism,* promoted by Bogdan and Biklen (1977) is revised herein in light of current preferred usage. Similar to *racism, sexism,* and *ageism, disablism* results in mistaken beliefs (stereotyping); irrational, preconceived opinions (prejudice); and ill treatment (discrimination) on the part of individuals or society in a more widespread sense. Bogdan and Biklen defined *handicapism* as "a

Table 1.3

Number* and Percentage of Civilian Noninstitutionalized Persons Aged ≥ 18 Years with Disabilities Reporting Selected Conditions as the Main[†] Cause of the Disability—Survey of Income and Program Participation, United States, 1999

Main Condition	All Persons		
	No.	(%)	(95% CI[‡])
Arthritis or rheumatism	7,207	17.5	(±1.1)
Back or spine problem	6,780	16.5	(±1.0)
Heart trouble/hardening of the arteries	3,209	7.8	(±0.8)
Lung or respiratory problem	1,931	4.7	(±0.6)
Deafness or hearing problem	1,794	4.4	(±0.6)
Limb/extremity stiffness	1,747	4.2	(±0.6)
Mental or emotional problem	1,541	3.7	(±0.5)
Diabetes	1,399	3.4	(±0.5)
Blindness or vision problem	1,361	3.3	(±0.5)
Stroke	1,160	2.8	(±0.5)
Broken bone/fracture	885	2.1	(±0.4)
Mental retardation	827	2.0	(±0.4)
Cancer	792	1.9	(±0.4)
High blood pressure	692	1.7	(±0.4)
Head or spinal cord injury	452	1.1	(±0.3)
Learning disability	408	1.0	(±0.3)
Alzheimer's disease/senility/dementia	354	0.9	(±0.3)
Kidney problems	348	0.8	(±0.3)
Paralysis	310	0.8	(±0.3)
Missing limbs	299	0.7	(±0.2)
Stomach/digestive problems	279	0.7	(±0.2)
Epilepsy	217	0.5	(±0.2)
Alcohol or drug problem	210	0.5	(±0.2)
Hernia or rupture	210	0.5	(±0.2)
AIDS or AIDS-related condition	132	0.3	(±0.2)
Cerebral palsy	141	0.3	(±0.2)
Tumor/cyst/growth	116	0.3	(±0.2)
Speech disorder	101	0.2	(±0.1)
Thyroid problems	77	0.2	(±0.1)
Other	6,188	15.0	(±1.0)
Total	41,168	100.0	

*In thousands.

[†]Persons who reported difficulty with functional limitations (except vision, hearing, or speech), activities of daily living, instrumental activities of daily living, the inability to do housework or the inability to work at a job or business identified the "main" cause and up to two other causes of the disability from a list of 30 conditions.

[‡]Confidence interval.

Source: From "Prevalence of Disabilities and Associated Health Conditions Among Adults—United States, 1999," by J. M. McNeil and J. Bineete, 2001, *Morbidity and Mortality Weekly Report, 50*(7), pp. 120–125.

set of assumptions and practices that promote the differential and unequal treatment of people because of apparent or assumed physical, mental, or behavioral differences" (p. 59). The following is an example of how disablism works:

Stereotyping:	Viewing adults with mental retardation as childlike.
Prejudice:	Leading to the belief that they are incapable of being responsible for their own behaviors.
Discrimination:	Resulting in these adults being denied certain privileges (e.g., getting a library card).

Disablism can be manifested in many different ways. On a personal level, it can be displayed in avoidance behavior on the part of the person who is not disabled or by telling tasteless jokes that target people with disabilities. On a societal level, disablism can be seen in regulatory policies and practices such as in the examples of stereotyping, prejudice, and discrimination listed above. It can also be seen in the way individuals who are exceptional are portrayed in the media. From poster children used for fund-raising purposes to characters in motion pictures, ample evidence of disablist images abounds.

The portrayal of individuals who are exceptional in motion pictures is voluminous. As a matter of fact, 14 motion pictures that have won academy awards for best picture, best actor, or best actress have included characters who were disabled (Safran, 2001). The portrayals have ranged from disablist (e.g., *Dr. Strangelove, Young Frankenstein*) to inaccurate (e.g., *Charley, Molly*) to extremely realistic and well done (e.g., *My Left Foot, A Beautiful Mind*). Table 1.4 contains a sampling of many motion pictures that have significant characters who are exceptional or that address issues related to exceptionality. Entries in the table include information about the type of disability portrayed by one or more of the characters. Note that the films depicted in the table represent positive as well as negative character portrayals.

BACKGROUND INFORMATION

This section of the chapter addresses two key topics that are germane to the study of individuals who are exceptional. The first topic is about how the philosophy of service delivery has changed over time. In a world of thumbnail sketches and pictures, it can be considered a thumbnail piece on noteworthy historical changes. The second topic includes a brief introduction to the major legislation that has had a pronounced effect on individuals with exceptionalities.

Changes in Service Delivery

Service delivery to individuals who have disabilities has changed dramatically over the years. The various orientations to service delivery discussed in this section can

Table 1.4
Motion Pictures with Characters Who Are Disabled or Gifted

Title	Disability of Key Character	Title	Disability of Key Character
At First Sight	VI	Miracle Worker, The	VI, HI
As Good As It Gets	E/BD; OHI	Moby Dick	PD
Awakenings	E/BD	Mr. Holland's Opus	HI
Bad Boy Buddy	E/BD	My Left Foot	PD
Beautiful Mind, A	GT; E/BD	Nell	ASD
Bedlam	MR	Of Mice and Men	MR
Being There	MR	One Flew Over the Cuckoo's Nest	E/BD
Benny and Joon	E/BD	Ordinary People	E/BD
Best Boy	MR	Other Side of the Mountain	PD
Blackboard Jungle	AR	Other Sister, The	MR
Born on the Fourth of July	PD	Passion Fish	PD
Butterflies Are Free	VI	Patch of Blue, A	VI
Camille Claudel	E/BD	Philadelphia	OHI
Charley	MR	Piano, The	HI
Children of a Lesser God	HI	Places in the Heart	VI
Coming Home	PD	Powder	GT
Dancer in the Dark	VI	Rainman	ASD
Dominick and Eugene	MR	Regarding Henry	TBI
Dr. Strangelove	PD	Rudy	LD
Dream Team	E/BD	Scent of a Woman	VI
Edward Scissorhands	PD	Searching for Bobby Fischer	GT
Elephant Man, The	PD	See No Evil, Hear No Evil	VI
Fisher King	E/BD	Shine	GT
Forest Gump	MR	Sling Blade	MR
Gaby: A True Story	PD	Sneakers	VI
Good Will Hunting	GT	Stand and Deliver	AR
Hand That Rocks the Cradle, The	MR	Steel Magnolias	OHI
Heart Is a Lonely Hunter, The	HI	Sybil	E/BD
I Am Sam	MR	Terms of Endearment	OHI
I Never Promised You a Rose Garden	E/BD	There's Something About Mary	MR
If You Could See What I Hear	VI	Tim	MR
King of Hearts	E/BD	Tin Man	HI
King of the Jungle	MR	To Kill a Mockingbird	MR
La Strada	MR	To Sir With Love	AR
Last Picture Show, The	MR	Wait Until Dark	VI
Little Man Tate	GT	Whatever Happened to Baby Jane	PD
Lorenzo's Oil	OHI	What's Eating Gilbert Grape	PD, MR
Man Without a Face, The	PD	Young Frankenstein	PD
Mask	VI, HI	Zelly and Me	E/BD

Key: AR, at risk; ASD, autism spectrum disorder; E/BD, emotional/behavior disorder/psychiatric issue; GT, gifted and talented; HI, hearing impairment; LD, learning disability; MR, mental retardation; OHI, other health impaired; PD, physical disability; TBI, traumatic brain injury; VI, visual impairment.

be organized into three distinct phases, as depicted in Figure 1.4. All of the different orientations to providing services discussed below evolved with the best interest of individuals with exceptional needs in mind; however, over time, professional thinking and community attitudes have changed, reflecting a more progressive philosophy that centers on personal empowerment.

The first definable approach involved the use of some type of private or public facility as the primary venue for providing services. Characterized by institutional placements, sheltered employment, separate special schools, and totally segregated classes, the thrust was to remove the person or student and take him or her to a segregated setting where centralized services were located.

This first orientation, although still much in existence in some parts of the United States and many parts of the world, evolved into a services-based orientation. In this model, individuals might be pulled from the mainstream of society or general education, but an effort at integration (i.e., physical proximity) was made. This approach to service delivery could be seen in deinstitutionalization, transitional sheltered workshops, resource rooms, and self-contained classes in the neighborhood schools.

The current orientation to service delivery is characterized as inclusive and supports based. This approach advocates inclusion in the community and at school, accompanied by requisite supports, when needed, to assist and maintain the individual in these environments. Terms such as *supported employment, supported living,* and *inclusive education* are commonly heard these days. The difference between physical integration associated with a services-based paradigm and inclusion, which is being promoted now, is that the latter concept implies a degree of acceptance and sense that the persons are part of the "community" in which they find themselves. This orientation also values and underscores the importance of self-determination and empowerment, which are discussed later in this chapter.

Legislative Mandates

Legislation has played a major role in guaranteeing the rights and addressing the needs of individuals who are exceptional. Many pieces of legislation have contributed, and continue to contribute, to the outcomes noted above, including the Developmental Disabilities Assistance and Bill of Rights Act of 1990 (PL 101–496), the Carl D. Perkins Vocational and Applied Technology Education Act of 1990

Figure 1.4
Paradigm Shifts in Service Delivery

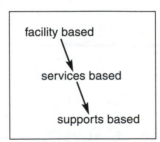

(PL 101–392), the Jacob K. Javits Gifted and Talented Students Act of 1988 (PL 100–297) (reauthorized in 1994), and the recently enacted No Child Left Behind Act (PL 107–110). However, three federal laws stand out and arguably have had the greatest impact on individuals with exceptional needs: Individuals with Disabilities Education Act (IDEA), Section 504 of the Vocational Rehabilitation Act, and Americans with Disabilities Act (ADA). These three laws are discussed briefly below and highlighted for comparison purposes in Table 1.5 on pages 16 and 17.

Individuals with Disabilities Education Act (IDEA).   IDEA is the most recent reauthorization of the original Education of All Handicapped Children's Act (EHA), signed into law in 1975 as PL 94–142. Since 1975, this law has been reauthorized four times (1983, 1986, 1990, 1997), with each set of amendments having significant effects on the education of students with disabilities. When EHA was reauthorized in 1990 (PL 105–47), the name of the law changed to its current title. Also at that time, two additional disabling conditions (autism and traumatic brain injury) were added resulting in 13 categories, as listed earlier in Table 1.2. Although attention deficit/hyperactivity disorder was not added as a specified disabling condition in the 1990 reauthorization, it was recognized as a disability under the category of "Other Health Impaired," as substantiated by a policy memorandum from the U.S. Department of Education in 1991.

The major provision of IDEA is that all students, ages 3 through 21, who have disabilities and who need special education and/or related services, are entitled to a free, appropriate public education in the least restrictive environment. Incentives exist for serving young children ages 0 to 2, and all states are providing such services. Key features of IDEA, along with a short description of what they mean, are listed in Table 1.6 on page 18. The various programs and services associated with IDEA are covered in the next chapter.

Section 504 of the Vocational Rehabilitation Act.   In 1973, amendments to the Vocational Rehabilitation Act (PL 93–112) were enacted. This law was most recently amended as the Rehabilitation Act Amendments of 1992 (PL 102–569). Section 504 of this act is really a broad civil rights law that has become the "bill of rights for people with disabilities" by ensuring that individuals with disabilities could not be discriminated against, particularly in the areas of education and employment. The legislation specifically protects any individual who has a physical or mental impairment that limits one or more major life activities, who has a record of such an impairment, or who is regarded as having such an impairment. Major life activities include, but are not limited to, areas such as caring for one's self, performing manual tasks, walking, seeing, hearing, speaking, breathing, learning, and working.

The significance of this legislation continues to this day. It should be noted that, as Table 1.5 highlights, Section 504 only applies to programs, agencies, or organizations that receive federal financial assistance. However, given that most educational settings receive federal dollars in some fashion, the reach of this law is extensive. The next chapter highlights how this particular legislation applies to students with special needs who are in education settings.

Table 1.5
Comparison of IDEA, Section 504, and ADA

	The IDEA	Section 504	The ADA
Mission	To provide a free, appropriate public education (FAPE) in the least restrictive environment.	To provide persons with disabilities, to the maximum extent possible, the opportunity to be fully integrated into mainstream American life.	To provide all persons with disabilities broader coverage than Section 504 in all aspects of discrimination law.
Scope	Applies to public schools.	Applies to any program or activity that is receiving federal financial assistance.	Applies to public or private employment, transportation, accommodations, and telecommunications, regardless of whether federal funding is received.
Coverage	Only those who are educationally disabled, in that they require special education services, ages 3–21 years.	All qualified persons with disabilities, regardless of whether special education services are required in public elementary, secondary, or postsecondary settings.	All qualified persons with disabilities, and qualified nondisabled persons related to or associated with a person with a disability.
Disability Defined	A listing of disabilities is provided in the act, including specific learning disabilities.	No listing of disabilities is provided, but inclusionary criteria of any physical or mental impairment that substantially limits one or more life activities, having a record of such an impairment, or being retarded as having an impairment.	No listing of disabilities provided. Same criteria as found in Section 504. HIV status and contagious and noncontagious diseases recently included.
Identification Process	Responsibility of school district to identify through "Child Find" and evaluate at no expense to parent or individual.	Responsibility of individual with the disability to self-identify and to provide documentation. Cost of the evaluation must be assumed by the individual, not the institution.	Same as Section 504.

	IDEA	Section 504	ADA
Service Delivery	Special education services and auxiliary aids must be mandated by Child Study Team and stipulated by the Individual Education Program.	Services, auxiliary aids, and academic adjustments may be provided in the general education setting. Arranged for by the special education coordinator or disabled student services provider.	Services, auxiliary aids, and accommodations arranged for by the ADA coordinator. Requires that accommodations do not pose an "undue hardship" to employers.
Funding	Federal funds are conditional to compliance with IDEA regulations.	No authorization for funding attached to this civil rights statute.	Same as Section 504.
Enforcement Agency	Office of Special Education and Rehabilitative Services in U.S. Department of Education.	The Office for Civil Rights (OCR) in the U.S. Department of Education.	Primarily the U.S. Department of Justice, in conjunction with the Equal Employment Opportunity Commission and Federal Communications Commission. May overlap with OCR.
Remedies	Reimbursement by district of school-related expenses is available to parents of children with disabilities to ensure a FAPE.	A private individual may sue a recipient of federal financial assistance to ensure compliance with Section 504.	Same as Section 504 with monetary damages up to $50,000 for the first violation. Attorney fees and litigation expenses are also recoverable.

Source: Adapted with permission of the *Section 504 Compliance Handbook*. © Thompson Publishing Group, Inc., (800) 677-3789.

Table 1.6

Key Components of the Individuals with Disabilities Education Act

Provisions	Description
Least restrictive environment	Children with disabilities are educated with nondisabled children as much as possible.
Individualized education program	All children served in special education must have an individualized education program (IEP).
Due-process rights	Children and their parents must be involved in decisions about special education.
Due-process hearing	Parents and schools can request an impartial hearing if there is a conflict over special education services.
Nondiscriminatory assessment	Students must be given a comprehensive assessment that is nondiscriminatory in nature.
Related services	Schools must provide related services, such as physical therapy, counseling, and transportation, if needed.
Free appropriate public education	The primary requirement of IDEA is the provision of a free appropriate public education to all school-age children with disabilities.
Mediation	Parents have a right, if they choose, to have a qualified mediator attempt to resolve differences with the school. Using mediation should not deny or delay a parent's request for a due-process hearing.
Transfer of rights	When the student reaches the age of majority, as defined by the state, the school shall notify both the parents and the student and transfer all rights of the parents to the child.
Discipline	A child with a disability cannot be expelled or suspended for 10 or more cumulative days in a school year without a manifest determination as to whether the child's disability is related to the inappropriate behavior.
State assessments	Children with disabilities must be included in districtwide and statewide assessment programs with appropriate accommodations. Alternative assessment programs must be developed for children who cannot participate in districtwide or statewide assessment programs.
Transition	Transition planning and program development begin when students with disabilties reach age 14.

From Smith, T., Polloway, E., Patton, J., Dowdy, C. *Teaching Students with Special Needs In Inclusive Settings,* 2/e © 2001. Published by Allyn and Bacon, Boston, MA. Copyright © 2001 by Pearson Education. Reprinted by permission of the publisher.

Americans with Disabilities Act (ADA). Considered to be the most important piece of civil rights legislation to be enacted since the Civil Rights Act of 1964, the ADA provides similar protections for and opportunities to individuals with disabilities. The law was enacted in 1990 (PL 101–336) and has provided protections for adults with disabilities in a wide range of settings, particularly in the workplace. The scope of the law extends to both public and private settings, and affects employment, public services, transportation, public accommodations (e.g., restaurants), and telecommunications. Although some concern has arisen regarding how much of an impact this law has made on the lives of persons with disabilities and some criticism has arisen from certain employers, the intent of the law is well founded, and it continues to receive support from the public. In fact, according to a Harris poll conducted in 1999, 90 percent of adults who have heard of the ADA support it (Talyor, 1999).

RECURRENT THEMES

Certain themes are woven throughout this book. They represent prevailing trends that are noticeable in the field of human exceptionality today. It is our opinion that these topics should guide our thinking as we begin to look more closely at the specific categorical areas that follow.

Inclusion

The intent of inclusion, as discussed previously, is for individuals who are different to be welcomed, accepted, and encouraged to participate as equal members of a group—whether the setting is the school, the workplace, or the community. The following inclusionary practices are preludes to more elaborate coverage of these ideas throughout the book:

School-based inclusion practices:
- Educating students with disabilities in general education classrooms
- Creating opportunities for students with disabilities to make friends with students who are not disabled
- Allowing students with disabilities to participate in all facets of school life
- Providing needed supports to students so they can be successful in general education settings
- Teaching general education students about disabilities and individual differences
- Emphasizing that differences enrich us all

Workplace-based inclusion practices:
- Preparing for and placing workers with exceptional needs in competitive work situations
- Welcoming and supporting newly hired workers who have disabilities
- Providing needed supports to workers so they can be successful in the work setting

❏ Educating coworkers about disabilities and how to become supports for their fellow workers who have special needs
❏ Allowing workers with disabilities to participate in all facets of the workplace (e.g., lunch, breaks, company functions)
❏ Educating employers about ADA

Community-based inclusion practices:

❏ Creating opportunities for adults who have disabilities to participate with those who do not have disabilities
❏ Educating the public about disabilities and individual differences and providing opportunities for interaction
❏ Encouraging friendships between adults with disabilities and others who are not disabled
❏ Ensuring that adults with disabilities are involved in age-appropriate activities

Self-Determination and Empowerment

Many professionals and parents realize that it is in the best interests of those with disabilities to be more in charge of their lives and better prepared to make decisions about their own lives. Concerted efforts have been made to teach skills related to self-determination, thus empowering these persons to be more in control of their lives.

According to Wehmeyer (1993), self-determination refers to "the attitudes and abilities necessary to act as the primary causal agent in one's life, and to make choices and decisions regarding one's quality of life free from undue external influence or interference" (p. 6). In this definition, attitudes correspond to the personal beliefs and perceptions one has of oneself as well as the degree of control one has in a given environment. Abilities relate to the skills and proficiencies that are needed to be able to act as the causal agent in one's life.

In addition to having the self-confidence and skills to make decisions about one's life, it is equally important to have options from which to choose. The following excerpt from a position paper on self-determination developed by The Arc of Texas (1995) illustrates this point:

> *Integral to the notion of self-determination and choice is the necessity of having options. If there is only one option presented, there is no real choice. Choice requires personally meaningful options, access to information about the choices, and the skills and experiences to make responsible decisions.* (p. 1)

Multicultural Considerations

In a pluralistic society where linguistic and cultural diversity is the norm, it is critically important that exceptionality always be considered in the context of a person's language and culture. From an educational perspective, school personnel must be sensitive to a student's values and background. Such an understanding must guide assessment, curriculum, management, and instruction. Without question, it is often very difficult to determine the needs of a student whose language is not English and whose culture differs from what is expected at school.

Multidisciplinary Nature of Exceptionality

Given the range of needs that are demonstrated by individuals who are exceptional, many different professionals may be involved in working with such individuals. These professions include the following:

❏ *Medicine and Allied Health:* neonatologists, pediatricians, neurologists, geneticists, psychiatrists, pharmacists, physical therapists, occupational therapists, speech/language pathologists, audiologists, and school nurses
❏ *Psychology:* school psychologists, clinical psychologists, psychometrists, child mental health specialists, and art and music therapists
❏ *Social Work:* school social workers, medical social workers, and case managers
❏ *Education/Training:* general educators, special educators, vocational educators, correctional educators, transition specialists, assistive technology specialists, behavior specialists, school guidance counselors, employment specialists/job coaches, vocational rehabilitation counselors, vocational evaluators, and recreation therapists

With such an array of professionals potentially involved in the day-to-day lives of persons with exceptional needs, it is essential that collaborative working relationships develop and continue over time.

Technological Applications

Technology has had a significant impact on individuals with exceptional needs. From low-tech devices like tape recorders to more sophisticated computer-based communication systems, technology, in general, has improved the quality of life of many individuals. In regard to the use of the Internet, a recent Harris poll (Talyor, 2000) found that the Internet "allows adults with disabilities to be better informed, more connected to the world around them, and puts them in touch with people who have similar interests and experiences" (p. 1).

Family Considerations

The impact of a disability on a family is tremendous—physically, emotionally, and financially. Family involvement has changed over the years from a passive role to one of encouragement to participate much more actively. From IDEA's emphasis on parent participation in their child's programs, particularly as a key member of the individualized education program (IEP) team, to the reality that parents may be the only case manager for their adult child, a need to get families involved has emerged.

A change can also be noticed in that professionals are now focusing on families rather than on parents only. The needs of siblings and extended family members have been identified as critical elements of working with families. Much like the individual, families may need varying levels and durations of support in coping with a member of their family who has a disability. The importance of family issues in the context of exceptionality promulgated us to include a new chapter (Chapter 15) dedicated to this topic.

Life-Span Perspective

The field of human exceptionality has been somewhat forced to expand its focus beyond the issues of childhood and adolescence. The significant number of adults who have disabilities, as presented in Table 1.3, creates a great need to look at disability from a life-span perspective. Even for those disability areas that do not have large identifiable groups in adulthood, increased professional interest can be detected.

The main motivation of studying exceptionality across the life span is that disability that manifests in childhood in most cases does not disappear with the onset of young adulthood. Moreover, ample evidence exists to indicate that the incidence of many disabling conditions is a function of age, particularly middle age and older. A great need now exists to study how various normative and nonnormative events in a person's life affect the daily functioning of those with exceptional needs.

It is important to stress that the issues of adulthood are vastly different from those of childhood. With this in mind, it is understandable that models of intervention used with children and youth are typically not appropriate for adults. If one studies adults with disabilities, then one must be sensitive to the complexities of adulthood.

FINAL THOUGHTS

As indicated in the preface to this book, our approach to human exceptionality is a personal one. The many personal vignettes that begin each of the following chapters are evidence of this. By sharing these stories that either we or our closest colleagues have experienced, we want to give the reader a "feel" for people who are exceptional and what it is like to work with them.

PONDER THESE

1. In your opinion, what arguments for and against the continuation of annual telethons, such as the one for muscular dystrophy that is held every Labor Day weekend, can you suggest?
2. Why do you suppose federal legislation has played such an important role historically in the provision of services to individuals with exceptional needs?
3. What are some technological applications that we encounter everyday that have special usefulness to individuals with certain physical or sensory needs?

REFERENCES

The Arc of Texas (1995). *Self determination* [*Position paper*]. Austin, TX: Author.

Bogdan, R., & Biklen, D. (1977). Handicapism. *Social Policy, 7*(5), 59–63.

McNeil, J. M., & Bineete, J. (2001). Prevalence of disabilities and associated health conditions among adults—United States, 1999. *Morbidity and Mortality Weekly Report, 50*(7), 120–125.

Orlansky, M. D., & Heward, W. L. (1981). *Voices: Interviews with handicapped people.* Upper Saddle River, NJ: Merrill/Prentice Hall.

Safran, S. P. (2001). Movie images of disability and war: Framing history and political ideology. *Remedial and Special Education, 22,* 223–232.

Smith, T. E. C., Polloway, E. A., Patton, J. R., & Dowdy, C. (2004). *Teaching students with special needs in inclusive settings* (4th ed.). Boston: Allyn & Bacon.

Talyor, H. (1999). Overwhelming majority of Americans continue to support the Americans with Disabilities Act [Harris Poll #30]. Retrieved May 12, 1999, from Harris Interactive website.

Talyor, H. (2000). How the Internet is improving the lives of Americans with disabilities. [Harris Poll #30]. Retrieved June 7, 2000, from Harris Interactive Web site.

U.S. Department of Education. (2001). *To assure the free appropriate public education of all children with disabilities: Twenty-third annual report to Congress on the implementation of the Individuals with Disabilities Act.* Washington, DC: Author.

Wehmeyer, M. (1993). Self-determination as an educational outcome. *Impact, 6*(4), 16–17, 26.

CHAPTER **2**

Programs and Services

This chapter focuses on specific programs and services that exist for addressing the needs of individuals with exceptional needs by expanding on some of the key topics initially presented in Chapter 1. Note that specific services that attend to the issues of gifted students and those children and youth placed at risk will be discussed in their respective chapters. The primary orientation of this chapter is on programs and services provided to children, youth, and adults with disabilities. Particular emphasis is given to the educational mandates of IDEA and Section 504.

The first part of the chapter highlights general programs and services to individuals with special needs from a life-span perspective. The second major section examines how services are typically delivered to school-age populations. The last section discusses topics related to the delivery of services in school settings.

NATURE AND TYPES OF SERVICES ACROSS THE LIFE SPAN

Programs and services available to individuals and their families vary noticeably across the life span. This section provides a primer on many of the most important services, most of which will be revisited in subsequent chapters. A more elaborate explanation of school-based services is undertaken in the next section of this chapter.

Infants and Toddlers

Early intervention (EI) represents a coordinated system of services that are available for young children, birth to age 3, who have disabilities or delays. Provided through federal funds (Part C of IDEA) and state funds, EI provides needed assistance to families who must deal with the real issues of having an infant and toddler with special needs.

Eligibility for services varies from state to state. However, in most cases, an infant or toddler who has a medically diagnosed condition (e.g., cerebral palsy) or developmental delay in the areas of cognition, motor, communication, socioemotional, or self-help will qualify for services. In some states, such as Texas, a third category, atypical development (e.g., inappropriate affective development), may be considered as well.

The general goal of IE is to provide needed supports to families and to minimize or prevent future problems of the child. A few of the special features of EI include the following:

❏ Family-centered philosophy, with parents being important team members and attention given to all family members
❏ Specific services and therapies implemented based on family and child needs (see Table 2.1)
❏ Services provided in natural environments (i.e., where families live, learn, and play)
❏ Services provided at no cost to families, regardless of income level
❏ Services provided in the family's native language

Table 2.1
Examples of Early Intervention Services

- Assistive technology—services and devices
- Audiological services
- Family counseling
- Medical services
- Nursing services
- Nutrition services
- Occupational therapy
- Physical therapy
- Psychological services
- Service coordination
- Social work services
- Special instruction
- Speech/language services
- Vision services

❏ Service coordination provided to all families, allowing for a single point of contact for families, providing assurance that the individualized family service plan (see below) is implemented properly, and assisting families in accessing needed community services/resources

❏ Transition planning provided to maintain needed services when IE is no longer available

The individualized family service plan (IFSP) serves as a guide for providing requisite early intervention services. The intent of the IFSP is to focus on the family unit and to support the natural caregiving role of families. Many of the components of the IFSP are similar to those of the individualized education program (IEP) (presented later in the chapter); however, several important differences exist. For example, the goals in the IFSP are called *outcome statements,* not *annual goals* as in the IEP. These statements reflect changes that families want to see for their child and for themselves. As a result, one of the most important differences between the two types of plans is that the outcome statements of the IFSP are family centered rather than child focused.

Early Childhood

When young children with special needs reach the age of 3, they must qualify for special education and/or related services under a different system related to IDEA (Part B). Simply stated, these young children must be determined eligible under the more school-related provisions of IDEA. Interestingly, some students served under EI will not qualify for services under the different eligibility criteria used for this age group. This is particularly true for many children who were served through EI primarily for communication difficulties.

Some families decide not to place their children in early childhood special education programs, even when they qualify, preferring to have their son or daughter in a private child care setting. Some families will pay for private services on their own. Similarly, some families may choose to have their son or daughter in a Head Start program.

Young children with disabilities who are determined eligible for and placed in preschool special education settings will be provided a free, appropriate education based on their individual needs. These young children are likely to be taught by certified special education teachers who have been prepared to work with this age group.

Most preschool special education classes will be located at the neighborhood school, close to where the student lives. Efforts are often made by the local school to provide opportunities for these students to spend time with other children their age who do not have disabilities. This goal can be difficult, because publicly supported preschool is not available to students without special needs. As a result, creative options have emerged in which preschool children with disabilities receive their education in private settings (e.g., child care) with other students.

School Age

Most students with special needs will attend public schools, although some students will attend private schools. Many students who will eventually receive special education are not identified and evaluated until they are in elementary school. For many students, especially those who have a learning disability or attention problems, their presenting problems are not "discovered" until they begin to encounter difficulties with the academic demands of school (e.g., reading, math, writing).

Placement.   If students are determined eligible for special education services during the school years, they will receive their specialized instruction in a variety of settings. A continuum of placement options exists in most schools where students who qualify for special education may receive instruction. Increasingly, more students are being placed in the general education classrooms. These inclusive settings are highly desirable, because they provide students with disabilities with ongoing opportunities to interact with their nondisabled peers; however, certain factors need to be in place for these settings to be effective. Smith, Polloway, Patton, and Dowdy (2004) point out that five essential features characterize successful inclusion of students with special needs:

❑ A sense of community and social acceptance must dominate the classroom.
❑ Student diversity must be acknowledged and appreciated.
❑ The curricular needs of the included student must be recognized and addressed.
❑ Effective teaching practices in terms of curriculum and instruction must be operative in the classroom.
❑ The general education teacher must have sufficient supports and collaborative opportunities with specialized staff.

Other educational environments within the local school where instruction might be provided include resource rooms, content mastery programs, or self-contained classrooms. Other segregated settings exist outside the neighborhood school. Some school districts maintain special schools that are separate from other schools in the system. These schools may have students who have severe disabilities or serious behavior disorders. Some students with disabilities may receive their education on a homebound basis. This option is often used with students who have serious and chronic health issues.

Most states continue to have schools designed for specific populations such as students who are deaf or hard of hearing or students who are blind or partially sighted. These schools are typically located in one city in the state and require students to reside there.

Curricular and Instructional Issues.   Under IDEA, students who receive special education should be exposed to and have access to the general education curriculum. What this means is that a student in special education should not have a different set of educational standards than other students. However, by the nature of a student's disability, certain curricular areas may need additional or more intensive attention. Instructional goals might need to be written to cover more than the obvious academic areas. The most common curricular areas for which goals may be needed are listed in Table 2.2

As mentioned earlier, goals based on student need should be generated for all appropriate areas and should be included in the IEP that is developed for each student. The actual program planning process and the essential components of the IEP are covered in the next section of the chapter.

In most situations, teachers determine how instruction is to be delivered. In some cases, however, the nature of instruction is determined by the specific program being used. For instance, if a school decides to use a specific reading program such as the Wilson Reading Program with students having difficulties in this area, the teacher is instructed in how to deliver the various lessons by the author of the program. The bottom line is that effective instructional techniques must be identified and utilized.

Table 2.2
Curricular Areas for Developing IEP Goals

- Academic areas (reading, written expression, spelling, math)
- Problem solving/reasoning
- Communication skills (speech, language)
- Motor development
- Personal/emotional/affective development
- Social skills
- Self-determination skills
- Study skills/learning strategies
- Life skills
- Vocational skills

Private School Settings.   A growing number of students with disabilities may attend private schools. Although many private schools have been established solely to serve students with disabilities, most have traditionally served a nondisabled population and, therefore, may not be set up to accommodate the needs of students with disabilities.

Some students with disabilities are placed in private settings by a public school system when the school system is unable to address the needs of these students (e.g., students who are extremely violent). Other students are placed in private settings as a result of due process proceedings that have decided that an appropriate education can only be provided in this type of setting. In such cases, the school system covers the costs. Other students are placed in private schools by parents who feel that it is in the best interest of their child to be taught in a non-public school setting. When parents choose to put their son or daughter in a private school, even though the public school is willing to provide services, the parents are obligated to pay for this schooling.

Other program options that are now available are charter schools and home-schooling. Charter schools operate under the same mandates of IDEA as do regular public schools. Parents who choose to homeschool children with special needs are afforded special services; however, the public school does not have to provide those services in the home.

The actual special education process is complicated yet can be very valuable to many students and their families. A key feature of the special education services that was introduced in the 1990 amendments to IDEA was the need for transition services. Although this topic is covered in more detail later in the chapter, it is useful to introduce this important concept here. One of the main goals of special education is to prepare students for life after school is over. To do this, activities are now required that will establish a seamless transition from school to whatever settings a student will find himself or herself in the near future.

Adulthood

When students with special needs complete their schooling, they encounter a new and different system of service delivery that they and their families must understand and master. To gain access to certain services and programs in higher education or the workplace, an individual will have to disclose that he or she has a disability. A significant number of young adults for a variety of reasons choose not to disclose this information. As a result, they will not receive certain services or accommodations.

A vast array of services, both public and private, is available in most urban settings for adults with disabilities. Certain types of public services are provided by agencies located in every state. Selected state agencies that provide important services to adults with disabilities in the state of Texas are listed in Table 2.3. Note that the names of these agencies do vary from state to state. For instance, as noted in Table 2.3, in Texas, vocational rehabilitation services are provided by the Texas

Table 2.3
Adult Service Agencies—Texas

Agency	Eligibility	Services
Texas Rehabilitation Commission (TRC)	• mental or physical disability—substantial problems—job • can get a job after services • requires services—to prepare for, get, and keep job	• vocational assessment, vocational guidance and direction, training, postsecondary education support • assistive devices • job guidance and counseling • supportive employment
Texas Department of Mental Health and Mental Retardation (TXMHMR)	• mental illness, mr, or related condition • eligibility differs as a function of service	• case management • home and community-based services (HCS) • in-home and family support • intermediate care facilities (ICF-MR)
Texas Commission for the Blind (TCB)	• any person who is blind or visually impaired	• orientation and mobility • career exploration and guidance • vocational assessment and training • technology assessment and equipment
Texas Department of Human Services (TDHS)	• person eligible for Supplemental Security Income (SSI) • income, resource, and other conditional requirements	• respite services • adult foster care • client managed attendant services • day activity and health services • community living assistance and support services program (CLASS) • in-home and family support services • Medicaid services
Texas Workforce Commission (TWC)	• anyone seeking employment	• job placement and referral
Texas Department of Protective and Regulatory Services (TDPRS)	• youth who are under their conservatorship	• participation in transition planning

Rehabilitation Commission (TRC). In many other states, this agency is referred to as the Department of Vocational Rehabilitation (DVR).

What is often overlooked is the reality that the delivery of services to adults with special needs is a lifelong issue. Far too often, transitioning planning, as noted above and described in more detail below, fails to consider long-term needs of students, focusing almost exclusively on short-term needs (Price & Patton, in press).

PROVIDING SERVICES TO SCHOOL-AGE STUDENTS WITH SPECIAL NEEDS

The actual process for addressing the needs of students with special needs used in most school settings today is depicted in Figure 2.1. The process begins with efforts to address student needs within the context of the general education classroom. If this level of intervention does not produce the result desired, the formal special education process commences when a referral is made for consideration. If a student is determined to be eligible, then special education/related services and all of the related provisions mandated by IDEA are implemented. If the student is not eligible under IDEA, then other options such as eligibility for services under Section 504 are pursued.

A number of school-based professionals play key roles in this process and form part of the team that is crucial in providing an appropriate education to students with special needs. Members of the team include special and general education teachers, administrative staff, other professional staff (e.g., school psychologists; various therapists—speech/language, occupational, physical; school social workers; school nurse), parents, and the student. Thus, a team, representing various disciplines and relationships with the student, makes key decisions in regard to the student throughout the process.

All teams, when dealing with the important issue of a student's educational program, should be guided by certain tenets. Some key principles follow that should guide all decisions regarding students with disabilities (Smith, Polloway, Patton, & Dowdy, 2004):

❏ The best interests of the student should dictate all aspects of the decision-making process.
❏ Sensitivity to family values and cultural differences must pervade all activities.
❏ Ongoing and effective home–school collaboration efforts should be established.
❏ Parents and students have a right to and should be given information about the educational performance of the student, the special education programs and services to which the student is entitled and may receive benefit, and what will happen after formal schooling ends.
❏ Students should be taught to and encouraged to participate as an active, contributing member of the team.
❏ Programs and services, including the rules and regulations that apply, should be reviewed regularly, and improvements should be made whenever possible and allowable under the law.

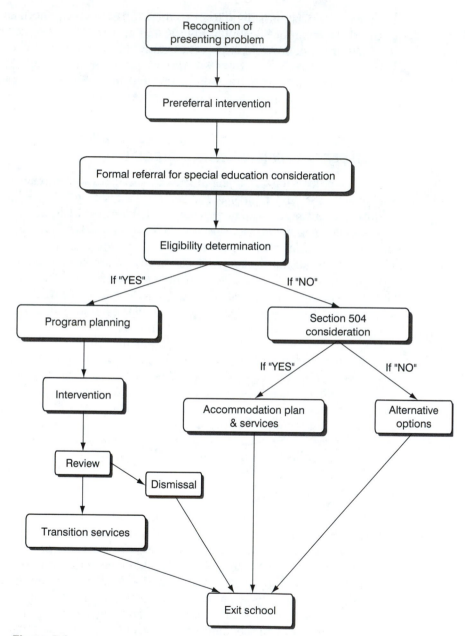

Figure 2.1
Special Education Process

As of this writing, IDEA is undergoing another reauthorization. The major intent of the law will not change and the major programs and services mandated by IDEA are not likely to change. However, the next reauthorization of IDEA will likely include some procedural refinements in areas such as reducing paperwork requirements, accentuating a more proactive and early approach to intervention, using different methods for identification, and providing better teacher preparation/professional development.

Recognition of a Potential Problem

The first step of the process, as noted in Figure 2.1, involves recognition that a student has some type of problem. Some students have already been identified and determined eligible—those who entered the system at an earlier age. Identification of need for many students, however, occurs as a result of their performance in school.

The person most likely to recognize that something is suspicious is the general education teacher. With this in mind, the importance of general education teachers having accurate information about exceptionalities is obvious. However, others may also initiate action on behalf of a student. Other sources could be parents, end-of-year reviewers of student progress, or an external service provider.

Once a potential problem is noted, the next step depends on the type of system that is in place at a particular school. Many schools these days use a system that attempts to study and intervene within the context of the existing classroom setting using prereferral intervention (i.e., actions that precede a formal referral to special education). Some schools do not use this system, and, as a result, the next step is formal referral for special education consideration.

Prereferral Intervention

The prereferral intervention process is designed to address the needs of students who exhibit learning and behavioral problems and who have not yet been referred for special education. Intervention focuses on providing assistance to the classroom teachers and the student. A major goal of this intervention is to provide solutions to problematic classroom-based situations so that a formal referral for special education services will not be needed. Interestingly, prereferral intervention is not required by IDEA at the present time. As a result, it is up to the local educational agency to decide to use this system and develop ways to implement it.

The prereferral intervention process should be considered a first level, or first line, of intervention. Other action may be needed if prereferral efforts are not successful in achieving the intervention goals that have been developed. According to Buck, Polloway, McConnell, and Patton (in press), the prereferral process involves four major components.

1. Initial indication that a classroom-based problem exists
2. Systematic examination of the presenting problem(s) that have been indicated by the referral source
3. Development of an intervention plan that contains strategies and other suggestions for addressing the presenting problem
4. Evaluation of the effectiveness of the interventions and decision on what to do next if the interventions have not yielded the outcomes originally desired

A referral is typically submitted to a group of school-based personnel, often referred to as the *child study team,* which reviews available information provided in the initial referral. Other terms such as *child assistance team, teacher intervention team, teacher assistance team, support team,* or *prereferral intervention team* may be used to refer to an in-school team (Buck, Wilcox-Cook, Polloway, & Smith-Thomas, 2002).

The main goal of the team is to generate suggestions to address the student's difficulties. Initially, the team targets the most significant problems and generates intervention goals. Then, the team usually will identify strategies to address the intervention goals. These strategies are subsequently implemented for a reasonable amount of time. The strategies used are monitored over time and at some designated date, the team evaluates the success of the prereferral intervention to determine if the intervention goals have been met and whether a formal referral for a comprehensive special education evaluation is warranted.

The learning and behavioral needs of many students can, and should, be handled in the general education classroom. To do so, however, requires a system (i.e., prereferral) that is responsive to teachers' dilemmas and that is able to provide the requisite supports to achieve the defined intervention goals.

Formal Referral for Special Education Consideration

When prereferral intervention is not able to address effectively the presenting problems a student has, a referral for special education consideration is initiated, marking the official beginning of the special education process. Inherent in this process are specific timelines and actions that must be followed to be compliant with federal and state law.

The first major decision regarding qualifying for special education services is made at this stage of the process. A school-based team, including the parents and the student, when appropriate, convenes to review existing data and to determine if the referral will be accepted for a formal evaluation to decide eligibility for special education services. As might be expected, the ramifications of this initial decision to proceed with an evaluation are significant for a student and his or her family. If the decision is "yes," then information is gathered to determine whether a student meets the criteria for a particular disability. If the decision is "no," then no further action is taken. However, parents do have the right to appeal this decision under the procedural safeguards provided by IDEA.

The actual formal referral is submitted to a designated school official. This person will contact the parents if a decision not to proceed is made. This person will also provide written notice to the parents, document the time and purpose of the eligibility meeting, and provide the parents with information regarding their rights in the special education process.

Eligibility Determination

The second major decision occurs after a comprehensive evaluation is conducted. At this point, various school-based professionals are involved in the process as members of the special education eligibility team.

The primary activity during this phase is to collect all necessary information to determine whether a student's presenting problem meets the criteria for a specific disability. The comprehensive evaluation that is conducted involves the collection of a range of information including existing assessment and classroom performance data. In addition, most evaluations will also involve the administrations of tests (standardized and nonstandardized), interviews, and observations. The assessment regimen that is chosen must be sensitive to age, grade level, and culture, and must be comprehensive and flexible enough to address the learning and behavioral difficulties of any student referred.

The general education teacher is likely to be actively involved during this phase. The teacher might be (1) asked to provide background information on the student, (2) interviewed, (3) asked to complete rating scales or checklists, or (4) asked to conduct some observations of a student.

After all of the assessment and fact finding are completed, the team responsible for making the eligibility decision compiles all of the pertinent information on a student. The team examines the data to determine whether a disability exists, whether the student meets the state eligibility guidelines for the particular disability, and whether, even if the student has a disability, the student needs special education. Then, a determination of whether a student qualifies for special education is made and the decision is conveyed to the family according to procedural guidelines.

If a student does qualify for special education, then the program planning phase begins (i.e., development of the IEP). Some of the data collected during the eligibility determination phase can be useful for generating instructional programs; however, typically, additional assessments will have to be conducted to determine actual present levels of performance on which goals are developed.

If the student does not meet the eligibility requirements, then the parents are notified. As mentioned previously, they have the right to appeal this decision under IDEA. However, consideration for eligibility under Section 504 should occur at this time, although the reality of this occurring in most school systems is slight. In most cases, the parents may need to request this consideration. Doing so creates another avenue for addressing the needs of students, as discussed later in this chapter.

Program Planning

The next step in the process, as illustrated earlier in Figure 2.1, is the development of the individualized education program. The IEP, as required by IDEA, is the document that guides programs and services for students receiving special education services. The IEP is developed soon after a student becomes eligible for special education, and it is reviewed at least once annually thereafter. Needed related services are also included in the IEP. The overriding concept behind the IEP is that all educational programming should be driven by the needs of the student, not by the availability of services. Goals should be developed for any of the areas highlighted in Table 2.2.

IEP Team.   The educational program designed for each student is developed and monitored by the IEP team. The federal regulations of IDEA specify that the team include the following people:

❑ The parents of the student
❑ At least one general education teacher of the student (if the student is in general education classrooms)
❑ At least one special education teacher
❑ A representative of the school district who is
  • Qualified to provide or supervise the provision of specially designed instruction to meet the unique need of students with disabilities
  • Knowledgeable about the general education curriculum
  • Knowledgeable about the availability of resources of the school district
❑ An individual who can interpret the instructional implications of evaluation results
❑ Other individuals who have knowledge or special expertise regarding the student, including related service personnel as appropriate (at the discretion of the parent or the school district)
❑ The student, if appropriate

IEP Components.   The IDEA Amendments of 1997 specify that each IEP should contain the following components:

❑ A statement of present levels of performance and how the disability affects the student's progress in the general education curriculum (or appropriate activities for preschoolers)
❑ Measurable annual goals including short-term benchmarks or objectives enabling the student to be involved in and progress in the regular curriculum (as appropriate) and meet the annual goals
❑ Special education and related services for the student and supplemental aids
❑ Program modifications or supports for school personnel to help the student be involved in and progress in both the curriculum and extracurricular and nonacademic activities

❑ An explanation of the extent, if any, to which the student will not participate in regular education classes

❑ Modifications to be used in statewide or district-wide assessment of student achievement or an explanation of how the student is to be assessed if different from nondisabled peers

❑ Projected dates for beginning of services and the frequency, location, and duration of services and modifications

❑ How progress toward annual goals and modifications is to be measured

❑ How parents will be regularly informed (must be at least as often as parents of nondisabled students) of progress toward the annual goals and whether progress will enable the student to meet goals by year end

❑ For students age 14 or younger, if appropriate, a statement of transition needs that focuses on the student's course of study (e.g., advanced classes or a vocational program)

❑ Beginning at age 16 or younger, if appropriate, in addition to the preceding information, a statement of interagency responsibilities or linkages if needed

Other special considerations include these:

❑ For students whose behavior impedes their learning or that of others, behavior strategy supports and interventions, when appropriate

❑ For limited English proficient students, language needs as they relate to the IEP

❑ For a child who is blind or visually impaired, Braille instruction, unless the IEP team determines that use of Braille is not appropriate

❑ For students with hearing impairments and language and communication needs, opportunities for communication with peers and teachers in the student's language and communication mode, including direct instruction in the mode

❑ Assistive technology devices and services for eligible students

Teacher Involvement and Responsibilities.   The extent of involvement of the general education teacher in the development, review, and revision of IEPs is determined on a case-by-case basis, but is likely to be significant. However, as a member of the IEP team, the active involvement of the general education teacher is crucial, particularly for those students who are in inclusive settings for most of their instructional day. All teachers who have contact with a student who is receiving special education and/or related services should have a copy of the IEP or have immediate access to it, as a reference tool throughout the year.

Teachers should refer to the IEP periodically to ensure that instruction is consistent with the long-term needs of the student. When a significant variance is noted, it may become the basis for a correction in instruction or perhaps a rationale for a change in the goals or objectives of the IEP.

Epstein, Patton, Polloway, and Foley (1992) remind us that teachers must not forget the theme of individualization that should guide the IEP process. Teachers need to view the IEP not just as a document that is compliant with the law but as a tool for meeting students' individual needs.

Intervention

After an appropriate IEP is developed, activities should commence to address the annual goals that have been identified. At the heart of the intervention is the notion that the techniques selected should reflect best practice and be shown effective, as validated by empirically based (i.e., science-based) evidence.

A general model of effective practice is shown in Figure 2.2 The figure highlights three related phases: management considerations, instructional practices, and evaluative and collaborative activities. The specific elements listed under each of these three areas demonstrate the complexity that is associated with effective instructional practice.

Review and Dismissal

Two additional critical features of the special education process are (1) the ongoing monitoring of a student's progress in special education and (2) continued need for special education services. By law, a student's IEP must be reviewed and revised on an annual basis. Every 3 years, however, a comprehensive reevaluation must be undertaken.

The annual review of the IEP is essential for updating the student's goals and writing new ones if needed. With this in mind, the IEP team should not only look closely at existing goals but also be open to the development of new goals in areas of need. For example, new goals may need to be written into the IEP during the transition planning process.

As a result of being exposed to effective instructional practices, many students can and should reach levels of competence in those areas specified in their IEPs whereby they will no longer need special education or related services. Sometimes services are discontinued when a student reaches a plateau of skill attainment—a situation where a student may still be skill deficient but has not shown any progress over time even when robust interventions have been tried. Both scenarios lead to the cessation of special education and related services.

Transition to Postschool Settings

Based in part on the less than favorable adult outcome data that were brought to light in the late 1980s and early 1990s, the IDEA amendments of 1990 and 1997 required activities that better prepared students for life after high school. Specifically, transition planning was now required. Some states chose to include transition plans as part of the IEP; other states decided to require a separate individual transition plan (ITP).

The 1990 amendments to IDEA required that a statement of needed transition services be identified and developed by age 16. The 1997 reauthorization of IDEA, however, lowered the age when action must occur. The 1997 amendments

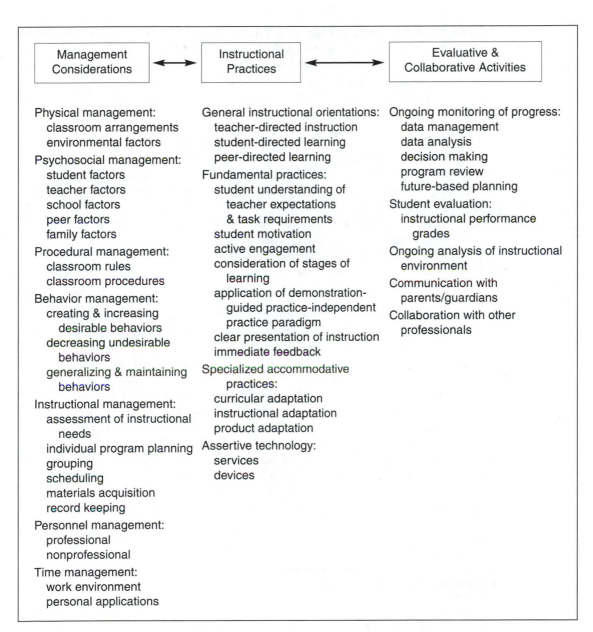

Management Considerations	Instructional Practices	Evaluative & Collaborative Activities

Physical management:
   classroom arrangements
   environmental factors

Psychosocial management:
   student factors
   teacher factors
   school factors
   peer factors
   family factors

Procedural management:
   classroom rules
   classroom procedures

Behavior management:
   creating & increasing
     desirable behaviors
   decreasing undesirable
     behaviors
   generalizing & maintaining
     behaviors

Instructional management:
   assessment of instructional
     needs
   individual program planning
   grouping
   scheduling
   materials acquisition
   record keeping

Personnel management:
   professional
   nonprofessional

Time management:
   work environment
   personal applications

General instructional orientations:
   teacher-directed instruction
   student-directed learning
   peer-directed learning

Fundamental practices:
   student understanding of
     teacher expectations
     & task requirements
   student motivation
   active engagement
   consideration of stages of
     learning
   application of demonstration-
     guided practice-independent
     practice paradigm
   clear presentation of instruction
   immediate feedback

Specialized accommodative
   practices:
   curricular adaptation
   instructional adaptation
   product adaptation

Assertive technology:
   services
   devices

Ongoing monitoring of progress:
   data management
   data analysis
   decision making
   program review
   future-based planning

Student evaluation:
   instructional performance
   grades

Ongoing analysis of instructional
   environment

Communication with
   parents/guardians

Collaboration with other
   professionals

Figure 2.2
Dimensions of Effective Practice

Source: From *Strategies for Teaching Learners with Needs,* 7th ed., by E. A. Polloway, J. R. Patton, and L. Serna, © 2001. Reprinted by permission of Pearson Education, Inc., Upper Saddle River, NJ.

now required that a statement of transition needs, which integrates transition planning within the process of educational planning, must be in a student's IEP by age 14. The 1997 amendments made it very clear that a student's program of study must be related to the general education curriculum as well.

The definition of transition services provided in the IDEA of 1990 and retained in the 1997 amendments describes transition as

> *a coordinated set of activities for a student, designed within an outcome oriented process, which promotes movement from school to post-school activities, including post-secondary education, vocational training, integrated employment (including supported employment), continuing and adult education, adult services, independent living or community participation.*
>
> *The coordinated set of activities shall be based upon the individual student's needs, taking into account student preferences and interests and shall include instruction, community experiences, and the development of employment and other post-school objectives, and if appropriate, acquisition of daily living skills and functional vocational evaluation.* [§300.18]

Transition planning and services are characterized by a number of key features (Patton & Dunn, 1998). First, planning must be comprehensive. In other words, the postschool needs of students must be considered across a range of adult, or transition, domains, as indicated in Table 2.4. Second, the student and his or her parents need to be actively involved in the process. Parents need information about a range of postschool options and services and their opinions must be sought and respected during the planning process. Third, the transition-related activities should begin early in a student's school career. Realistically, this process should begin at the elementary level (Patton, Cronin, & Wood, 1999). Fourth, the transition needs of a student should be reflected by the inclusion of goals in the IEP that relate to postschool outcomes. Fifth, for the transition process to work effectively, coordination, communication, and cooperation between schools and adult agencies and organizations is critical. Sixth, the transition planning process

Table 2.4
Transition Domains

- Community participation
- Daily living
- Employment
- Financial/income management
- Health
- Independent living (includes living arrangements)
- Leisure/recreation
- Postsecondary education
- Relationships/social competence
- Transportation/mobility
- Vocational training

should capitalize on the strengths of the student in addition to recognizing and addressing areas of need.

Transition planning is a good idea for all students. However, the only students for whom formal transition plans have to be developed are those who remain eligible for special education services. If a student who previously qualified for special education is dismissed from the system, as discussed in the previous section, then the student would not have a transition plan developed.

Exit School

Students with special needs, at some point, exit the school system. Increasingly, more students with disabilities, regardless of whether they are in special education or not, are graduating with diplomas. Some students leave school with certificates of completion, or a similarly designated document. Others stay in school until they reach the age of 22, at which time the school under IDEA is no longer responsible for providing services to the student. Too many students, however, drop out of school prior to completing their program of studies.

After school formally ends, young adults with special needs will encounter a new world. Some will qualify for adult services, as described earlier in this chapter and in Chapter 14. The demands of adulthood are complex and can be overwhelming. The process just described in this section was designed to prepare students for the challenges of life in today's world as a contributing member of the community.

Services Under Section 504

Section 504 was introduced briefly in the previous chapter, and its relationship to IDEA and ADA was documented in Table 1.5. The point has been made that some students who do not qualify for services under IDEA may do so under the provisions of this law.

Eligibility is based on a student having a physical or mental impairment that results in a substantial limitation in one or more major life activities (e.g., seeing, hearing, learning). A "substantial limitation" is related to two primary factors: severity of the impairment and duration (i.e., permanence of the condition).

As presented earlier and depicted in Figure 2.1, Section 504 consideration should be given to any student who is referred for special education services but does not qualify under IDEA.

Every public school should have in place a committee and process for handling Section 504 matters. Schools need to be able to document that a logical and reasonable process for determining eligibility is used. Someone on staff should be identified who is knowledgeable about Section 504 and who can develop a coherent system for addressing queries about it.

If a student qualifies for services under Section 504, schools are required to provide reasonable accommodations in all academic and nonacademic areas in which accommodations are needed. Examples of accommodations that might be provided range from providing extended time on tests for a student with attention deficit/hyperactivity disorder to providing dry marker boards for a student with severe allergies to chalk dust. Most accommodations are easy to implement and do not cost much money. Occasionally a needed accommodation may require some expenditures.

Each student who receives services under Section 504 should have a written accommodation plan that specifies the nature and scope of the accommodations to be implemented. This document differs significantly from an IEP required under IDEA for a number of reasons—one of which is that Section 504 does not specify any required components. As a result, accommodation plans vary greatly in format from one school district to another.

Alternative Options

For the student who is experiencing learning-related problems but does not qualify for services under either IDEA or Section 504, other options do exist that the family can pursue, as depicted in Figure 2.1. As mentioned earlier and explained further below, parents can appeal the decision that has been made. Doing so does not guarantee that services will be provided; however, the due process provisions of IDEA do allow for reexamination of the case.

Many parents whose child does not qualify for services, as noted above, will decide to place their son or daughter in a private setting. The costs of doing this are the responsibility of the family, unless it is determined at some later time that their child was denied an appropriate education under IDEA.

Another option that some parents choose is to keep their child in the public school setting and secure tutoring services. Again, the costs associated with this option must be covered by the family.

RELATED TOPICS

Behavioral Intervention Planning

The requirement that a behavioral intervention plan (BIP) be developed for some students receiving special education services was introduced in the 1997 amendments to IDEA. Although the fundamental concept of behavioral intervention is not new and has been used in various settings previously, especially settings that included students with severe behavioral difficulties, the fact that BIPs are now required for certain students was a new feature.

In general, behavioral intervention plans are required for (a) students whose behaviors impede their learning or that of others, (b) students who put peers at risk because of their behaviors, and (c) students with disabilities for whom serious disciplinary action is being taken. The major assumptions underlying the development of BIPs include the following points:

❏ Behavior problems are best addressed when the causes (i.e., function) of the behaviors are known.

❏ Interventions that are based on positive intervention strategies are more effective than punitive ones.
❏ Dealing with difficult behaviors demands a team approach.

Age of Majority

IDEA also requires that a student be notified of the transfer of his or her rights at least 1 year prior to reaching the age of majority specified by law in his or her state. For example, in many states, the age of majority is 18; so, by this age, the student must sign the IEP verifying that this right has been explained. After this birthday, students can make decisions regarding school, independent living, and work. In extreme cases, when students are judged incapable of making their own decisions and protecting their own rights, the courts will award guardianship to parents or another advocate.

Teacher Needs

Despite the availability of a wide range of resources in schools, teachers need support in order to address the needs of students with special needs. Smith and colleagues (2004) have identified five essential features that must be present if this system is to work properly:

❏ Teachers need comprehensive training in how to work with students who have special needs.
❏ Teachers need certain knowledge and skills to be successful with these students.
❏ Teachers need a wealth of information about the students they teach.
❏ Teachers need adequate time to collaborate with other school-based staff.
❏ Teachers need appropriate supports to be successful—an "it takes a village" approach is required.

Teacher preparation and professional development will remain an important topic for years to come.

FINAL THOUGHTS

The intent of this chapter was to provide an overview of the programs and services available to individuals with special needs across the life span. Particular attention was given to the school-based process of providing services to student with disabilities.

Chapters 3 through 13 focus on specific areas of exceptionality. The material covered in this chapter will be useful in understanding how best to provide needed services to these populations.

PONDER THESE

1. Debate the merits of disclosing or not disclosing your disability in college or the workplace.
2. Which is a better document to use for programming needs: one like the IEP, which specifies required elements, or one like a Section 504 plan, which is very unstructured?
3. Would the philosophy behind early intervention services and the IFSP work with school-age students and their families?
4. From a school system's perspective, what are some compelling reasons for and against establishing a prereferral intervention process?

REFERENCES

Buck, G. H., Polloway, E. A., McConnell, K., & Patton, J. R. (in press). *Prereferral intervention resource guide.* Austin, TX: PRO-ED.

Buck, G. H., Wilcox-Cook, K., Polloway, E. A., & Smith-Thomas, A. (2002). *Prereferral intervention process: A survey of practices.* Manuscript submitted for publication.

Epstein, M. H., Patton, J. R., Polloway, E. A., & Foley, R. (1992). Educational services for students with behavior disorders: A review of individualized education programs. *Teacher and Special Education, 15,* 41–48.

Patton, J. R., & Dunn, C. (1998). *Transition from school to young adulthood: Basic concepts and recommended practices.* Austin, TX: PRO-ED.

Patton, J. R., Cronin, M. E., & Wood, S. J. (1999). *Infusing real-life topics into existing curricula: Recommended procedures and instructional examples for the elementary, middle, and high school levels.* Austin, TX: PRO-ED.

Price, L., & Patton, J. R. (in press). A new world order: Connecting adult development theory to learning disabilities. *Remedial and Special Education.*

Smith, T. E. C., Polloway, E. A., Patton, J. R., & Dowdy, C. A. (2004). *Teaching students with special needs in inclusive settings* (4th ed.). Boston: Allyn & Bacon.

PART I

Learning and Behavioral Disorders

CHAPTER 3

Learning Disabilities

Anna was in the sixth grade. She was a good student in most respects. She tried hard and did acceptable work in most areas. She was easy to get along with and related well to her peers, but she just couldn't spell.

Most sixth-grade classes love art projects and mine was no exception. I had acquired a kiln and some clay discarded by another school in the district, and we were having a really great time making all kinds of things. Anna brought me a beautiful slab pot that she had just finished. It was about 2 inches high and 6 inches in diameter, and I commented on its nice form and proportion in addition to the quality of construction. Obviously elated, Anna said that she was going to label her bowl so that everyone would know what it was (she didn't like having it called a "pot") and hurried off to do the job. About 20 minutes later she was back with her bowl. In perfectly formed, 2-inch letters, she had written on the side of her treasure, BOWEL.

I worked with Josh for 8 months on penmanship. I felt he was really making progress. His writing was more legible, he reversed fewer letters, and he could now mark within the lines. On the last day of the school year, a small box was left anonymously on my desk. Inside was a small figurine of an owl with the following note:

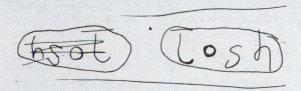

Now that I think about it, it really wasn't bad when you realize that at the beginning of the year, he couldn't even hold a pencil.

Eddie could count and add. If you showed him 3 dots plus 5 dots, he would say 8. However, when presented with any numeral, he experienced difficulty identifying it. After 1 year, I was exhausted and frustrated with the entire process of teaching him the identification of numbers. As he arrived for the first day of school for the second year, he dropped by my resource room and asked, "Am I going to learn the names of my numbers this year?"

I responded, "I sure hope so."

He quickly replied, "Don't worry about it, there is always another year."

Dr. Fonerden:

I wish to explain to you a strange mental weakness, to which I have all my life been a victim. At the age of seven or eight, I could read quite well, but shut the book and I could not spell the smallest words. My aunt who instructed me, beleeveing that it was obstinacy on my part, turn me over to my grandfather, and he having punished me severely gave me a collum of words to commit by a certain time; but alas, when the time had expired, I could not spell the first word, which was urn. Hour after hour and day after day was I compeled to study over this word; but let me shut the book for ten minutes and I could not spell it right, except by chance, and to my utter mortification a little collored boy was called up to spell it for me, he having lurned it from hearing it repeated to me so often. At last to such an extent was I persicuted on account of this word that I deturmined to run away. . . . Now this peculiarity of my youth sticks by me still. When I went to sea, I toodk a dictionary, with the determination never to return home until I had lurned to spell; but it was no use. If I had kept my resolve I should never have returned. The hours of study I have wasted in endeavoring to become a good speller would have given me a profession. For that which I read, if it excite any interest, becomes stamped upon my memory indelibly, with this single exception, that which I wonce lurne I never forget. When I left school I wrote a very good hand, but spoilt it in endeavoring so to disguise the letters, that they might pass for what they should be, instead of what they were. I had occasion very recently, to direct a letter to my sister, but could not do so untill I had looked over many books to find the name Rachal, which I could not spell. I have been puzzled to distinguish between the agative too and preposition to, and between the article the and the pronoun thee. Were I to write this over from memory a great majority of the words would be spelled differently.

. . . The chief difficulty that I have to contend with is this; that when I write the most familiar words, and then ask myself are they spelt right, some jugling friend whispers in my ear many ways of spelling them, and I became lost in a maze of doubt and conjecture. To no other than yourself would I make this humuliating confession; and only to you in the faint hope that you may suggest a remedy. If you can, all that you have done to develope my mind, and to strengthen my character, will be as nothing in comparison.

Yours, truly[1]

_____

Patrick Milton Wills frowned as he closed the file folders containing the information presented at the eligibility meeting for Edwin and J. C. Fifteen years ago, when he first became director of special education for the Marion County Schools, he had anticipated that his job would become easier as the years rolled by. Instead, it seemed to him that the decisions he faced were getting tougher all the time. True, the decisions about Edwin and J. C. were not his alone. He was only one member of the eligibility committee that was to decide whether these students qualified as handicapped under PL 94–142, and therefore, were eligible for special education. But that didn't make it any easier for him to decide how he felt about these boys' education. "Fact is," he thought to himself, "I have my hunches about them both. But if I were cross-examined in court, I'd have an awfully hard time defending any decision on either of them with hard facts and figures that make sense."

_____

[1]From *American Journal of Insanity* (pp. 61–63), author unknown, 1850.

Mr. Wills let his mind drift back to the state's adoption of the LD definition under which Edwin and J. C. were being considered for special education. After seemingly interminable wrangling among state officials and LD experts, the state education department decided that the proposed federal formula for defining LD was too complicated and unreliable. Learning disability, the state decided, meant a difference of 20 or more points between Full-Scale WISC-R IQ and standard scores for the Woodcock-Johnson achievement test in written language or mathematics, or the Peabody Individual Achievement Test in math or reading. Seemed simple enough, he thought at the time. He remembered how the superintendent had slapped him on the back and said, "Well, P. M., I think we've finally got us a definition that'll cut out a lot of this needless haggling about who belongs in our LD classes."

Only it hadn't proved to be so simple. Take Edwin, for example. He was a third grader with a Full-Scale WISC-R IQ of 74. His W-J standard scores were lower than his IQ, 19 points in written language and 17 in mathematics. He didn't quite qualify for LD services under the definition, but he was certainly having lots of trouble in school. His teacher was at his wit's end to know what to do with Edwin. He was a constant behavior problem, according to the teacher—nearly always out of his seat, taunting and teasing his classmates, bullying smaller children on the playground, making life miserable for everyone. This was not a teacher whose class was generally disorderly or who had difficulty managing and teaching most children. Obviously, Edwin was not a bright child, though he didn't quite qualify as mentally retarded. And he was having more academic difficulty than one would expect based on his IQ. A lot more difficulty, in fact. His parents were extremely concerned and wanted him placed in one of the county's self-contained LD classes. But the classes were already filled. Besides, nearly 4 percent of the county's students were already identified as LD, many of them with test score discrepancies smaller than Edwin's.

Then there was the case of J. C., a bright and talented sixth grader. J. C. had a Full-Scale WISC-R score of 129. Here was a highly motivated, well-adjusted boy who was well liked by his peers, well liked by his teachers, and well read on nearly every topic. But he had only third-grade math skills. On all achievement tests, he scored about two standard deviations above the mean in written language; but his math scores were consistently 40 or more standard points below his IQ. He seemed not to care; his peers seemed not to notice; his parents were convinced that the problem was simply poor teaching and strongly resisted the notion of his being identified as LD. They gave permission for J. C.'s formal evaluation for special education only with great reluctance. And, to make matters worse, P. M. Wills knew that J. C.'s math instruction had been, for the past 3 years, anything but exemplary. "Perhaps," he thought, "J. C. does not belong in an LD program even though he does technically fit the definition. I think his problems could quickly be resolved by a skilled tutor. And if he were my son, I don't think I'd want him in special education either."

P. M. Wills sighed. "Where are all those nice, neat cases I was taught about in graduate school?" he asked himself.[2]

---

[2]From *Introduction to Learning Disabilities* (pp. 293–294) by D. P. Hallahan, J. M. Kauffman, and J. W. Lloyd, 1985, Upper Saddle River, NJ: Prentice Hall. Copyright 1985 by Prentice Hall. Reprinted by permission.

DEFINITION AND PREVALENCE

The idea that some people have specific disabilities in learning is not new. The term *learning disability,* however, is only a little over 25 years old. Besides being the most recently labeled, learning disability (LD) is certainly the most controversial and least understood special education category. Ironically, nearly everyone has heard the term *learning disability*—and most people who talk about LD use the term as *if* they understand it. Some estimates have indicated that perhaps 1,000 people *per day* in the United States alone are newly and officially classified as learning disabled (Mercer, 1997; Reeve & Kauffman, 1988). And LD is now by far the largest category of special education in terms of the number of children and amount of money involved. Yet the definition of learning disability is still being debated. As one leading scholar and his colleagues put it, "though even the most illiterate student of education is likely to know the term, even the most literate scholar is likely to have difficulty explaining exactly what a learning disability is" (Hallahan, Kauffman, & Lloyd, 1985, p. 2).

Why do we have so much difficulty defining a problem that is so widely recognized and deciding the precise meaning of such a popularly applied label? Probably we find the definition difficult because the *idea* of a learning disability is pretty straightforward but application of the concept to real people is extremely complex. The same is likely true for the difficulty we have in trying to decide how many children have a learning disability: The abstract formula is a neat gadget, but it doesn't work very well in the real world of schools and children. As Hallahan et al. (1985) explain:

> *Learning disability is easy to define as an abstraction. When we consider flesh and blood children, however, our abstract definition that seemed so adequate, or even elegant, on paper becomes a house of cards. The moment we try to apply our neatly written criteria to an actual child, our definition collapses around us, a casualty of the child's living, breathing individuality. Naturally, if we have difficulty deciding that any given child fits our definition, then we have little basis for stating how many children possess a LD. Our estimation of the prevalence of learning disability often is based on a statistical probability that, like our definition, is attractive in the abstract but unworkable in practice.* (pp. 292–293)

In the abstract, experts estimate that 1 percent to 3 percent of the school-aged population (ages 6 to 17) has a learning disability. In the real world of classrooms, about 5.68 percent of the U.S. school population has been identified as learning disabled (U.S. Department of Education, 2000). Meanwhile, controversy about the definition of LD continues. The current federal definition of LD, which is included in PL 94–142 and its subsequent amendments, reads as follows:

> Specific learning disability *means a disorder of one or more of the basic psychological processes involved in understanding or in using language, spoken or written, which may manifest itself in an imperfect ability to listen, think, speak, read, write, spell, or do arithmetic calculations. The term includes such conditions as perceptual handicaps, brain injury, minimal brain damage, dyslexia, and developmental aphasia.*

The term does not include children who have learning problems which are primarily the result of visual, hearing, or motor handicaps, of mental retardation, or environmental, cultural, or economic disadvantage. (U.S. Office of Education, 1977, p. 42478)

Although language and academics remain major areas of concern related to defining learning disabilities (Lerner, 2003; Mercer, King-Sears, & Mercer, 1990), most children with learning disabilities, in essence, have been defined by exclusion. These are not people who are emotionally disturbed, culturally disadvantaged, retarded, visibly crippled (although the term *invisibly crippled* has been used), deaf, or blind. They simply do not learn some specific, basic developmental and academic tasks as most children do. And nobody knows why for sure. Although this continues to be the situation in most cases reported by Lerner (2003), the author also reports that there is a growing consistency among and between the states as to the factors critical to defining learning disabilities. This line of thinking, however, precludes the possibility of a person with learning disabilities being multiply handicapped. Hammill, Leigh, McNutt, and Larsen (1981) offer a good example of why this interpretation is not accurate. "Take for example a blind 14-year-old child who lost spoken language as a consequence of a brain tumor. This would be a clear-cut case of a multiply handicapped LD child" (p. 338).

Because learning disabilities are a relatively new area of study, service, and research, definitions must be considered to be in an experimental, developmental stage. Other attempts at definition have been offered as well. Hallahan and Kauffman (1977) suggested that much more specificity is needed in labeling each person's particular problem, for example, "specific learning disability in remembering the spelling of words" (p. 29).

Of particular note to anyone interested in learning disabilities is the emergence of other definitions. Representatives from major professional and parent organizations forming the National Joint Committee on Learning Disabilities[3] (NJCLD) were motivated by displeasure with the definition used in PL 94–142, and as a result, approved the following definition in 1981 (Hammill et al., 1981):

Learning disabilities *is a generic term that refers to a heterogeneous group of disorders manifested by significant difficulties in the acquisition and use of listening, speaking, reading, writing, or mathematical abilities. These disorders are intrinsic to the individual and presumed to be due to central nervous system dysfunction. Even though a learning disability may occur concomitantly with other handicapping conditions (e.g., sensory impairment, mental retardation, social and emotional disturbance) or*

---

[3]The National Joint Committee on Learning Disabilities represents the following organizations: American Speech-Language-Hearing Association; Association on Higher Education and Disability; Council for Learning Disabilities; Division for Communicative Disabilities and Deafness, Council for Exceptional Children; Division for Learning Disabilities, Council for Exceptional Children; International Dsylexia Association; International Reading Association; Learning Disabilities Association, formerly the Association for Children and Adults with Learning Disabilities; National Association of School Psychologists; and the National Center for Learning Disabilities.

environmental influences (e.g., cultural differences, insufficient/inappropriate instruction, psychogenic factors), it is not the direct result of those conditions or influences. (p. 336)

The NJCLD modified the 1981 definition twice, adding new content as well as changing some of the wording.[4] The most recent revised definition was accepted by this organization in 1997 and reads as follows:

Learning disabilities *is a general term that refers to a heterogeneous group of disorders manifested by significant difficulties in the acquisition and use of listening, speaking, reading, writing, reasoning, or mathematical abilities. These disorders are intrinsic to the individual, presumed to be due to central nervous system dysfunction, and may occur across the life span. Problems in self-regulatory behaviors, social perception, and social interaction may exist with learning disabilities but do not by themselves constitute a learning disability. Although a learning disability may occur concomitantly with other handicapping conditions (for example, sensory impairment, mental retardation, serious emotional disturbance) or with extrinsic influences (such as cultural differences, insufficient or inappropriate instruction), it would not be the result of those conditions or influences.* (p. 2)

Etiology

As mentioned previously, learning disabilities have traditionally been defined by exclusion. Consequently, it has been denied that children can be learning disabled due to mental retardation, emotional disturbance, visual or hearing impairment, crippling conditions, or environmental disadvantage (lack of appropriate stimulation or opportunity to learn). What is left? As the argument goes, if the child is not learning and the lack of achievement cannot be explained in any other way, there must be something wrong in the child's head—there must be brain dysfunction.

As will be mentioned in the discussion of the etiologies of other exceptionalities, brain damage can result from a very large number of factors. But knowing that brains *can be* injured by many factors does not prove that a given child's brain *has been* injured. It is also extremely difficult to provide conclusive evidence that a learning disability is the direct result of brain injury, even if it is known that the brain has been damaged. Consequently, it is safe to say only that brain injury is a suspected etiological factor in many cases of learning disability.

By most definitions, children with serious emotional disturbance are excluded from the learning disabled population; however, there is little doubt that emotional factors are involved in learning disabilities. Children with mild emotional disturbance and children with learning disabilities do exhibit many similar characteristics, but it is not clear whether emotional disturbance is an etiological factor in or a consequence of a learning disability (Hallahan et al., 1985; Kauffman, 2001).

---

[4]Position paper of the NJCLD, 1997.
Source: Collective Perspectives on Issues Affecting Learning Disabilities: Position Papers, Statements, and Reports, by National Joint Committee on Learning Disabilities, 2001, Austin, TX: PRO-ED.

There is a third possible etiological factor in learning disabilities that special educators are only now beginning to face squarely: instructionally related problems such as inadequate teaching (Wallace & Kauffman, 1986). Although it would be ridiculous to suggest that *all* children with learning disabilities have been poorly taught, it seems likely that in a significant number of cases the problem is as much one of providing appropriate instruction as of finding the child's disability. This line of thought places a lot of responsibility on the teacher, but that is where it should be. If a child is not learning, it may be concluded that the teacher has not found an effective way of teaching. The malady may be as much in the teacher's lack of instructional prowess as in the child's lack of ability to perform (see Engelmann & Carnine, 1982).

LEARNING DISABLED OR LEARNING DYSLABELED?

Given the ambiguities and controversy surrounding the definition of learning disabilities, it is not surprising that arguments have arisen about what the children in question should be called. Concern for the label to be attached to those who have only recently been recognized as a distinct group of handicapped individuals is heightened by the realization that other special education labels seem to have a deleterious effect on children. It is no secret that *retarded* can be a bad name, and it does not take a Rhodes scholar to recognize that *emotionally disturbed, autistic, stutterer, crippled, hyperactive,* or any other special term used to describe a handicapped individual can likewise become an epithet designed to hurt or degrade the person. Many of the people who were instrumental in developing the "new" field of learning disabilities in the 1960s were also determined to avoid stigmatizing still another group of children. In a frantic effort to foil the pernicious influence of labels known to carry negative connotations, these people thought up a wide variety of new ones, all of them used at some time or another, to refer to essentially the same type of child or condition. Moreover, many of the terms used to describe individuals who experience difficulty in learning-related endeavors reflect a given professional orientation or affiliation. A sample of such terms follows:

Attentional Deficit Disorder	Dyslexia
Atypical Child	Dyssychronous Child
Brain Damaged	Educationally Handicapped
Brain Injured	Educationally Maladjusted
Choreiform Child	Hyperactive Behavior Disorder
Developmental Aphasia	Hyperkinetic Child
Developmentally Imbalanced	Interjacent Child
Driven Child	Invisibly Crippled Child

Language Disordered	Problem Reader
Learning Disabled	Psycholinguistic Disability
Learning Disordered	Psychoneurological Disorder
Learning Impaired	Psychoneurological Learning Disability
Minimal Brain Dysfunction	Reading Disability
Minimal Cerebral Dysfunction	Remedial Education Case
Organic Brain Syndrome	Special Learning Disability
Performance Deviation	Specific Learning Disability
Performance Disabled	Strauss Syndrome
Performance Handicapped	Underachiever
Problem Learner	

Predictably, as soon as people found out what these labels really meant, the names became noxious. Of course, what is derogatory in a name is the social role, quality, deviancy, or conformity it suggests. In our society the imagery conjured up by *any* label for a handicapping condition tends to be stigmatizing, not because of the label itself, but because of our archaic attitudes toward handicaps. The stigma of being exceptional will not go away, no matter what the label, until a handicap is no longer the reason for pity, mourning, disgust, humor, segregation, or reverence. When we can laugh, cry, teach, learn, struggle, and enjoy life with persons who have handicaps as we do with other individuals who share our human limitations, there will be no pain in labels (see Burbach, 1981).

But stigma is not the only problem with labeling. We need to classify people in order to avoid total confusion and miscommunication. The real issues in labeling are these: Labeled according to what criteria? Labeled by whom? Labeled for what purpose? When labels are based on objective and relevant criteria, are applied by responsible professionals, and are used to communicate essential information about an individual, they can even be helpful to the individuals involved.

Numerous factors are known to influence how a child is perceived and categorized including (a) the social role and cultural context of children's behavior, (b) the fads and predispositions of labelers, (c) the legislation and legal rules regarding exceptional children, and (d) the awareness or unawareness of environmental cues for children's behavior on the part of diagnosticians. Some of these factors inevitably contribute to "dyslabelia."

Social and Cultural Contexts

Social and cultural contexts vary from location to location and change over time. In our country, attitudes toward the behavior of children in school have changed dramatically during the last century. Gnagey (1968) reports that S. L. Pressey found a list of misbehaviors and recommended punishments published in North Carolina in 1848. Among them were:

Playing cards at school (10 lashes)

Swearing at school (8 lashes)

Drinking liquor at school (8 lashes)

Telling lies (7 lashes)

Boys and girls playing together (4 lashes)

Quarreling (4 lashes)

Wearing long fingernails (2 lashes)

Blotting one's copybook (2 lashes)

Neglecting to bow when going home (2 lashes)

Today, many Americans would be more likely to recommend lashes for playing too many video games or for a student's *insistence* on bowing when going home. The important thing to remember is that whether or not a child is considered disturbed, retarded, learning disabled, speech impaired, gifted, and so forth, depends to a significant degree on when, where, and with whom the individual lives and works (i.e., on the demands and expectations of the environment). A case in point is that most mildly retarded children are not considered retarded until they enter school and are not thought of as retarded by most people after they leave the school environment.

Learning disabilities tend to be "invisible disabilities." In essence, because students with learning disabilities do not have any severe or obvious physical or mental abnormalities, the expectations of teachers, administrators, parents, employers, and even other students are consistent with those expectations for the average student. The failure of students with learning disabilities to meet the expectations of others in their various "life environments" (school, work, etc.) often results in perceptions of laziness, lack of motivation, disinterest, and even rebelliousness. Such perceptions on the part of teachers and administrators can lead to a limiting or absence of effective classroom intervention or accommodation. Social dysfunction, as a major problem for students with learning disabilities (Baum, Duffelmeyer, & Geeland, 1988), and the efficacy of teaching social skills to this population (Bender & Wall, 1994; Blackbourn, 1989) are well documented.

Ellis (1991) suggests a model of the negative effect of poor classroom skills (related to social interaction) on the perception of teachers and other students (see Figure 3.1). He also outlines a model of the possible positive outcomes available to students with learning disabilities if they are prepared to interact effectively with the material, the teacher, and the students in regular classrooms (see Figure 3.2). These models, developed by Ellis, explain the dynamics of the classroom and how they impact the social and academic status of the student with learning disabilities.

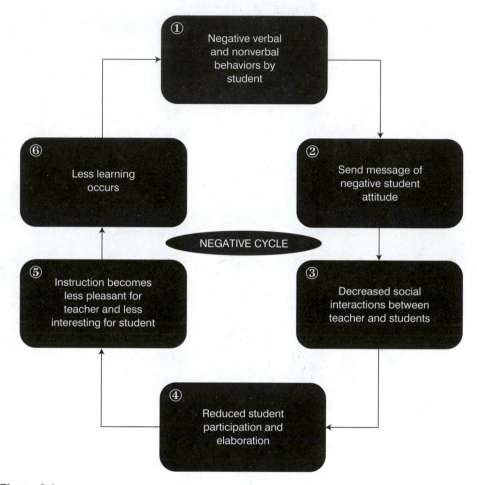

Figure 3.1
Negative Effect of Poor Classroom Skills

Source: From SLANT: *A Starter Strategy for Class Participation,* by E. Ellis, 1991, Lawrence, KS: EDGE Enterprises. Used by permission.

Fads and Predispositions

Like clothes and furniture, labels for exceptional children become fashionable and then go out of style. People who label children—physicians, psychologists, educators—are influenced by "in" terms. A child may receive a certain label because it "sounds right" or because it is more acceptable to parents than another term that seems to be more denigrating. White and Charry (1966) studied approximately 3,000 referrals to school psychologists. They found a significant relationship between the child's socioeconomic level and IQ and the label given. Children low in IQ and socioeconomic level more often were labeled *culturally disadvantaged* or *educationally inadequate,* while children high in IQ and socioeconomic level were more often labeled *brain injured* or *emotionally*

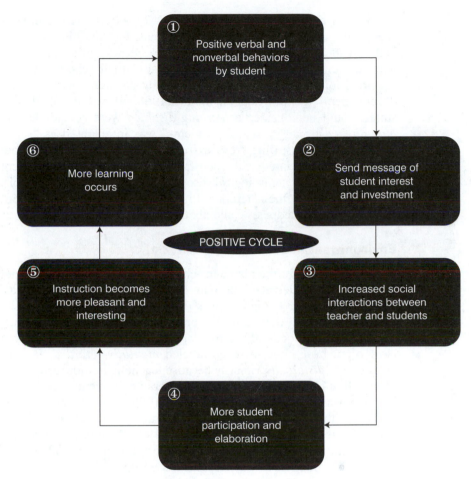

Figure 3.2
Positive Cycle

Source: From *SLANT: A Starter Strategy for Class Participation,* by E. Ellis, 1991, Lawrence, KS: EDGE Enterprises. Used by permission.

disturbed. It seemed clear to these investigators that the labelers had definite biases or expectations that influenced how they chose to interpret and label children's behavior.

Legislation and Legal Rules

It is not a complete distortion of reality to say that legislation and school codes sometimes "make" children exceptional. It is obvious to most of us which children need help, but what to call them is a problem. Now, if a state legislature decides that money and services will be available for *educationally handicapped* children, then *educationally handicapped* children will be identified and served in the schools of that state, regardless of the fact that in another state they would be labeled *learning disabled, maladjusted,* or *Type 600.* For example, for a number of years the state of Illinois decided that "maladjusted children . . . means children between the ages of 5 and 21 years who, because of social and emotional problems, are unable to make constructive use of their school experience and require the provisions of special services designed to promote their educational growth and development" (School Code of Illinois, 1988, 14–1, par. 2). Children who in most states would be considered *learning disabled* were considered, in Illinois, to be *maladjusted* because "social problems" was interpreted as "serious educational maladjustment resulting from extreme discrepancy between ability and school achievement associated with such factors as perceptual impairment, severe learning disorders, and neurological disorders" (School Code of Illinois, 1988, Article VII, Rule 7.01b). One is tempted to speculate that if funds were provided for "sinful" children, wickedness would abound among our youngsters.

Environmental Cues

No one likes to take the blame for children's educational deficiencies—not parents, and certainly not teachers who are always tempted to look outside the classroom for the reasons for the child's lack of success. The mind, the intelligence, the culture, the emotions, the family, the brain—certainly, somehow, somewhere, teachers hope to find the locus of the problem and avoid having the buck stop with them. How often have children been labeled *mentally retarded, learning disabled,* or *emotionally disturbed* primarily because teachers did not recognize their own ineptitude? It is clear that many times teachers inadvertently reinforce the very behavior they want to stop (Axlerod & Hall, 1999; Kazdin, 2001; Miltenberger, 2001; D. D. Smith, 1984; Wallace & Kauffman, 1986) or simply do not know how to teach effectively (Engelmann & Carnine, 1982; Mercer & Mercer, 2001).

Furthermore, we want to emphasize the point that labels themselves do not add any information to our store of knowledge, offer any explanation of what is observed, or provide new insights. Labels are only succinct ways of communicating a concept or set of expectations. There is danger in thinking that once a problem is classified or labeled, a solution has been found and appropriate intervention will automatically follow. There is also danger in using labels as explanations for behavior, a type of circular reasoning known as *reification*:

> "Why isn't this child, who appears to be of normal intelligence, learning to read?"
>
> "Well, because he has a learning disability."
>
> "But how do you know that he is learning disabled?"
>
> "Because he appears to have normal intelligence but he isn't learning to read."

The danger in reification or in labeling for its own sake is that sloppy thinking will prevent children from being helped. Exceptional children have suffered too many indignities and have waited too long for effective education for us to play word games.

CURRENT DEVELOPMENTS

Within the last few years, a number of important events have occurred that have influenced the field of learning disabilities. Services to students with learning disabilities have expanded to include children at a preschool level as well as college students. Although there is still a paucity of information about the corresponding services for adults with learning disabilities, some attention is beginning to be directed in this area (Lerner, 2003; Mercer & Mercer, 2001; Patton & Polloway, 1982).

The sophistication of various organizations concerned with learning disabilities has also been witnessed. The Learning Disabilities Association of America has continued to be concerned with the problems faced by LD citizens. The Council for Learning Disabilities, the Division for Learning Disabilities of the Council for Exceptional Children, and the International Dyslexia Association also have continued to be professionally involved by encouraging research, sharing information, and furthering the development of the field. In addition, in various locations throughout the nation, other organizations are forming. These groups, however, differ from those previously mentioned in that they are composed of adults with learning disabilities (e.g., groups such as Time Out to Enjoy).

A current controversy in the field of learning disabilities involves the inclusion movement. The basic premise of this movement is that many students who are served in pull-out programs (i. e., resource settings) for part of the day could be better educated in the regular classroom. Inclusion involves the merger of special education and regular education and requires that regular educators assume primary responsibility for the education of all students, including those with disabilities or special needs.

Implementation of inclusionary practices would require the following: (a) extensive in-service and preservice training for regular educators in special education competencies, (b) collaboration and shared responsibility between regular and special educators, and (c) a restructuring of regular education settings to accommodate the needs of all children.

Opponents of inclusion cite lack of research support, erroneous assumptions about the basis of the program, and the potential for failure of the program and an associated negative impact on integration/mainstreaming efforts as reasons to maintain the current service delivery models. Proponents of inclusion point to the inappropriateness of all pull-out (resource room) programs for children with mild handicaps (Lewis & Doorlag, 2003; Smith, Polloway, Patton, & Dowdy, 2004; Will, 1986; Wood, 2002), the mandate to educate children with disabilities in the least restrictive environment, and the increased number of at-risk students served by the public schools as major components in their rationale. Such inclusionary programs require that teachers and administrators be well trained in inclusion practices (Boyer & Bandy, 1997), be committed to the principle of inclusion (Wigle & Wilcox, 1997), and be focused on individualizing all instructional modifications and accommodations (Bryant, Dean, Elrod, & Blackbourn, 1999). Regardless of one's perspective related to inclusion, the program seems to be taking root

(Bartlett, Weisenstien, & Etscheidt, 2002; Baum & Duffelmeyer, 1990; Smith et al., 2004).

Major research efforts have also focused on individuals with learning disabilities. In 1977, the federal government funded five major research projects specifically focusing on students with learning disabilities. The five institutes were located at the University of Illinois at Chicago Circle, the University of Kansas, the University of Minnesota, the University of Virginia, and Columbia Teachers College in New York. All of these LD institutes developed multifaceted research programs, the results of which are having a major impact on the field of learning disabilities (Kneedler & Hallahan, 1983). By no means do we want to imply that the only notable research is emanating from these sources. On the contrary, many other significant research efforts have been conducted by various research groups and other individuals as well.

Two of the most prominent have been the learning strategies approach (Alley & Deshler, 1979; Deshler, Ellis, & Lenz, 1996) and the learning styles approach (Dunn, 1990). Although both approaches have gained a good deal of acceptance, they differ significantly in the theory and means employed in intervening with students who have learning disabilities. Also, several special education professionals question the legitimacy of the learning styles approach (Kavale & Forness, 1987, 1990) (see Figure 3.3).

The learning strategies approach focuses on teaching the student with learning disabilities specific ways to process information. The goals of the learning strategies approach are to (a) provide students with learning disabilities with those skills necessary to function in the regular classroom and (b) facilitate generalization of these skills to "normal" academic settings. Strategies that focus on test taking, paraphrasing, sentence writing, and social interaction are all included in the learning strategies approach.

The learning styles approach focuses on modifying instruction according to an individual student's learning style. In this approach, the teacher assesses the student to determine how he or she learns best and then modifies materials, methods, and the classroom environment to meet the student's needs. The primary goal of the learning styles approach is to make the classroom environment more responsive to the student with learning disabilities' needs.

Both the learning styles and learning strategies approaches to instruction have given support to the inclusion movement for students with learning disabilities. This movement, which is an outgrowth of the mainstreaming movement of the 1970s and the regular education initiative of the 1980s, contends that students with disabilities can learn most effectively in regular classroom settings with their age-appropriate peers. For the inclusion movement to succeed, teachers must possess the necessary skills to create a facilitative classroom environment and provide effective instruction to students with disabilities. Indeed, the American Federation of Teachers has recently adopted a position in opposition to inclusive education due to the lack of preparedness among regular teachers to effectively manage and teach students with disabilities. The learning strategies and learning styles

	Learning Styles	Learning Strategies
Goal	Create classroom environments that are responsive to the specific learning needs of students.	Provide the students with critical skills necessary to process classroom content.
Responsibility for academic success	The teacher.	The student.
Advantages	1. Puts the student at the center of the instructional process. 2. Focuses on individualization of intervention. 3. Ties weaker modalities into the instructional process to develop student proficiency in these areas.	1. Strong, longitudinal research base. 2. Focuses on generalization of the skills acquired to a variety of environments. 3. Can facilitate transition from class to class and/or school to school. 4. Ties content and strategies together in the instructional setting.
Disadvantages	1. May inhibit effective transition due to a lack of consistency between teachers and/or schools. 2. Theoretical underpinning and research-base controversial.	1. Requires linguistic ability appropriate to a 9-year-old. 2. Requires intensive, long-term intervention to teach specific strategies.

Figure 3.3
A Comparison of the Learning Styles and Learning Strategies Approaches to Instruction

approaches to instruction could offer the regular classroom teacher viable alternative means for accomplishing the goals of the inclusive education movement.

At the present time, professionals and nonprofessionals alike are tackling some major questions confronting the field. These issues include the following:

How are services best delivered to students with learning disabilities?

Which model of intervention (remedial, compensatory, vocational, functional skills, or learning strategy) is most appropriate for students with learning disabilities?

How should persons with learning disabilities be identified?

Are various intervention techniques and therapies (e.g., pharmacological, dietary, and megavitamin) effective or warranted?

How do students with learning disabilities process information?

What impact and implication does the competency movement have on students with learning disabilities?

How should we prepare professionals to work with students who possess learning disabilities?

Attempts to ameliorate the confusion and indefiniteness of the concept of learning disabilities and efforts to research the nature of this condition must be encouraged, supported, and continued. Yet we must always be mindful of the specific individuals toward whom such endeavors are directed. The problems that they face daily can have profound social, academic, and vocational repercussions. Let us not fail to realize a learning disability is not something that a person merely outgrows.

SUGGESTIONS FOR WORKING WITH PEOPLE WITH LEARNING DISABILITIES

1.   Always remember the major purpose or objective of the child's effort. It is easy to lose sight of the relative unimportance of some of the things we expect from nondisabled children. For example, if the goal is to have the child write a composition, do not be obsessive about neatness and spelling; rather focus on the expression and flow of ideas.

2.   Be sure you do not expect the child to perform beyond his or her capacity. A child cannot be expected to perform tasks *just because he or she is intellectually bright.* Some individuals have specific learning problems even though they are generally bright. Expect the child to try and make a little improvement in the area where you are offering instruction.

3.   Realize that working in the area of disability is frustrating. Remember that some things are very hard for you to do, and you probably have found successful ways of avoiding them. When you are pushed to do things you find very difficult (singing, swimming, reading, or math, for example), you probably tend to become emotional about it rather quickly. You should not be surprised if a child responds in the same way.

4.   Try another way. See if you can find a different method of teaching the skill, one that might be simpler or easier for the child. Or try to substitute a slightly different skill for the one that seems so difficult to learn. For example, if the child has great difficulty writing things by hand, try letting her or him type or use a word processor.

5.   Be sure the environment is conducive to learning and successful performance. Give clear instructions. Comment positively on the child's efforts. Eliminate distractions by working in a quiet, uncluttered place.

6.   Try to figure out what strategies the child is using to learn or perform. If he or she does not appear to be using a strategy or is using one that is ineffective,

try to think through and teach the child a new and more effective approach to the task. For example, the child may not be aware of the common strategies people use to try to remember things, like saying things to themselves and making associations between what they can and are trying to remember.

PONDER THESE

1. If you were in Patrick Milton Wills' shoes, how would you handle the cases of Edwin and J. C.? (See the vignette at the beginning of this chapter.)
2. Professionals in the field of assessment and special education often have difficulty deciding whether a student is learning disabled or merely low achieving as a result of any number of environmental, economic, or cultural reasons. What would be the advantages and disadvantages of using a term like *educationally handicapped* to describe all students who are having learning-related problems in school?
3. Federal and some state governments are considering putting a "cap" on the LD category—that is, passing laws or regulations that would prohibit school districts from receiving funding for services to more than a certain percentage of students placed in LD programs. For example, a district might receive special education funding for LD programs for no more than 2 percent of its enrollment. Debate the merits of such a cap.

INFORMATION/RESOURCES

1. The Center on Learning
   3061 Dole Center
   University of Kansas
   Lawrence, KS 66045
2. Center for the Study of Learning and Teaching Styles
   St. John's University
   Jamaica, NY 11439
3. The Slingerland Institute
   One Bellevue Center
   411 108th Avenue N.E.
   Bellevue, WA 98004
4. Council for Learning Disabilities
   P.O. Box 40303
   Overland Park, KS 66204

Online Resources

Council for Exceptional Children/Division for Learning Disabilities http://www.teachingld.org

International Dyslexia Association http://www.interdys.org

Kansas Center for Research on Learning http://www.ku-crl.org

Learning Disabilities Association http://www.ldanatl.org

National Center for Learning Disabilities http://www.ld.org

National Dropout Prevention Center http://www.dropoutprevention.org

REFERENCES

Alley, G. R., & Deshler, D. (1979). *Teaching the learning disabled adolescent: Strategies and methods.* Denver, CO: Love Publishing Company.

Axelrod, S., & Hall, R. V. (1999). *Behavior modification: Basic principles.* Austin, TX: PRO-ED.

Bartlett, L. D., Weisenstien, G. R., & Etscheidt, S. (2002). *Successful inclusion for school leaders.* Upper Saddle River, NJ: Merrill/Prentice Hall.

Baum, D. D., & Duffelmeyer, F. (1990). The regular education initiative: Is it developing roots?

National Forum of Special Education Journal, 2, 4–11.

Baum, D. D., Duffelmeyer, F., & Geeland, M. (1988). An investigation of the prevalence of social dysfunction among learning disabled students. *Journal of Learning Disabilities, 21,* 380–381.

Bender, W. N., & Wall, M. E. (1994). Social-emotional development of students with learning disabilities. *Learning Disabilities Quarterly, 17,* 323–341.

Blackbourn, J. M. (1989). Acquisition and generalization of social skills in elementary-age children with learning disabilities. *Journal of Learning Disabilities, 22,* 28–34.

Boyer, W. A. R., & Bandy, H. (1997). Rural teachers' perceptions of the current state of inclusion: Knowledge, training, teaching practices, and adequacy of support systems. *Exceptionality, 7*(1), 1–18.

Bryant, R., Dean, M., Elrod, G. F., & Blackbourn, J. M. (1999). Rural general education teachers' opinions of adaptations for inclusive classrooms: A renewed call for dual licensure. *Rural Special Education Quarterly, 18*(1), 5–11.

Burbach, H. J. (1981). The labeling process: A sociological analysis. In J. M. Kauffman & D. P. Hallahan (Eds.), *Handbook of special education* (pp. 361–377). Upper Saddle River, NJ: Merrill/Prentice Hall.

Deshler, D. D., Ellis, E. S., & Lenz, B. K. (1996). *Teaching adolescents with learning disabilities: Strategies and methods* (2nd ed.). Denver, CO: Love Publishing Company.

Dunn, R. (1990). Bias over substance: A critical analysis of Kavale & Forness' report on modality based instruction. *Exceptional Children, 56,* 352–356.

Ellis, E. (1991). *SLANT: A starter strategy for class participation.* Lawrence, KS: EDGE Enterprises.

Engelmann, S., & Carnine, D. (1982). *Theory of instruction: Principles and applications.* New York: Irvington.

Gnagey, W. J. (1968). *The psychology of discipline in the classroom.* Upper Saddle River, NJ: Merrill/Prentice Hall.

Hallahan, D. P., & Kauffman, J. M. (1977). Categories, labels, behavioral characteristics: ED, LD, and EMR reconsidered. *Journal of Special Education, 11,* 139–149.

Hallahan, D. P., Kauffman, J. M., & Lloyd, J. W. (1985). *Introduction to learning disabilities.* Upper Saddle River, NJ: Merrill/Prentice Hall.

Hammill, D. D., Leigh, J. E., McNutt, G., & Larsen, S. C. (1981). A new definition of learning disabilities. *Learning Disability Quarterly, 4,* 336–342.

Kauffman, J. M. (2001). *Characteristics of emotional and behavioral disorders of children and youth* (7th ed.). Upper Saddle River, NJ: Merrill/Prentice Hall.

Kavale, K. A., & Forness, S. R. (1987). Substance over style: Assessing the efficacy of modality testing and teaching. *Exceptional Children, 54,* 228–239.

Kavale, K. A., & Forness, S. R. (1990). Substance over style: A rejoinder to Dunn's animadversions. *Exceptional Children, 56,* 357–361.

Kazdin, A. E. (2001). *Behavior modification in applied settings* (6th ed.). Belmont, CA: Wadsworth.

Kneedler, R. D., & Hallahan, D. P. (Eds.). (1983). Research in learning disabilities: Summaries of the institutes. *Exceptional Education Quarterly, 4*(1), 43–51.

Lerner, J. (2003). *Learning disabilities: Theories, diagnosis, and teaching strategies* (9th ed.). Boston: Houghton Mifflin.

Lewis, L. D., and Doorlag, D. H. (2003). *Teaching special students in general education classrooms* (6th ed.). Upper Saddle River, NJ: Merrill/Prentice Hall.

Mercer, C. D. (1997). *Students with learning disabilities* (5th ed.). Upper Saddle River, NJ: Merrill/Prentice Hall.

Mercer, C. D., King-Sears, P., & Mercer, A. R. (1990). Learning disabilities definitions and criteria used by state education departments. *Learning Disabilities Quarterly, 13*(2), 141–152.

Mercer, C. D., & Mercer, A. R. (2001). *Teaching students with learning problems* (6th ed.). Upper Saddle River, NJ: Merrill/Prentice Hall.

Miltenberger, R. G. (2001). *Behavior modification: Principles and procedures* (6th ed.). Belmont, CA: Wadsworth.

Patton, J. R., & Polloway, E. A. (1982). The learning disabled: The adult years. *Topics in Learning and Learning Disabilities, 2*(3), 79–88.

Reeve, R. E., & Kauffman, J. M. (1988). Learning disabilities. In V. B. Van Hasselt, P. S. Strain, & M. Hersen (Eds.), *Handbook of developmental and physical disabilities* (pp. 316–335). New York: Plenum.

Smith, D. D. (1984). *Effective discipline.* Austin, TX: Pro-Ed.

Smith, T. E. C., Polloway, E. A., Patton, J. R., & Dowdy, C. A. (2004). *Teaching children with special needs in inclusive settings* (4th ed.). Boston: Allyn & Bacon.

U. S. Department of Education. (2000). *Twenty-second annual report to Congress on the implementation of the Individuals with Disabilities Education Act.* Washington, DC: Author.

U. S. Office of Education (1977). *Education of all handicapped children: Implementation of Part B of the Education of the Handicapped Act. Federal Register, 42*, 42474–42518.

Wallace, G., & Kauffman, J. M. (1986). *Teaching students with learning and behavior problems* (3rd ed.). Upper Saddle River, NJ: Merrill/Prentice Hall.

White, M. A., & Charry, J. (Eds.). (1966). *School disorder, intelligence, and social class.* New York: Teachers College Press.

Wigle, S. E., & Wilcox, D. J. (1997). Teacher and administrator attitudes toward full inclusion in rural mid-America. *Rural Special Education Quarterly, 16*(1), 3–7.

Will, M. (1986). *Educating students with learning problems: A shared responsibility.* Washington, DC: U.S. Department of Education.

Wood, J. W. (2002). *Adapting instruction to accommodate students in inclusive settings* (4th ed.). Upper Saddle River, NJ: Merrill/Prentice Hall.

CHAPTER 4

Attention Deficit/Hyperactivity Disorder

This chapter has been adapted from *Attention Deficit Hyperactivity Disorder in the Classroom: A Practical Guide for Teachers*, by C. A. Dowdy, J. R. Patton, T. E. C. Smith, and E. A. Polloway, 1998, Austin, TX: PRO-ED. Adapted by permission.

Sam, a very bright fourth grader, was found to have attention deficit/hyperactivity disorder (ADHD). He had an extremely difficult time paying attention to what was going on in the classroom. In a previous school, his resulting frustration with not being able to follow a discussion or teacher presentation led to some strange and inappropriate behaviors. These behaviors had become so extreme (e.g., getting on the floor and barking like a dog—his creativity allowed him to imitate a variety of breeds) that he was considered emotionally disturbed.

A number of months after he had been diagnosed as ADHD and had been on Ritalin, he approached his teacher and asked if he could stop taking the medication because he did not like the way it made him feel. Although it was not the teacher's call nor were his attention problems and hyperactivity completely under control, the teacher did contact Sam's mother and physician to discuss an idea she had. The teacher was comfortable with trying a behavioral program with Sam in the absence of any pharmacological intervention. She felt that Sam had demonstrated the incentive necessary to make such a system work.

The intervention was based on cueing Sam when his behavior was getting "out of control." When Sam started losing it, the teacher would briefly stop what she was doing, get his attention, and say "Sam, you need to get in control." She would also fingerspell the letters i and c as a paired association for "in control." Sam's response was typically an immediate attempt to get his behavior under his own control because he knew that otherwise he would have to get back on medication.

The goal of the program was self-control. The verbal reminder was faded out, so the teacher—never breaking her instructional stride—would simply fingerspell the letters i and c whenever necessary. Over the course of a few weeks, Sam was able to control his inattentive behaviors at levels comparable to his classmates. He never had to take medication for his attention problems again.

With his ability to control his own behaviors successfully, he was able to engage in schooling in ways he had not been able to do previously. He graduated from high school with honors and went on to attend one of the most prestigious institutions in the United States, majoring in engineering. There is no question that, even after he was able to self-regulate his behaviors, he still had his share of educational mishaps. However, his education journey turned out to be quite different from what had been predicted by observers during his dog days of elementary school.

Attention deficit/hyperactivity disorder is one of the most intriguing, beguiling, and complicated topics in the field of education. This condition has had a fascinating history and remains controversial today, mainly because professional perspectives and personal opinions vary greatly regarding the nature and treatment of ADHD. Both popular and scholarly media are replete with discussions about this disorder, sometimes contributing to the confusion surrounding its diagnosis and treatment. The last decade has witnessed an increased awareness of and activity regarding this disorder. Currently, ADHD is the most commonly diagnosed childhood mental health condition in the United States (LeFever, Villers, Morrow, & Vaughn, 2002).

BASIC CONCEPTS

Definitional Perspective

Attention deficit/hyperactivity disorder is an invisible disability that affects a significant number of individuals. As a developmental disability, it can be identified in childhood, continue into adulthood, result in significant problems in many functional life activities, and require disability-related services. For students, functional limitations will be reflected in difficulty with an assortment of school-related activities, both academic and nonacademic. ADHD is considered hidden, or invisible, because there are no specific physical characteristics associated with the condition; it is only through behavioral manifestations that it becomes recognizable.

Initial discovery of the disorder was made at the turn of the 20th century, and subsequent study of ADHD has refined both diagnostic criteria and the etiology of the disorder (Mercugliano, 1999). Fundamentally, however, the condition has referred to problems in attention, impulsivity, and hyperactivity. The predominance of any one of these features at a given period of time is a function of the professional thinking at that time.

Currently, the term *attention deficit/hyperactivity disorder* is being used most frequently in the United States. This terminology is used in the fourth edition of the *Diagnostic and Statistical Manual of Mental Disorders* (DSM-IV), published in 1994—the most frequently cited reference on this condition (American Psychiatric Association, 1994). From a global perspective, the World Health Organization's 10th edition of the *International Classification of Diseases* (ICD-10), published in 1992, is typically used and promotes the term *hyperkinetic disorders* to describe conditions related to problems in attention and hyperactivity.

Diagnostic Criteria

According to the DSM-IV, ADHD is classified as a disruptive disorder characterized by persistent patterns and inappropriate degrees of inattention and/or hyperactivity-impulsivity. These principal features distinguish ADHD from other disruptive disorders such as conduct order (i.e., physical fighting) and oppositional defiant behavior (i.e., recurrent pattern of disobedience).

The major criteria contained in DSM-IV are likely to guide diagnostic practice in the near future. The final criteria evolved from extensive committee work and changed throughout the process of revision. According to DSM-IV, ADHD can be one of four types that are based on two sets of symptoms. The diagnostic criteria are presented in Table 4.1.

Table 4.1
DSM-IV Diagnostic Criteria for Attention-Deficit/Hyperactivity Disorder

A. Either (1) or (2):
   (1) six (or more) of the following symptoms of **inattention** have persisted for at least 6 months to a degree that is maladaptive and inconsistent with developmental level:

   Inattention

   (a) often fails to give close attention to details or makes careless mistakes in schoolwork, work, or other activities
   (b) often has difficulty sustaining attention in tasks or play activities
   (c) often does not seem to listen when spoken to directly
   (d) often does not follow through on instructions and fails to finish schoolwork, chores, or duties in the workplace (not due to oppositional behavior or failure to understand instructions)
   (e) often has difficulty organizing tasks and activities
   (f) often avoids, dislikes, or is reluctant to engage in tasks that require sustained mental effort (such as schoolwork or home-work)
   (g) often loses things necessary for tasks or activities (e.g., toys, school assignments, pencils, books, or tools)
   (h) is often easily distracted by extraneous stimuli
   (i) is often forgetful in daily activities

   (2) six (or more) of the following symptoms of **hyperactivity-impulsivity** have persisted for at least 6 months to a degree that is maladaptive and inconsistent with developmental level:

   Hyperactivity

   (a) often fidgets with hands or feet or squirms in seat
   (b) often leaves seat in classroom or in other situations in which remaining seated is expected
   (c) often runs about or climbs excessively in situations in which it is inappropriate (in adolescents or adults, may be limited to subjective feelings or restlessness)
   (d) often has difficulty playing or engaging in leisure activities quietly

   (e) is often "on the go" or often acts as if "driven by a motor"
   (f) often talks excessively

   Impulsivity

   (g) often blurts out answers before questions have been completed
   (h) often has difficulty awaiting turn
   (i) often interrupts or intrudes on others (e.g., butts into conversations or games)

B. Some hyperactive-impulsive or inattentive symptoms that caused impairment were present before age 7 years.
C. Some impairment from the symptoms is present in two or more settings (e.g., at school [or work] and at home).
D. There must be clear evidence of clinically significant impairment in social, academic, or occupational functioning.
E. The symptoms do not occur exclusively during the course of a pervasive developmental disorder, schizophrenia, or other psychotic disorder and are not better accounted for by another mental disorder (e.g., mood disorder, anxiety disorder, dissociative disorder, or a personality disorder).

Code based on type:
314.01 Attention-Deficit/Hyperactivity Disorder, Combined Type: if both Criteria A1 and A2 are met for the past 6 months
314.00 Attention-Deficit/Hyperactivity Disorder, Predominantly Inattentive Type: if Criterion A1 is met but Criterion A2 is not met for the past 6 months
314.01 Attention-Deficit/Hyperactivity Disorder, Predominantly Hyperactive-Impulsive Type: if Criterion A2 is met but Criterion A1 is not met for the past 6 months
Coding note: For individuals (especially adolescents and adults) who currently have symptoms that no longer meet full criteria, "In Partial Remission" should be specified.
314.09 Attention-Deficit/Hyperactivity Disorder Not Otherwise Specified: This category is for disorders with prominent symptoms of inattention or hyperactivity-impulsivity that do not meet criteria for Attention-Deficit/Hyperactivity Disorder.

Source: Reprinted with permission from the *Diagnostic and Statistical Manual of Mental Disorders,* Fourth Edition. Copyright 1994 American Phychiatric Association.

Based on the criteria listed in Table 4.1, four types of ADHD are possible. The DSM-IV codes for these four are listed in brackets.

❑ Attention-deficit/hyperactivity disorder, combined type (if criteria A1 and A2 are met for the past 6 months) [314.01]
❑ Attention-deficit/hyperactivity disorder, predominantly inattentive type (if criterion A1 is met but criterion A2 is not met for the last 6 months) [314.00]
❑ Attention-deficit/hyperactivity disorder, predominantly hyperactive-impulsive type (if criterion A2 is met but criterion A1 is not met for the last 6 months) [314.01]
❑ Attention-deficit/hyperactivity disorder not otherwise specified (for disorders with prominent symptoms of inattention or hyperactivity-impulsivity that do not meet criteria for ADHD) [314.09]

Teachers should be familiar with the symptoms that are associated with the criteria listed in Table 4.1 and with the different types of ADHD. Since the diagnosis of ADHD typically occurs outside of educational settings by psychologists or medical personnel, students so identified will bring with them a dossier of information about their condition that most likely will be based on DSM-IV criteria.

Prevalence of ADHD

Estimates of the existence of attention deficit/hyperactivity disorder in the school-age population range from conservative figures under 2 percent to liberal ones of 30 percent. These extreme variations in prevalence rates reflect the lack of an exact definition and problems in identification. Nevertheless, even more conservative estimates suggest that a substantial number of individuals may have this condition. The presence of ADHD has been documented in other cultures and countries, including Germany, Korea, India, Brazil, and Norway, to name only a few (Weyandt, 2001). Boys are three times as likely to be diagnosed with ADHD than are girls (Barkley, 1995). Some research, however, suggests that the prevalence of ADHD in girls is more comparable to boys, yet the disorder remains undiagnosed because girls are less hyperactive and more inattentive (Hinshaw, 2002). Inattention may be less obvious than hyperactivity to teachers and parents.

Legal Bases for Service Delivery and Protection

Individuals with ADHD struggle with the presence of this disorder throughout their life spans; therefore, protection of their individual rights may be necessary throughout their lives. The legal rights of individuals with ADHD are protected by three pieces of federal legislation (Weyandt, 2001). Whereas IDEA and Section 504 legislation protect the educational rights of school-aged children with ADHD, the Americans With Disabilities Act may offer protection in postsecondary and work environments during adulthood.

Individuals with Disabilities Act (IDEA) (PL 101–476). Attention deficit/hyperactivity disorder is recognized as a disability under IDEA; however, it has not been added as a separate disability category in the reauthorizations of this law. Some people are pleased that ADHD has finally been recognized under IDEA; others are very disappointed that it did not become a distinct category of disability.

In 1991, the U.S. Department of Education (DOE) issued a policy memorandum that indicated that students with attention deficit disorder (the terminology used by DOE) who need special education and/or related services can qualify for such services under existing categories. Students whose primary disability is ADHD are eligible under the category Other Health Impaired (OHI). This category includes all chronic and acute conditions that result in limited alertness and that adversely affect educational performance. Evidence is accumulating to suggest that the OHI categorical designation is being utilized for students identified as ADHD; however, 50 percent of children with ADHD do not qualify for special education (Reid & Maag, 1998).

Students whose primary disability is not ADHD, although they display the symptoms highlighted in Table 4.1, may be likely to qualify under other categories. For instance, Reid, Maag, Vasa, and Wright (1994), in their school-based study of students with ADHD who were receiving special education services, found that nearly 52 percent identified as behaviorally disordered, 29 percent identified as learning disabled, and 9 percent identified as mentally retarded possessed characteristics related to ADHD.

During the last few years, many professionals have come to realize that many students with ADHD were floundering in school and not qualifying for services that might be beneficial to them. As a result, changes in policy and thinking have occurred prompted by the 1991 DOE policy memorandum, which drew attention to this underserved population. Unfortunately, policy and thinking do not always result in best practice.

Section 504 of the Vocational Rehabilitation Act (PL 93–112). Many students with ADHD qualify for services under Section 504 of the Vocational Rehabilitation Act. The intent of the law, as it applies to schools, is to provide general or special education and related aids and services that are designed to accommodate the individual educational needs of students with disabilities as adequately as the needs of those who are not disabled. This is not a "special education" law but a civil rights law that covers the entire educational system.

Section 504 includes a larger group of persons who are disabled than are covered by IDEA and differs in some respects from IDEA as highlighted in chapter 1. This law protects all students who have disabilities, defined as any physical or mental impairment that substantially limits one or more major life activities. Since one of the stated life activities is learning, it becomes obvious that it also applies to schools. If a school has reason to believe that a student has a disability as defined under Section 504, the school must evaluate the student. If it is determined that the student has a disability under this law, then the school must develop and implement a plan for the delivery of services that are needed (Council of Administrators in Special Education, 1992). However, a written individualized education program is not required.

If a student with ADHD does not qualify for services under IDEA, it might be possible to do so under Section 504. However, many of the substantive and procedural components found in IDEA are either different or missing. Nevertheless, Section 504 provides another avenue for accommodating the needs of students with ADHD.

Americans with Disabilities Act of 1990 (PL 101–336).   When high school students with ADHD transition into postsecondary or employment settings, they may continue to need accommodations or modifications. In 1990, the Americans With Disabilities Act (ADA) was enacted to provide protection against discrimination for all people with disabilities. Rather than the entitlement (guaranteed protection, the onus for which is on the schools and teachers) provided by IDEA, ADA, like Section 504, provides protection against discrimination, but the responsibility for disability disclosure and requests for accommodations remain squarely on the shoulders of the individual with disabilities. Therefore, if a college student with ADHD needs to have preferential seating near the instructor in a large lecture hall, the student must seek such an accommodation through the proper channels at the university or college he or she attends.

Causes of ADHD

Like the causes of other developmental disabilities of students, the precise etiology of ADHD is complex and remains under investigation. Generally, researchers have acknowledged that the causes of this disorder are a result of the interaction of neuropsychological (i.e., damage to a specific part of the brain), neurochemical (i.e., chemical imbalance), genetic (i.e., familial predisposition), and physiological variables (i.e., atypical brain activity in certain lobes of the brain) (Weyandt, 2001). Some evidence suggests that certain environmental factors (i.e., exposure to toxins such as lead and cigarette smoke) may contribute to the presence of ADHD (Mercugliano, 1999). A key point here is to note that many myths regarding the causes of ADHD that have been introduced through the popular press (i.e., high-sugar diets) have not been substantiated by research (Weyandt, 2001). Similarly, parenting skills are not the cause of ADHD; however, it is true that some parenting styles and interactions have been observed to either exacerbate or prohibit problematic ADHD-related behaviors in children (Mercugliano, 1999).

Historically, ADHD has been researched from a medical perspective (Reid & Maag, 1998). The vast majority of information and research about ADHD has focused on the etiology rather than on treatment and intervention. As a result, little of this information is of immediate or practical use for teachers, parents, and students. The remainder of the focus here is on characteristic behaviors and challenges of students with ADHD and interventions designed to meet their needs.

CHARACTERISTICS

Attention deficit and hyperactivity disorders impact peoples' lives across the life span. The characteristic manifestations of the disability, however, may differ according to the developmental stage of the person with ADHD. Additionally, the setting demands of home, school, and work can impact the ADHD-related symptoms and expressions of the disorder.

Classroom Manifestations

The specific characteristics of ADHD that manifest themselves in the classroom can vary greatly. Recognizing them and knowing how to accommodate them are challenges that confront teachers. Behaviors that might be associated with ADHD and manifested in classroom settings can be grouped into the following categories: attention/concentration, reasoning/information processing, memory, executive functions (e.g., planning/organizing actions), social/emotional areas, communication, and academic performance. Most of the suggested ways for accommodating each presenting behavior are relatively minor modifications and can be accomplished easily. However, the payoff for taking the time to make these accommodations is well worth the effort. Specific techniques for addressing various classroom manifestations of ADHD can be found in other sources (Dowdy, Patton, Smith, & Polloway, 1998).

A classroom behavior that is often misinterpreted by teachers is a lack of competence. As Goldstein and Goldstein (1990) point out, what is often seen as purposeful noncompliance is actually better viewed as a lack of competence. In other words, many students with ADHD will seem to defy teacher directives when in fact they really are not able to react in a competent way. The misinterpretation of a lack of confidence and the likely punishment that follows it create problems for students who are really not trying to defy their teachers. For this reason, it is important for teachers to be aware of this phenomenon and be able to distinguish between the two behaviors.

Identifying Features

Assessment and diagnosis of the presence of ADHD during each of the developmental stages discussed next follow a similar pattern. A physician's diagnosis is necessary. Often, a pediatrician or a developmental psychiatrist can provide assessments for such a diagnosis. Typically, these professionals rely on physical examinations, the collection of medical, social, and developmental histories, and neurodevelopmental assessments (Accardo, 1999). Referrals of students to medical doctors by parents and teachers should include the use of behavioral checklists and rating scales to determine to what extent ADHD is being exhibited in the classroom and home settings. For adults, self-referrals may occur and adult patients would be asked to rate their own behavior. Assessment of this disorder is based on the coexistence of observable ADHD-related behaviors that occur across settings (i.e., home and school) and throughout a person's life span.

Infancy and Early Childhood.   Mothers of children with ADHD have reported high activity levels for their children *in utero,* during the final stages of pregnancy (Accardo, 1999). Although these babies generally match developmental milestones of typically developing infants, they tend to be fussy, require lots of attention, and do not adhere to sleeping patterns typical of infancy.

Most young children are frequently characterized as having poor attention spans, acting impulsively, and maintaining high levels of activity at some point during their development. For young children with ADHD, however, these characteristics are noticeably more pronounced than in typically developing children. In fact, for young children with ADHD, high activity levels, more than inattention and impulsivity, are reported by parents and teachers. Children with ADHD are the children who run through the house/park/classroom at breakneck speeds seemingly never to tire. They pursue physical activity (i.e., climbing and jumping) more than quiet, low-energy activities (e.g., listening to a story). Toddlers with ADHD may stop napping earlier than those without ADHD.

Childhood.   Elementary and early middle school–aged children with ADHD have problems staying on task and completing assigned work. They tend to be restless and may be physically active at their desks (e.g., fidgeting, leaning back in chair) or they may move about the classroom excessively. They may be poor turn-takers and may often speak without raising their hands. Because of these impulsive behaviors, peers without ADHD may react negatively toward students with ADHD, and social interaction problems can occur.

Adolescence.   Although adolescents with ADHD often experience diminished symptoms of hyperactivity, inattention, and impulsivity, these characteristic features are generally still present and may be the source of academic and social difficulties experienced by teens with ADHD. These students are more likely to fail courses, get suspended, score lower on achievement tests, and engage in substance abuse than are their peers without ADHD (Schwiebert, Sealander, & Dennison, 2002).

Secondary students with ADHD can struggle with distractibility and disorganization, as well as social/emotional problems associated with depression and low self-esteem (Barkley, 1995). Conduct disorders are more common among students with ADHD, and parents report more difficulty controlling the behavior of their children with ADHD during this developmental stage (Weyandt, 2001). Furthermore, teens with ADHD often impulsively engage in risky behavior.

Adulthood.   Originally ADHD was conceptualized as a childhood disorder that disappeared during adulthood. Current theories, however, reflect the increasing documentation of ADHD in adults (Franklin & Bender, 1997). It is important to note that ADHD is not an adult-onset disorder; rather, an adult with ADHD may have been undiagnosed during childhood. Assessments for adults will reflect the presence of ADHD symptoms over a lifetime, as respondents typically report childhood manifestations of the disorder.

Typical problems associated with the disorder (i.e., inattentiveness, impulsivity) can cause problems in both postsecondary education and employment settings. Academic skills necessary to succeed in colleges and university settings may be lacking if, as an adolescent, the adult with ADHD did not develop study skills and academic content mastery. Furthermore, adult settings demand independent and social behavior that is conducive to collaboration, including self-regulation, self-assessment, acceptance of constructive criticism, and goal setting and attainment. Each of these skills may be challenging to a person who acts on impulse and struggles to maintain task persistence.

As students with ADHD mature, two noteworthy scenarios can result: (a) The characteristics associated with one's condition continue to be problematic for the individual and (b) the residual effects of previous problems associated with ADHD linger. Either scenario can have a profound effect on the adult outcomes of individuals with ADHD. Follow-up studies reveal that both negative (i.e., increased substance abuse problems, lack of completion of college) and positive outcomes (i.e., successful employment in high-intensity jobs and jobs that require creativity and innovation) for adults with ADHD have been reported (Weyandt, 2001). Successful adult adjustment is determined by the following general variables: intelligence, socioeconomic status, socialization, activity level, tolerance of delayed rewards, aggression, and family mental health.

INTERVENTIONS

The medical model that guides the treatment of ADHD includes the use of medication to control symptoms of hyperactivity, impulsivity, and inattention. Yet, the most successful interventions for students with ADHD, regardless of their developmental stage, involve an additional component of combined school-based (our focus here) and home-based efforts. At various points in a person's life, options to forego medication therapy in favor of environmental interventions, accommodations, and modifications may be explored. Similarly, medication may provide sufficient support, particularly in adulthood, so that certain interventions, accommodations, and modifications are not necessary. A key point to remember is that consideration must be given to each component in order for the best choices to be made.

Placement Realities

Most students with ADHD are in general education classrooms and do not need to be removed from these settings. However, certain accommodations may need to be made to address their needs. Reid et al. (1994) found that the majority of students with ADHD who were receiving special education services were in general education most, or all, of their school day.

That most students with ADHD are in general education suggests that classroom teachers need to understand this condition and know how to deal with it.

Special educators must be prepared to collaborate with general educators in this venture and know how to modify curriculum, instruction, and assignments. Special education teachers also need to be competent managers of behavior and adept at teaching students how to manage their own behavior.

School-Based Model of Intervention

Even though it has been established that ADHD is not just a childhood condition, it is also true that most intervention efforts, when they are implemented, occur in school settings. This is not to suggest that adult issues are not as important, because various facets of ADHD can significantly affect the lives of adults, as discussed in the previous section.

A school-based approach to addressing the needs of students with ADHD must be comprehensive to ensure appropriateness. A model of educational intervention that covers a full range of target areas is depicted in Figure 4.1. This model is built on four fundamental intervention areas: environmental management, instructional accommodations, student-regulated strategies, and medical management. It also contains two mediating variables (identification procedures and placement/programmatic considerations) that influence how the four major areas are invoked. The model also has two supportive features (counseling and collaboration) that enhance the overall quality of intervention services. A brief explanation of the four major intervention areas is provided next.

Environmental Management.   Environmental management relates closely to the concept of classroom management, which can be defined as "all teacher-directed activities that support the efficient operations of the classroom and that help establish optimal conditions for learning" (Smith, Polloway, Patton, & Dowdy, 2004, p. 414). Changes to the classroom setting and implementation of behavior management systems are examples of environmental management.

Figure 4.1
Model of Educational Intervention

Source: From *Attention Deficit Hyperactivity Disorder in the Classroom: A Practical Guide for Teachers,* by C. A. Dowdy, J. R. Patton, T. E. C. Smith, and E. A. Polloway, 1998, Austin, TX: PRO-ED. Reprinted by permission.

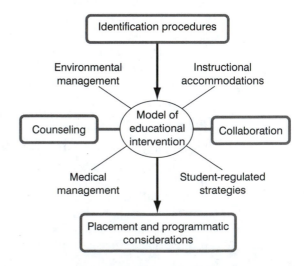

Classroom or environmental management is made up of the following seven dimensions, all of which should be considered when addressing the needs of students with ADHD (also given are select examples that relate to students with ADHD):

1. *Psychosocial:* student, teacher, peer, family factors
2. *Physical:* arrangement of classroom, seating, assistive technology
3. *Instructional:* scheduling, transitions, grouping, lesson planning, homework
4. *Procedural:* classroom rules and procedures
5. *Behavioral:* creating and increasing desirable behaviors, decreasing undesirable behaviors, generalizing and maintaining behaviors
6. *Personnel:* teaching assistance, peer tutors, volunteers
7. *Organizational:* work environment of teacher, instructional applications

A working understanding of and proper application of behavior management principles are extremely important. Emphasis should be on the use of positive behavioral interventions and supports and movement toward a system where students self-regulate their behaviors.

Instructional Accommodations.　Students with ADHD may benefit greatly from certain accommodations that are made to their instructional programs. Such accommodations can involve curriculum, materials, instructional processes, and the products students produce as a result of instruction. Examples of accommodations that may be appropriate for students with ADHD include the following:

1. *Curriculum:* life skills, study skills, and social skills instruction
2. *Material:* use of a variety of media, advanced organizers, multilevel materials, graphic aids, highlighting
3. *Process:* active involvement in the lesson; use of a demonstration/guided practice/independent practice paradigm; clearly stated directions; cooperative learning situations; adaptations regarding speed, accuracy, and amount of assigned work
4. *Products:* alternative final products, portfolios, testing accommodations, grading considerations

Student-Regulated Strategies.　These strategies, though initially taught by the teacher, can be viewed as interventions that are intended to be implemented independently by students. Characteristically, students with ADHD display certain behaviors (e.g., various attentional problems) for which self-regulatory interventions (e.g., self-monitoring) are appropriate and warranted. These strategies offer the promise of enhancing the educational development of students with ADHD by

❏ Increasing their selective attention/focus
❏ Modifying their impulsive responding

❏ Providing them with verbal mediators to assist in academic and social problem-solving situations
❏ Teaching them effective self-instructional statements to enable them to "talk through" tasks and problems
❏ Providing strategies that may lead to improvement in peer relations and the development of prosocial behaviors (Rooney, 1995)

Medical Management.   Although school personnel are not responsible for the prescription of medication for students with ADHD, they do play an important role in its usage. Monitoring students who are on medication is probably the most critical aspect of being part of the treatment team. It is essential that school personnel communicate with parents and physicians regarding the effects of the medications that a student is taking.

Stimulants are commonly prescribed for the treatment of ADHD. The most commonly used medication is methylphenidate (the brand name is Ritalin), which is a mild stimulant. In fact, Ritalin production increased 650 percent between 1990 and 1997 (Moline & Frankenberger, 2001). Other medications used with children and adults with ADHD include amphetamines such as Cylert, Dexadrine, and Adderall.

The medications prescribed to address the behaviors associated with ADHD have a number of possible positive and negative outcomes. Some of the desirable outcomes of using medication with students who have ADHD are increased attention, improved academic performance, and increased appropriate behaviors. Some of the negative outcomes are the side effects of the medications, which can include weight loss, irritability, behavior swings, nausea, organ damage, and dizziness. Everybody involved with the treatment program must be alert to all of these factors and be willing to make adjustments as necessary.

TRENDS AND ISSUES

Attention deficit/hyperactivity disorder is a "hot" topic in education, medicine, and U.S. popular media. Like any controversial subject, there are many trends and issues that indicate current thinking. Brief discussion of some of the most prominent trends and issues follows:

❏ Properly identifying girls with ADHD is of current concern to teachers and researchers (Hinshaw, 2002). Girls may be less likely to act out than their male peers. If girls are not diagnosed and treated for ADHD, serious academic and social implications of the disorder may be misunderstood and go untreated, leaving young girls with ADHD with little self-awareness and few compensatory strategies.
❏ Grand-scale use of stimulant medications to treat ADHD is a controversial topic in the medical treatment of the disorder (Moline & Frankenberger, 2001). The prescription drugs used to treat ADHD are U.S. Drug Enforcement

Agency controlled substances. Long-term effects, both positive and negative, have not been clearly delineated by existing medical studies. Furthermore, students' attitudes about taking medication, stopping medication, and illegally sharing or selling medication are all key issues in need of further investigation.

❏ Helping students with ADHD develop social skills, in addition to academic skills, is a major concern when one considers that most adults with special needs lose jobs as a result of negative social interactions rather than an inability to perform job-related tasks. Increasing the social competencies of students with ADHD is key to ameliorating the negative social outcomes characteristically associated with this disorder (Stormont, 2001).

❏ Formal disciplinary procedures for students with disabilities attending public schools have been the subject of policy, legislation, and litigation (Yell, Drasgow, & Rozalski, 2001). When implementing suspensions and expulsions, for example, schools must determine whether the infraction is related to the student's disability (this is called *manifestation determination*). For students with ADHD, this may be particularly difficult to discern and, therefore, appropriate behavioral management (which may include suspension) may be contentious.

FINAL THOUGHTS

Attention deficit/hyperactivity disorder is a condition that has been discussed for some time now, but it still remains elusive. ADHD continues to mystify the teaching profession, families, and those who have it. From a school perspective, students with ADHD present a real challenge, because their problems create critical barriers to learning. From an adult perspective, these same characteristics, plus the baggage that comes with living with these problems for many years, can have a significant effect on major life functions. For these reasons, we must take this condition seriously and strive to do the following:

❏ Create accommodative environments in which persons with ADHD can thrive.
❏ Teach self-regulatory behaviors that create independence.
❏ Provide appropriate supports, as needed.
❏ Link individuals with requisite services.

SUGGESTIONS FOR WORKING WITH PEOPLE WITH ADHD

1. Consider the physical arrangements in which the person will be, for instance, a classroom or the workplace.
2. Present both verbal and nonverbal information in a clear and organized fashion.

3. Understand that certain behaviors should not be interpreted as noncompliance.
4. Allow individuals who are hyperactive to have opportunities to be active.
5. Refrain from using a behavioral intervention system that is largely dominated by the use of negative reinforcement (e.g., threats).
6. Teach individuals to manage their own behaviors.
7. Be an active member of the person's intervention team.
8. Prevent potential problems by considering them ahead of time and instituting appropriate accommodations.
9. Monitor the outcomes of a prescribed medication closely, and report this information regularly to parents and the treating physician.
10. Help individuals gain a realistic understanding of their strengths and limitations.

PONDER THESE

1. Consider the cross-cultural implications of ADHD. Are the criteria established in DSM-IV valid in other parts of the world?
2. Can you think of any television personalities—either actors or characters portrayed by actors—whose behaviors suggest a possible ADHD label?
3. Explain why students with ADHD continue to be underidentified and underserved in schools today.

4. How might the following areas of adult functioning be affected for someone with ADHD?
   ❑ Interpersonal relationships
   ❑ Personal responsibility
   ❑ Personal financial management
   ❑ Job seeking
   ❑ Leisure pursuits

INFORMATION/RESOURCES

1. National attention disorders associations are particularly helpful in providing information on all aspects of attention problems, as well as links to support groups:
   ❑ Attention Deficit Disorder Association
   http://www.add.org
   ❑ Children and Adults with Attention Deficit Disorder
   http://chadd.org

2. More general information about the spectrum of attention disorders and ADHD as a national health concern is available from:
   National Institutes for Health
   http://www.nimh.nih.gov/publicat/adhdmenu.cfm
3. Teacher and parent resources can be ordered from:
   Attention Deficit Information Network, Inc.
   http://www.addinfonetwork.com

REFERENCES

Accardo, P. (1999). A rational approach to the medical assessment of the child with attention-deficit/hyperactivity disorder. *Pediatric Clinics of North America, 46,* 845-856.

American Psychiatric Association. (1994). *Diagnostic and statistical manual of mental disorders* (4th ed.). Washington, DC: Author.

Barkley, R. A. (1995). *Taking charge of ADHD: The complete, authoritative guide for parents.* New York: Guilford Press.

Council of Administrators in Special Education. (1992). *Student access: Section 504 of the Rehabilitation Act of 1973.* Reston, VA: Author.

Dowdy, C. A., Patton, J. R., Smith, T. E. C., & Polloway, E. A. (1998). *Attention deficit hyperactivity disorder in the classroom: A practical guide for teachers.* Austin, TX: PRO-ED.

Franklin, L. M., & Bender, W. N. (1997). The adult with ADHD. In W. Bender (Ed.), *Understanding ADHD: A practical guide for teachers and parents.* Upper Saddle River, NJ: Merrill/Prentice Hall.

Goldstein, S., & Goldstein, M. (1990). *Managing attention disorders in children.* New York: Wiley.

Hinshaw, S. P. (2002). Preadolescent girls with attention-deficit/hyperactivity disorder: Background characteristics, comorbidity, cognitive and social functioning, and parenting practices. *Journal of Consulting & Clinical Psychology, 70,* 1086–1098.

LeFever, G. B., Villers, M. S., Morrow, A. L., & Vaughn, E. S. (2002). Parental perceptions of adverse educational outcomes among children diagnosed and treated for ADHD: A call for improved school/provider collaboration. *Psychology in the Schools, 39,* 63–71.

Mercugliano, M. (1999). What is attention-deficit/hyperactivity disorder? *Pediatric Clinics of North America, 46,* 831–843.

Moline, S., & Frankenberger, W. (2001). Use of stimulant medication for treatment of attention-deficit/hyperactivity disorder: A survey of middle and high school students' attitudes. *Psychology in the Schools, 38,* 569–584.

Reid, R., & Maag, J. W. (1998). Functional assessment: A method for developing classroom-based accommodations and interventions for children with ADHD. *Reading & Writing Quarterly, 14*(1), 9–15.

Reid, R., Maag, J. W., Vasa, S. F., & Wright, G. (1994). Who are the children with attention deficit-hyperactivity disorder? A school-based survey. *Journal of Special Education, 28,* 117–137.

Rooney, K. J. (1995). Classroom interventions for students with attention deficit disorders. *Focus on Exceptional Children, 26*(4), 1–16.

Schwiebert, V. L., Sealander, K. A., & Dennison, J. L. (2002). Strategies for counselors working with high school students with attention-deficit/hyperactivity disorder. *Journal of Counseling & Development, 80*(1), 3–10.

Smith, T. E. C., Polloway, E. A., Patton, J. R., & Dowdy, C. A. (2004). *Teaching students with special needs in inclusive settings* (4th ed.). Boston: Allyn & Bacon.

Stormont, M. (2001). Social outcomes of children with AD/HD: Contributing factors and implications for practice. *Psychology in the Schools, 38,* 521–531.

Weyandt, L. L. (2001). *An ADHD primer.* Boston: Allyn & Bacon.

Yell, M. L., Drasgow, E., & Rozalski, M. E. (2001). Disciplining students with disabilities. *Focus on Exceptional Children, 33*(9), 3–8.

CHAPTER 5

Emotional/Behavioral Disorders

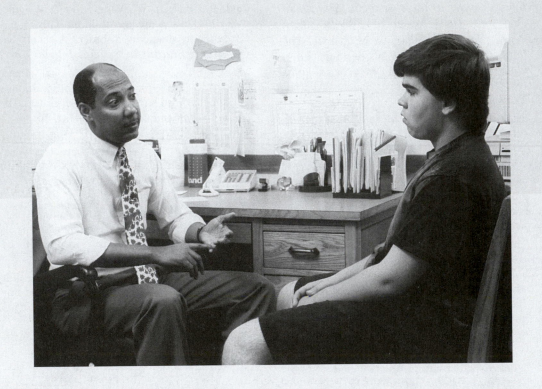

Wesley is 16 years old and has been labeled emotionally disturbed since he was 6 years old. That year, when he was in first grade, he attacked his elementary school principal and tried to kill him. During the next several years, he progressed from a regular class to a resource room to a self-contained class to a class on a separate campus, where he goes to school now. Wesley is very bright (his measured IQ is about 135), but he often refuses to complete assignments. He dresses in baggy pants and black t-shirts, has long hair and tattoos, and looks bored with the world. At his last ARD meeting, we were working with him to set some social/behavioral goals. Since he's always had problems with authority figures and frequently threatens or curses them, we thought it would be a good idea to write a goal addressing the skill of speaking respectfully to adults, including teachers and principals. We were in the middle of a discussion of why it's important not to curse at your boss, a policeman, or your school principal when his father interrupted us. Wesley's dad commented, "Of course I want Wesley to get along with people. But if somebody gets in his face, then they should expect Wesley to get right back in their face, and sometimes that might mean he cusses someone out. That's what I would do, and that's what I've taught my son to do. He's not going to take any *$#^ from anybody." It was one of the first times I remember that a room full of educators had nothing to say.

In all of my years of teaching, James was one of my favorite students. James lived with his mother. His father had been charged with the sexual abuse of James's sister. Their dad would force his daughter to have sex with him and make home videos, which he would force James to watch. Whenever anything went wrong, James got blamed and punished for it. He was a very quiet boy, thin and shy, but very kind and loving. After James's father got arrested, he was dishonorably discharged from the Air Force and forbidden to come near James's home. Because James was so quiet and so reluctant to ask for help, we had to keep a close eye on things. The last month of school, the child protective workers came to see me. We had noticed that James had been very tired in school and having a hard time getting his work done. As it turned out, James's mother had rented out his room to a stranger. James had nowhere to sleep or do his homework except in the living room. He did his best to sleep while his mother and her friends watched TV and socialized. When the social worker told his mom that she needed to give James his room back, she couldn't understand why. She said that she needed the money and that James should be willing to help out.

John was almost 14. Academically, he was at a low second-grade level. He had been expelled from a special public school class for children with brain damage because he threatened the teacher and other children and had actually beaten another child with a chain. He was on the waiting list to be admitted to the state mental hospital, but he was to be enrolled in my public school class for children with emotional disturbances because there was nowhere else for him to go. When his mother brought him to school the first day, he refused to get out of the car. She coaxed and pleaded, but he refused to budge. She got the principal, and he coaxed and pleaded, but John would not talk to him. John's mother and the principal came to me. I went out to the car and coaxed and pleaded, but he would

83

not even look at me. Now what? We decided that we would tell him it was time to come in and that he was going to come into the building now. He could choose the way he was going to come in—he could walk or we would carry him. Once he had come in and looked over the classroom, he would have another choice—to stay or to go home—and the decision would be his alone. We told him, but he did not appear to listen, and he did not budge. We pulled him out of the car, and he stood up and walked into the building. Five minutes later we were showing him the classroom; he was smiling and talking and decided to stay. John tested me out in several other ways, and I was beginning to wonder if I was getting anywhere with him. About a month later a new boy entered the class and began the usual testing. Did I mean what I said and would I level appropriate consequences for behavior? At a beautifully timed moment, John went over to the new boy and said, "Look, you might as well do what Mr. Phillips tells you to, because it's for your own good. Besides, he means what he says, and if you don't do it, you'll only be hurting yourself."

It's hard to know who is emotionally disturbed and who isn't. When I was in high school, the valedictorian of our class of 412 students was always a little different. Sarah had few friends and never seemed to fit in with any of the normal high school social groups. She seemed to learn things without effort and so much more quickly than the rest of us could that we were in awe of her. After I went to college, I didn't hear much about Sarah, except that she still lived with her parents, never dated, and had few, if any, friends. In the fall of my junior year in college, I opened the newspaper and saw her picture. She had gone to the park near our high school and shot herself in the head. Nowadays, the teen suicide rate is so high that most people pay attention when teenagers are withdrawn and depressed and watch for signs of suicide. I wish that someone had paid some attention to Sarah. I figured that she was one of those people who could have discovered a cure for cancer or composed a symphony or written a Pulitzer prize winning novel. Instead, she was dead at age 19.

DEFINITION AND PREVALENCE

Emotional disturbance and *behavioral disorders* are two of a confusing array of terms used to describe children who have difficulty relating to others or behaving acceptably. While the federal law governing special education describes this category of students as seriously emotionally disturbed, an increasing number of professionals and many state regulations describe similar students as behaviorally disordered. The terminology for this category of special education is in transition, and this chapter uses *emotionally disturbed* and *behaviorally disordered* (ED/BD) interchangeably.

Definition

Descriptions and definitions of students who are ED/BD are confusing because of the overlap with other disciplines, especially psychiatry and psychology.

Psychiatrists and psychologists usually refer to descriptors and categories in the fourth edition of the *Diagnostic and Statistical Manual of Mental Disorders* (DSM-IV). Educators have had to write their own definitions to fit children's behavior in school. Essentially, teachers have defined children with ED/BD as those who behave in harmful or inappropriate ways that cause them academic and social problems. The current federal definition was based on one written by Bower (1959, 1982) and defines students who are seriously emotionally disturbed as follows:

> *The term means a condition exhibiting one or more of the following characteristics over a long period of time and to a marked degree, which adversely affects educational performance: (a) an inability to learn that cannot be explained by intellectual, sensory, or health factors; (b) an inability to build or maintain satisfactory interpersonal relationships with peers and teachers; (c) inappropriate types of behavior or feelings under normal circumstances; (d) a general pervasive mood of unhappiness or depression; or (e) a tendency to develop physical symptoms or fears associated with personal or school problems. (Education of All Handicapped Children Act of 1975 [PL 94–142]; Individuals with Disabilities Education Act, 1990 [PL 101–476]; Individuals with Disabilities Education Act Reauthorization, 1997 [PL 105–17]).* (Bower, 1982, p. 57)

Unfortunately, the federal definition has several clauses that are vague and confusing. Sometimes it is of little help in deciding who is and who is not disturbed (Kauffman, 2001). Its flaws seem to allow many children with ED/BD to go unserved, while perhaps overidentifying students who fit certain patterns of acting out behavior.

The definition is also difficult to specify because it excludes students who are socially maladjusted, unless they are also emotionally disturbed. The exclusion of social maladjustment from the category of emotional disturbance is a significant concern because the difference between social maladjustment and emotional disturbance is not clear. Many professionals would agree with Nelson, Rutherford, Center, and Walker (1991), who pointed out that one of the major factors affecting the abilities of policy makers and researchers to clarify this issue is the lack of a generally accepted definition of social maladjustment. In other words, the definition excludes a group of students without defining who they are. A socially maladjusted child will often exhibit some of the characteristics that are used to define emotional disturbance, and it is difficult to know how to differentiate the two disorders.

The National Mental Health and Special Education Coalition has proposed a definition that addresses many of the shortcomings of earlier ones (Forness & Kavale, 2000; Kauffman, 1999; McIntyre & Forness, 1996). It outlines a category called *emotional or behavioral disorder* (EBD). The definition qualifies the condition so that transient, expected responses to stressors are excluded and allows for an EBD label along with other disabilities. The new definition would also emphasize a two-step diagnostic process similar to that used in the learning disability and mental retardation categories. It includes ethnic and cultural considerations, suggests some clinical diagnoses that could perhaps create eligibility if concomitant with learning problems, and does not require the distinctions between social and emotional maladjustment.

Identification of Emotional/Behavioral Problems

Algozzine, Serna, and Patton (2001) and Whelan (1980, 1990) point out that the behavior of students in and of itself is not a problem. The effects of the behavior for students identified as ED/BD are the source of concern. While all children behave inappropriately *sometimes,* children with ED/BD exhibit behavior that goes to an extreme: They are too aggressive or too withdrawn, too loud or too quiet, too euphoric or too depressed. Furthermore, they exhibit these extreme behaviors over a long period of time, not just for a short while. In addition, they tend to exhibit behaviors in strange contexts—there is often nothing wrong with what they are doing, only with when and where they are doing it. In short, children with ED/BD *behave in ways their teachers consider undesirable or inappropriate, and their behavior differs from that of normal children along three crucial dimensions:* (a) *severity*—the extremes to which their behavior goes; (b) *chronicity*—the period of time over which they exhibit inappropriate behavior; and (c) *context*—the time and place they do certain things. Whelan (1990) states that such students are not "disturbed," but are rather "disturbing" to teachers, administrators, other students, and the classroom operation.

For more than 20 years, the federal estimate of the prevalence of serious emotional disturbance among school-aged children and youth was about 2 percent. Nowadays, estimates of the prevalence of ED/BD vary from less than 1 percent to more than 25 percent of the student population, depending on the individual state. Nationally, less than 1 percent of public school students, or about 8.3 percent of all special education students, are served in the ED/BD category (U.S. Department of Education, 2000).

Still, many authorities in the field believe that realistically, as many as 12 percent to 18 percent of students under the age of 18 are mentally ill. A report by the Associated Press in 1989 indicated that children with emotional problems are significantly underidentified and underserved. Those students who are served in the ED category are just a small part of an ever growing population of children in America who have emotional and behavioral problems ("Problems found," 1990). The fact that less than half the number of children *conservatively* estimated to fall into this category are receiving services means that children with ED/BD are one of the most neglected, underserved groups of children in American schools today.

It is not difficult to guess why estimates of the prevalence of ED/BD vary so greatly and why so few of the estimated number of eligible children receive special education. When you have a very vague, jumbled, and subjective definition, it is next to impossible to make an accurate count of the number of children who fit it. If there is a lot of room for argument about whether or not a child qualifies under the label of ED/BD, then the school officials responsible for special education may have difficulty identifying and serving many children (Kauffman, 2001). Because of money and personnel constraints, school officials may feel that they must overlook students who arguably do not have a disability. The question of prevalence of ED/BD sometimes seems in practice to be less "How many children with ED/BD are there?" than "How many children with ED/BD can we afford?"

ETIOLOGY

The causes of erratic, disturbing, debilitating human behavior have always been a puzzle. All that is clear is that such behavior stems from a complex interaction of many factors (Kearney, 1999). These factors have long been known, but the exact role of each has never been fully understood.

The devil made him do it has always been one of the explanations for aberrant and disturbing behavior. The idea that God and the devil battle for control of the mind and body has been with us for centuries. It is not uncommon, even today, to hear spiritual explanations of and cures for troublesome behavior. Although we no longer burn people at the stake or leave them in the wilderness to die when their behavior is significantly different from that of their peer groups, many people still believe that demonic or divine powers control behavior.

Something just snapped in his head is another popular explanation of deviant behavior. Some individuals with severe psychopathology, such as schizophrenia and autism, may also have abnormal levels of specific biochemicals (hallucinogens and neurotransmitters); however, not all individuals with those disorders demonstrate such abnormal biochemistry (Algozzine et al., 2001). Nutrition may also play a role in behavior problems. The *quantity* of a person's intake of food, as in malnutrition, can cause some behavioral disorders. Likewise, the *quality* of a person's food input can also affect behavior. Vitamin deficiencies and food allergies have been suggested as causes for some behavioral disorders, especially some variations of hyperactivity and attention deficit disorder. Central nervous system dysfunction and brain injuries may also be related to aberrant behavior. Yet, in the vast majority of cases, even those involving severe disorders, there is no clear evidence of a specific biological etiology. The search for medical explanations and cures remains, to this day, mostly a matter of speculation.

It runs in the family, the genetic or hereditary explanation, is in operation for some psychological disorders. For example, an individual's chances of developing schizophrenia are much higher if he or she has parents with schizophrenia. Other types of severe disorders such as psychoses are also found more often among close blood relatives. However, some disorders may result from child-rearing practices as well as from genetic factors. Obtaining family histories and seeking genetic counseling are some of the ways in which families can investigate these relationships. The search for genetic contributions to the development of disordered behavior, like the search for other biological causes, is still going on.

He has a sick mind is often the ultimate explanation of those who approach behavior from a psychoanalytic perspective. Algozzine et al. (2001) explain that in this view, emotional development, just like physical development ". . . is viewed as progressing through stages of development from immaturity and psychological dependency toward emotional maturity and independence" (p. 38). Childhood behavior disorders are thought to be the result of exaggerations in normal developmental stages, and deviant behavior is considered to be symptomatic of underlying disturbances in development caused by failure to resolve important conflicts. To put it simplistically, emotional disorders result from early experiences that later cause anxiety, stress, or other unresolved emotions. There is not a great deal of scientific evidence for this point of view, but it is deeply and pervasively entrenched in our culture.

He just can't seem to find himself suggests that a person does not know or understand his own feelings or perceptions or has not developed an adequate self-concept. Deviant behavior supposedly arises because the person has not learned introspection, self-awareness arenas, self-regard, sensitivity, and the like. The role of one's feelings and lack of self-awareness *as a cause* of emotional or behavioral disorders has not been demonstrated in any scientific manner.

He never learned how to get along implies that deviant patterns of behavior are learned and that appropriate behavior can be taught. A body of scientific evidence indicates that this may be correct, particularly for mild disorders; however, evidence is not conclusive that *all* emotional problems (especially those that are more serious) are learned behaviors. Behavioral theory is especially important to educators because they are in the business of teaching children new patterns of behavior. When behaviors are considered to be the result of prior learning, then the learning environment can be arranged and teaching strategies can be used that will increase desirable behaviors or decrease undesirable ones. Students' problems are solvable (Algozzine et al., 2001).

The disturbing versus disturbed question represents an ecological perspective on behavioral disorders. Ecological theorists believe that deviant behavior depends as much on where and with whom a child interacts as it does on the type of interactions of the individual. According to Algozzine et al. (2001), the ecological perspective is that "deviance, disturbance, and behavior problems are as much a function of reactions to behavior as they are the behavior in and of itself. Emotional disturbance is behavior that is poorly fitted to circumstances and setting" (p. 158). Even though ecological theorists agree that deviance is a misfit between a person's behavior and the expectations of the immediate environment, they do not necessarily agree on the source of the problem.

Most likely, behavioral disorders and emotional disturbance result from the interaction of many factors, including a genetic predisposition, a biophysical basis, family and societal factors, expectations of school and community, and stresses that may trigger or precipitate behavior problems. We do know that certain factors predispose children to greater long-term risk for emotional and behavioral problems. Today's society is often a dangerous place for children.

Garwood and Sheehan (1989) summarized the conditions that are most likely to put infants and children at great risk for emotional as well as physical problems: poverty, single and teenage parent families, low birth weights, congenital anomalies, fetal alcohol syndrome, failure to thrive, abuse and neglect, poor nutrition, and environmental poisons. In addition, risk factors such as homelessness, substance abuse, and violence challenge an individual's mental health (Kauffman, 2001). It sometimes seems that environmental conditions in some children's lives make it impossible *not* to have emotional or behavioral problems.

CLASSIFICATION SYSTEMS/CHARACTERISTICS

Classification of children with ED/BD has not been very meaningful for special educators. The traditional psychiatric categories have been of almost no value whatsoever in teaching (Wicks-Nelson & Israel, 2003). Some systems of classification (Achenbach & Edelbrock, 1983; Quay, 1979) have identified children as primarily (a) aggressive, rude, attention seeking, and hyperactive; (b) anxious, hypersensitive, fearful, and withdrawn; or (c) delinquent, truant, or antisocial (according to middle-class standards). The simplest and most productive classification system for *educators* has traditionally involved two categories: mild or moderate and severe. Though this distinction is not included in the definition in IDEA (the title of the category is Emotionally Disturbed), it is one way to practically differentiate children based on the type and scope of educational intervention they require. Students who have mild or moderate problems can usually be taught in regular public school classes if the teacher gets some advice and consultation in behavior management; or they can be taught in resource rooms, where the child spends only part of the day with a specially trained teacher (Mercer & Mercer, 2001; Wood, 2002). Occasionally, these children (who are often labeled *neurotic, personality disordered,* or *behavior disordered*) must be taught in segregated special classes, but they are ordinarily returned to a regular class in 2 years or less (Kauffman, 2001). Children with severe problems, often classified as psychotic, frequently must be educated in special classes in public schools or sometimes in special schools or in institutions (Whelan, 1998). Some children with severe ED/BD may never enter the educational mainstream (Whelan, 1999).

Because the law requires that students be served in the least restrictive environment possible, it is important to consider the advantages and disadvantages of various placements before making a decision. Table 5.1 represents some of the advantages and disadvantages of various placement options for students with ED/BD.

Table 5.1

Advantages and Disadvantages of More Restrictive and Less Restrictive Placements for Students With Serious Emotional Disturbance

	Advantages	Disadvantages
Less Restrictive Placements • Regular classrooms (with or without support) • Resource rooms	1. Prevents the regular educator from giving up on the child and turning to "experts." 2. Permits students to model appropriate behavior of their peers; increased interaction. 3. Possibly less expensive. 4. May be able to serve more students. 5. Students do not experience problems with reintegration. 6. Students follow general education curriculum.	1. Expense and time required to train regular educators to work with students and special educators and special educators to work as consultants to regular educators. 2. Problems with classroom management and discipline. 3. Lack of consistent expectations for the students. 4. Time and materials required for individualization. 5. Fear and frustration of teachers.
More Restrictive Placements • Hospitals • Residential facilities • Separate campuses • Separate classes	1. Flexibility to provide different curricula and different goals. 2. Progress can be more closely monitored. 3. Accountability of program is more clearly defined. 4. Intervention can be more consistent. 5. Student follows only one set of guidelines and expectations. 6. Teacher's time goes to instruction only, not consultation. 7. One team for consistent discipline.	1. Student's opportunities for peer interactions are limited, especially when student is not at neighborhood school with peers from his neighborhood. 2. Travel time for students can be excessive. 3. No possible modeling of appropriate peers; no opportunities for socialization with nondisabled peers. 4. Difficulties with reintegration back into regular school or class.

Source: From "Placement," by Kathleen McConnell, 2001. In B. Algozzine, L. Serna, and J. Patton (Eds.), *Childhood Behavior Disorders*. Austin, TX: PRO-ED.

CONCEPTUAL MODELS OF INSTRUCTION AND TREATMENT

Different conceptual models—sets of assumptions about what the problem is, how it came about, and what can be done about it—can be adopted in working with children with ED/BD (Gallagher, 1988; Whelan, 1998, 1999). In fact, there are so many different models, each having proponents who claim their ideas are best and that the advocates of other models are ignorant or malicious, that the field is confusing for a beginning student. We will try to guide you through this array of models.

You should keep three things in mind. First, there are many ways to group models that conceptually "slice" the field. Ours is not the only way to do it; other sources may give descriptions of more or fewer models or use different terminology. Second, relatively few professionals let themselves become the prisoners of a single model even though they think one model is better. Most thoughtful people realize that each model has its limitations and that it is an attempt to impose a useful order on information and events, but that it is not a full and complete description of reality. Third, you can get into trouble by being mindlessly eclectic. Many students and some professionals try to take the position that they see merit in *every* conceptual model. And because they want to maintain a friendly neutrality on all issues, they fail to make necessary judgments on the basis of research evidence or common sense. Our contention is that if you are going to help children with ED/BD most effectively, you have to have your feet on the ground *and* be guided by the findings of research.

Psychoanalytic Model

The psychoanalytic model, based on the ideas of Freud and other psychoanalysts, has its biggest appeal for psychotherapists and social workers. Educators who respond to this model tend to advocate a permissive classroom in which the child can "work through" or express his underlying problems freely. A premium is placed on two things: (a) an accepting attitude of the teacher toward the child's feelings and (b) an understanding of the unconscious motivation of the child's behavior. Several problems arise, however, from relying on the psychoanalytic model.

First, there is very little empirical research showing that it works. You may find anecdotal reports of successes or cases reporting favorable results, but few of these reports are based on scientific research. In most of them, the effects of "treatment" are not clearly and reliably measured or demonstrated. Second, this model does not focus on improving the student's actual behavior. It is very difficult for teachers to focus on *internal* changes in students when the students' behaviors are disruptive, aggressive, antisocial, or dangerous. The third limitation of the psychoanalytic model is that the process of psychoanalysis is very time consuming, and its time lines are not always realistic. Waiting months or even years for the change process endorsed by this model may be impractical and frustrating.

Psychoeducational Model

Psychoeducation is not well defined, even by the people who are identified with it. Implying a combination of psychological and educational concepts, this model includes psychoanalytic ideas about unconscious motivation and puts a premium on the teacher–pupil relationship. There is a concern for "surface behavior" (what children *do*) and for academic progress, primarily achieved by talking to children and getting them to achieve insight into their own problems. This model offers most of its teaching through projects and creative arts. Although we think the psychoeducational approach is far more sensible than the psychoanalytic model, it still suffers from the same flaw—little or no supporting data from empirical research. However, it does represent some commonsense approaches to talking to children about their behavior, including the *life-space interview,* developed by Long. Another strategy that has its roots in the psychoeducational model is cognitive behavioral modification training, which is supported by scientific research data.

Humanistic Model

Nonauthoritarian, self-directed, self-evaluative, affective, open, personal—these words are often used to describe the humanistic model. This model grew out of humanistic psychology and the development of open schools, alternative schools, and other nontraditional practices of the late 1960s and early 1970s. These approaches represent an attempt to give more attention to the affective side of education and to get children more involved in their own education. Humanistic educators made important contributions to society by highlighting how it feels to learn, succeed, fail, be a pupil, be a teacher—in other words, how it feels to be human. Unfortunately, the proponents of this model seem too often satisfied with merely developing a nontraditional educational setting and have not always documented its effectiveness in helping children improve their academic learning and behavior.

Ecological Model

Many concepts of the ecological model were adapted from research in biological ecology and ecological psychology. Every child is enmeshed in a complex social system. Consequently, one has to consider the entire social system, not just the child in isolation. Educators should be concerned with the child in the classroom, the family, the neighborhood, and all other arenas of the social environment. The value we see in this model is not in the specific tactics it offers for teaching or managing behavior, but in its overall approach or strategy for dealing with the child's problems. For example, one might use behavior modification tactics for teaching and managing the child, but use an ecological strategy that involves the child's family and community. The ecological view seems very sensible to many educators and is also supported by some research.

Behavioral Model

The behavioral model includes these fundamental ideas: (a) behavior can be observed and directly and reliably measured; (b) behavioral excesses and deficits *are* the problem, not underlying or unconscious feelings; and (c) behavior is a function of its consequences and can be modified by changing the consequences. If children's behavior is learned, then the problem with children with ED/BD must be that they have learned the wrong behaviors. The solution is to teach them new, more appropriate ones. In classrooms operated according to a behavioral model, specific behavioral goals are achieved by using specific teaching and management techniques. Also, a careful daily measurement of behavior is designed to tell the teacher to what extent the techniques are leading to an achievement of the goals (Breen & Fielder, 2003).

The behavioral model seems to be the most valuable model for teachers for two reasons: (a) It is supported by more scientific research than any of the others, and (b) it is compatible with certain sensible, research-supported aspects of other models. One can talk meaningfully with children about their behavior (psychoeducational), care about their feelings and individuality (humanistic), deal with all aspects of their social environment (ecological), and still be a good behaviorist. *But without the behavioral model as a basis, the components of the other models are relatively much less significant or useful.*

Because children with ED/BD come to the attention of teachers, parents, peers, and others as a result of their behavioral excesses and deficiencies, many professionals remain firmly committed to working with students' observable behaviors. Kauffman's 1986 challenge to educators is still pertinent:

> *Not to define precisely and measure these behavioral excesses and deficiencies, then, is a fundamental error: It is akin to the malpractice of a nurse who decides not to measure vital signs (heart rate, respiration rate, temperature, and blood pressure), perhaps arguing that he/she is too busy, that subjective estimates of vital signs are quite adequate, that vital signs are only superficial estimates of the patient's health, or that the vital signs do not signify the nature of the underlying pathology. The teaching profession is dedicated to the task of changing behavior demonstrably for the better. What can one say, then, of educational practice that does not include reliable and forthright measurement of the behavior change induced by the teacher's methodology? I believe simply this:* It is indefensible. (pp. 339–340)

ISSUES IN THE EDUCATION OF CHILDREN WITH ED/BD

One of the foremost challenges to both regular and special educators today is how to best serve the growing numbers of students with emotional and behavioral problems. For a long time, their treatment was the domain of psychotherapists, usually psychiatrists (medical doctors with training in psychiatry), psychoanalysts (psychiatrists with a special training in psychoanalysis), or clinical psychologists (nonphysicians with advanced graduate training in psychology). Fortunately, most psychotherapists now readily admit that teachers are also equipped to offer significant assistance to these students. Despite the best efforts of mental health professionals and educators, the outlook for students with emotional and behavioral problems is bleak due to an ongoing lack of wrap-around services (school, community, and family) and a fragmentation of those services that do exist (Wicks-Nelson & Israel, 2003). Some of the problems for students in this category are detailed in the following:

❏ Students with emotional and behavioral problems seem to be significantly underidentified and underserved. The Council for Children with Behavioral Disorders (CCBD) estimates that less than half of the eligible students in this category are receiving services.

❏ Students with emotional and behavioral problems are the worst of all 13 special education categories on several key indicators: *days absent per year, grade-point average, drop-out rate,* and *productive involvement after high school.* They are also very likely to be involved in criminal activity after leaving school (U.S. Department of Education, 2000).

❏ The placement information for students with emotional and behavioral problems demonstrates a pattern of very restrictive placements. More than 54 percent of students in this category are in separate classes, separate schools, or residential or homebound placements.

❏ The "social maladjustment" issue is a serious concern. CCBD believes that this exclusionary clause denies services to students with underlying emotional disorders such as depression or anxiety because those students often demonstrate serious acting out behaviors and are discipline problems.

❏ The educational services provided for students with emotional problems often do not meet their needs. Epstein, Foley, and Cullinan (1992) surveyed teachers about their ED/BD students. Their survey indicated that teachers often have no systematic, well-thought-out, justifiable program for these students, relying instead on a hodgepodge of features that may or may not be effective.

❏ One of the biggest problems for professionals who deal with students who are emotionally disturbed/behaviorally disordered is prevention. We have not really done a very good job with early identification and prevention of problems *before* they get serious. Recently, several studies have investigated the factors that put students at greatest risk for serious problems. Not surprisingly, these factors, which are presented in Table 5.2, have a lot to do with students' families. Because the number of students with serious emotional disturbance is increasing, communities are likely to experience an ever increasing need to attend to some of these risk factors while children are still young and before they develop serious behavioral problems.

Table 5.2

Factors That Put Students at Risk for Serious Emotional or Behavioral Problems

Percent of Sample	
Family-Setting Risk Factors	
52.4%	Family income below poverty level
52.4%	Divorce between natural parents
30.0%	Three or more siblings
11.5%	Adopted
16.3%	Parent psychiatric hospitalization
18.7%	Parent convicted of felony (current or previous)
14.2%	Siblings institutionalized (current or previous)
17.2%	Siblings in foster care
37.8%	History of family mental illness
58.1%	History of family violence
48.1%	History of family chemical dependence
11.2%	Family unavailable for aftercare
40.3%	Negative peer influence
Child Risk Factors	
59.6%	Previous psychiatric hospitalization
40.3%	Physically abused (reported)
36.3%	Sexually abused (reported)
15.7%	Chronic runaway (more than three prior attempts)
20.6%	Suicide attempt(s)
29.0%	Chronic school truancy
69.6%	Below-grade-level school achievement
8.7%	Drug/alcohol dependency
36.3%	Frequent suspension/expulsion
18.1%	Other handicapping conditions (e.g., physical, sensory)
Child Dangerousness	
4.8%	Sexually abusive (adjudicated)
1.8%	Previous felony conviction
65.1%	Dangerous to others (history of aggression/violence)
41.8%	Dangerous to self (self-injurious)
20.6%	Fire-setting

Source: From *Integrating Services for Children and Youth with Emotional and Behavioral Disorders* (p. 6), by C. M. Nelson and C. A. Pearson, 1991, Reston, VA: The Council for Exceptional Children. Reprinted by permission.

INCLUSION OF STUDENTS WITH EMOTIONAL/BEHAVIORAL PROBLEMS

There is increased pressure today to include all students with disabilities in regular education environments (Smith, Polloway, Patton, & Dowdy, 2004). However, since students with ED/BD often display challenging or disruptive behaviors, regular educators may be reluctant to include them in regular education situations. In addition, their educational needs, which often include a structured environment and instruction emphasizing social competencies, cannot always be met in regular education. In the spring of 1993, the Executive Committee of the CCBD met and discussed the group's position on "full inclusion." The resulting CCBD position on inclusion of students with emotional and behavioral disorders follows:

> *Consistent with IDEA, CCBD supports a full continuum of mental health and special education services for children and youth with emotional and behavioral disorders. We believe that educational decisions depend on individual students' needs. Consequently, in contrast to those individuals and groups who advocate for full inclusion, CCBD does **not** support the notion that all special education students, including those students with emotional and behavioral disorders, are always best served in general education classrooms.* (1993, p. 1)

The requirements of the law are clear: A full continuum of services must be available and decisions about students' programs must be made on an individual basis.

SUGGESTIONS FOR WORKING WITH PEOPLE WITH ED/BD

1. Children with ED/BD are masters at making their problems your problems. Make sure you do not let yourself get caught up in their "pathology." For example, such children may try to drag you into senseless arguments or make you feel that their problems with following classroom rules are your fault. You must emotionally distance yourself from interactions with children to be able to tell their difficulties from yours.

2. Children should know what you expect from them. Children with ED/BD especially need to know what is and is not OK. Do not keep them guessing.

 3. When you make a rule or give an instruction, make it stick. By this we mean think through the rule or instruction before you give it, tell the child the consequences of meeting or not meeting your expectation, and be consistent in applying the consequences. Before you tell the child what to do, you must consider whether doing it is appropriate and important, whether the consequences are reasonable and desirable, and whether or not you can follow through with the consequences.

4. Do not expect love and attention in return. If all that children with ED/BD needed was someone to love them, we could cure most of them next year (maybe even this year!). If you want to help them, you must be willing to extend love, affection, and *structure*—appropriate rules, clear expectations, and consistent consequences—without the expectation that you will receive respect, love, or gratitude in return.

5. Do not demand perfection or steady progress; do expect gradual improvement. Remember that we all have our quirks and our bad days. Life for most children with ED/BD is especially rocky. The goal is to help them get their behavior smoothed out enough to live happily and independently in the mainstream of society.

The goal cannot be reached overnight, and it leaves a lot of room for imperfection by most people's standards.

    6.   Try very hard to work with the families of ED/BD students. Communication is very important. Behavior change will come more quickly when parents and teachers are consistent in their expectations and with their consequences. When in doubt, communicate!

PONDER THESE

1. Study the following behaviors. According to your interpretation of the definition, which behaviors indicate emotional disturbance or a behavioral disorder? Under what conditions, if any, would you consider the behaviors normal? Rank order them from most serious to least serious.
   - ❏ Interrupting conversations
   - ❏ Banging head against the wall
   - ❏ Screaming
   - ❏ Killing another person
   - ❏ Refusing to work
   - ❏ Eating paper
   - ❏ Swearing
   - ❏ Saying, "I'm no good. I hate myself. I wish I were dead."
   - ❏ Sleeping in class
   - ❏ Setting fire to the bathroom

2. Consider the following scenario, and then describe ways you could respond to the situation:

   Elmer has a pair of scissors. He is making deep scratches on the wall of the classroom. You tell him to stop, but he pays no attention. You go to him and take hold of his arm and matter-of-factly say, "No, Elmer, you can't do that." He flies at you, tries to scratch you with the scissors, and screams, "Let me go, you *$!" You loosen your grip on Elmer, and he runs out of the room. You follow, but lose sight of him as he rounds the corner at the end of the hall. You suspect that he has gone into the boys' rest room. As you enter the rest room, you see Elmer perched on top of the stall partition. He has taken off one shoe and is about to throw it at you. As you approach him he shouts, "Get away from me. You can't make me come down. I'll kill you, you *$!. I'll break my leg, and then my dad will sue you. You come any closer and I'll knock your teeth out."

3. Children with ED/BD have a way of forcing other people to make decisions for them or about their behavior. Much of the controversy in the field concerns the child's right to make her own decisions versus the teacher's responsibility to make decisions for the child. For each of the following problems, specify the decisions you would be willing to make for a child and those you believe should be left to her:
   - ❏ The student is not coming to class on time.
   - ❏ The student refuses to read.
   - ❏ The student hits others.
   - ❏ The student makes loud animal noises in class.
   - ❏ The student takes things that are not hers.
   - ❏ The student does not bathe and smells so bad no one will sit by her.

ONLINE RESOURCES

Center for the Study and Prevention of Violence
http://www.colorado.edu/cspv

Council for Exceptional Children/Division for Children with Behavioral Disorders
http://www.ccbd.net

Discipline Associates
http://www.disciplineassociates.com

Institute for Violence and Destructive Behavior
http://www.darkwing.uoregon.edu/~ivdb

National Dropout Prevention Center
http://www.dropoutprevention.org
Oregon Social Learning Center
http://www.oslc.org

Technical Assistance Center on Positive Behavioral
Interventions and Supports
http://www.pbis.org

REFERENCES

Achenbach, T. M., & Edelbrock, C. S. (1983). Taxonomic issues in child psychopathology. In T. H. Ollendick & M. Hersen (Eds.), *Handbook of child psychopathology* (pp. 65–93). New York: Plenum.

Algozzine, B., Serna, L., & Patton, J. R. (2001). *Childhood behavior disorders*. Austin, TX: PRO-ED.

Bower, E. M. (1959). The emotionally handicapped child and the school. *Exceptional Children, 26,* 6–11.

Bower, E. M. (1982). Defining emotional disturbance: Public policy and research. *Psychology in the Schools, 19,* 55–60.

Breen, M. J., & Fielder, C. R. (1996). *Behavioral approach to assessment of youth with emotional/behavioral disorders: A handbook for school-based practitioners* (2nd ed.). Austin, TX: PRO-ED.

Council for Children with Behavioral Disorders. (1993, June). Staff position statement: Inclusion. *CCBD Newsletter,* p. 1.

Epstein, J. H., Foley, R. M., & Cullinan, D. (1992). National survey of educational programs for adolescents with serious emotional disturbance. *Behavioral Disorders, 17*(3), 202–210.

Forness, S., & Kavale, K. (2000). Emotional or behavior disorders: Background and current status of the E/BD terminology, and definition. *Behavior Disorders, 25,* 264–269.

Gallagher, P. A. (1988). *Teaching students with behavioral disorders. Techniques and activities for classroom instruction.* Denver, CO: Love Publishing Company.

Garwood, S. G., & Sheehan, R. (1989). *Designing a comprehensive early intervention system: The challenge of Public Law 99–457.* Austin, TX: PRO-ED.

Kauffman, J. M. (1986). Educating children with behavior disorders. In R. J. Morris & B. Blatt (Eds.), *Special education: Research and trends* (pp. 249–271). New York: Pergamon.

Kauffman, J. M. (1999). Educating students with emotional or behavioral disorders: What's over the horizon? In L. M. Bullock and R. A. Gable (Eds.), *Educating students with emotional and behavioral disorders: Historical perspectives and future directions* (pp. 38–59). Reston, VA: Council for Children with Behavioral Disorders.

Kauffman, J. M. (2001). *Characteristics of emotional and behavioral disorders of children and youth* (5th ed.). Upper Saddle River, NJ: Merrill/Prentice Hall.

Kearney, C. A. (1999). *Casebook in child behavior disorders.* Belmont, CA: Wadsworth.

McIntyre, T., & Forness, S. (1996). Is there a new definition yet or are kids still seriously emotionally disturbed? *Beyond Behavior, 7*(3), 4–9.

Mercer, C. O., & Mercer, A. R. (2001). *Teaching students with learning problems.* Upper Saddle River, NJ: Merrill/Prentice Hall.

Nelson, C. M., Rutherford, R. B., Center, D. B., & Walker, H. M. (1991). Do public schools have an obligation to serve troubled children and youth? *Exceptional Children, 57*(5), 406–415.

Problems found in 1 to 5 children. (1990, December 9). The *Washington Post,* p. A27.

Quay, H. C. (1979). Classification. In H. C. Quay & J. S. Werry (Eds.), *Psychopathological disorders of childhood* (2nd ed., pp. 1–42). New York: Wiley.

Smith, T. E. C., Polloway, E. A., Patton, J. R., & Dowdy, C. A. (2004). *Teaching children with special needs in inclusive settings* (4th ed.). Boston: Allyn & Bacon.

U.S. Department of Education. (2000). *To assure the free appropriate public education of all children with disabilities. Twenty-second annual report to Congress on the implementation of the Individuals with Disabilities Education Act.* Washington, DC : Author.

Whelan, R. J. (1980). *Human understanding of human behavior.* Unpublished manuscript, University of Kansas, Lawrence.

Whelan, R. J. (1990). Education of students with behavior disorders: Theories and practices. *National Forum of Special Education, 1*(1), 11–17.

Whelan, R. J. (1998). *Emotional and behavioral disorders: A 25-year focus.* Denver, CO: Love Publishing Company.

Whelan, R. J. (1999). Historical perspective. In L. M. Bullock and R. A. Gable (Eds.), *Educating students with emotional and behavioral disorders: Historical perspectives and future directions* (pp. 3–36). Reston, VA: Council for Children with Behavioral Disorders.

Wicks-Nelson, R., & Israel, A. C. (2003). *Behavior disorders of childhood* (5th ed.). Upper Saddle River, NJ: Prentice Hall.

Wood, J. W. (2002). *Adapting instruction to accommodate students in instructive settings* (4th ed.). Upper Saddle River, NJ: Merrill/Prentice Hall.

CHAPTER **6**

Mental Retardation

Harvey is an enthusiastic, polite child who entered a new school district in the fifth grade. The previous year, Harvey had been tested, found to have a measured IQ of 57, and placed in a self-contained class for students with mental retardation. When Harvey entered his new school, he did not know his alphabet and could count only to 20. He was assigned to an inclusion class that has a regular education teacher all day and a special education teacher for half a day. In this class abilities and labels range from *talented and gifted* to *mentally retarded*. The two teachers share teaching and tutoring responsibilities for all of the students. Because Harvey was so limited in his academic skills in language arts and math, he was assigned additional tutoring on a daily basis. The language arts tutoring focused on acquisition of basic English skills—letter identification, letter sounds, and basic words. During the first 6 weeks, his teachers decided that Harvey's oral comprehension was at grade level, so they modified their science and social studies materials to include a generous amount of oral instruction and group work. Harvey was able to join in group projects for presentation before the entire class. Before long, Harvey began to shine. The other students began to benefit from Harvey's easygoing way of responding to difficulties and his impeccable manners. They also became more sensitive to the reality that although some people may have intellectual limitations, they all have something to offer others.

One day in language arts tutoring, Harvey exclaimed in a rush of words, "I got it! I got it! Mr. Wayne, I got it! Do you want to hear?" Harvey proceeded to read all of the words in a sentence, then all of the sentences in a short story. Harvey was reading and understanding what he read for the first time in his life! Never limit what someone can do on the basis of tests. Expose all children to the wonders of learning. They may surprise themselves and delight you![1]

———————————————————————

I worked with Allen every day for 6 months, teaching him how to garnish sandwiches in a high-volume restaurant. He learned very slowly, but he was fun and interesting to work with. We always joked with one another. Not even I would ever have guessed that he had a tested IQ of 52. By about the sixth month, Allen was doing his job without my assistance, except during the rush periods. Over the next 3 months, Allen became very skillful and could garnish at an impressive rate—except during the very busy times when it was sometimes too hectic, even for me. Slowly, day by day, pressure began to build. One night when tempers were short at cleanup time, Allen started yelling, "Don't touch me! Push, push, push, that's all you do. Don't come close to me. I hate this place! I hate hamburgers! I hate salads! I hate mustard!" With this outcry, he flung the mustard container against the kitchen wall and ran out the back door. Impulsively, I took off after him. Finally, I caught him down by the incinerator in the back lot. He yelled, his voice shaking and hands trembling, "You'd better leave me alone!" Fearing that he might run in front of a car, I stepped closer to reach him. He pulled a kitchen knife about 10 inches long from his pocket and said, "Don't come near me, I hate you. Take another step and I'll kill you!" Then he dropped the knife to the ground, fell to his knees, and wept. He pulled me close to him, held my legs, and murmured, "I'm sorry. I

———————————————————————

[1]This story was contributed by Lynne Lewis, MSW and LPC, Lockhart Independent School District, Lockhart, Texas.

love you. I'm sorry." Before the night was over, we had talked it out and completed our cleanup duties together. That was over 5 years ago. Today, he is still garnishing sandwiches at the same high-volume restaurant, and we are still the closest of friends.

Bobby was diagnosed as having mild mental retardation when he was in the second grade. His parents had been surprised at the diagnosis, but agreed to special education placement. Bobby seemed like a normal child. He played with the other children in the neighborhood, he had no speech or physical problems, and his interests/activities were age appropriate. Bobby spent the next 9 years in special education classrooms. When he reached the age of 16, he immediately quit school. Bobby went to work for a local discount store that was part of a national chain. At night Bobby worked on his GED (general educational development) high school equivalency diploma, which he finished in 4 years. As time went on, Bobby advanced in his career, married, and had three children. At 26 years of age—10 years after quitting school—Bobby became manager of his own discount store in the chain. His six-figure salary was far superior to that of most persons labeled mildly mentally retarded.

Most people are aware of the Special Olympics, although some people may not realize that there is more to it than just track and field events. Other sports (e.g., skiing, soccer, and basketball) are also part of this program. Nevertheless, this story concerns the track and field competition. For months, a friend of mine, a teacher of students with moderate mental retardation, had been preparing them for the district-level meet. They practiced every day. As every track runner knows, "getting out of the blocks" is a critical part of any running event. This teacher consistently worked on this aspect with her students. She would yell, "Get on your mark, get set, GO!" After months of training, her students were ready. The district meet approached. They were "psyched"—they wanted to do well so they could go to the state meet. Although they had entered a number of different events, they were most excited about the running. The truth of truths—athlete versus athlete—had arrived. The officials lined up the runners in their appropriate positions. The adrenaline was flowing. The excitement was building to a climax. The official starter asked if the runners were ready. They or their sponsors indicated that they were. The starter then began the countdown: "Get on your mark, get set . . . " "BLAM!" The race had begun! Unfortunately, the participants from my friend's class were still at the starting line, startled by the loud sounds that had just thundered from the starter's gun to be sure, but still waiting anxiously for him to say, "GO!"

Almost 20 years ago, long before the current inclusion movement, I worked part time as a one-on-one tutor/assistant. The student I worked with, Nancy, was 11 years old and had Down syndrome. She was born when her parents were in their mid-forties. Both were well-educated professionals and were strong advocates for their daughter. Instead of spending her whole school day in a self-contained class, which was common at the time, Nancy was in some regular education classes and a resource room on a regular elementary campus. Nancy's parents were always on the lookout for something that would improve her functioning level. The year I worked with her, she had already been through patterning training in Philadelphia and was in the process of taking megadoses of vitamins.

Nancy's parents were also very concerned about her social interactions. Every Halloween, they had a big party and invited all the kids from their neighborhood, as well as teachers. However, whenever it was time to eat, Nancy would disappear. Even though they wanted Nancy to be a part of school and community peer groups, her parents were embarrassed by her table manners and wouldn't let her eat with any of her friends—they set up a table for her in a separate room.

DEFINITION

Special education textbooks typically devote a considerable amount of space to discussions of the *definitions* of mental retardation, both from a historical and a functional perspective. One reason for such lengthy considerations may be that although the concept of a normal distribution of intelligence and abilities has long been accepted, society's view of what constitutes *normal* functioning continues to change over time. (In any population, there are a very small number of individuals with extraordinarily high or low abilities and a large number of individuals with average abilities.) As a culture, our views on disabilities and the role of people with disabilities in society has certainly undergone dramatic adjustment during the past decade. The way that we view individuals with mental retardation is shaped by many variables in our culture, including our current (a) values, (b) willingness to tolerate and appreciate diversity, (c) requirements for conformity, (d) expectations for achievement, and (e) definition of *normal*.

Various definitions of mental retardation have been used over the years. Public Law 94–142, now the IDEA, refers to mental retardation in basically the same terms as the 1983 definition by Grossman: "significantly subaverage general intellectual functioning resulting in or associated with concurrent impairments in adaptive behavior and manifested during the development period" (p. 11). *Subaverage intellectual functioning* refers to a score on an intelligence test that is approximately two or more standard deviations below the mean. *Adaptive behavior* refers to one's ability to cope with the demands of daily life and is manifested in such things as sensorimotor, communication, self-help, socialization, academic, and vocational skills. The *development period* consists of the time span between conception and the 19th birthday.

For many years prior to the Grossman definition, emphasis was placed solely on an intelligence test score for classifying a person as mentally retarded. If children scored in the retarded range on an IQ test, they were classified as mentally retarded even if they functioned adequately in the community, at school, on the job, or with peers. They were placed in special classes for students with mental retardation simply because they scored in the retarded range on standardized tests and had trouble with academic learning. Many of these children were able to get along well in their community and with their peers. After leaving school, they functioned successfully in their jobs, and in some cases have married and raised fine families (see the vignette about Bobby at the beginning of this chapter).

For these individuals, being labeled mentally retarded served no constructive purpose. If consideration had been given to adaptive behavior, they would not have met the criteria nor been labeled as mentally retarded. It is important to emphasize that in determining eligibility for educational services, the definition of mental retardation assigns equal weight to both the intellectual functioning and the adaptive behavior dimensions. In other words, to be classified as mentally retarded, a person must show deficits in both areas. For individuals who have left school after experiencing academic difficulties, yet who can get along well on a job in the community, the label of mental retardation would no longer apply (Beirne-Smith, Ittenbach, & Patton, 2002).

Although the IDEA definition is operative in the *federal* law, many states have their own definitions of mental retardation. For years, a new definition has been considered, discussed, and finally proposed. In 1992, the American Association on Mental Retardation (AAMR) Ad Hoc Committee on Terminology and Classification published its ninth manual on classification and terminology. The most recent definition appears in *Mental Retardation: Definition, Classification, and Systems of Support* (2002). This new definition of mental retardation is as follows:

> *Mental retardation is a disability characterized by significant limitations both in intellectual functioning and in adaptive behavior as expressed in conceptual, social, and practical adaptive skills. This disability originates before age 18.*

Five assumptions are essential to the application of the AAMR definition:

1. Limitations in present functioning must be considered within the context of community environments typical of the individual's age, peers, and culture.
2. Valid assessment considers cultural and linguistic diversity as well as differences in communication, sensory, motor, and behavioral factors.
3. Within an individual, limitations often coexist with strengths.
4. An important purpose of describing limitations is to develop a profile of needed supports.
5. With appropriate, personalized supports over a sustained period, the life functioning of the person with mental retardation generally will improve.

Table 6.1
Framework for Assessment of Mental Retardation

Function	Primary Purposes
Diagnosis	Establishing eligibility: • Services • Benefits • Legal protections
Classification	Grouping for: • Service reimbursement for funding • Research • Services • Communication about selected characteristics
Planning Supports	Enhancing personal outcomes: • Independence • Relationships • Contributions • School and community participation • Personal well-being

Source: From *Mental Retardation: Definition, Classification, and Systems of Supports,* 10th ed. (p. 12), by the Association on Mental Retardation (AAMR),1992, Washington, DC: Author. Reprinted by permission.

This new definition proposes some very significant changes from its predecessors. It is much more *functional* than previous definitions because it (a) stresses the interaction among three major dimensions: a person's capabilities, the environments in which the person functions, and the individual's need for support; (b) refines the concept of adaptive behavior; (c) institutes a framework for assessment, which includes: diagnosis, classification, and planning supports; and (d) espouses a multidimensional approach to mental retardation (intellectual abilities; adaptive behavior; participation, interactions, and social roles; health; context-environments and culture). The new definition also recommends that former levels of severity (mild, moderate, severe, and profound) be discontinued. Table 6.1 lists the three key functions related to the framework for assessment. Table 6.2 defines and provides examples of the intensities of supports that may be required by various individuals.

PREVALENCE

Estimates of what percentage of the population is mentally retarded vary from one source to another. Beirne-Smith et al. (2002) point out that prevalence variations are impacted by numerous factors, including differences in criteria and methodologies of the researchers and gender, age, community, race, and sociopolitical

Table 6.2
Definition and Examples of Intensities of Supports

Intermittent

Support on an "as-needed basis," characterized by their episodic person not always needing the support[s]; or short-term nature (supports needed during life-span transitions, e.g., job loss or an acute medical crisis). Intermittent supports may be high or low intensity when provided.

Limited

An intensity of supports characterized by consistency over time; time-limited but not of an intermittent nature, may require fewer staff members and less cost than more intense levels of support (e.g., time-limited employment training or transitional supports during the school to adult provided period).

Extensive

Supports characterized by regular involvement (e.g., daily) in at least some environments (e.g., school, work, or home) and not time limited nature (e.g., long-term support and long-term home living support)

Pervasive

Supports characterized by their constancy, high intensity, provision across environments, potential life-sustaining nature. Pervasive supports typically involve more staff members and intrusiveness than do extensive or time-limited supports.

Source: From *Mental Retardation: Definition, Classification, and Systems of Supports,* 10th ed. (p. 152), by the Association on Mental Retardation (AAMR), 2002, Washington, DC: Author. Reprinted by permission.

factors of the individuals being considered for identification in this category. If IQ were the only criterion for defining mental retardation, about 2 percent of the population would be considered mentally retarded. The federal government reported that for the 1990–1991 school year, slightly fewer than 600,000 children were classified as mentally retarded. This represents a little more than 1.5 percent of the school age population (U.S. Department of Education, 2000) and about 10.5 percent of students with disabilities. According to Beirne-Smith et al. (1998), most professionals would suggest prevalence figures of less than 1 percent. The majority of students in this category have *mild* rather than moderate or severe mental retardation.

One of the more interesting trends in special education since the implementation of PL 94–142 has to do with the mental retardation category. Since the U.S. Department of Education began collecting and compiling data on special education services, there has been a dramatic *decrease* in the number of students in the mental retardation category. From the 1976–1977 school year until the 1990–1991 school year, the number of students identified and served as mentally retarded has declined by about 319,000 (or 39 percent). This decline is likely due to a number of factors. One is sociopolitical; that is, many school districts may be more conservative in identifying students as mentally retarded, especially if those students are from culturally diverse backgrounds and minority ethnic groups. Another possible reason is that many higher functioning students who were formerly labeled as mentally retarded may now be called learning disabled. The learning disability category is thought to be less stigmatizing than mental retardation, and the students may be able to function very well in resource settings. The third reason for the decline in the number of students labeled mentally retarded may be that recent efforts at prevention and early intervention may be having a significant impact. Increasing awareness of prenatal and postnatal risk factors as well as early childhood intervention programs may be resulting in less serious problems in learning and development.

ETIOLOGY

Mental retardation is caused by a number of variables, many of which are unknown. It is likely that for many individuals who are mentally retarded, specific causal factors may not be apparent; or several causes that interact can be identified. In general, however, two categorical schemes can be used to describe the many causes of mental retardation: biological or organic causes and sociocultural causes (Hardman, Drew, Egan, & Wolf, 1993).

Biological or organic causes of mental retardation include maternal infections (e.g., rubella or syphilis), maternal intoxication (resulting in fetal alcohol syndrome), and postnatal infections (e.g., encephalitis). Mental retardation can also be due to chromosomal abnormalities (e.g., trisomy 21, which results in Down's syndrome). Physical traumas (e.g., anoxia [oxygen deprivation]) and metabolic disorders (e.g., phenylketonuria) also can cause mental retardation. In addition, disorders such as neurofibromatosis or tuberous sclerosis can also contribute to mental retardation. Environmental toxins (e.g., excessive amounts of lead) and low birth weight are also contributing factors. Furthermore, unknown factors may result in serious conditions such as anencephaly (partial or complete absence of brain tissue) (Hardman et al., 1993).

Despite these many serious biological or organic causes of mental retardation, most individuals who are classified as mentally retarded are considered to have *mild* mental retardation, and the causes of their learning problems are not apparent. It is commonly assumed that the mental impairment of these individuals is due to sociocultural factors (sometimes referred to as *psychosocial* variables). Many individuals with mild mental retardation come from low socioeconomic and/or culturally or linguistically different backgrounds. In situations where children do not have adequate nutrition, access to health care, exposure to stimulating educational opportunities, or positive influences or role models who value education, it may be very difficult for them to learn well in school.

For many individuals, there are both sociocultural factors and genetic factors that interact. The term used to described students whose retardation is likely due to both categories of problems is *cultural-familial*. The term implies that the causation is a complex interaction of both environmental and hereditary factors. In fact, there has been a long-standing discussion in special education about whether intelligence is innate or acquired. Often referred to as the *nature versus nurture debate,* the controversy has been important because it impacts educators' beliefs about the efficacy of education and treatment, that is, whether students can benefit significantly from intervention and education. Most authorities agree that intelligence is complex and that it is both acquired and inherited. Nevertheless, environmental influences are extremely important, and educators usually realize that they can have a very powerful impact on students' progress. When individuals with mental retardation are properly taught and given carefully planned assistance, their potential for achieving, learning, and living is enhanced. In this section, realistic expectations for people labeled mildly or moderately retarded are described, along with the types of treatment and care that are essential for furthering their cognitive, affective, social, motor, and vocational development.

Before proceeding, it is important to emphasize that regardless of the severity of retardation, an individual can be helped and can develop new skills. The child with mental retardation is not likely to blossom or intellectually unfold without special help. With proper intervention, undesirable behaviors can be ameliorated and desirable behaviors can be taught. Moreover, the earlier we get involved, the greater our chance of witnessing improvement.

EARLY INTERVENTION, EXPECTATIONS, AND SOCIOCULTURAL INFLUENCES VERSUS HEREDITY

The Wild Boy

One way to understand the complex nature of sociocultural influences on educational programming for students with mental retardation is to look at some of the landmark historical studies investigating the effects of intervention. The creative and partially successful attempts of Jean Marc Gaspard Itard to educate a 12-year-old *homme sauvage* deserve mention in any discussion of mental retardation. In 1799, a wild boy was captured in the forest of Aveyron, France. The boy, later named Victor, behaved in many ways like a wild animal. Victor did not speak or respond to the sound of gunfire, yet he quickly startled at the sound of a cracking nut. Victor did not seem to feel differences between hot and cold, or smell differences between foul and pleasant odors. His moods swung from deep depression to hyper excitement. Itard believed that with proper education Victor could be cured. For 5 years, he worked intensively with Victor and then abandoned his goals, concluding that he had failed. Later, the French Academy of Science recognized Itard's significant accomplishments and requested that he publish a report of his work. The result was a classic for the field of education, *The Wild Boy of Aveyron* (Itard, 1962).

Although Itard had failed to "cure" Victor, many very dramatic changes in the boy were evidenced. Victor's behavior was greatly changed, and after much training, he was taught to identify various vowel sounds. Ultimately, he learned to read and write a few words; however, he remained mute. Although Itard regarded his work with Victor unsuccessful, the strategies and activities that he developed are the basis for many of the interventions educators use today.

Studies Related to Sociocultural Influences

Several noted researchers have attempted to determine the relative importance of environmental influences in causing mental retardation. When investigating environmental impact on learning, studies have usually looked at the role of unstimulating, poor environments. It is important to remember that the effects of poverty are different from the effects of cultural minority status (Chan & Rueda, 1979; Garber, 1988). Because culturally, linguistically, and ethnically diverse individuals are so often overrepresented in poverty groups, this may be difficult to do. The effects of a poverty culture seem to be significant and pervasive, stemming in part from factors such as inconsistent parenting practices, lack of stability, stressors related to finding and keeping jobs and paying bills, a sense of fatalism, health problems, and a lack of educational opportunity.

Some of the most interesting research related to environmental influences was performed by Harold Skeels. His early research, begun in the 1930s, is the basis for many of the early intervention programs begun in the 1960s. The Skeels and Dye study (1939) investigated the reversibility of the effects of nonstimulating orphanage environments on children. The study contrasted two groups of children: One group was left in an unstimulating environment with minimal health and medical services and the other group received one-on-one care from a surrogate mother trained in how to nurture and care for them. When the groups were retested, the experimental group showed a significant gain in IQ (about 28 points). A follow-up study 25 years later (Skeels, 1966) confirmed that the improvements of the experimental group were lasting and were accompanied by educational progress, stable employment and marriages, and functional independent living. The majority of the contrast group, on the other hand, had a low level of education and were either unemployed or institutionalized. Skeels (1966) concluded:

> It seems obvious that under present-day conditions there are still countless infants with sound biological constitutions and potentialities for development well within the normal range who will become mentally retarded and noncontributing members of society unless appropriate intervention occurs. It is suggested by the findings of this study and others published in the past 20 years that sufficient knowledge is available to design programs of intervention to counteract the devastating effects of poverty, sociocultural, and maternal deprivations. The unanswered questions of this study could form the basis for many life-long research projects. If the tragic fate of the 12 contrast group children provokes even a single crucial study that will help prevent such a fate for others their lives will not have been in vain. (pp. 54–55)

Another research and intervention program that addressed the question of the relationship between environment and mental retardation was the Milwaukee Project. The project was a longitudinal study examining the influence of family and/or home environments on the intellectual development of young children. The program focused on attempts to (a) train mothers to better care for their families and (b) increase the amount of stimulation provided to infants. Early results of the project were very encouraging. The experimental children made significant gains in IQ and were performing better on language, motor, and cognitive tasks (Garber & Heber, 1973). Unfortunately, follow-up studies were not as hopeful. Both experimental children and control children tended to do poorly later in school, and the majority of both groups were below-average achievers in reading and mathematics by fourth grade (Garber, 1988). There has also been considerable criticism of the experiment because of possible bias and poor experimental procedures. Despite the overwhelming skepticism regarding the integrity of the Milwaukee Project, for many years it had considerable influence on the development of early intervention programs.

Studies Related to Heredity

Significant studies have also been conducted that addressed the role of heredity in mental retardation. Perhaps the most famous of these was the work of Jensen (1969), who examined the possible correlation between intelligence and the genetic base of social classes. The idea that inherited gene pools determine the genetic makeup of future generations has remained a controversial issue. Questions about genetic determinism based on membership in a class or group and the consequent implications for genetic engineering are inherently distasteful to many individuals. Historical movements like the *eugenics* movement, which advocated mass sterilization of individuals with mental retardation, have reinforced many people's opinion that viewing intelligence as a genetically determined quality leads to unwarranted and dangerous social policies.

Most professionals seem to believe in a middle ground that credits the interaction of both genetic and environmental factors. With such a highly complex construct as intelligence, it is likely that this moderate point of view is the most accepted.

CHARACTERISTICS OF INDIVIDUALS WITH MENTAL RETARDATION

In presenting some of the characteristics and behaviors exhibited by people labeled mentally retarded, we will discuss some objectives that we believe to be representative of realistic expectations for many of them. Realizing that individuals with mental retardation differ from one another as much as nondisabled people differ among themselves, it is essential to recognize that the following discussion will not apply to *all* individuals classified as retarded. The behaviors described are typically displayed at some age level by all people; those with mental retardation often develop at a slower rate or later than do most people.

Mild Mental Retardation

Generally speaking, people with mild retardation are usually quite capable of caring for their own personal needs. They should be able to carry out everyday activities without the assistance of family, friends, or benefactors. A terminal goal for individuals classified as mildly mentally retarded is often employment and successful adjustment to community living on the completion of formal schooling.

In terms of cognitive functioning, individuals with mild mental retardation will often have problems in several distinct areas, including memory, generalization ability, and use of learning strategies. Developing learning strategies involves *metacognitive* processes, that is, *learning to learn*. Without these metacognitive skills, which are critical for acquiring new information, school can be a source of difficulty. The demands of school may turn a student with mild mental retardation into what the President's Committee on Mental Retardation called "the six-hour retarded child" (1970). Being classified as mentally retarded may only be appropriate for these students when they are attending school. In *real-life* situations requiring social and vocational competencies rather than academic skills, individuals with mild retardation are often very successful.

Other domains may also be problematic for people who are mildly mentally retarded, including

1. *Personal and motivational competencies:* self-concept, dependency, failure syndrome
2. *Social and behavioral skills:* self-direction, responsibility, social relationships
3. *General learning problems:* attentional variables, mediational strategies
4. *Speech and language skills:* articulation, receptive and expressive language ability
5. *Physical and health dimensions:* body measurements, motor skills

Almost all children with mild mental retardation can be effectively educated. In the elementary grades, many students with mild mental retardation can be fully or partially included (i.e., *integrated*) into regular classrooms when these settings are determined appropriate. In a partially self-contained arrangement, students spend some of their instructional day in the regular education setting and the remainder of their time in a special setting with a trained special education teacher. The special education time is usually devoted to helping the student with language, reading, math, or social skill development. During the latter elementary grades, and certainly by the junior high level, special provisions must be made for teaching the essential and practical academic subjects. Students should remain with their normal peers as much as possible, but they may require special programs in language arts, reading, and math.

As children with mental retardation grow to adulthood, the ability to handle leisure time and to enjoy recreational activities can also have a significant impact on their lives. Although they may be able to dance or bowl in organized group situations, too many adults with mental retardation often end up spending their days watching television. To have a balanced, enjoyable life, it is important to develop hobbies and interests and to participate in recreational activities. With appropriate education and training, adults with mild mental retardation can master the life skills necessary for well-rounded, satisfying lives.

Cronin and Patton (1993), in their book on life skills instruction, have provided a thorough guide for professionals who work with adults. Figure 6.1 provides a look

Life Skills Course	Select Topics
Personal Finance 	maintaining a budget filing tax submitting an application for a loan using credit cards
Practical Math 	performing home repairs/maintenance estimating travel time cooking measuring dosage of prescribed medicine
Health & Hygiene 	dealing with illness administering first aid maintaining one's personal appearance handling stress
Everyday Science 	gardening identifying how things work controlling pests using science in the kitchen
Practical Communication 	using resource materials requesting information writing personal cards and notes taking phone messages
Community Awareness and Involvement 	registering to vote using community resources (e.g., library) attending neighborhood association meetings knowing one's legal rights
Occupational Development 	identifying personal interests and aptitudes preparing a career planning packet practicing interview skills identifying available jobs in the community
Interpersonal Relations 	getting along with others accepting criticism complimenting others engaging in social conversation

Figure 6.1
Life Skills Courses and Select Sample Topics

Source: From *Life Skills Instruction for All Students With Special Needs: A Practical Guide for Integrating Real Life Content Into the Curriculum* (p. 31), by M. E. Cronin and J. R. Patton, 1993, Austin, TX: PRO-ED. Reprinted by permission.

at some of the topics pertinent in a life skills course, including personal finance, health and hygiene, and community awareness.

Career education is essential and should begin in the elementary grades and continue throughout the students' schooling and lives. Attention to prevocational and vocational skill development should be programmed into the students' academic plans. Instruction in the areas of general job skills and specific vocational training is essential. By high school, students with mild retardation may remain with their peers in some subjects and focus on vocational training. They should be given an opportunity to learn various types of job skills and be allowed to realistically demonstrate their competence by working on various jobs in the community (i.e., community-based training). Job training can be accomplished through programs that allow students to attend school for part of the day and participate in job training and evaluation and actual employment.

Postsecondary programs and continuing educational opportunities are also important. These programs should teach the person with mild mental retardation to cope with personal problems and provide opportunities for socialization and recreation. Programs should be comprehensive (cover social, motor, cognitive, and academic skills) and continuous (begin early and continue well into adulthood).

Moderate Mental Retardation

It is not always helpful or accurate to express people's abilities in either age or grade equivalents because we overlook individual strengths and deficits. However, sometimes people can understand individuals' characteristics when they are viewed developmentally. People with *moderate* mental retardation can sometimes be considered developmentally as approximately 3 or more years behind those who are diagnosed as *mildly* retarded.

Identification of children with more moderate retardation may occur very early. By about age 3, children with moderate mental retardation are so significantly delayed in their development that most are already diagnosed as retarded. At this age, educational programs should include training in self-care skills such as independent bathroom and eating skills, so that children can move toward independence. Preschool children who have moderate mental retardation can usually stand and walk alone but may need help in climbing steps. They generally have a vocabulary of from four to six words, recognize others, play for short periods of time with peers, and communicate many needs with gestures. By age 6, children with moderate mental retardation can usually feed themselves with a spoon (although this may still be messy) and can drink unassisted. They can climb up and down stairs, but still not with alternating feet. They can speak two- or three-word sentences and name simple common objects. Individuals with moderate mental retardation will remain developmentally delayed into their adult lives.

Individuals with moderate mental retardation have traditionally not been placed in regular school classrooms for academic instruction but are often integrated for nonacademic courses. Including children with moderate or severe disabilities into regular classrooms for *all* instruction is part of the political and social movement in education toward *full inclusion*. Research on the effects of inclusion are not conclusive, but many states have made significant efforts at integrating all students into regular education classes in their home schools. The socialization benefits of increased integration is perhaps the important result when students with disabilities and students without disabilities interact.

Educationally, the program emphasis should be *functionality,* that is, improving skills necessary to take care of oneself, to get along with others, and to display other requisite community living and vocational skills. It is very important that transitional planning occur for this group of students. Moreover, the program should strive to get the students or clients to feel good about themselves and ultimately to enjoy their lives.

We typically think of adults with moderate mental retardation as individuals who are capable of varying degrees of employment, including sheltered, supported, or competitive situations. Nevertheless, even into adulthood, these individuals may need supervision in carrying out routine daily activities. Many adults with moderate mental retardation are able to recognize written words and read simple sentences but, for all practical purposes, do not evidence great academic achievement. They can carry on simple conversations and can perform such household chores as dusting, mopping, and cleaning. They can feed, bathe, and dress themselves. By adulthood their gross and fine motor coordination will be developed to the point where they will have good body control. However, social life will be a constant problem. Although individuals with moderate mental retardation are limited in some respects, they typically are interesting, challenging, and enjoyable company; however, if left alone they may end up socially isolated.

Severe Mental Retardation

Individuals with the lowest functional level of mental retardation have been labeled as severely or profoundly retarded. However, Sailor, Gee, Goetz, and Graham (1988) state that the dichotomy between severe and profound mental retardation is unnecessary. Usually these persons are referred to collectively as having severe mental retardation and (at the lowest levels) as possessing the most severe disabilities. Ryndak and Alper (2003) currently propose the label of *persons with significant disabilities* to refer to this population.

Individuals who are severely mentally retarded are often served by public schools in self-contained classes. These classes may be located in special schools or residential institutions. However, even in these settings inclusion into normalized settings such as regular classrooms, community environments (restaurants, buses, stores, etc.), or group homes is a key objective that should guide intervention.

As with individuals who are moderately mentally retarded, students with severe retardation have difficulty mastering many basic self-help, social, and communication skills. The basic difference between the two groups involves the number and complexity of the functional skills aquired and mastered, as well as the degree of proficiency in these skills each type of student displays. Instruction focuses on skills that are both age appropriate and functional in the severely retarded person's current environment and the generalization of these skills to future environments (Ryndak & Alper, 2003). Most academic skills will be absent or appear only in an attenuated form. Whereas persons with moderate mental retardation may be able to live in the community with a minimum of supervision, persons with severe retardation often require direct supervision and/or prompting even to carry out the simplest domestic or self-help skill. Work environments for this group range from supported to sheltered settings. Individuals with severe mental retardation may live and work in a community setting, but not without ongoing care and management.

An individual with mild mental retardation usually *looks* normal. That is, you probably would not be able to tell if someone you have merely seen on the street is mildly retarded. This may not be the case for people with moderate or severe mental retardation. These individuals often look like something is different about them and may have one or many observable, distinctive features (e.g., language problems, poor motor coordination, physical differences, or inappropriate stereotypical behaviors). The distinctive physical characteristics become more prevalent the more severe the retardation.

FINAL THOUGHTS

The characteristics and behaviors that we have reported for people with mild, moderate, and severe mental retardation do not represent each and every possibility on the continuum of characteristics. For instance, it is not unusual to find a person with mild mental retardation who is incapable of holding a job and who may even experience a great deal of difficulty remaining employed in more sheltered settings. The important thing to remember is that individuals with mental retardation can acquire new skills, can learn, and can grow intellectually and personally. This developmental process is greatly enhanced when adequate services are provided as early as possible and continue into adulthood.

It is obvious that being retarded is not something one chooses. Having a child with mental retardation is something parents neither hope for nor, in most cases, prepare for. The difficulties that parents encounter are sometimes compounded by the absence of appropriate services or the difficulty of obtaining information and services that are available. The adjustment of parents to the birth of a child with a disability can be made worse by insensitivity and misinformation. Physicians, who are often the first to notice a problem, may not always know what to expect and so cannot tell the parents. By anyone's standards, the birth of a child with mental retardation is a significant event, often leading to joy and fulfillment as well as difficulties. Individuals with mental retardation are people who are more like than unlike the rest of us. Although they often get caught in life's absurdities and amusing circumstances, they can lead successful and rewarding lives. Because individuals with mental retardation themselves do not enjoy strong political clout, it is important that we act as advocates for them and teach them to act as advocates for themselves. We must ensure that the public in general and legislators, policy makers, and judges in particular realize that people with mental retardation are entitled to the same rights that every citizen enjoys and the same human dignity that you and I continually demand.

SUGGESTIONS FOR WORKING WITH PEOPLE WITH MENTAL RETARDATION

1. Set goals that are realistic for the individual and the community in which the individual lives.
2. Assign tasks that are personally relevant, are carefully sequenced from easy to difficult, and allow the learner to be highly and frequently successful.
3. Recognize the individual's strengths and weaknesses, provide incentives for performance, and establish necessary rules for behavior. Maintain high expectations and do not teach the student to be helpless.
4. Explain required tasks in terms of concrete concepts.
5. When giving instructions, be specific: "John, go to the principal's office, give Mrs. Smith the absentee sheet, and come back here."
6. When giving instructions, briefly summarize: "Remember, John: First, go to the principal's office. Second, give the sheet to Mrs. Smith. Third, come back."
7. When giving instructions, ask what is to be done: "John, tell me what you are to do."
8. When praising, be specific, not general: "John, you did a good job taking the absentee sheet to Mrs. Smith. You went directly to the office, and you came straight back." Do not just make a generic statement about doing a good job.
9. When praising, emphasize "you" rather than "I": "John, you got nine out of ten math problems correct. That took a lot of effort. Keep up the good work."
10. Give constant praise and feedback, especially when the individual is learning a new task.

PONDER THESE

1. What are the arguments for and against the following actions:
   - ❏ Sterilizing adults with mental retardation
   - ❏ Encouraging matrimony among individuals with mental retardation
   - ❏ Advocating for a community home for adults with mental retardation in your neighborhood
   - ❏ Allowing the initiation of a child with mental retardation into your son's or daughter's Cub Scout or Brownie troop

2. Think about how you could convince a businessperson to hire an adult with mental retardation. For example, how would you do the following?
   - ❏ Request cooperation (by phone or personal contact—Would you take your client with you?)
   - ❏ Describe your client (Would you use the term retarded?)
   - ❏ Ask questions about the job description
   - ❏ Describe the competencies of your client
   - ❏ Guarantee success

3. You are a first-grade teacher in a public school. Included in your class is a student (Bill) who is classified as mentally retarded. Bill has some behavioral problems. For example, when he wants something, he takes it, whether another student is using it or not. He is difficult to understand because his speech is not clear. The other students are beginning to make fun of him and are angry at him because he does not share. How will you deal with this situation?

4. What are some everyday living skills necessary for successful functioning in your community?

ONLINE RESOURCES

American Association on Mental Retardation
http://www.AAMR.org

The ARC of the United States
http://www.thearc.org

The Association for Persons with Severe Handicaps
http://www.tash.org

Beach Center on Disabilities
http://www.beachcenter.org

Center for Applied Special Technology
http://www.CAST.org

Center on Human Development and Disability
http://www.depts.washington.edu/chdd

Council for Exceptional Children/Division on Developmental Disabilities
http://www.dddcec.org

John F. Kennedy Center for Research on Human Development
http://www.vanderbilt.edu/kennedy

T. K. Martin Center for Technology and Disability
http://www.tkmartin.msstate.edu

REFERENCES

American Association on Mental Retardation. (1992). *Mental retardation: Definition, classification, and systems of supports* (9th ed.). Washington, DC: Author.

American Association on Mental Retardation. (2002). *Mental retardation: Definition, classification, and systems of supports* (10th ed.). Washington, DC: Author.

Beirne-Smith, M., Ittenbach, R., & Patton, J. R. (2002). *Mental retardation* (6th ed.). Upper Saddle River, NJ: Merrill/Prentice Hall.

Chan, K. S., & Rueda, R. (1979). Poverty and culture in education: Separate but equal. *Exceptional Children, 45,* 422–428.

Cronin, M. E., & Patton, J. R. (1993). *Life skills instruction for all students with special needs: A practical guide for integrating real life content into the curriculum.* Austin, TX: PRO-ED.

Garber, J. L. (1988). *The Milwaukee Project: Preventing mental retardation in children at risk.* Washington, DC: American Association on Mental Retardation.

Garber, J. L., & Heber, R. F. (1973). *The Milwaukee Project: Early intervention as a technique to prevent mental retardation.* Storrs: University of Connecticut.

Grossman, H. J. (Ed.). (1983). *Classification in mental retardation.* Washington, DC: American Association on Mental Deficiency.

Hardman, M. L., Drew, C. J., Egan, M. W., & Wolf, B. (1993). *Human exceptionality: Society, school, and family* (4th ed.). Boston: Allyn & Bacon.

Itard, J. M. G. (1962). *The wild boy of Aveyron.* New York: Appleton-Century-Crofts.

Jensen, A. R. (1969). How much can we boost IQ and scholastic achievement? *Harvard Educational Review, 39,* 1–123.

President's Committee on Mental Retardation. (1970). *The six-hour retarded child.* Washington, DC: U.S. Government Printing Office.

Ryndak, D. L. & Alper, S. (2003). *Curriculum and instruction for students with significant disabilities in inclusive settings.* Boston: Allyn & Bacon.

Sailor, W., Gee, K., Goetz, L., & Graham, N. (1988). Progress in educating students with the most severe disabilities: Is there any? *Journal of the Association for Persons with Severe Handicaps, 13,* 87–99.

Skeels, H. M. (1966). Adult status of children with contrasting early life experiences: A follow-up study. *Monographs of the Society for Research in Child Development, 31*(3, Whole No. 105), 1–26.

Skeels, H. M., & Dye, H. B. (1939). A study of the effects of differential stimulation on mentally retarded children. *Convention Proceedings of the American Association on Mental Deficiency, 44,* 114–136.

U.S. Department of Education. (2000). *To assure the free appropriate public education of all children with disabilities. Twenty-second annual report to Congress on the implementation of the Individuals with Disabilities Education Act.* Washington, DC: Author.

CHAPTER 7

Pervasive Developmental Disorders/ Autism Spectrum Disorders

Kimberly G. Carper

William is 57 years old. Each day he attends a well-established sheltered workshop in the county where he lives. To attend the workshop, William rides the bus for 2 hours in the morning, making four separate transfers; and 2.5 hours in the afternoon, making six separate transfers. He has worked at this particular sheltered workshop for the past 20 years, and spends most of his time there sorting objects, completing piecemeal projects, and drawing pictures of places he remembers living or visiting. William sketches and draws in a freehand style, utilizing colored pencils as well as regular pencils. He produces very intricate pictures and demonstrates a clear artistic talent. Recently, he won a local art contest and was recognized in a ceremony attended by hundreds of people throughout the community. Though unable to independently dress himself, grocery shop, or successfully attend to his medications, he is able to ride public transportation across town to attend the sheltered workshop. When William was 3 years old, his parents committed him to an institution based upon the recommendation of their family doctor; he spent nearly 30 years there. For the past 24 years, William has resided with his parents, who are in their late eighties and in extremely poor health. There is valid concern among those at the sheltered workshop concerning William's living situation when his parents are no longer able to care for him within their home. William was diagnosed with autism when he was 2 years old.

Now finished with an intensive, vocational preparatory program, Peter spends much of his time sitting at home watching television and cleaning his mother's house. Though he was provided extensive vocational training in high school and has worked successfully at several jobs in restaurants during the past 7 years, his vocational rehabilitation (VR) counselor has yet to place him within a paid work situation. The VR counselor was supposed to have found Peter a job matched to his specific skills prior to Peter's high school graduation. After 6 months Peter's mother is growing impatient while waiting for VR to assist him in procuring a job. At 22 years old, Peter stands 6′2″, and weighs nearly 300 pounds. He engages in many odd behaviors and mannerisms including screaming when he is happy, organizing any area he is in, and antagonizing those around him by providing tidbits of information that are socially inappropriate. He appears fond of jumping up and down squealing, slapping his legs while twisting and contorting his body, and speaking to himself in low tones when he is happy about something. When Peter is angry or frustrated he will often slap his head and use profane language; when he becomes highly agitated, he sometimes engages in physical aggression. Peter has a photographic memory, never forgetting the face or name of someone he has met. When he navigates the community, people are often surprised that he calls them by name, even if he has not seen them in a number of years or has only met them on one occasion. Peter was diagnosed with PDD-NOS when he was 3 years old.

I am often amazed at how far Tracy has progressed since our first meeting. When I first met him, he was in elementary school, and was often highly agitated and so physically aggressive that restraint was required to keep him (and those around him) safe.

During his elementary experience, Tracy demonstrated great behavioral difficulty at school, as well as within his home. His single mother often had to endure intense tantrums, and she spent a great deal of time working with Tracy on his behavioral and social problems. Additionally, they both had to deal with the chronic poor health of Tracy's grandmother who also lived with them during this period. From the start, it was clear that Tracy's cognitive and verbal abilities were highly developed, in spite of his inability to socialize appropriately with his peers or demonstrate empathy for others when necessary. Following a brief stint in a self-contained classroom and a great deal of intensive intervention, Tracy successfully navigated elementary school in a regular education classroom with a support assistant. During this time, Tracy underwent major surgery for an injury that he had previously sustained in an accident. Following elementary school, Tracy made the transition to middle school and continues to do exceptionally well in regular education classes, most of which are gifted classes. He still has a support assistant, though does not often utilize her help. He is now able to socialize appropriately with both peers and teachers most of the time. Tracy enjoys playing on his computer, spending time with his friends, and engaging in his newest hobby, golf. Tracy was diagnosed with Asperger syndrome when he was 5 years old.

The device he carries is the only indication that something is different about Mark. He carries a dynovox, an automated voice-output device that allows Mark to communicate with others because he is unable to speak. The device resembles a small computer and has picture icons that Mark is able to manipulate on different screens for communicative purposes or expression. Mark is now in sixth grade and has been fully included in his regular elementary school since kindergarten. The elementary school he attends has a full-inclusion policy for all students, even those with significant disabilities. Karen, Mark's one-to-one assistant, has been working with him since he was in the first grade and has grown accustomed to frequent outbursts of aggression, self-injurious behavior, and crying. She is very dedicated to Mark and treats him as if he were her own child. Karen is patient, firm, and compassionate, and she works diligently with him on the basic skills necessary for reading and mathematics. She keeps all of his instruction functional and relevant and allows Mark to move at his own pace within the school's mandated curriculum. Several agencies are involved with Mark and his family, including the local augmentative specialists, developmental services, intervention services, and the Center for Autism and Related Disabilities. Recently, Mark's father was killed in an accident. The school and support staff struggled to make visual supports that would allow Mark to communicate his grief with those around him and to express any sorrow, frustration, or loss he was feeling. Mark was diagnosed with autism when he was a year and a half old.

Pervasive developmental disorders, also known as autism spectrum disorders, are a class of developmental disorders that are neurological in nature. They are characterized as a spectrum of disorders that vary in individual symptoms, age of onset, and association with other disorders (Committee on Educational Interventions for

Children with Autism, 2001). Under this global category, the manifestations of autism vary abundantly among individuals and have lifelong implications on learning and development.

BASIC CONCEPTS

Terminology

The term *pervasive developmental disorder* (PDD) was first utilized to provide a formal diagnosis for individuals who exhibited behavior similar to those with autism, but failed to meet eligibility criteria for a specific diagnosis of autism (Chakrabarti & Fombonne, 2001). Emphasis was placed on the pervasiveness of these particular impairments, with the express purpose of differentiating autism from general cognitive disabilities.

In 1943, Leo Kanner first wrote about children with autism, describing them as a unique group of children whose behavioral abnormalities made them qualitatively different from other children with identified disabilities (Simpson & Smith-Myles, 1998). Though Kanner described children with autism according to a specific set of symptoms, the current definitions and conceptualizations of autism reverberate with many of Kanner's earliest observations. In 1944, just one year after Kanner's groundbreaking paper on autism, Hans Asperger described four socially impaired children with idiosyncratic, narrow interests who suffered from "autistic psychopathy" (Klin, Volkmar, & Sparrow, 2000). Now identified as Asperger syndrome, it is listed under the same diagnostic category (pervasive developmental disorders) as autism. Historically, autism and other PDDs were considered a form of mental illness, with a universal recommendation of institutionalization by the medical and educational communities. Pervasive developmental disorders are now widely recognized as syndromes emanating from brain-based etiology (Cohen & Volkmar, 1997; Smith & Luckasson, 1995), and they are considered by many researchers to be a neurobiological disorder.

During the past 60 years, the study of autism has extended well beyond the conceptual and definitional ideas about this particular form of a pervasive developmental disorder. The product of this evolution appears to be a scientific consensus that autism is only one of several autism spectrum disorders (ASDs) (Wetherby & Prizant, 2000). Specifically, ASD refers to the five subcategorical diagnoses that encompass the domain of a PDD: autistic disorder, childhood disintegrative disorder, Rett's disorder, Asperger syndrome, and pervasive developmental disorder–not otherwise specified. The acronyms PDD and ASD are often used interchangeably; in fact, the current trend within the field appears to favor the use of ASD rather than PDD when referring to spectrum-related disorders.

Debate continues among scientists regarding which disorders should be included under the category of PDDs and the exact scope of the "spectrum." Few dispute the notion of a "spectrum" of autism-related disorders (Wetherby & Prizant, 2000), and all agree that a great deal of collaborative work is necessary to clarify the diagnostic criteria for any future classifications or diagnostic definitional changes.

Several acronyms are used regularly in the field of autism spectrum disorders. Knowing them helps to facilitate a better understanding of the common terms utilized by professionals within the medical, educational, and community support systems. Table 7.1 includes important acronyms not included in the original list presented in chapter 1 (see Table 1.1).

Definitional Perspective

PDD is defined by observed or described behavior specific to distinct categories. Affected behaviors are defined by the American Psychiatric Association (APA, 1994) and encompass three distinct categories of marked impairment. Largely theoretical, the involvement of some type of genetic component in the etiology of PDDs is widely accepted, although biological markers have not yet been identified (Wetherby & Prizant, 2000).

The PDD classification has five distinct subcategories: autistic disorder, childhood disintegrative disorder, Rett's disorder, Asperger syndrome, and pervasive developmental disorder–not otherwise specified. Each of these developmental disorders originates prior to birth or within early infancy. Regardless of which of the five types of PDD an individual is diagnosed with, three primary categories of symptoms exist: pervasive delays in language, intense difficulty with social skills, and an extreme maladaptive behavioral demonstration, as expanded on in Table 7.2. Descriptions by caregivers and observations of specific symptoms are utilized to establish a specific diagnosis under the category of a pervasive developmental disorder. Specifically, these are impaired social interaction, impaired communication, and characteristic behavior problems (Powers, 2000).

Table 7.1
Acronyms Used in the Field of ASD

ABA	Applied behavioral analysis
AS	Asperger syndrome
ASA	Autism Society of America
CDD	Childhood disintegrative disorder
DS	Developmental services
DSM-IV	*Diagnostic and Statistical Manual of Mental Disorders, fourth edition*
DTT	Discrete trial training or discrete trial teaching
EEG	Electroencephalogram
HFA	High functioning autism
MRI	Magnetic resonance imaging (brain scan)
PDD	Pervasive developmental disorders
PDD-NOS	Pervasive developmental disorder–not otherwise specified
PECS	Picture exchange communication system
PRT	Pivotal response training
SI	Sensory integration

Table 7.2
Common Symptoms of Pervasive Developmental Disorders

___

Social Interaction

Shows little or no interest in making friends.
Prefers own company, rather than that of others.
Does not imitate the action of others.
Does not interact playfully.
Avoids eye contact.
Does not smile at familiar people.
Appears unaware of others.

Communication

Has difficulty maintaining a conversation.
Reverses pronouns (specifically "you" and "I").
Repeats words (echolalia).
Lacks imagination or the ability to pretend.
Does not use symbolic gestures.
Cannot communicate with words or gestures.

Unusual Interests

Is fascinated by facts about specific topics.
Reads words at a very early age (hyperlexia).
Is intensely interested in the mechanics of objects.
Lines toys up in neat rows.

Behavioral Symptoms

Is physically inactive—prefers to be indoors.
Does not respond to requests (selective listening).
Engages in picky eating habits (self-restricts).
Throws tantrums (screaming, kicking, crying, etc.).
Behaves aggressively.
Injures self.

___

Source: Adapted from *Children with Autism: A Parents' Guide,* by M. D. Powers, Ed., 2000, Bethesda, MD: Woodbine House.

The most widely recognized definition of PDDs is described in the fourth edition of the *Diagnostic and Statistical Manual of Mental Disorders* (DSM-IV) (APA, 1994), a clinical guide utilized by psychiatrists, psychologists, and physicians to accurately diagnose specific disorders. According to the DSM-IV, individuals identified with pervasive developmental disorders "are characterized by severe and pervasive impairment in several areas of development: reciprocal social interaction skills, communication skills, or the presence of stereotyped behavior, interests, and activities" (APA, 1994, p. 65). The demonstration of these behavioral patterns, atypical in relation to a child's mental or developmental age, often appear within the first few years of life. Contrary to the popular opinion that PDD symptoms manifest between 18 and 24 months of age, several researchers have indicated strong evidence of symptoms that begin to occur during the first year of a child's life. As might be expected, an increasing number of very young children are being served by early intervention programs.

Prevalence

Long considered a low-incidence disability, PDDs have effectively joined the ranks of more commonly occurring disabilities. Reportedly, there are now more individuals with autism than with Down syndrome or blindness (Janzen, 1999; Westling & Fox, 2000). Reported figures and epidemiological studies on the prevalence of PDDs indicate a vast array of findings. Statistics that have been reported range from 2 per 10,000 to as high as 11.6 per 10,000 (Mesibov, Adams, & Klinger, 1997). Notably, some researchers have published staggering figures reporting as many as 9 affected individuals with PDDs per 1,000 births (Wing, 1997). The DSM-IV reports the prevalence of autism to be 2 to 5 cases per 10,000 people, though one must bear in mind this statistic was published in 1994, when the most recent edition of the DSM-IV was published. In a recent study conducted by Chakrabarti and Fombonne (2001) in the United Kingdom, a prevalence rate of 62.6 per 10,000 (or 5 to 6 per 1,000) was determined for ASDs. A breakdown of these findings indicated that 16.8 per 10,000 (or nearly 2 per 1,000) of these individuals had an autistic disorder, with the remaining 45.8 per 10,000 (or nearly 5 per 1,000) having a range of PDDs.

In addition to these recent prevalence findings, the researchers reported a 26 percent occurrence rate (comorbidity) of mental retardation with a PDD. This finding is particularly startling because previous studies have indicated this occurrence rate to be as high as 75 percent, 55 percent, and 40 percent (Chakrabarti & Fombonne, 2001).

Though the media, and some people within school systems and community agencies, have reported an epidemic of PDDs during the last several years, much of the literature supports the notion that medical practitioners are now more aware of PDDs and are making accurate diagnostic assessments. Historically, many psychiatrists, psychologists, and medical professionals would wait for a child to reach 5 or 6 years of age before committing to a PDD diagnosis. Most recently, young children are being diagnosed at an earlier age, because doctors appear to be less apprehensive regarding any perceived stigma attached to such a diagnosis. Further, a dramatic increase has been seen in the number of medical personnel receiving ongoing education and information regarding PDDs and accurate diagnostic protocols.

Etiology

For nearly three decades ASDs have been associated with neurobiological correlates and central nervous system (CNS) dysfunctions, including high rates of seizure activity in individuals with autism and other PDDs. Several investigators have documented the onset of seizures once children with PDDs reach adolescence, specifically, one quarter to one third of those with autism have reported this phenomenon, further solidifying the possible indication of a neuropathological problem (Cohen & Volkmar, 1997; Schopler & Mesibov, 1983).

Currently accepted by most as disorders of the brain, PDDs clearly demonstrate a specific neurological origin. Strong evidence indicates that PDDs originate at the level of DNA or within its transcription process for brain development (Cohen &

Volkmar, 1997). Lending additional support to this theory is the demonstration of consistent symptoms and pathology among individuals with PDDs in case after case.

Symptoms demonstrated by individuals with ASD, including behavioral, emotional, and cognitive difficulties indicate a compromised function of the CNS. Further indicators of brain abnormality are the early onset, pervasive nature, and chronicity of PDDs (Cohen & Volkmar, 1997). An understanding of the role genetic factors contribute to autism and other PDDs has increased greatly within the medical and research communities during the past decade. Though basic questions have yet to be answered, it is now clear that genetic factors do indeed play a crucial role in the etiology of PDDs.

CHARACTERISTICS

A great deal of variance is seen in the characteristics and manifestations of symptoms in persons with PDDs; no one person will necessarily display all aspects or symptomatic possibilities of a specific diagnostic category (Koegel & Koegel, 1995). For instance, behaviors people exhibit may look similar, but individuals will display great fluctuation in the demonstration of categorical symptoms. Moreover, it is important to note that each of the diagnostic subcategories of PDDs differs by classification, *not* by severity. For example, a diagnosis of autistic disorder will not necessarily indicate a more severe impairment than someone with a PDD-NOS. Recognition of the immense variability over the autism spectrum is particularly useful to those within community and educational settings.

According to the DSM-IV, *autistic disorder* is characterized by displays of social interaction impairments, communication impairments, and repetitive, stereotypic, and restricted interests and activities prior to an individual becoming 36 months of age. Table 7.3 lists the diagnostic criteria for autistic disorder. Reportedly, most children diagnosed with autistic disorder tend to be moderately to severely impaired, the majority having IQs in the range of moderate to severe mental retardation (Simpson & Smith-Myles, 1998).

Research literature suggests that the language development of individuals with autism improves slowly and consistently. Half of the individuals identified as having autism do not develop functional speech by adolescence; the other half who do develop speech by the time they are an adolescent acquire it after the age of 5 (Schopler & Mesibov, 1983).

Individuals with *childhood disintegrative disorder* have characteristics similar to those with autism. The marked difference between these two disorders is the age of onset of the disability. Those with autism demonstrate pervasive developmental disorders prior to the age of 3 (many from birth), whereas those with childhood disintegrative disorder demonstrate a period of normal growth and development prior to the manifestation of social, communicative, and behavioral impairments. Occurring for 2 to 10 years, an apparently normal period of growth and development abruptly ceases, along with a significant loss of previously acquired skills (Simpson & Zionts, 2000).

Table 7.3
Summary of Diagnostic Criteria for Autistic Disorder

Criteria include social interaction impairments as shown by at least two of the following characteristics:
- Significant impairment in the use of nonverbal behaviors, including eye-to-eye contact, facial expression, body posture, and social interaction gestures
- Inability to develop developmentally appropriate peer relationships
- Failure to spontaneously seek opportunities to interact with other people (e.g., by a lack of identifying objects of interest)
- Poor social or emotional reciprocity

Criteria include communication impairments as shown by at least one of the following characteristics:
- Delay in, or total lack of, spoken language development (not accompanied by an attempt to use alternative modes of communication such as gestures)
- In persons with adequate speech, significant impairment in the ability to initiate or maintain a conversation with others
- Stereotyped and repetitive language use or idiosyncratic language
- Lack of varied, developmentally appropriate spontaneous make-believe play or social imitative play

Criteria include repetitive and restricted stereotyped patterns of behavior, activities, and interests, as shown by at least one of these characteristics:
- Marked preoccupation with one or more stereotyped and restricted patterns of interest that is abnormal either in focus or intensity
- Inflexible adherence to nonfunctional routines or rituals
- Stereotyped and repetitive motor movements such as hand or finger flapping or twisting, or complex whole-body movements
- Persistent preoccupation with objects/components

Source: Reprinted with permission from the *Diagnostic and Statistical Manual of Mental Disorders,* 4th ed. Copyright 1994 American Psychiatric Association.

Rett's disorder is a rare genetic condition that only occurs in females. Typically, the age of onset is reported at 1 or 2 years of age. This disorder is characterized by head growth deceleration, loss of previously acquired hand movements and other motor skills, stereotypic hand wringing or hand washing, various motor impairments, and social and communication impairments (Simpson & Zionts, 2000).

Though the prevalence of *Asperger Syndrome* (AS) appears to be increasing, individuals who exhibit characteristics associated with this PDD frequently remain undiagnosed until their teenage years (Smith-Myles & Simpson, 1998, 2002). Common characteristics of this syndrome include social impairments, verbal and nonverbal communication problems, stereotypic behaviors, and a restricted range of interests (Freeman, Cronin, & Candela, 2002; Ghaziuddin, 2002; Gutstein & Whitney, 2002). (See Table 7.4 for a description of the diagnostic criteria for AS.) Individuals diagnosed with AS commonly exhibit the following clinical features according to Klin, Volkmar, and Sparrow (2000):

❑ Difficulty forming friendships
❑ Difficulties with social cognition

Table 7.4
Diagnostic Criteria for Asperger Syndrome

A. *Social interaction impairment as shown by at least two of the following:*
1. Significant impairment in nonverbal behavior use, including social interaction gestures, facial expression, eye-to-eye contact, and body postures
2. Inability to form developmentally appropriate relationships with peers
3. Failure to spontaneously seek out others for interaction, including sharing interests, enjoyment, or achievements
4. Difficulty with social or emotional reciprocity

B. *Repetitive and restricted stereotyped patterns of behavior, activities, and interests, as shown by at least one of the following:*
1. Significant preoccupation with one or more stereotyped and restricted interest patterns whose focus or intensity makes it abnormal
2. Significant display of nonfunctional routines or inflexible adherence to rituals
3. Repetitive and stereotyped motor movements such as complex whole-body movements, or hand or finger flapping or twisting
4. Significant and persistent preoccupation with parts of objects

C. *Clinically significant social, occupational, or other impairment in functioning.*

D. *Absence of a clinically significant general language delay.*

E. *Absence of a clinically significant delay in cognitive development or in development of age-appropriate adaptive behavior (other than social interaction), self-help skills, and childhood curiosity about the environment.*

F. *Failure to meet diagnostic criteria for schizophrenia or another pervasive developmental disorder.*

Source: Reprinted with permission from the Diagnostic and Statistical Manual of Mental Disorders, 4th ed. Copyright 1994 American Psychiatric Association.

❑ Diminished capacity for empathy
❑ Poor nonverbal communication
❑ Restricted or repetitive patterns of interests and behavior
❑ Frequent, intense absorption in circumscribed topics

The subcategory of *pervasive developmental disorder–not otherwise specified* is utilized as a diagnostic subtype when an individual does not meet the criteria for any other form of a PDD. Moreover, this diagnosis is reserved for individuals who manifest "severe and pervasive impairment in the development of reciprocal social interaction or verbal and nonverbal communication skills, or when stereotyped behavior, interests, and activities are present" (APA, 1994, p. 77).

Sensory issues are often included among the list of symptomatic problems experienced by individuals with PDDs. These may range from strong aversions to specific smells, tastes, textures, or environments to an intense desire to engage in repetitive sensory stimulation within one (or all) of the sensory areas. Families with children and also adults with PDDs report that many functional abilities are negatively affected by the need for some type of unusual sensory stimulation (Simpson & Smith-Myles, 1998). Further, many seek specific types of sensations to satisfy needs that are unclear to an observer. The diagnostic criteria for PDDs identify the area of sensory issues under the specific categorization of restricted, repetitive

Table 7.5
Location and Functions of the Sensory Systems

Visual (sight)

Retina of the eye—stimulated by light.

Provides information about objects and persons. Helps us define boundaries as we move through time and space.

Proprioception (body awareness)

Muscles and joints—activated by muscle contractions and movement.

Provides information about where a certain body part is and how it is moving.

Gustatory (taste)

Chemical receptors in the tongue— closely entwined with the olfactory (smell) system.

Provides information about different types of taste (sweet, sour, bitter, salty, spicy).

Auditory (hearing)

Inner ear—stimulated by air/sound waves.

Provides information about sounds in the environment (loud, soft, high, low, near, far).

Olfactory (smell)

Chemical receptors in the nasal structure—closely associated with the gustatory system.

Provides information about different types of smell (musty, acrid, putrid, flowery, pungent).

Vestibular (balance)

Inner ear—stimulated by head movements and input from other senses, especially visual.

Provides information about where our body is in space, and whether or not we or our surroundings are moving. Tells about speed and direction of movement.

Tactile (touch)

Skin—density of cell distribution varies throughout the body. Areas of greatest density include mouth, hands, and genitals.

Provides information about the environment and object qualities (touch, pressure, texture, hard, soft, sharp, dull, heat, cold, pain).

interests, with specific allusion to "stereotyped and repetitive motor mannerisms (e.g., hand or finger flapping or twisting, or complex whole-body movements" [APA, 1994, p. 67]).

Many individuals with PDDs engage in finger flapping and twisting, rocking behavior, swaying behavior (moving back and forth from one foot to another foot in a standing rocking position), and repetitive movements including a vast array of manifestations. A. Jean Ayres (1972, 1979) developed the theory of *sensory integration,* which is a reference to a neurological process and the theory of the relationship between that neurological process and behavior. This theory is based on the notion that we are all constantly bombarded by external and internal sensory input.

According to Murray-Slutsky and Paris (2000), "The process of *sensory integration* involves receiving the sensory information from one or more of our sensory systems, registering the stimuli, and constantly analyzing which stimuli are important or unimportant. On a conscious or unconscious level, we make decisions about which stimuli to attend or react to and how much of our attention to direct to it" (p. 136). According to these same experts, problems occur when people with PDDs have difficulty organizing the information coming into their system. Consequently many display a strong aversion to loud sounds, fluorescent lights, rough or smooth textures, and specific clothing or shoes. Conversely, individuals who lack some type of necessary stimulus may spend copious amounts of time in the pursuit of objects, foods, or environments that can provide them needed internal stimulation. Table 7.5 illustrates the location and the functions of the sensory systems.

INTERVENTIONS

Assessment procedures employed by professionals, in an attempt to determine appropriate intervention, often target deficits rather than skills individuals are capable of completing. This focus, based on a traditional "medical model," tends to accentuate what a person cannot do, with a specific focus on the remediation of skill-deficit areas (Leaf & McEachin, 1999). Historically, intervention programs have conducted protocols that lack individual or family input regarding values or functionality, regardless of the feelings of the individual or family (Downing, 1996; Lovaas, 2003). Further, many assessments require the demonstration of skills outside of a normal context for individuals with PDD, only serving to frustrate those receiving testing in nonfamiliar settings on unfamiliar material.

Encouraging data exist regarding the success of early intervention programs for young children with PDDs, particularly programs that demonstrate data-based treatment models with specific focus on successful student outcomes (Dunn, Saiter, & Rinner, 2002; Handleman & Harris, 2001; Lovaas, 2003).

Since we know that the brain and CNS of a newborn child are not fully developed, and that brain development is most active during the first 5 or 6 years of life, it is crucial that individuals with PDDs receive intensive, outcome-based, early

Table 7.6
Research-Based Interventions

Augmentative and alternative communication (AAC)
Applied behavior analysis (ABA)
Discrete trial teaching (DTT)
Direct instruction (DI)
Incidental teaching (IT)
Pivotal response training (PRT)
Project TEACCH (in North Carolina)
UCLA Early Intervention Project

---

intervention (Handleman & Harris, 2001). By the time a child has reached 6 years of age, most major brain structures are in place, limiting the possibilities of long-term, effective intervention. To assist young children with PDDs in the development of functional neurological pathways and structures that will enhance complex learning, professionals must present multiple, consistent stimuli.

Because children with PDDs do not respond in typical ways to commonly occurring stimulation, such as television, music, other people interacting, or sounds, it is necessary to present them with all types of natural stimuli that will assist them in making sense of their world (Janzen, 1999).

Families, schools, and agencies are constantly bombarded with outlandish claims of novel "scientific" treatments and interventions for individuals with ASDs. Many of these "new" treatments lack empirical evidence, have not employed rigorous scientific standards, or have failed to demonstrate valid outcome measures that precisely document specific improvements. Moreover, numerous "treatments" have not been analyzed within peer-reviewed mediums and are based on scant theories driven by implausible, unscientific, and unproven theoretical constructs.

Table 7.6 provides a list of the research-based interventions that have demonstrated statistically significant, positive improvements in many individuals with PDDs. Though not intended to provide a comprehensive listing of all research-based interventions, Table 7.6 does identify many of the most notable and successful programs to date. Several additional interventions indicate great promise, yet lack quantitative data (to date) to support their efficacy. These include social skills intervention, medical intervention, sensory intervention, specific language intervention, and community-based intervention.

TRENDS AND ISSUES

The meteoric rise in the use of unproven and controversial treatments such as facilitated communication, biologic interventions, special diets, auditory integration training, rhythmic or music-based treatments, and outlandish pharmacological treatments for individuals with PDDs continues at an alarming rate. Use of the term *controversial treatments* refers to the use of unproven methods of treatment, particularly those promising extraordinary results. Speculation regarding the use of such controversial methods appears to be grounded in the general theory that the efficacy of such interventions will be proven at some later date. Many studies documenting the lack of effect or harm in specific alternative treatments have done little to sway those who seek intervention and treatment for PDDs. Reportedly, one of every three persons living in the United States uses unconventional therapies for ailments and more than $14 billion is spent annually on unproven treatments (Simpson & Smith-Myles, 1998).

Due to the unique qualities of ASDs, and the fact that relatively few of these disorders can be explained by modern medicine, it is not surprising that many families, medical personnel, and agencies turn to alternative treatments in a desperate attempt to "cure" or treat those they care most about (Maurice, Green, & Luce, 1996). To date, there is no known cure for PDDs, though the research is clear that early intervention and successful school and community-based programs increase the likelihood that individuals with even the most significant disabilities can be successfully included within their neighborhoods and communities (Maurice, Green, & Foxx, 2001).

SUGGESTIONS FOR WORKING WITH PEOPLE WITH PDDs

1. Set clear goals, and be consistent; make an individualized plan and then stick with it through mastery.
2. Teach perspective taking, specifically, the identification of false information, lying, and cheating, and the development of empathy and compassion.
3. Construct a framework for core skills intervention, focusing on areas of most need for an individual.
4. Understand the function of social and communicative behavior; always remember to look at the function of all behavior.
5. Monitor the acquisition, fluency, maintenance, and generalization of targeted skills, and teach in natural settings, at natural times whenever possible.
6. Make sure skills taught are individualized, person centered, functional/practical, adaptive, relevant to the student, and ecologically oriented.
7. Directly teach social skills in all settings.
8. Make sure you have a student's attention prior to beginning instruction.
9. Use teaching methods that minimize errors. When errors occur, provide immediate corrective feedback.
10. Communicate and cooperate with others. Parents, other caregivers, community agencies, and school system personnel can enhance any program.

PONDER THESE

1. Based on your knowledge of the three core deficits of PDDs, how would you go about designing an inclusive program for a student with a diagnosis of PDD-NOS?
2. You are out in the community and you witness a child engaging in what appears to be a significant tantrum. As you watch his mother struggle to get him under control you realize that the child most likely has an ASD. How would you handle the situation?
3. Many people favor the full inclusion of all individuals with disabilities, regardless of the severity of the disability or the services required. If you were a parent of a child with a PDD, specifically, autism, how would you feel about this approach?
4. To date, it is difficult to surmise all the factors contributing to the cause of PDDs. What advice would you give parents who sought your council regarding the use of "alternative therapies" for their child?

REFERENCES

American Psychiatric Association. (1994). *Diagnostic and statistical manual of mental disorders* (4th ed.). Washington, DC: Author.

Ayres, A. J. (1972). *Sensory integration and learning disorders.* Los Angeles: Western Psychological Services.

Ayres, A. J. (1979). *Sensory integration and the child.* Los Angeles: Western Psychological Services.

Chakrabarti, S., & Fombonne, E. (2001). Pervasive developmental disorders in preschool children. *Journal of the American Medical Association, 285*(24), 57–64.

Cohen, D. J., & Volkmar, F. R. (Eds.). (1997). *Handbook of autism and pervasive developmental disorders* (2nd ed.). New York: John Wiley & Sons.

Committee on Educational Interventions for Children with Autism, Division of Behavioral and Social Sciences and Education, National Research Council. (2001). *Educating children with autism.* Washington, DC: National Academy Press.

Downing, J. E. (1996). *Including students with severe and multiple disabilities in typical classrooms.* Baltimore, MD: Paul H. Brookes Publishing Company.

Dunn, W., Saiter, J., & Rinner, L. (2002). Asperger syndrome and sensory processing: A conceptual model and guidance for intervention planning. *Focus on Autism and Other Developmental Disabilities, 17*(3), 172–185.

Freeman, B. J., Cronin, P., & Candela, P. (2002). Asperger syndrome or autistic disorder? The diagnostic dilemma. *Focus on Autism and Other Developmental Disabilities, 17*(3), 145–151.

Ghaziuddin, M. (2002). Asperger syndrome: Associated psychiatric and medical conditions. *Focus on Autism and Other Developmental Disabilities, 17*(3), 138–144.

Gutstein, S. E., & Whitney, T. (2002). Asperger syndrome and the development of social competence. *Focus on Autism and Other Developmental Disabilities, 17*(3), 161–171.

Handleman, J. S., & Harris, S. L. (Eds.). (2001). *Preschool education programs for children with autism* (2nd ed.). Austin, TX: PRO-ED.

Janzen, J. E. (Ed.). (1999). *Autism facts and strategies for parents.* Tucson, AZ: Therapy Skill Builders.

Klin, A., Volkmar, F. R., & Sparrow, S. S. (Eds.). (2000). *Asperger syndrome.* New York: Guilford Press.

Koegel, R. L., & Koegel, L. K. (1995). *Teaching children with autism strategies for initiating positive interactions and improving learning opportunities.* Baltimore, MD: Paul H. Brookes Publishing Company.

Leaf, R., & McEachin, J. (Eds.). (1999). *A work in progress behavior management strategies and a curriculum for intensive behavioral treatment of autism.* New York: DRL Books.

Lovaas, O. I. (2003). *Teaching individuals with developmental delays basic intervention techniques.* Austin, TX: PRO-ED.

Maurice, C., Green, G., & Foxx, R. M. (2001). *Making a difference: Behavioral intervention for autism.* Austin, TX: PRO-ED.

Maurice, C., Green, G., & Luce, S. C. (Eds.). (1996). *Behavioral intervention for young children with autism: A manual for parents and professionals.* Austin, TX: PRO-ED.

Mesibov, G. B., Adams, L. W., & Klinger, L. G. (1997). *Autism: Understanding the disorder.* New York: Plenum Press.

Murray-Slutsky, C., & Paris, B. A. (2000). *Exploring the spectrum of autism and pervasive developmental disorders intervention strategies.* Tucson, AZ: Therapy Skill Builders.

Powers, M. D. (Ed.). (2000). *Children with autism: A parents' guide.* Bethesda, MD: Woodbine House.

Schopler, E., & Mesibov, G. B. (Eds.). (1983). *Autism in adolescents and adults.* New York: Plenum Press.

Simpson, R. L., & Smith-Myles, B. (Eds.). (1998). *Educating children and youth with autism: Strategies for effective practice.* Austin, TX: PRO-ED.

Simpson, R. L., & Zionts, P. (2000). *Autism: Information and resources for professionals and parents* (2nd ed.). Austin, TX: PRO-ED.

Smith, D. D., & Luckasson, R. (1995). *Introduction to special education teaching in an age of challenge* (2nd ed.). Needham Heights, MA: Allyn & Bacon.

Smith-Myles, B., & Simpson, R. L. (1998). *Asperger syndrome: A guide for educators and parents.* Austin, TX: PRO-ED.

Smith-Myles, B., & Simpson, R. L. (2002). Asperger syndrome: An overview of characteristics. *Focus on Autism and Other Developmental Disabilities, 17*(3), 132–137.

Westling, D. L., & Fox, L. (2000). *Teaching students with severe disabilities* (2nd ed.). Upper Saddle River, NJ: Prentice Hall.

Wetherby, A. M., & Prizant, B. M. (2000). *Autism spectrum disorders.* Baltimore, MD: Paul H. Brookes Publishing Company.

Wing, L. (1997). The history of ideas on autism: Legends, myths, and reality. In *Autism: The International Journal of Research and Practice* (Vol. 1, pp. 13–23). London, England: Sage.

PART II

Physical, Sensory, and Communicative Impairments

CHAPTER 8

Physical and Health Impairments

A young man, age 15, was being admitted to a short-term residential diagnostic center. The school was concerned because he was experiencing an increase in numbers of seizures and questioned the family's compliance with his drug regimen. As the interview with the parents proceeded, the mother expressed her belief about his "fits." "Yes," she said, "he done had more of 'em this last year, but they won't last much longer." When asked what she meant by that, she stated, "Well, he's getting older, you know. And once he's been with a woman, he won't have them fits no more!"
(Who knows, maybe sex is better than Dilantin!)[1]

People with disabilities are not to be abused, talked down to, or pitied. They are people just like you and me. The film *Leo Beuerman*[2] is about a man whose physical disabilities were so extensive that he was described sometimes as "grotesque" or "too horrible to look at." He was small, he weighed less than 90 pounds, and his legs were so bent out of shape that he couldn't walk. He also had poor eyesight and was hard of hearing. Leo lived on a farm in Kansas. Somehow, he learned to drive a tractor, and later he invented a hoist that allowed him to raise himself onto the tractor. He also invented and built a pushcart that enabled him to get around from place to place. Using a hoist to get his cart on the tractor, he would then get on the tractor and drive to town. In town Leo would park his tractor, lower himself and his cart down to the street, get in the cart, and propel himself down the sidewalk to the storefront where he repaired watches and sold pencils. The reason the movie about Leo had such an impact on me is that I can remember buying pencils from him as a kid in school. At that time, I didn't realize how remarkable Leo really was. He just wanted to talk to people, work, and do his own thing. He wanted to be self-sufficient and independent. Here was a man, deformed to the point that, to most people, he was a repulsive sight. However, he was more individual, more free, and more alive than most people.

It was Jimmy's first day in class. Jimmy could not walk due to spina bifida, but he didn't let that get in his way. He was a very proficient crawler. One day, after circle time, the kids were heading for the housekeeping center, and Jimmy was scooting right along with them—in fact, faster than many. One little girl, exasperated that he got to her favorite spot first, indignantly pointed her finger at Jimmy and informed him, "Little boy, we don't run in here."

Ms. Jones had just begun her first elementary teaching job when she went to her doctor complaining of numbness in her legs. After a series of treatments with no improvement, initial test results by the physician indicated multiple sclerosis. The diagnosis proved

[1]This story was contributed by Carol Grimm, Lockhart, Texas.
[2]*Leo Beuerman*, Centron Educational Films, 1621 West 9th Street, Lawrence, Kansas 66044 (13 minutes/color).

to be correct. Ms. Jones refused to let the disease end her career. As time went on, the progressive disease affected her arms and legs until she had to use a wheelchair. Ms. Jones continued to teach. The ramps, special toilet equipment, and self-opening doors, originally designed to provide access for students with disabilities in her school, now allowed her to reach her classroom. Not only did Ms. Jones continue her teaching career, but her disability made her more sensitive to the needs of all children. She began to organize her third-grade classroom to foster interactions between nondisabled children and their peers with disabilities. As a result of her innovative techniques and success with all her students, she was selected as her state's outstanding teacher.

I have a friend, Bobby, who has epilepsy. The medication he takes regularly seems to control the seizures to a great extent; however, he still experiences grand mal tonic-clonic episodes once in a while (approximately once a year). Bobby is athletic and enjoys sports. Interestingly, his favorite leisure time activity is surfing. Now, around here that is not unusual; but for someone who has seizures, it is a bit risky, especially when surfing alone. However, Bobby is not about to let his epilepsy control his life, so his frequent surfboard riding through the breaking waves does not surprise me a bit. Nevertheless, one day when Bobby was talking to my introductory class in special education, I asked him about the danger of going surfing alone and possibly having a grand mal seizure. After a brief hesitation, Bobby replied that he had thought about it and that if he did have a seizure he would probably drown unless someone else could pull him to safety. The class was confused by his matter-of-fact attitude, but they understood his strong feelings about doing what he wanted to do. Then Bobby made everyone sit back and reflect when he concluded his response to my question with this quip: "But at least I'd die happy!"

One summer, our university hosted the National Wheelchair Games by providing facilities, lodging, and assistance to the athletes and to the games. I gave students in my class the option of volunteering to help with the games or to complete another assignment for the course. Some of my students chose to spend a few afternoons being involved with the wheelchair games. After the games were over, we discussed in class the students' experiences.

One of my students noted that she had learned much through this experience but was a little confused at first by a term the wheelchair athletes used to describe her and most of the other volunteers. She said that the athletes kept referring to us as "TABs." Her observation had the entire class very interested in finding out what this was all about. She continued by explaining that TAB stood for "Temporarily Able Bodied." After further discussion, we decided that this was an acceptable, healthy, albeit uncommon, way to be perceived.

American society, perhaps more than any other culture, puts a premium on strong, healthy looking bodies. All forms of media, especially those used for advertising and entertainment, sell products and services by using images of health and attractiveness. We spend millions of dollars each year on beauty aids, cosmetics, tanning lotions, dietary products, running shoes, health equipment, and memberships to health spas, most of the time with the sole purpose to enhance our appearance. As a result, individuals with physical and health impairments often face a challenge when they attempt to find full acceptance in this type of culture. Integration into school, work, and a full social life can be difficult for everyone, but the physical and social barriers of our modern society can make the process complicated and overwhelming for persons with physical and health disorders. They must deal not only with their disabilities but also with our social attitudes toward appearances and good health.

BASIC CONCEPTS

Terminology

The terms *physical impairment, health impairment,* and *traumatic brain injury* refer to a very heterogeneous population that displays a wide range of strengths and challenges. As discussed in chapter 1, current attempts at political correctness have had an important impact on the way individuals with disabilities are described. When IDEA was amended in 1990, all references to "handicapped children" were replaced with "children with disabilities." These amendments to IDEA also added the category of traumatic brain injury as a distinct disability area. It had always included the categories of orthopedic impairments and other health impairments.

A variety of terms can be used to refer to physical and health conditions. The term associated with the actual condition (e.g., diabetes) often is the term of choice, because it most specifically conveys the nature of the condition. As mentioned in chapter 1, terms such as *physically challenged* have enjoyed more widespread use in recent times. This chapter uses the term *physical impairments* instead of *orthopedic impairments* and the term *health impairments* in place of *other health impairments* (OHI) to describe the general class of conditions covered in the next sections. The reason for this decision is that *orthopedic impairment* limits the conditions that are covered by this topic, as other neuromotor impairments must also be considered, as discussed later.

The term *traumatic brain injury* (TBI) is used in much of the professional literature and in IDEA. However, other terms such *head injury* and *closed-head injury* also are used to refer to individuals who have experienced insult to their brains. As might be expected, a significant amount of overlap exists with the presenting issues of TBI and the more global notion of physical impairment.

Definitional Perspectives

The definitions of physical impairments, health impairments, and traumatic brain injury can vary significantly across settings and age level. It is important to note that, for children and youth with conditions that fall under these topical areas to qualify for special education services, evidence must exist that the conditions *interfere with* educational performance. The point being made is that possession of a physical or health impairment does not mean that special intervention is needed.

Physical Impairments.   A physical impairment can be considered a disorder that interferes with a person's mobility and coordination as well as a person's capacity to communicate, learn, and adjust (Hardman, Drew, Egan, & Wolf, 1993). Physical impairments include both orthopedic and neuromotor conditions. Heward (2003) distinguishes between the two in the following way:

> An orthopedic impairment involves the skeletal system—bones, joints, limbs, and associated muscles. A neuromotor impairment involves the central nervous system, affecting the ability to move, use, feel, or control certain parts of the body. (p. 442)

Examples of physical impairments include cerebral palsy, muscular dystrophy, multiple sclerosis, spina bifida, spinal cord injuries, amputations, congenital limb deficiencies, and juvenile rheumatoid arthritis.

Health Impairments.   According to Smith (2004), a *health impairment* is a condition in which the body's physical well-being is affected, requiring some form of ongoing medical attention. Health impairments, as defined by IDEA, result in "limited strength, vitality or alertness, due to chronic or acute health problems such as a heart condition, tuberculosis, rheumatic fever, nephritis, asthma, sickle cell anemia, hemophilia, epilepsy, lead poisoning, leukemia, or diabetes which adversely affect education performance" (23 Code of Federal Regulations, Section 300.5 [7]). Other health impairments that can be found in children and youth populations include cancer, cystic fibrosis, chronic heart conditions, hemophilia, and HIV/AIDS.

Traumatic Brain Injury.   Traumatic brain injury implies damage, or insult, to the brain caused by an external event rather than by some type of congenital condition or degenerative disease. The definition of TBI used in IDEA is as follows:

> An acquired injury to the brain caused by an external force, resulting in total or partial functional disability or psychosocial impairments, or both, that adversely affects a child's educational performance. The term applies to open or closed head injuries resulting in impairments in one or more areas, such as cognition; language; memory; attention; reasoning; abstract thinking; judgment; problem-solving; sensory, perceptual, and motor abilities; psychosocial behavior; physical functions; information processing; and speech. The term does not apply to brain injuries that are congenital or generative, or brain injuries induced by birth trauma. (34 C.F.R. Sec. 300.7 [6] [12])

Prevalence

Examination of the data provided in chapter 1 (Tables 1.2 and 1.3) provides some interesting observations. First, these conditions are low-incidence disabilities in the school-age population. The categories of "Orthopedic Impairments" and "Traumatic Brain Injury" have 71,422 and 13,874 students ages 6 to 21, respectively. The fact that the category of "Other health impairments" has as many students identified as it does (254,110 students ages 6 to 21) is due to the influx of students with attention deficit/hyperactivity disorder into this category. When these students are excluded from this category, the numbers are more modest. Second, although the dramatic increase in the number of students classified as OHI is understood, the increase in the number of students classified "Orthopedic Impairments" since the early 1990s, albeit not as dramatic, is not clear. No discernable factor can be identified to explain the increase. Third, the nature of disability in adulthood, as indicated in Table 1.3, clearly underscores the reality that physical and health issues are predominant. More precise prevalence figures will be presented as selected disorders are described in this chapter.

Etiology

Physical or health impairments can result from many different causes and can be classified in many different ways. For example, impairments may be *congenital* (the child has it from birth) or *acquired* (the child is normal at birth but something happens later). Causes may include genetic factors, physical trauma, oxygen deprivation, chemical agents (poisoning), disease, or some combination of these or other factors. Impairments may also be classified according to the particular organ or organ system involved, for example, neurological impairments (involving the brain or spinal cord or peripheral nerves), cardiovascular conditions (involving the heart and blood vessels), hematological problems (involving the blood), orthopedic conditions (involving the bones and joints), and so on. Some types of disorders can be congenital or acquired, result from a variety of causes, and involve more than one organ system. The etiology of specific conditions discussed in this chapter will be addressed in the respective sections.

CHARACTERISTICS

The effects that a physical impairment, health problem, or traumatic brain injury has on an individual and his or her family vary widely. Each person's situation is different and requires individual attention. However, certain factors can, and do, play important roles in the way an individual handles and adjusts to his or her situation. These factors also have impact on the way others react to those with various physical and health conditions.

❏ Severity of the disability—relates to what a person might be able to do
❏ Age of onset—relates to experiences the person may or may not have had

❏ Visibility of the disability—relates to self-concept, acceptance, and expectations
❏ Circumstances when the condition was acquired—relates to emotional and psychological issues such as anger and guilt
❏ Progressive or degenerative nature of the impairment—relates to issues that have to be considered over time
❏ Support available in the community and from school system—relates to variables that are available to assist the individual and his or her family

Due to the varying impact that these factors can have on an individual, it is often difficult to make generalizations about individuals with physical impairments, health conditions, or brain injury. Nevertheless, there is value in looking more closely at selected conditions in these areas.

Physical Impairments

Two conditions are covered in this section: cerebral palsy and spina bifida. Although other physical impairments exist, these conditions have been selected because they are among the most common physical impairments.

Cerebral Palsy.   The term *cerebral palsy* is used to describe a condition with a wide range of characteristics and a varying level of severity. *Cerebral palsy* literally implies brain paralysis. According to Inge (1992), cerebral palsy is "a nonprogressive disorder caused by a lesion or defect to the brain occurring prior to birth, during the birth process, or during the first four years of life" (p. 30). Numerous causes, occurring before, during, or after birth, may be responsible for this condition. Some of the etiologies include anoxia, infection, intoxication, hemorrhaging, trauma, fever, and prematurity. The resulting physical impairment can range from slightly inhibiting to profoundly debilitating. Approximately 2 children in 1,000 (0.2 percent) are affected by some form of cerebral palsy (Inge, 1992). Prevalence figures, however, vary widely and may depend on level of family awareness and ability to seek attention.

Cerebral palsy can be categorized both by *type* (description of the movement disorder) and by *physical characteristics* (see Table 8.1). Perhaps the biggest problem facing individuals with cerebral palsy is abnormal muscle tone. The muscle tone of a person with cerebral palsy can be either excessive (spastic/hypertonic) or insufficient (hypotonic). Either way, muscle tone is critical for posture and movement. The other important consideration is the individuality of the person who has the condition. Two people can be categorized with exactly the same type or distribution of the disorder, yet have very different levels of functioning and abilities.

According to Prensky and Palkes (1982), many individuals with cerebral palsy also have associated problems. These can include mental retardation, seizure disorders, visual impairments, hearing loss, speech and language disorders, and cognitive limitations. Because of the many facets of related disorders, many individuals with cerebral palsy are considered to have multiple disabilities. About two

Table 8.1

Classifications of Cerebral Palsy (by Type and Distribution)

Descriptive Terminology	Characteristics
Monoplegia	One limb involved
Hemiplegia	One side of body involved
Triplegia	Three limbs involved
Paraplegia	Lower extremities (legs) involved
Diplegia	All limbs involved, but legs more than arms
Quadriplegia	Entire body involved, including all four limbs and trunk
Spastic	Increased muscle tone (hypertonic); slow movement
Athetoid	Involuntary, uncontrolled movements; difficulty maintaining stable posture
Dystonic	Distorted movement; muscle tone that varies between hypotonic and hypertonic
Rigid	Invariable muscle tone; stiff movement
Hypotonic	Low muscle tone; floppy movement
Mixed	More than one type; usually with one predominant

thirds of those with cerebral palsy have mental retardation (Pellegrino, 1997). Perhaps more than with any other physical disability, students with cerebral palsy require multidisciplinary interventions. Medical treatment by physicians and nurses, interventions for enhanced mobility provided by occupational and physical therapists, and speech-language therapy available from speech-language professionals are just some of the many interventions necessary for these students.

Advances in computer technology and augmentative communication devices have had an important and beneficial impact on the lives of individuals with cerebral palsy. Communication systems, touch screens for computers, light beam control devices, and lighter weight wheelchairs are just some of the inventions that have improved communication and mobility. As technological advances continue, it is likely that increased integration into school, community, and the workplace will be more common.

For teachers and teaching assistants, competencies required for effective education of students with cerebral palsy can include (a) skills required in moving and positioning; (b) abilities related to teaching activities of daily living, including dressing, feeding, and toileting; and (c) knowledge required for appropriate monitoring (for problems like gagging or jaw clenching). Looking ahead, we must focus on educational considerations that prepare individuals with cerebral palsy for life in the community. Employment, housing, leisure, and transportation (see Table 2.4, transition domains) are just a few of the areas of concern if the future is to include independent or interdependent living.

Spina Bifida. Spina bifida is the most common physical disability of childhood. Spina bifida is a birth defect caused by a prenatal malformation of the spine, resulting in an opening in the vertebral column. The central nervous system is often involved and symptoms can include (a) loss of sensation from the spina bifida protrusion to all areas of the body below it; (b) little or no bladder or bowel control; (c) hydrocephalus, which can be corrected through the implantation of shunts; (d) brittle bones in areas where there is poor circulation due to lack of sensation and physical movement; and/or (e) loss of muscle control below the spine lesion (Paasche, Gorrill, & Strom, 1990). The incidence of spina bifida is approximately 0.5 to 1.0 per 1,000 live births (Rowley-Kelly & Reigel, 1993). There appear to be multiple causes of spina bifida, including factors related to race, malnutrition, and poverty as well as a family tendency or predisposition. Recent research has focused on deficiencies in the diet of mothers during their pregnancies.

Most students with spina bifida have normal levels of intelligence and should be placed in inclusive educational settings. Those students with the more serious forms of spina bifida require modifications and adaptive equipment like braces or wheelchairs. Smith, Polloway, Patton, and Dowdy (2004) offer the following suggestions for educators of students with spina bifida:

❏ Maintain an environment that is conducive to the needs of individuals with motor impairments (e.g., remove loose floor coverings, make sure floors are not wet).
❏ Learn how to position students to develop strength and avoid sores.
❏ Understand the process of clean intermittent bladder catheterization and be ready to deal with occasional incontinence.
❏ Learn how to deal with seizures.
❏ Ensure full participation of the students in classroom activities.
❏ Help the student with spina bifida develop a healthy, positive self-concept.
❏ Communicate regularly with the parents.

Health Impairments

The section covers four specific health impairments: seizure disorders (epilepsy), human immunodeficiency virus and acquired immunodeficiency syndrome, asthma, and juvenile diabetes.

Seizure Disorders (Epilepsy).   A seizure is "any sudden attack of altered behavior, consciousness, sensation, or autonomical function that is produced by self-limited disruption of brain activity due to repetitive, simultaneous electrical discharges from hyperexcitable neurons in the cortex" (Brown, 1997, p. 554; Clancy, 1990). Brown also notes that about 8 percent of all children in the United States will have at least one seizure by the time they reach 15 years of age. Many of the seizures are due to high fever or some type of brain insult and may only occur once. *Epilepsy* is the term used to describe a disorder that involves recurrent episodes of seizure activity. The prevalence of epilepsy can range from 0.15 to 1 percent of the population, depending on the definition used.

Epilepsy can be caused by any event that results in brain damage, such as brain lesions, anoxia, trauma, poisoning, or tumors. If etiology can be determined, the term *symptomatic epilepsy* is used; however, if causation cannot be determined, which is true the majority of the time, the appropriate term used is *idiopathic epilepsy*. Even if the original cause of the problem can be determined, the reason for the abnormal discharge of electrical energy under certain conditions (i.e., what triggers a seizure) may remain unknown.

One system for classifying the various forms of epilepsy is based on the localization of the seizure activity in the brain, as presented next. Note that the following system focuses on cases where recurrent seizures (i.e., epilepsy) are present; as mentioned, other seizures are possible due to high fever (febrile seizure) or other cause.

❑ *Generalized seizures:* Discharge is bilateral and symmetrical or is nonlocalized (40 percent of all cases of epilepsy).
❑ *Partial seizure:* Discharge is localized (60 percent of all cases of epilepsy).

Included in the generalized seizure category are *grand mal, petit mal, myoclonic,* and *akinetic* seizures. The generalized seizure is characterized by a spontaneous loss of consciousness of varying length and expression.

The generalized tonic-clonic seizure (grand mal seizure) is the type most people think of when they think of epilepsy. The person having a grand mal attack, which is convulsive in nature, usually lets out a cry, loses consciousness, falls, and goes through a short period of muscle contractions of the extremities, trunk, and head. This type of seizure may be preceded by an *aura* (an unusual sensory perception) that can serve as a warning of the onset of a seizure. The tonic-clonic seizure also may include facial contortions, heavy breathing, perspiration, foaming at the mouth, loss of bladder and bowel control, and physical injury if the person strikes against an object while falling or convulsing. This behavior may last up to 5 minutes, after which the individual falls into a deep sleep that is followed by natural sleep. On regaining consciousness, the individual may display the following characteristics: disorientation, depression, amnesia of the seizure, nausea, soreness, and exhaustion.

The absence seizure (petit mal seizure) is less dramatic but can have a devastating effect on a student's educational progress. Berg (1982) describes the typical petit mal seizure as "the momentary suspension of all activity, a staring spell, or as some have called them, lapses or absence attacks" (p. 104). Often, this form of epilepsy is misperceived in a classroom setting as daydreaming, inattention, or misbehavior. The lapse of consciousness may last only a few seconds or may continue for up to 30 seconds. Unlike the grand mal seizure, the onset of a petit mal seizure will not be accompanied by the aura phenomenon. Frequently, children will grow out of this type of seizure.

Partial (focal) seizures involve a focal discharge in a localized part of the brain, and as a result they produce a specific motor or sensory effect. A *Jacksonian seizure* is an example of a partial seizure and involves a pattern of rhythmic movements that start in one part of the body and progressively spread to other parts.

Although not fully understood, psychomotor seizure (complex partial) is considered to be a type of focal seizure and is characterized by inappropriate behaviors such as being verbally incoherent, verbally abusive, or violent. Even though this type of seizure is brief, the behaviors nevertheless are socially unacceptable, and there is a good chance that they will be misinterpreted.

There have been many misconceptions about epilepsy throughout history. Unfortunately, some of these misconceptions still exist. Seeing someone have a convulsion is upsetting and frightening to many people, especially to those uninformed or misinformed about the nature of seizures. Individuals with epilepsy are no more disposed to mental illness than other individuals, and they function quite normally between seizures. Mental retardation occurs in only 10 percent of this population; most people with epilepsy (approximately 70 percent) have average or above-average intelligence. Most seizures (80 percent) can be totally or partially controlled with proper medication. Teachers can assist children who have seizures by ensuring their safety during seizures, by attempting to correct the misperceptions of others, and by being prepared to deal with learning problems that may arise.

Human Immunodeficiency Virus.   The human immunodeficiency virus (HIV) causes the disease AIDS. Individuals can be HIV positive and show no signs of the disease; however, children with HIV are likely to develop symptoms of AIDS. It is estimated that more than 30 million people are infected worldwide. AIDS is growing fastest among women, adolescents, and young adults. It is difficult to obtain accurate information about the number of AIDS-infected children and youth and even more difficult to accurately describe the specific relationships of the disease to disability issues.

HIV is transmitted only through an exchange of body fluids, such as semen, blood, and breast milk. In adults and adolescents, the most common causes of infection are the use of contaminated needles or through sexual contact. Batshaw (2002) estimated that about 80 percent of children diagnosed with HIV acquired the infection from their mothers, either prenatally or during the birth process. The other 20 percent of cases in children are either the result of receiving contaminated blood or from sexual partners. There is less likelihood of acquiring the disease from blood products now that they are screened regularly. Infants with HIV will likely develop AIDS before the age of 2, and most will die about a year later. It is expected that as treatments advance, there will be more survivors from this population. Adolescents who acquire HIV are less likely to develop symptoms while still in school, but they still carry the virus (LeRoy, Powell, & Kelker, 1994).

According to LeRoy et al. (1994, p. 40), some of the typical symptoms of childhood AIDS include

- ❏ Attention difficulties
- ❏ Cardiac disease
- ❏ Central nervous system damage
- ❏ Cognitive deficits
- ❏ Cold sores

❑ Coughing
❑ Diarrhea (acute and chronic)
❑ Emotional problems
❑ Fine and gross motor difficulties
❑ Hearing problems
❑ Infections, including frequent bacterial and viral infections; middle ear, eye, and joint infections
❑ Seizures
❑ Shortness of breath
❑ Speech and language delays
❑ Visual problems
❑ Weakness
❑ Weight loss

Some of the unique complications for children with health impairments include social isolation, the effects of long-term hospitalization, parental illness and death (of parents who also have AIDS), family problems, a lack of understanding from the community, and associated learning problems. Children with HIV can be developmentally delayed at birth or may develop normally for a number of years and then begin to evidence delays at a later age. Cognitive impairments such as decreased intellectual levels, specific learning disabilities, mental retardation, visual or spatial deficits, and decreased alertness can cause academic problems in school. Social or behavioral problems can also develop and can range from lethargy to hyperactivity (Seidel, 1992).

Teachers and administrators should keep abreast of information about the disease and follow the guidelines suggested by the Centers for Disease Control and Prevention (CDC) and the National Institute of Allergy and Infectious Diseases regarding precautions for prevention of HIV. These precautions include (a) careful handling (with nonpermeable gloves) of blood, feces, nasal secretions, sputum, sweat, saliva, tears, urine, and vomitus; (b) use of receptacles with tightly fitting lids and cleanup with a bleach-water combination; and (c) hand washing when skin is exposed to contaminated fluids and drug treatment if an open lesion is exposed to contamination (CDC, 1993). In addition, teachers should maintain ongoing communication with parents and physicians, maintain confidentiality of records, reevaluate frequently, and obtain updated training on a regular basis. Table 8.2 presents a teacher checklist for accommodating students with AIDS (Kelker, Hecimovic, & LeRoy, 1994).

Asthma.   Asthma has been described as the leading cause of absenteeism among schoolchildren. Estimates are that approximately 3 million children and youth under the age of 15 have asthma. Characteristic problems include shortness of breath, coughing, and wheezing due to irritation of the bronchial mucus from allergens or other infections. For some children, asthma attacks are a nuisance; for others, the attacks are life threatening.

Table 8.2
Teacher Checklist for Accommodating Students with HIV

- Observe guidelines for confidentiality of information.
- Assess the student for eligibility under IDEA or Section 504.
- Obtain copies of state and local policies for inclusion of students with HIV.
- Get the facts about HIV and how it affects learning.
- Assemble a team to develop an individualized education program (IEP) that addresses educational needs and health-related supports.
- Plan modifications of instructional methods and curriculum to meet the student's individual needs.
- Design ways to include the student who has HIV in typical classroom activities.
- Build flexibility into the student's IEP to allow for hospitalizations and frequent absences.
- Arrange for training in infection control procedures (e.g., universal precautions).
- Educate parents about communicable disease policies and the use of universal precautions.
- Answer students' questions about terminal illness.

Source: From "Designing a Classroom and School Environment for Students with AIDS," by K. Kelker, A. Hecimovic, and C. H. LeRoy, 1994, *Teaching Exceptional Children, 24*(4), p. 52. Reprinted by permission.

Teachers who have students with asthma in their classes should be aware of the side effects of the medications used by students, including headaches, hand tremors, stomachaches, lethargy, and reduced stamina. Allowances should be made for absences, which may be excessive for individual students. In addition, the classroom may harbor many allergens such as chalk dust or animal hair.

Juvenile Diabetes.   Juvenile diabetes is less familiar to educators. It is a metabolic disorder. Because of insufficient insulin production, individuals with diabetes do not process sugar in a normal way. For many students, management of diabetes includes careful attention to diet and exercise. Urine or blood tests to monitor insulin levels and injections of insulin may be a typical routine for students with more serious diabetes.

Students with diabetes may have problems concentrating and remaining alert in class. According to Paasche et al. (1990), students with juvenile diabetes may also be thin and pale and have abnormal increases in thirst and appetite. Teachers must closely monitor these symptoms and be sure that dietary schedules and restrictions are followed carefully. A student with diabetes should wear a *Medic Alert* bracelet. If a child has received too much insulin or if insulin has been ingested too quickly or without adequate caloric intake, an insulin reaction may occur. Symptoms include tremors, sweating, weakness, dizziness, odd behavior, and (later) unconsciousness or convulsions. Teachers and others should know the procedures for responding to an insulin reaction and should take the child to the hospital quickly if he or she does not improve within a few minutes.

Traumatic Brain Injury

During the 1991–1992 school year, the first year that traumatic brain injury was used as a category of disability under IDEA, approximately 330 students with TBI were served in special education. That figure has now risen to 13,874, based on counts from the 1999–2000 school year. Prior to the 1991–1992 school year, many students with severe traumatic brain injuries were served in programs for students with mental retardation and severe disabilities; those with milder long-term problems may have been placed in programs for students with learning disabilities or serious emotional disturbance. However, students in the TBI category require appropriate educational programs that often will include a variety of related services.

According to the National Head Injury Foundation, a traumatic brain injury is "an insult to the brain caused by an external force that may produce diminished or altered states of consciousness, which results in impaired cognitive abilities or physical functioning" (1989, p. 2). Traumatic brain injuries include both *closed-head* injuries (such as those often caused by impact accidents) and *open-head* injuries (such as gunshot wounds), depending on whether there is penetration of the skull. Brain damage can be either *primary*, which is a direct result of the impact, or *secondary*, which occurs after the initial injury but is still related to it. Knowledge about traumatic brain injuries is valuable for teachers, because students often have significant *residual* impairments that may last for a long time.

Unfortunately, traumatic brain injury is not a rare occurrence among children. Note that even a slight concussion is a form of brain injury. Each year, about 1 million children sustain traumatic brain injuries. According to Tyler and Mira (1999), this means that 1 in 500 children is hospitalized with a head injury. About 3 percent of school-age children still have residual impairments from brain injuries. Young people between the ages of 15 and 24 face the greatest risk of traumatic brain injury. Among older students, motor vehicle accidents are the leading cause of TBI, but sports-related injuries, especially those associated with popular extreme sports, are also common. The other high-risk age group for brain injuries is very young children (preschoolers). Causes of brain injury for this group include child abuse and falls. The number of boys who sustain brain injuries is about twice that of girls.

The majority of brain injuries are *mild,* meaning concussions, dizziness, or loss of consciousness without skull fracture. Although not as serious as other brain injuries, mild brain injuries can still result in residual memory and attention problems. *Moderate* brain injuries involve a loss of consciousness from 1 to 24 hours or a skull fracture. Children with moderate head injuries often develop secondary neurological problems such as swelling within the brain and usually have long-term residual effects. In *severe* brain injuries, there is a loss of consciousness for more than 24 hours, bruising of the brain tissue, or bleeding within the brain. Children with severe brain injuries are often hospitalized in critical condition and are very likely to have motor, language, and cognitive problems after regaining consciousness. They will likely experience life-long deficits that impact their learning (Tyler & Mira, 1999).

As emphasized previously, conditions and factors in students' lives will play a role in the outcome of traumatic brain injuries. According to Tyler and Mira (1999), children who sustain brain injuries reportedly have a higher incidence of prior behavior problems. Overactive and impulsive children often take risks that predispose them to brain injuries. Other risk factors in a child's environment include high levels of family stress, including marital instability and economic problems.

Interventions for TBI vary, depending on the stage of injury. Immediately after injury, the focus is often on sustaining life and minimizing complications, especially if the injury results in coma (unconsciousness lasting more than a short period of time). There seems to be a direct relationship between the length of the coma and the level of cognitive impairment. If the child remains in a coma, therapists may use special stimulation to arouse him or her. After the coma, children often experience post-traumatic amnesia and are seriously disoriented. Efforts must be made to reorient them to their surroundings. Children who sustain traumatic brain injuries may also have other serious medical problems that require intensive intervention.

In the first few months after a traumatic brain injury, children often make rapid recoveries. Many of the initial effects of the injury diminish. However, 6 months to 1 year after the injury, many children still evidence a wide range of medical, motor, cognitive, behavioral, and language problems. These problems may persist for many years. Some of the common residual physical problems are seizures, loss of stamina, headaches, hearing or vision impairments, growth problems, and a variety of other effects. Long-term cognitive effects often include problems with memory, attention, language processing, problem solving, and general intellectual functioning. Of the resultant problems highlighted above, memory problems are often the most troublesome. Because success in school requires significant long- and short-term memory skills, lingering memory problems can have a serious impact on students' academic achievement.

Language problems are also critical for students. Many school tasks involve written or oral language, often in conjunction with other skills. In many ways, students with residual effects of traumatic brain injury resemble their peers with learning disabilities. Expressive and receptive language problems, word retrieval (remembering commonly used words), sequencing skills, and general disorganization are common.

Behaviorally, students with brain injuries may display problems similar to those of students with emotional and behavioral disorders. Students often display impulsivity, hyperactivity, poor social interaction skills, and inconsistency of responses. The interesting and often problematic fact is that a student who suffers a traumatic brain injury can experience significant changes in his or her personality, as reflected in outward behaviors. This change can be difficult for friends and classmates to understand and adapt to.

School personnel, who have the charge of attending to the needs of students with traumatic brain injuries, must recognize their responsibilities. Hardman et al. (1993) have suggested some relevant interventions, including providing counseling and therapy to help the child cope with the injury and its effects, assisting the child and family in maintaining the gains achieved, and referring the child and family to community agencies for additional services that may be needed. A well-informed staff, a structured, controlled environment, and adaptive equipment and devices are also important in schools. Educators must also be sensitive to the emotional reactions of families. Parents of a child with a brain injury will face a grieving process and an adaptation to loss and may need assistance and understanding from teachers and administrators. Some general suggestions for school personnel who work with students who have had brain injuries are included in Table 8.3.

Table 8.3
Classroom Suggestions for Teaching Students with Traumatic Brain Injury

---

Receptive Language

Limit the amount of information presented at one time.
Provide simple instructions for only one activity at a time.
Have the student repeat instructions.

Expressive Language

Teach the student to rehearse silently before verbally replying.
Teach the student to look for cues from listeners to ascertain that the student is being understood.
Teach the student to ask directly if he or she is being understood.

Maintaining Attention

Provide a study carrel or preferential seating.
After giving instructions, check for proper attention and understanding by having the student repeat them.
Teach the student to use self-regulating techniques to maintain attention (e.g., asking "Am I paying attention?" "What is the required task?")

Impulsiveness

Teach the student to mentally rehearse steps before beginning an activity.
Reduce potential distractions.
Frequently restate and reinforce rules.

Memory

Teach the student to use external aids such as notes, memos, daily schedule sheets, and assignment sheets.
Use visual imagery, when possible, to supplement oral content.
Teach visual imaging techniques for information presented.
Provide repetition and frequent review of instructional materials.
Provide immediate and frequent feedback to enable the student to interpret success or failure.

Following Directions

Provide the student with both visual and auditory directions.
Model tasks, whenever possible.
Break multistep directions into small parts and list them so that the student can refer back to them when needed.

Motor Skills

Allow the student to complete a project rather than turn in a written assignment.
Have the student use a typewriter or a word processor to complete assignments.
Allow extra time for completing tasks requiring fine motor skills.
Assign someone to take notes for the student during lectures.

Source: Adapted from *Traumatic Brain Injury in Children and Adolescents: A Sourcebook for Teachers and Other School Personnel,* 2nd ed., by J. S. Tyler and M. P. Mira, 1999, Austin, TX: PRO-ED.

INTERVENTIONS

Academic Concerns

An important point that has been made previously is that having a physical or health impairment does not automatically imply a limitation in cognitive functioning. Although it is true that some children with physical or health impairments also have mental retardation and/or sensory disabilities, many do not. The intellectual ability of most individuals with physical or health impairments is no different from their normal peers. In the past, a physical or health disorder usually resulted in a separate, restrictive placement for students; however, schools today are providing instruction in less restrictive, inclusive environments in ever increasing numbers. The movement toward inclusion of students with severe disabilities is occurring in many situations, often with increased support of technology and personnel. However, some students with physical or health issues, who otherwise do not need special education–related services, still miss school frequently because of medical problems. In these cases, their academic achievement may suffer and remedial efforts may be indicated.

Activities of Daily Living

Individualization of instruction is critical for students with physical and health conditions. Adaptive measures that facilitate communication (e.g., use of computers and modified input devices) and movement (e.g., use of myoelectric arms and wheelchairs controlled by sipping and puffing techniques) are available and can provide children with physical or health disorders with access to information, which is the key to learning. Educational programming for students with physical impairments should make sure that these students acquire the necessary skills needed to function successfully with the tasks of everyday living. If needs are identified, then instruction should be designed to improve skills in the following areas:

❏ Occupational and vocational training
❏ Self-help
❏ Daily living
❏ Mobility training
❏ Communication

Individualized programs should be guided by the long-term goal of independent functioning. This goal usually implies the need for high-level skills, so not every individual with a physical impairment will be able to function independently in everyday life. Thus, a program that stresses sequential programming of skills from the most basic to the more advanced is essential.

Psychological Concerns

The successful adjustment of a child or youth with a physical impairment, health impairment, or traumatic brain injury depends in large part on the actions and attitudes of significant people such as parents, siblings, teachers, peers, neighbors, and others in the community whom the student encounters in everyday life. Children and youth with physical, health impairments, or traumatic brain injury may experience feelings of insecurity, hopelessness, embarrassment, rejection, guilt, low self-esteem, and fear. These feelings may result in efforts to withdraw from interaction (avoidance), hide the stigmatizing impairment, or become overly dependent on others. These reactions can be minimized by sincere and thoughtful intervention, including school situations in which the student is accepted, integrated, and included in the ongoing activities of the classroom and school building. In addition, it is also essential that realistic goals be set for the student. Often, the student with a physical impairment, health impairment, or traumatic brain injury will fantasize about being "normal" and participating in activities in which "normal" kids usually engage.

We are often guilty of reacting to individuals who differ from us physically with fear, rejection, pity, discrimination, low expectations, or awkwardness. We are probably just uncomfortable! We need to realize that these individuals, although limited in some ways, can nonetheless be valuable contributors to society. Providing opportunities for typical interactions and relationships can minimize the effects of the disability and enhance our own personal growth.

Service Delivery Issues

To provide appropriate services to children with physical or health impairments, changes in the way services and program are delivered may sometimes be required. The reorganization of schools and redesign of school buildings has been mandated by the Americans with Disabilities Act. Barrier-free environments, improved communication, and provisions for transportation are all important in schools, just as in the workplace. The successful coordination of many different ancillary services, necessitated by the pervasive nature of certain impairments, must also be addressed. Depending on the severity of the impairment, the delivery of educational services may include a hospital program, home-bound education, a special school setting, or a regular school setting. Considerations of mobility, transportation, medical services, and adaptive equipment are also important for school administrators. However, including the student with a physical impairment, health impairment, or traumatic brain injury into general education settings requires more than making the building accessible. Successful inclusion, as stressed in chapter 2, requires preparing the school as a whole for inclusion, and efforts must focus on education, training, and support.

TRENDS AND ISSUES

Emergent Technologies

Significant advances have been made in recent years in the areas of medicine, prosthetics/orthotics, adaptive technology, and cosmetology. These advances have had positive effects for many individuals with health and physical impairments. The field of medicine has had a significant impact on this disability group by preventing and treating physical impairments (with surgery, drug therapy, etc.), health problems (through the use of fetal monitoring, immunizations, and other techniques), and traumatic brain injury (through interventions such as cognitive retraining). In the area of prosthetics, the artificial replacement of missing body parts has enabled many individuals to regain some of the functioning necessary for daily living. The use of prosthetic limbs and other adaptive technological advances, including devices that allow persons with physical impairments to perform many everyday self-help tasks, are constantly being developed and improved. Other examples of engineering advancements are wheelchairs that are operated by miniature computers that can be told what to do; mouth-operated electronic devices that allow persons who have quadriplegia to perform certain actions from bed by varying their breathing patterns; puffing and sipping devices that can operate a telephone, radio, TV, lamp, keyboard, or door. Cosmetological intervention is also helping some individuals with physical impairments through plastic and reconstructive surgical procedures and through techniques that attempt to minimize the visibility of an impairment (e.g., individuals who have been severely burned).

Costs

Costs for supporting research and providing services for this population can be significant. However, these economic matters should be considered from a long-term perspective. For instance, a computerized wheelchair, although expensive, may enable a person to work and function in society. In the long run, this is a cost-effective approach. Of even more importance are benefits gained by the individual. It is hard to put a price on someone's independence and long-term adjustment.

FINAL THOUGHTS

The myriad problems that persons with physical impairments, health impairments, or traumatic brain injury face can seem overwhelming. The benefits of appropriate education and training must be followed by opportunities to work and live as independently as possible in the community. We must foster a society receptive to individuals with physical impairments, health impairments, or traumatic brain injury and find ways for them to become more included and more accepted. In introducing the reader to the various topics in this chapter, we are unable to provide you with a *real* understanding of what it is like to be physically or health impaired. So, we would like to conclude with the following thought:

> *Physical disability is a minority problem among the young and middle-aged, but among those who reach the life expectancy age of 70, it is a problem of the majority. A very small percentage of us will experience loss of mobility because of diseases like multiple sclerosis or muscular dystrophy; a somewhat larger, but still small percentage, will experience this loss because of accidents; most of us, however, will become old.* (Cohen, 1977, p. 136)

SUGGESTIONS FOR WORKING OR INTERACTING WITH PEOPLE WHO HAVE PHYSICAL IMPAIRMENTS, HEALTH IMPAIRMENTS, OR TRAUMATIC BRAIN INJURIES

This section is divided into categories based on the specific suggestions relevant to each area.

General Suggestions

1. Treat people with physical or health impairments as normally as possible.
2. Do not underestimate their abilities because of their physical and/or health limitations.
3. Be aware of the individual's specific situation and the special needs and precautions that are warranted.
4. Be concerned about the psychosocial ramifications associated with the acquisition of a physical or health impairment.

For Individuals Who Use Wheelchairs

1. Ask wheelchair users if they would like assistance before you help.
2. If conversation lasts more than a few minutes, consider sitting down or kneeling to get yourself on the same level as the wheelchair user.
3. Do not demean or patronize wheelchair users by patting them on the head.
4. Give clear directions, including distance, weather conditions, and physical obstacles that may hinder travel.
5. When wheelchair users "transfer" out of the wheelchair to a chair, toilet, car, or bed, do not move the wheelchair out of reaching distance.
6. Do not assume that using a wheelchair is in itself a tragedy. It is a means of freedom that allows the user to move about independently.

For Individuals with Traumatic Brain Injury

1. Expect inconsistency, including memory and organizational problems.
2. Help the student by providing structure and support in his or her environment.
3. Try to attend to the student's needs for stress management and social skills training.
4. Modify assignments whenever the student's individual needs require it.

For Individuals with Severe Forms of Cerebral Palsy

1. If the person has difficulties communicating clearly, do not be afraid to ask the person to repeat what was said.
2. Do ask persons with cerebral palsy if they need assistance if they are experiencing difficulty in performing certain activities.
3. Be aware of the person's special needs (e.g., special chair for sitting).
4. Allow for additional time that will probably be needed for accomplishing various tasks (e.g., walking, writing).
5. Individualize the format for assignments, especially requirements for written work.

For Individuals Who Have Convulsive Types of Seizures

1. Remain calm if a person has a seizure.
2. Try to prevent the person from injury by safeguarding the immediate environment.
3. Do not interfere with the person's seizure-related behaviors. Do not force anything into the person's mouth (i.e., between the teeth).
4. If possible, place something soft beneath the person's head and, if possible, turn the person's face to one side to drain saliva.
5. Let the person rest after regaining consciousness.
6. Seek medical assistance if the person seems to pass from one seizure to another without regaining consciousness.

For Individuals with HIV/AIDS

1. Respect the student's and family's right to confidentiality.
2. Train everyone in preventive procedures for handling bodily fluids.
3. Stay in close touch with medical personnel, including the school nurse and the student's physician.
4. Be sensitive to other students' attitudes and behavior toward the student with AIDS. Educate *all* students to avoid prejudicial actions.
5. Make sure that illness-related absences are taken into consideration.

PONDER THESE

1. Imagine that you must use a wheelchair for one day; list all the barriers or obstacles that you would encounter in the course of your typical daily schedule.

2. If you catastrophically lost the use of your arms or legs, what functions would you first want to be able to reacquire or relearn?

3. Suppose you invited a friend who uses a wheelchair over to your home or apartment for dinner. What modifications to your residence would you have to make to accommodate your guest?

4. Consider how individuals with physical disabilities have been portrayed in the various forms of media (films, television, cartoons, comics, advertisements, etc.). In general, have these portrayals been positive or negative?

5. If you were a classroom teacher and you learned that a student in your class had HIV, but you were not told who it was, how would you feel? How would you handle the situation?

6. Assume you have a student in your class who was in a car accident and, as a result, has a traumatic brain injury. He has regular, frequent outbursts of anger, often with no apparent provocation. What would you do? From whom would you seek advice and assistance?

REFERENCES

Batshaw, M. L. (2002). *Children with disabilities: A medical primer* (5th ed.). Baltimore: Paul H. Brookes.

Berg, B. O. (1982). Convulsive disorders. In E. E. Bleck & D. A. Nagel (Eds.), *Physically handicapped children: A medical atlas for teachers* (2nd ed., pp. 101–108). New York: Grune & Stratton.

Brown, L. W. (1997). Seizure disorders. In M. L. Batshaw (Ed.), *Children with disabilities* (4th ed., pp. 553–593). Baltimore: Paul H. Brookes.

Centers for Disease Control and Prevention. (1993). *HIV/AIDS Surveillance Report* (Vol. 5, No. 2). Atlanta, GA: U.S. Department of Health and Human Services, Public Health Service.

Clancy, R. R. (1990). Valproate: An update: The challenge of modern pediatric seizure management. *Current Problems in Pediatrics, 20,* 161–233.

Cohen, S. (1977). *Special people.* Upper Saddle River, NJ: Prentice Hall.

Hallahan, D. P., & Kauffman, J. M. (1988). *Exceptional children: Introduction to special education* (4th ed.). Upper Saddle River, NJ: Merrill/Prentice Hall.

Hardman, M. L., Drew, C. J., Egan, M. W., & Wolf, B. (1993). *Human exceptionality* (4th ed.). Boston: Allyn & Bacon.

Heward, W. L. (2003). *Exceptional children: An introduction to special education* (7th ed.). Upper Saddle River, NJ: Merrill/Prentice Hall.

Individuals with Disabilities Education Act of 1990, PL 101–476, §602(a)(19).

Inge, K. J. (1992). Cerebral palsy. In P. J. McLaughlin & P. Wehman (Eds.), *Developmental disabilities: A handbook for best practices* (pp. 30–53). Boston: Andover Medical Publishers.

Kelker, K., Hecimovic, A., & LeRoy, C. H. (1994). Designing a classroom and school environment for students with AIDS: A checklist for teachers. *TEACHING Exceptional Children, 26*(4), 52–55.

LeRoy, C. H., Powell, T. H., & Kelker, P. H. (1994). Meeting our responsibilities in special education. *TEACHING Exceptional Children, 26*(4), 37–44.

National Head Injury Foundation Task Force on Special Education. (1989). *An educator's manual: What educators need to know about students with traumatic brain injury.* Southborough, MA: Author.

Paasche, C. L., Gorrill, L., & Strom, B. (1990). *Children with special needs in early childhood settings.* Menlo Park, CA: Addison-Wesley.

Pellegrino, L. (1997). Cerebral palsy. In M. L. Batshaw (Ed.), *Children with disabilities* (4th ed., pp. 499–528). Baltimore: Paul H. Brookes.

Prensky, A. L., & Palkes, H. S. (1982). *Care of the neurologically handicapped child: A book for parents and professionals.* New York: Oxford University Press.

Rowley-Kelly, F. L., & Reigel, D. H. (1993). *Teaching the student with spina bifida.* Baltimore: Paul H. Brookes.

Seidel, J. F. (1992). Children with HIV-related developmental difficulties. *Phi Delta Kappan, 72,* 38–56.

Smith, D. D. (2004). *Introduction to special education: Teaching in an age of opportunity* (6th ed.). Boston: Allyn & Bacon.

Smith, T. E. C., Polloway, E. A., Patton, J. R., & Dowdy, C. A. (2004). *Teaching students with special needs in inclusive settings* (4th ed.). Boston: Allyn & Bacon.

Tyler, J. S., & Mira, M. P. (1999). *Traumatic brain injury in children and adolescents: A sourcebook for teachers and other school personnel* (2nd ed.). Austin, TX: PRO-ED.

U.S. Department of Education. (1993). *To assure the free appropriate public education of all children with disabilities. Fifteenth annual report to Congress on the implementation of the Individuals with Disabilities Education Act.* Washington, DC: Author.

CHAPTER 9

Blindness and Low Vision

A young couple with visual impairments, with whom my wife and I were friends and professional associates, invited us during the Christmas holidays to an evening at their home. After a time of visiting, we went to the dining area where we enjoyed some refreshments. The colored holiday lights in the windows created a perfect effect for the late evening treats. The next morning, my wife received a very apologetic phone call from an embarrassed hostess. It was not until our host and hostess were retiring for the night that they discovered their light switch was in the off position. It was then that they realized they had fed us in a very dark room.

What I remember most from my philosophy class in my junior year of college is Joe, a student with a visual impairment who sat behind me. He was a likable guy—good sense of humor and very bright. I think he was unable to see at all. He walked with a cane and took all his class notes in Braille—I can still hear the peck, peck, peck of his stylus. One class session about midway through the semester, the professor was flamboyantly explaining a complex theory. He scribbled on the chalkboard to assist him in his instruction. As the professor paused for a moment, Joe raised his hand.

"Yes, Joe."

"I don't quite understand."

"What don't you understand, Joe?"

"The whole thing. It doesn't make any sense."

At this, the professor spun on his heel and frantically drew diagram after diagram, at the same time eloquently explaining the theory. After about 15 minutes, the professor turned around and gasped, "Now do you see?"

Joe stopped pecking with his stylus and calmly replied, "No, I still can't see, but I understand."

The professor cried, "Good!" and then wheeled around and started drawing again.

The Helms were concerned about Susan, their 4-year-old daughter, who was lagging in several developmental areas. Although she seemed to be normal in terms of physical and language development, some of her cognitive skills were far below normal. For example, she couldn't identify letters, shapes, or numbers and could identify only a few common household items (e.g., spoons, knife, chair, bed). An in-depth assessment resulted in a measured IQ of 68 for Susan and a label of mild mental retardation.

Susan was placed in an early childhood program for children with mild handicaps. She remained in special education for several years. At the age of 8, Susan was moved from her early childhood special education program to a primary special education classroom at a local elementary school.

Susan's new teacher, Mr. Williams, soon became convinced that she was not mentally retarded. He enlisted the help of other professors in his school to conduct further evaluations of his student. These assessments revealed that Susan had a serious visual problem. A ophthalmologist eventually discovered that Susan suffered from congenital cataracts.

Surgery soon corrected Susan's primary disability. Susan was reassigned to a program for children with visual problems. Special services and intervention eventually allowed Susan to enter the regular classroom where today she functions well.

Sue, a young college student, desired a means of independent travel that would permit her greater range than by foot. Being legally blind, she obviously could not obtain a driver's license. However, she did have enough remaining vision to ride a bicycle. She purchased a bike and began making frequent trips about the college town and into the surrounding country, often riding several miles. On one occasion she made a visit to our home and decided to return to her dormitory by a new route that took her through the downtown area. As she rode the streets through the main business district, she began noticing numerous friendly people waving and smiling from the sidewalks. They seemed to be waving at her. As she continued, the number of people increased. Then there were crowds, looking, waving, and clapping—for her? Finally, she realized the reason for all the attention. She was riding in the middle of a major holiday parade!

Two adolescent friends attending a school for the blind went for a brief walk on the familiar sidewalks of the immediate neighborhood and left their travel canes behind. During their walk, they encountered an unfamiliar patch of what felt to them like mud. They giggled and walked through it to "dry ground." Imagine the frustration on the face of the homeowner as he looked up from his troweling in time to see two young girls slogging through his freshly poured concrete driveway!

Little Teressa, a first grader, was examining the various objects in a touch-and-tell box. She extracted some shapes from the box—a square, a triangle, and a circle—and described or named them. Finally she came to a cube that was different in shape and texture from those objects she had already handled. She paused, felt it intensely on all sides, and said, "A block. What's this? An H and R Block?"

As a graduate student in special education, I had never met Debbie in person, but I had heard about how independent she was and wanted to be. Debbie, who was totally blind, was preparing to become a teacher of students with visual impairments. At this point in time, I still had much to learn about people with handicaps in general and individuals with visual impairments in particular.

It was an early winter morning and a fresh covering of snow blanketed the ground. I happened to be on my way to the campus center when I came upon Debbie. Debbie was on her way to breakfast; however, she seemed to be very disoriented and confused. Knowing that Debbie was a very independent person and fearing her wrath, I approached her somewhat timidly, not really sure whether I should ask her if she needed some assistance. Nevertheless, I introduced myself, highlighting our common bond or burden of being fellow graduate students. I then proceeded to ask her if she needed any help.

Debbie told me that she certainly could use some help because the snow had covered the walkway that she normally used to go to the campus center where breakfast was served, thus negating the usefulness of her cane. I was delighted that she had allowed me to provide some assistance. Having had no prior experience as a sighted guide, I was anxious to learn the proper techniques. Debbie told me how to act and so off we went.

Everything went smoothly at first, and I was proud of how well I was doing. Then we came to a set of steps that descended to a lower level. Here I was trying to be so careful that I lost my footing on the icy steps and literally dropped out of the picture. I picked myself up off the ground, climbed back up the steps I had just rocketed over, and regained my position next to Debbie. I was worried that she would simply tell me not to get within 10 feet of her as I was a menace to her safety. However, Debbie was most understanding, and after she realized the reason for my abrupt departure, she got a good laugh out of it.

After I finally escorted her to her destination, without any further mishaps, I realized that I might have needed Debbie's assistance in dealing with the hazards of mobility in the snow as much as she needed mine.

What sort of image does the word *blindness* evoke? Dark glasses, a guide dog, a tin cup, the groping tap of a red-tipped white cane? The word *blindness* has historically been associated with thoughts of helplessness, pity, and a life of eternal blackness. But is this really blindness? What does *blindness* mean? What does *low vision* mean? To us it means, in part, working with people who are blind or who have partial sight and forgetting that they have problems in seeing.

Vision problems are a result of a malfunctioning eye or optic nerve that prevents a person from seeing normally. An individual has a visual impairment whenever anomalous development, disease, or injury reduces the ability of the eyes to function. When an individual cannot see normally in at least one eye, the person is considered visually impaired. People who are visually impaired may find that things look dim, blurred, or out of focus. They may have the sensation of seeing only a part of an object or seeing everything masked in a cloud. They may see occasional dark blotches that float or appear to remain in front of the object they are viewing. It may be that they can see things clearly but only straight ahead, as if looking through a drinking straw. Just as there are varying degrees of vision, the ability to use what vision there is also varies among people.

BASIC CONCEPTS

Terminology

Various terms such as *visual impairment, blindness, legally blind, functionally blind, totally blind, low vision, limited vision, partially sighted, visually limited, visual disability,* and *visual handicap* are used to describe individuals with vision

Table 9.1
Terms Related to Visual Impairments

All Disciplines	Rehabilitation
Congenitally blind	Legally blind
Adventitiously blind	Medically blind
Visually handicapped	Economically blind
Residual vision	Vocationally blind
Clinical	**Education**
Partially blind	Educationally blind
Visually disabled	Functionally blind
Subnormal vision	Visually impaired
Remaining vision	Low vision
Visually defective	Braille blind

Source: From *Visual Impairments and Learning,* 4th ed. (p. 19), by
N. C. Barraga and J. N. Erin, 2001, Austin, TX: PRO-ED.

problems. As a result, a certain amount of confusion exists as to which term should
be used.

The specific use of a term has much to do with professional perspective. Barraga and Erin (2001) organized terms that have been used in the professional literature over the course of the last 150 years (see Table 9.1). Education in general prefers the term *visual impairment,* as evidenced by the fact that it is this term that is used in IDEA to cover the range of students with vision problems. Teachers who are trained in the field of vision education often use the terms *low vision, functionally blind,* and *totally blind,* indicating varying degrees of ability to use visual input. The next section clarifies the distinctions among the many terms that proliferate the field.

Definitional Perspective

Two definitions of visual impairment are discussed in this section. One definition, the older legal definition, is based on visual acuity and field of vision. The other definition, a more recent one, is based on functional vision for educational purposes.

Legal Definition.   The first definition, established by federal law, was needed to identify those people who were eligible for benefits through federal programs, such as additional tax exemption, free mailing privileges, special materials from the Library of Congress, the privilege of operating vending stands in federal buildings, the opportunity of receiving special educational materials, and benefits from rehabilitation programs. This definition is still considered the legal definition for receiving benefits:

> *The legally blind are defined as those with a central visual acuity for distance of 20/200 or less in the better eye with correction or, if greater than 20/200, a field of vision no greater than 20 degrees in the widest diameter.*

Acuity generally denotes sharpness or keenness with which one can recognize given objects at a stated distance. A visual disorder is usually thought of when visual acuity is less than 20/70 in the best eye after correction; that is, a person with 20/70 vision can see at a distance of 20 feet what the normally sighted person can see at approximately 70 feet. A visual acuity of 20/200 in the best eye after correction generally is used as the demarcation for legal blindness, meaning that this individual can see at 20 feet what the normally sighted person sees at approximately 200 feet. To illustrate, if two individuals were standing on the goal line of a football field and looking forward, the legally blind individual would see at 7 yards with the acuity that a normally sighted individual would see at 77 yards. The acuity range from 20/70 to 20/200 feet or more in the best eye after correction is referred to as *legally blind.*

Field of vision generally denotes the angle or surrounding field with which one can recognize familiar objects. This indicator of vision problems refers to the significant reduction of the peripheral field (i.e., peripheral vision), which is normally 160 degrees or better. If this field of vision falls to 20 degrees or less, an individual generally is classified as legally blind. This condition is commonly referred to as *tunnel vision.*

Educational Definition.   The second definitional perspective is a more functional approach to conceptualizing vision needs, focusing on how a particular vision problem affects learning and the ability to use print. Visual impairment, as defined in IDEA, means "an impairment in vision that, even with correction, adversely affects a child's educational performance. The term includes both partial sight and blindness" (34 CFR, Section 300.7 [c] [13]).

Those people who are partially sighted or suffer from low vision make up about 85 percent of those individuals labeled *legally blind.* These people have some degree of residual vision, but the limits of their sight restrict their mobility, orientation, academic performance, or vocational functioning. Thus, individuals whose vision does not permit the use of print for reading can be educated by the use of Braille and tactile and auditory devices. Persons with partial vision are educated by the use of materials that complement their residual vision, such as large-print books or special illumination.

School-based personnel find functional definitions far more useful than clinical definitions. Such definitions focus on *visual efficiency,* that is, how well a person with a visual disorder uses his or her existing sight. *Blind* individuals possess, at best, only light perception without projection or are totally lacking in sight. Those people with low vision may have significantly impaired sight after correction but possess enough residual vision to function successfully with instructional and occupational modifications, such as large print or tactile aids.

Individuals with *limited vision* are those people who are limited in their visual ability under average circumstances (Barraga, 1986). These people may need modification in lighting or high-contrast print to function successfully in the classroom.

Because the above definitions may appear overly technical, most educational practitioners prefer a simpler way of defining vision issues. The primary concern is the ability of a student to use print. As a result, many school-based professionals consider a student to be visually impaired if his or her vision is diminished so as to interfere with the reading of print in a book (near vision) or the reading of print on the chalkboard (distance vision).

Prevalence

The accuracy of estimates of prevalence in specific impairments is always subject to disagreement due to the ambiguity inherent in existing definitions, eligibility criteria, and identification procedures. Visual impairment is a disability that affects only a small number of the school-aged population. Recent statistics issued by the U.S. Department of Education (2001) indicate that 26,590 students ages 6 to 21 were served under the category "visual impairment" during the 1999–2000 school year. This is a relatively small percentage of the total school population. It should be pointed out that most students identified under IDEA as having some type of visual impairment could use printed materials for educational purposes.

Visual impairment becomes a much more prevalent condition when we look at the elderly population. Age becomes a significant factor that must be acknowledged when we speak of the prevalence of visual impairment.

Etiology

The eye is one of the more intriguing and complex organs of the body. Its derivation comes from the Latin word *oculus* and the Greek word *ophthalmos;* hence, the English terms *ocular* and *ophthalmologist*. Early civilizations referred to the eye as the window of the soul. As can be seen in Figure 9.1, the eye is a large sphere actually made up of three distinct layers: the *sclera* and *cones,* the *choroid,* and the *retina.* At the front of the eye is the *cornea,* which gives the sphere its oval shape. Then there is the *iris,* which is a flat bar with circular muscle fibers that dilate and contract the pupil or central opening of the eye. The *lens* is next, directing light rays back to the retina where a camera-like phenomenon transfers the image to the *optic nerve* and onto the *visual cortex* of the occipital lobe of the brain.

As reported by Livingston (1986), most visual problems can be attributed to malformations and malfunctions of the eye. The following list categorizes selected types of visual impairments and provides brief explanations of each:

❑ *Refractive problems:* Refractive problems occur when light coming through the lens and cornea is not focused precisely on the retina. Such errors are the result of the light being focused in front of or beyond the retina. Refractive errors are related to the shape of the eye itself.
  • Myopia—nearsightedness (eyeball too long)
  • Hyperopia—farsightedness
  • Astigmatism—unevenness in surfaces of cornea or lens

Figure 9.1
The Eye

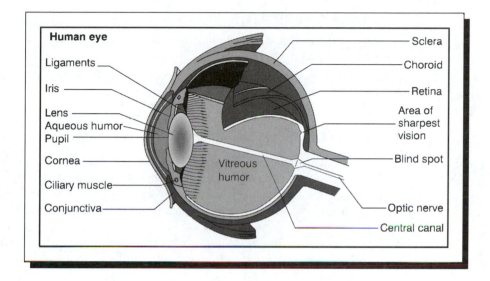

- *Lens abnormalities* (or accommodation errors): These errors are related to the way in which the lens of the eye changes during the process of focusing light waves.
  - Dislocation
  - Cataracts—clouding of the lens
  - Retinopathy of prematurity (retrolental fibroplasia)—scar tissue behind the lens (overconcentration of oxygen)
- *Retinal defects:* These defects are related to damage or destruction of the retinal portion of the eye. Visual acuity and reductions in the field of vision are the most common types of manifestations.
  - Retinitis pigmentosa—progressive degeneration of retina
  - Diabetic retinopathy—interference of blood supply to retina
  - Macular degeneration—blood vessels of macula (part of retina) are damaged (loss of central vision)
- *Muscle control problems:* These problems refer to the use and control of the six muscles that control eye movement. Double vision and many problems with depth perception are related to difficulties with muscular control.
  - Strabismus—cross-eyed
  - Nystagmus—involuntary, rapid, rhythmic, side-to-side eye movements
  - Amblyopia—"lazy eye"
- *Miscellaneous*
  - Glaucoma—pressure due to a buildup of eye fluid
  - Trauma—damage due to accidents, and so on
  - Color vision—inability to detect certain colors

CHARACTERISTICS

Individuals with vision problems vary greatly and each person's situation warrants attention. Some characteristics result from the nature of the specific vision condition (e.g., myopia). This section explores some of the characteristics that apply to many individuals with visual impairments.

General Characteristics

Turnbull, Turnbull, Shank, Smith, and Leal (2002) remarked that the following characteristics are important issues for many children, youth, and adults who have some type of significant visual impairment. Note that these issues are not insurmountable; however, they are challenges that must be acknowledged and dealt with.

❏ *Limitations in the range and variety of experiences.* Affects acquisition of knowledge, concept development, and ability to share and communicate about common experiences.
❏ *Limitations in the ability to get around.* Affects ability to move around one's environment as spontaneously as others who have functional vision.
❏ *Limitations in interactions with the environment.* Affects one's ability to monitor and comprehend the local environment in an immediate sense.

Other general characteristics of individuals with visual impairments may be observed in this population. Some of the more commonly found features include the following:

❏ They may experience difficulty with visual information, including the Internet and other forms of media.
❏ The language ability of school-age children and adults is similar to individuals with vision.
❏ Social skills may need to be taught (e.g., using various visual cues such as smiling when interacting).
❏ Stereotypic behaviors (variety of repetitive behaviors like body rocking) are displayed by some individuals.

Noteworthy Features

The vignettes at the beginning of this chapter illustrate several points about visual impairment; these and other points are further developed next.

Most individuals with visual impairments can see. Only a small portion of those who are legally or educationally blind are totally blind or without any usable vision.

Most individuals with visual impairments have all of their other senses; that is, they are normal. Having a visual impairment, even total blindness, does not impair or improve one's sense of hearing, smell, taste, or touch. An individual with a severe visual impairment is not endowed with a "sixth" sense, as some believe. If such a person does do some things in different ways from most, it may be a very natural way of using the other senses in place of lost vision.

Most people who are totally blind can learn much about their environments by making use of hearing, touch, smell, and kinesthetic perception. With good orientation and mobility skills and experience, those with little or no vision can use a cane as an aid for crossing intersections, taking walks, making shopping trips, and getting to just about any place within walking distance. Their hands help them to learn about a lot of things if they are just permitted to touch, handle, and move objects that are about them.

Often, the biggest barrier to living and learning naturally for persons with visual impairments is other people who have normal vision. Family and friends, in their attempts to be helpful, too often forget the needs of a person with a visual impairment. For example, rather than permit a person with a visual impairment to take an elbow, they may push him or her across the intersection (see Table 9.2 for tips on being a sighted guide); or they may take the same man's order from his sighted friend across the table; or they may insist on "look, but don't touch."

As a group, people who are visually impaired comprise a normal range of personalities, interests, and abilities. Some people with visual impairments are gifted, some have mental retardation, and most are intellectually normal. There are those who are emotionally disturbed and others with learning disabilities. We have athletes and scholars with visual impairments. There are those who are socially adept, delinquent, prolific, dull, fascinating, obnoxious, or any other combination.

People with severe visual impairments have been successful in nearly every activity and vocation. However, society still judges these people not so much by their abilities as by their perceived differences. Because they are judged incapable *before* the fact, far too often, adults with severe visual impairments find locating jobs and obtaining desirable employment very difficult.

Table 9.2
Tips for Being a Sighted Guide

- A person with the visual impairment should grasp the guide's upper arm firmly, just above the elbow, with the thumb on the outside and the fingers on the inside of the guide's arm.
- A young child should hold the guide's wrist.
- Both the individual and the guide hold their upper arms close to their bodies.
- The person with the visual impairment should be positioned one-half step behind the guide.
- The guide can press his or her arm closer to the body to indicate that a narrow area is approaching and must be navigated.
- The guide should approach squarely (i.e., not at an angle) all situations where there is a change in level—the guide will ascend or descend the first step.
- The guide should negotiate all hazards (e.g., low hanging branches) that would create a problem.
- The use of verbal cues is recommended—however, elaborate description is not necessary.

Adapted from Torres, I., & Corn, A. L. (1990). *When you have a visually handicapped child in your classroom: Suggestions for teachers.* New York: American Federation for the Blind.

Severe visual impairment can inhibit children in their early experiences and in their ability to get from place to place. Important early experiences can be denied to children with visual impairments if they are not permitted to be active and to use all of their senses to the maximum, thus often affecting concept and language development. Active early childhood and preschool experiences are important factors in assuring normal development for children with visual impairments.

The difficulty in establishing one's position in the environment (orientation) and in moving from place to place (mobility) are two of the most direct barriers created by visual impairment. Some individuals with visual impairments are limited only in their ability to operate a motor vehicle, whereas, for others, visual impairment may cause a major mobility impediment. Yet, mobility issues can be addressed and individuals can learn ways to deal with these issues (Corn & Rosenblum, 2000).

Visual impairment can occur as one of the impairments in a person with multiple disabilities. In about half the cases, severe visual impairment occurs as one of several difficulties in persons with multiple disabilities.

The child with multiple impairments (e.g., deaf–blind) presents a unique educational problem. Impairments come in all degrees of severity and in nearly every possible combination. In many cases, particularly if the impairments are severe, instruction must be highly individualized. Furthermore, teachers who work with this population must be highly trained.

To date, too little is still understood about children with multiple disabilities. This misunderstanding has led in some cases to the misplacement and inappropriate treatment of these individuals. There are cases of persons who are deaf–blind with normal cognitive abilities being placed in special units of residential institutions designed for individuals who are mentally retarded. It is probably safe to say that, for some people with multiple disabilities, much more could be done to ensure their maximum potential for development.

INTERVENTIONS

Education

This section discusses three major components of intervention at the school level: curriculum, instructional methodology, and placement.

Curricular Issues.   The curriculum for students with visual impairment should be consistent with the general education curriculum, as specified by the 1997 amendments of IDEA. However, additional instruction in certain areas of specific need may also be necessary. Barraga and Erin (2001) acknowledge that a specialized curriculum may be needed for many students with visual problems. In their opinion, several major issues require attention and inclusion in the curriculum. The curricular areas are listed in Table 9.3.

Table 9.3
Components of a Specialized Curriculum

- Communication
- Orientation and mobility
- Social interaction skills
- Independent living skills
- Recreation and leisure skills
- Visual efficiency skills
- Career-vocational preparation
- Use of assistive technology

Source: From *Visual Impairments and Learning,* 4th ed., by N. C.
Barraga and J. N. Erin, 2001, Austin, TX: PRO-ED.

Instructional Methodology.   Most teaching methods found effective with normal-seeing students are effective with students with visual impairments. The obvious difference occurs with visual presentations that must be adapted or modified to utilize auditory or tactile sensory channels.

Among the majority of those persons identified as visually impaired, the utilization of residual sight is a key component in any intervention. Such practices as frequent breaks to reduce eye fatigue, a mixture of multisensory activities (i.e., visual, auditory, tactile), and the use of materials that offer a high visual contrast are among the practical and viable instructional adaptations available to the teacher.

In addition, optical aids (some requiring a prescription) and nonoptical aids are available to teachers. These aids include such things as large-print textbooks, bold-lined paper, closed-circuit television, and text magnifiers (special lenses). Further, a variety of technologies, including Braille keyboards for computers or specialized monitor adaptations for enlarging the screen, are now available.

Placement.   The issue of best placement of students who are visually impaired has provoked much debate over the years. With the implementation of PL 94–142, more students with milder problems have been provided services in the regular school settings, typically in general education classrooms. However, this has not always been the case. Furthermore, the question of best placement is more complicated for those students with more severe forms of impairment.

A question of which setting, residential versus day or public school, is the better setting to deliver an appropriate education to students with visual impairments remains unanswered. For many decades, the majority of children with severe visual impairments who received a specialized education were educated at residential schools for the blind. Most states still to this day maintain these schools. However over the years, increased numbers of children with severe visual impairments are being educated at schools closer to their homes, including regular public schools. As a result, the number of students attending state residential schools has decreased. A discussion of the major arguments for these educational arrangements follow.

Arguments favoring local day schools or neighborhood schools include these:

❑ It is important that children live at home with their families.
❑ Segregation from normally seeing peers deprives children with visual impairments of important experiences needed for normal development.
❑ Larger local high schools can provide a wider range of curricular offerings than most small residential schools.

Arguments favoring residential schools include these:

❑ Only the residential school is in a direct position to influence what learning takes place between the end of one school day and the beginning of the next.
❑ The student can receive more individualized instruction than in the day or public schools where classes are often much larger.
❑ Education will be better when the teachers can devote their entire interest and training to working with persons who are visually impaired.
❑ If the number of children or the number of disabling conditions increases, those with visual impairments will become a neglected minority, eventually losing out on educational services and materials as money is spent elsewhere.

To ensure a nonrestrictive environment for persons with visual impairments, it is necessary (a) to provide placement alternatives that are flexible and varied and (b) to consider the skill level of the person when selecting the most appropriate setting. The needs of children and youth who are visually impaired must not be overlooked in the selection of educational placement.

Activities of Daily Living

In addition to the educational needs of individuals who are visually impaired, other practical considerations must be addressed. Many everyday activities sighted persons routinely perform may have to be done in different ways by those with limited or no vision. For example, the selection and matching up of clothes will have to be determined in alternative ways. Some individuals use Braille tags; others simply buy clothes of certain colors that always go together, then organize their closets accordingly. The acts of eating and drinking will be executed in modified ways. Telling time is accomplished by using specially designed watches with hands and raised dots (not Braille configurations) that can be touched. Many typical household appliances may also need to be modified.

TRENDS AND ISSUES

As is the case in all areas of exceptionality, many critical issues and emerging trends exist. Barraga and Erin (2001), in referring to the status of present knowledge and practices for individuals with visual challenges, note that "not all of the information available is being utilized fully, and numerous unresolved issues remain" (p. 163). They go on to identify seven critical issues that currently face the field of vision and visual impairments. These issues include the use of print versus Braille materials, acquisition of Braille literacy, the need for early intervention, complexities related to individuals with multiple disabilities, various aspects associated with orientation and mobility, appropriate placement and service delivery, and the use of technology.

We now elaborate on two of the issues raised by Barraga and Erin (2001): placement/service delivery and the use of technology. We also discuss two other topics of importance: accessibility and transition to adulthood.

Placement and Service Delivery

One issue that continues to receive discussion involves the best setting in which to teach students with visual challenges. Although a significant number of students are included in general education classrooms, some professionals and parents argue that other settings—often special school settings—are preferable. To a great degree, the issue is related to the severity of the visual problem, because many students with low vision who are able to use print materials are able to handle the demands of the general education setting.

The argument for special day schools and residential facilities gets stronger when the point is made that a cadre of specially trained teachers and staff and a centralization of specialized equipment and materials are needed for those with severe visual problems. Obviously, being included with other peers of the same age who do not have visual problems is not as easily achieved in this type of situation.

A related issue to the placement and service delivery question is the availability of support personnel who can assist general education teachers in meeting the needs of students with visual needs. Although most of the accommodations that might be needed for these students are not complex or difficult to implement, they may take time. Having support is an essential ingredient in meeting the needs of the student and the teacher.

Technology

The positive effects of recent technological developments on the lives of everyone are widespread. This includes both high- and low-tech applications. For instance, new tools have been developed to address many of the activities of daily living (ADL) such as talking watches and instruments that assist with a variety of kitchen tasks. Magnification devices now exist that allow individuals with vision problems to use regular print materials. Many periodicals are now available in large-print format.

For persons with visual challenges, certain recent technological developments have proven invaluable. Heward (2003) notes two examples of electronic and bio-medical technologies that might have a dramatic impact on the lives of individuals with visual impairments. The first one is an affordable, talking global positioning system (GPS) device. This type of device provides audible information that can be of great use in determining present location as well as identifying specific locations such as pay phones or restrooms. The second development is the possibility of artificial sight. Similar on a general level to cochlear implants, this biomedical technology involves implanting electrodes into the brain and connecting them to an artificial eye.

It is important to note that technology will not solve all of the issues that face individuals with visual challenges. As Hallahan and Kauffman (2003) suggest, at times technology actually creates some difficulties. They discuss the limitations of using a tape player when dealing with textual material. For example, skimming or scanning text for information is much more difficult when using a tape recording rather than print or Braille materials.

Accessibility

Although the issue of physical accessibility is improving, new issues have emerged in recent times. More Braille labels are now found in and on buildings throughout communities in which we live. More restaurants have made the effort to offer a Braille version of their menus. A variety of greeting cards are now available in formats that can be used by people with vision problems.

The new area that is presenting a real challenge for many persons who have visual problems is the Internet and other graphics-based materials like CDs. Many Web sites are not set up in a way that allows this population to use them appropriately. The graphic nature of most Web sites provides the central problem. Good Web design suggests that a text-based alternative be made available for all graphics included on a Web site. Many institutions (e.g., universities) require that all Web site development take into consideration the needs of individuals whose vision precludes them from using graphics-based information.

Transition to Adulthood

The adult outcomes for persons who are blind or who have low vision are not as good as those of us in the field would like. Hallahan and Kauffman (2003) remark that "many working-age adults with visual impairment are unemployed, and those who do work are often overqualified for the jobs they hold" (p. 369). In addition, they note that "achieving independence is often difficult" (p. 367).

What is needed is more systematic planning for the transition from school to living and working in the community. Such transition planning must be comprehensive (i.e., more than just vocational preparation) and it must start early (i.e., at least by middle school). Transition efforts should strive to involve actively the student and his or her family, taking into consideration family values, attitudes, and capabilities. The recommended and best practices identified in the transition literature apply to students with visual issues and their families. However, some special considerations are noteworthy for this group of students, as noted by Erin and Wolffe (1999).

SUGGESTIONS FOR WORKING WITH PEOPLE WHO HAVE VISUAL IMPAIRMENTS

The following suggestions have been divided into sections based on the nature of the recommendation.

General Suggestions

1. If a person with a visual impairment seems to be having problems (e.g., disorientation), ask whether you can be of any assistance. The worst that can happen is that she or he will say "no."
2. When acting as a sighted guide (a) let the person who is visually impaired take your arm rather than grabbing his or her arm and pushing and (b) approach steps and other similar environmental realities at right angles.
3. Assist persons in getting into a chair or a car by placing their hands in the appropriate location (i.e., on the back of the chair or on the roof of the car).
4. Be sure to talk directly to the person and not to other companions. This is especially important for people working in restaurants who sometimes avoid talking to persons with visual impairments.
5. When you enter or leave a room in which the only other person present is visually impaired/blind, let the other person know you have come in or are leaving.

Educational Suggestions

1. Seat students with visual impairments in settings that maximize any residual vision and that avoid glare from the sun or lighting.
2. Try to minimize the reliance on visual materials when lecturing and, if they are needed, explain them fully.
3. Be careful not to talk at too quick a pace for students who use a slate and stylus for taking notes in Braille.
4. Avoid using materials that have low-contrast features (such as purple ditto sheets) or glossy surfaces.
5. It may be necessary to allow students with visual impairments to take more breaks than usual. Their eyes may fatigue at quicker rates than students without visual impairments.
6. For students with visual impairments who can use printed materials, use large-print materials and broad-tipped markers that contrast with the color of your materials.
7. Encourage students to tape record your presentations and to use readers if available.
8. Utilize the services of Recordings for the Blind and Dyslexic. This organization has put much printed material on tape.

PONDER THESE

1. If a child without orientation and mobility skills entered your class, what specific things would you have to teach him in order for him to adapt successfully to the classroom? How might you and the children in your class have to change your habits or behaviors to facilitate the child's adaptation?
2. Imagine that you are a self-sufficient adult who is blind. How would you feel about receiving a special tax exemption simply because you are categorized as legally blind? Would you work for legislation providing special exemptions for persons categorized as disabled.

3. If you suddenly lost your vision, what special problems would you encounter in performing such everyday activities as eating, dressing and grooming, toileting, communicating, and getting around? What would you do for recreation?
4. Highlight the advantages and disadvantages of the following mobility techniques used by people who are blind or visually limited: sighted guide or cane.
5. Find out how a person with congenital blindness dreams.

REFERENCES

Barraga, N. C. (1986). Sensory perceptual development. In G. T. Scholl (Ed.), *Foundations of education for the blind youth: Theory to practice.* New York: American Federation for the Blind.

Barraga, N. C., & Erin, J. N. (2001). *Visual handicaps and learning: A developmental approach* (4th ed.). Austin, TX: PRO-ED.

Corn, A. L., & Rosenblum, L. P. (2000). *Finding wheels: A curriculum for nondrivers with visual impairments for gaining control of transportation needs.* Austin, TX: PRO-ED.

Erin, J. N., & Wolffe, K. E. (1999). *Transition issues related to students with visual disabilities.* Austin, TX: PRO-ED.

Hallahan, D. P., & Kauffman, J. M. (2003). *Exceptional learners: Introduction to special education* (9th ed.). Boston: Allyn & Bacon.

Heward, W. L. (2003). *Exceptional children: An introduction to special education.* Upper Saddle River, NJ: Merrill/Prentice Hall.

Livingston, R. (1986). Visual impairments. In N. G. Haring & L. P. McCormick (Eds.), *Exceptional children and youth* (4th ed., pp. 397–429). Upper Saddle River, NJ: Merrill/Prentice Hall.

Turnbull, R., Turnbull, A., Schank, M., Smith, S., & Leal, D. (2002). *Exceptional lives: Special education in today's schools* (3rd ed.). Upper Saddle River, NJ: Merrill/Prentice Hall.

U.S. Department of Education. (2001). *Twenty-third annual report to Congress on the implementation of the Education of the Handicapped Act.* Washington, DC: U.S. Government Printing Office.

CHAPTER 10

Deaf and Hard of Hearing

Barbara J. Dray
Lee Dray

At the age of 3, David began undergoing speech therapy. Each week his mother took him to the session, sat through as an observer, and then took him home. At the first visit, the therapist, who was aware of the fact that David had a little experience in speech reading (lip reading), chose to test the skills by initiating a simple command, "Close door." David watched the therapist's face intently but made no move to carry out the command. The command was repeated and, again, no response. This continued for a while until it became obvious that both the therapist and David were confused. Not daring to initiate other commands or try other words under the circumstances, the therapist suggested to the mother that perhaps David was disturbed by the new situation. Calmly looking into the therapist's eyes, the mother patiently suggested, "Try 'shut door.' "[1]

We were being trained to be teachers of deaf and hard of hearing children. We had completed our course work and were preparing to do student teaching at a residential school. We had been trained strictly in teaching speech and speech reading (lip reading) without the use of signs or gestures. However, students and staff at the school made considerable use of various forms of communication such as Signing Exact English, home signs, fingerspelling, and American Sign Language (ASL)—none of which we understood. A few of us were given assignments at the secondary level, which was particularly difficult since the use of signed communication at that level was considerable.

We were all having difficulty mastering different sign systems and ASL in addition to our student teaching assignments. To improve our ability, we practiced these skills by reading the Ann Landers column to our fellow student teachers in the evening. It was a laborious task and each day's column seemed to take forever.

During our learning period, one of my fellow student teachers returned to our dormitory at the end of an exhaustive day. She was embarrassed, concerned, and wondering aloud, "What do they think of me?" Only after considerable coaxing did the story come out. Her responsibility was to teach arithmetic. Because of her difficulty with communicating in sign and the inability of many students to speech read, she had devised a plan to use the overhead projector in writing out each problem for the students. Things went well until she indicated the operation of addition by writing the plus sign. This was greeted by a room full of blank faces. Try as she might, she was unable to make the children understand that they were to add. Exasperated, she finally decided to resort to fingerspelling the word "add." Suddenly the room was astir with children's snickering and laughing. What had she done? There in the middle of a lesson, standing before all those young attentive faces, she suddenly realized that she had just signed the letters "a-s-s"!

When my daughter was just 3 months old, she lost her hearing due to meningitis. At the time we lived in Mexico City, and had heard of an experimental procedure being used in the United States called a cochlear implant. We came to the United States to

[1]Special gratitude is extended to Lois Schoeny and Lynn Mann, experienced teachers of deaf and hard of hearing children, who kindly contributed some of the anecdotal material used in this chapter.

find out more about this procedure. At first, we were overwhelmed by the cost and the controversy. We even read about deaf people from Gallaudet University who were very angry and insistent that this surgery would rob children of their culture. We also visited the Central Institute for the Deaf in St. Louis, Missouri. We did not want to rob our daughter of an opportunity to connect with who she was as a deaf person. At the same time, being from Mexico, we were experiencing a loss of our own culture as the doctors strongly advised that we only speak English to our daughter, so she could learn to read lips and more easily transition into the larger society. We thought this made sense so we began to only use English with our children. In addition, we were strongly encouraged not to use signs, so that Stephanie would have to learn to lip read. To this day none of my children speak Spanish and for that I wonder about all that they are missing.

You might ask, why did we ultimately decide to go ahead with the cochlear implant, especially since we fully understood our options and the role of culture in developing a sense of identity? In the end, it was simple. I remember we had just met with a woman from Gallaudet. We were in a park and my daughter started running toward a busy street distracted in her playfulness. We kept yelling to her, we were yelling her name and she could not hear us and she kept running toward the busy street. Soon the cars were honking and my daughter kept going toward the street—she could not hear the horns honking. Finally the cars came to a screeching halt and I grabbed my daughter from the street. It was at that moment that we decided what it meant to hear. Hearing is more than communicating and culture; it is about safety too. We thought why not give her all the options possible; after all, she could always turn off the device if she chose not to hear. But at least she would have the option to live in both worlds, to benefit from her deafness and experience the safety of hearing. We knew that if we did not get the device then, she would have fewer options in the long run.[2]

I had just completed a university program in teaching children who are deaf, and the summer was mine to relax and prepare specifically for my first teaching experience in the fall. I was well armed with techniques and materials and very anxious to apply them to my class of early elementary children.

The first day of school finally arrived. Was I prepared! The room was ready, and I was at school well before the hour. My course work and student teaching experiences had taught me well that children who were prelingually deaf have difficulty in reading and communicating, so early intervention is key in developing these skills. I also knew that a part of teaching children who are deaf involves surrounding them with a world of language. I thought that while my children might be unable to hear me, I would greet each child at the door with a "good morning." As they entered the room, I positioned myself so that my face was clearly visible, and I carefully spoke and formed the words "good morning." I anxiously watched each small face for any sign of recognition or attempt at response. Response I got! To each greeting there was a well-spoken "Good morning, Mr. —." I had just introduced myself to my class, only to discover that they were not

[2]A special thanks to Christian Martin for sharing his story.

deaf, but were an excited, talking, hard of hearing group of children with mild to moderate hearing losses.

As a deaf adult looking back on my educational experiences, I have to say I wish they had been better. I began my learning in an all-oral approach classroom setting for 10 years, relying solely on what hearing I had left by using a hearing aid. From time to time, I tried using the phonic ear to help me out when I couldn't lip read the teachers, but because of social stigma, I refused to wear it most of the time. I also had a lot of "resource help" where I was taken out of class to see a speech therapist. It was interesting that I spent so much time learning how to speak yet so little on how to write! As I got older, I struggled understanding that there were several writing styles that we were supposed to learn. Basically, the way we communicate verbally is very different from how we write on paper. I even had a harder time trying to grasp other subjects such as math and science. The turning point was when I got to 10th grade; it took a great effort for me to keep up with the rest of the class. As the subject matter got more advanced, understanding my teachers via lip reading became problematic. As a result, I slowly faltered in grades. I began to wonder "How would I survive if I were going to go to college?"

That summer, I met some deaf people who exposed me to ASL. So, I decided I needed to learn ASL and "the other side" of being a deaf person. After much haggling with my mother, I was able to transfer to a school for the deaf and finish my high school education. It was extremely hard to succeed at the school for the deaf because I faced culture shock and rejection, but I managed. I was able to learn sign language and deaf culture there. This experience taught me the advantages and disadvantages of an exclusive oral versus a sign communication approach. As a result, I would have preferred to have been exposed to ASL first then learn English. In addition, speech therapy and audio equipment could have been minimized. Especially since, as an adult, I can no longer benefit from such devices. Rather, a more balanced approach that developed my identity as a deaf person along with tools for integration into the hearing world should have been utilized. It would have made my educational experiences easier, if not happier.[3]

BASIC CONCEPTS

In recent times the term *hearing impairment* has been phased out with the shift in the 1990s of disability law to place "people first" and assert what individuals with disabilities *can do* rather than what they *cannot do*. Deaf and hard of hearing individuals believe that their "deafness" and use of American Sign Language are a source of cultural identity. Thus hearing loss should not be viewed as a "problem to be fixed" but rather a cultural difference to be celebrated. In this

---

[3]This story was contributed by Lee Dray.

chapter we attempt to present a balanced perspective of the medical and cultural aspects of deaf and hard of hearing issues related to the education of such individuals.

Definition

Two perspectives should be considered when labeling individuals with hearing losses. The medical perspective labels individuals based on the type and severity of hearing loss and relies mainly on audiological information. The cultural perspective considers four major factors to labeling an individual: (a) audiological or the type and severity of hearing loss, (b) linguistic or proficiency in American Sign Language, (c) level of social participation within the deaf community, and (d) political ability to influence matters of the deaf community at local, state, and national levels (Baker-Shenk & Cokely, 1980).

Terminology

From an audiological perspective, a child who is born with little or no hearing, or whose loss occurs early in infancy before speech and language patterns are acquired, is said to be *prelingually deaf.* One who is born with normal hearing and loses hearing after language and speech are acquired is said to be *late-deafened* or *postlingually deaf. Hearing loss* is a generic term indicating an inability to hear that may range in severity from mild to profound. It consists of two categories, *deaf* and *hard of hearing.* A person who is *deaf* typically has moderate to profound hearing loss and does not benefit from the use of a hearing aid. A person who is *hard of hearing* is one who, generally with the use of a hearing aid, has enough residual hearing to process information through audition (Martin, 1994).

One would think that being deaf would automatically warrant membership in the Deaf community. That may be true if you are talking about the community as a whole, because of the characteristics of deafness and the experiences they have socially. However, Deaf community membership entails much more than being deaf. In fact, not only can an individual with a hearing loss belong, so can a hearing person. The deaf community (lowercase *d*) at large refers to individuals with hearing losses, their hearing family members, and the professionals who serve them. In all there are 11 groups within the deaf community. They are American Sign Language users, bilingual users of ASL and written English, minimal language users, oralists, early and late-deafened individuals, older adults with hearing loss, hard of hearing individuals, deaf-blind individuals, cochlear implantees, family members, and professionals who serve the deaf community (Hagemeyer, 2001). The Deaf community (uppercase *D*) refers to the 10 percent of deaf individuals who are audiologically deaf, primarily use American Sign Language, and are socially and politically involved in the Deaf community (Baker-Shenk & Cokely, 1980).

Prevalence

Approximately 1 million children under the age of 18 experience some sort of hearing loss in their lifetimes (Easterbrooks, 1999). It is estimated that 5 percent of the school-age population possesses some degree of hearing loss (Martin, 1994; Silverman & Lane, 1970). Of this 5 percent, approximately 0.13 percent of the school population was receiving special education services as reported by the Department of Education to Congress in the 1989 annual report. Of the school-age students with hearing losses, approximately 25 percent had other disabilities with the most (9 percent) having learning disabilities (Easterbrooks, 1999). Keep in mind that a great number of children with hearing losses *benefit from accommodation* but *do not require special education placement* because their losses do not negatively affect their ability to learn in an inclusive environment.

Let it be known that of people who are deaf or hard of hearing, only a small percent use American Sign Language because most are born to hearing parents. Thus, many deaf and hard of hearing individuals learn ASL and learn about their culture as adults, but this is slowly changing. In fact from 1988 to 1996 there was a 4 percent increase in the number of school-age children who use sign as their primary mode of communication (Easterbrooks, 1999).

Etiology

Hearing loss occurs when individuals cannot hear due to damage or blockage in the ear or of the associated nerves. Hearing losses can be temporary or permanent, mild to profound. Myklebust (1964) proposed that four variables be considered: (a) degree of loss, (b) age at onset, (c) cause, and (d) physical origin. The variables of degree of loss and age at onset have the most direct relevance for education. In a study of school-age children with hearing losses enrolled in special education programs, more than half had impaired hearing at birth (Myklebust, 1964). Reviews of the literature indicate 25 to 50 percent of all childhood deafness is due to heredity (Hoemann & Briga, 1981). This figure is explained to a certain degree by the high incidence of marriage among people who have hearing losses.

The ear itself consists of three parts: the outer ear, the middle ear, and the inner ear (see Figure 10.1). Damage or malfunction in the middle and/or inner ear can result in hearing loss. The middle ear consists of four parts: the tympanic membrane (ear drum), the malleus (hammer), the incus (anvil), and the stapes (stirrup). These organs transmit sound waves through vibration to the inner ear. The inner ear consists of the vestibular mechanism made up of the semicircular canals (related to balance) and the cochlea, which is involved in hearing. It is the cochlea that receives the vibrations from the middle ear and transmits a signal to the brain via the auditory nerve.

Figure 10.1
The Ear

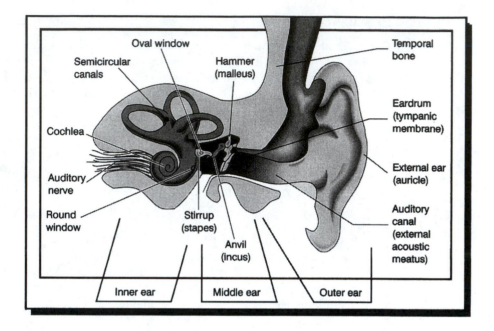

Damage or blockage in the outer or middle ear is considered a *conductive* hearing loss and it is possible with the use of surgery and/or assistive devices for hearing to be restored. Inner ear or nerve damage that results in hearing loss is called *sensorineural* hearing loss and can be a more serious, irreversible type of hearing loss.

Conductive hearing loss can result from a variety of causes. Excess ear wax and placement of small objects in the ear by children are frequent causes of conductive hearing loss, as is otitis media, an inflammation of the middle ear or, as more commonly referred to, an earache (Davis, 1970). Pregnant women contracting rubella during the first trimester frequently give birth to children with sensorineural hearing loss (Northern & Downs, 1974). Some childhood diseases that involve viral infections of the upper respiratory tract also can cause hearing loss. Other causes include the use of certain antibiotics (McGee, 1968), excessive exposure to loud noises, viral infections of the pregnant mother prior to the child's birth, and Rh incompatibility (Davis, 1970).

Assessment

Although parents, teachers, and other key individuals in a child's life may suspect that a hearing loss exists, it is usually an audiologist who conducts the more accurate and elaborate assessment procedures. As Hallahan and Kauffman (2003) have pointed out, there are three general types of hearing tests: pure-tone audiometry, speech audiometry, and specialized tests designed for use with very young children.

Pure-tone audiometry assesses an individual's hearing sensitivity (loudness) at various frequencies. Intensity of sound is measured in decibel (dB) units and frequency is measured in Hertz (Hz) units. The intensities of sounds that we come into contact with every day range from 0 dB (the zero hearing threshold) to well over 100 dB (very loud sounds like auto horns). The frequencies of most speech sounds that are important to humans fall between 125 and 8,000 Hz. Pure-tone tests can be administered either by earphones (air conduction) or by placing a vibrating device on the person's forehead (bone conduction). By administering these two types of tests, an audiologist can determine if the hearing loss is conductive or sensorineural.

Speech audiometry is a test of whether a person can understand speech. At the heart of this procedure is an attempt to determine at which decibel level the examinee is able to understand speech (known as the *speech reception threshold*).

Inherent in these assessment techniques is the examinee's ability to respond to the stimulus situation. For very young children, this voluntary response may not be possible. Two techniques that have been developed for utilization with this age group include play audiometry and evoked-response audiometry (Hallahan & Kauffman, 2003).

Other *specialized audiometric tests* are used with individuals who have multiple disabilities or who have severe disabilities. These tests do not require a specific behavioral response from the child and therefore can facilitate assessment.

Tympanometry is an auditory test that yields information related to the resistance of the tympanic membrane or its ability to conduct vibrations into the middle ear mechanism. Stapedial reflex testing employs pure-tone signals and measures the reflex response of the stapedial muscle to these signals. Both of these auditory tests use an impedance audiometer as the instrument of evaluation. An additional auditory assessment technique, which requires the use of an electroencephalograph and a computer, is the evolved response technique. This technique is used to examine changes in brain wave patterns in response to specific sound stimuli.

CHARACTERISTICS

Hearing people have many myths and misconceptions about deaf and hard of hearing children. Some of the most common are (a) children who are deaf cannot hear, (b) children who cannot hear cannot talk, and (c) children who are deaf have cognitive disabilities. These three notions have direct educational and social implications; therefore, they will receive focal attention in this chapter.

Children Who Are Deaf Typically Can Hear.   Children with a profound hearing loss may still have some ability to hear. They may be able to hear loud noises such as automobile horns or slamming doors. The ability to hear even this much may provide vital information to alert or warn the child of danger. Of all children with hearing losses, only small percentages are profoundly deaf. Many have enough usable hearing to develop language. The typical breakdown of degrees of hearing losses is as follows:

Classification	Degree of Decibel Loss
Mild	26–54
Moderate	55–69
Severe	70–89
Profound	90+

There are two ways in which children with hearing losses can be taught to use their residual hearing to process auditory information. First, they can be taught to understand and use what sounds they can hear. Then, if the hearing loss is such that the individual would benefit from amplification of sound, they can be fitted with a hearing aid. However, it is worth noting that hearing aids amplify all sounds in the environment, which can be distracting. Also, hearing aids do not affect a person's ability to process sounds, and if a hearing loss distorts sound the hearing aid will not correct this and may make the distortion worse. As a result, although these devices provide a useful function to many people with hearing losses, they do have limitations. For these reasons, it is important that children with hearing losses be identified at an early age so that they may benefit from all possible interventions.

Children Who Are Deaf Typically Talk.   In language acquisition, receptive language precedes expressive language. Children who are profoundly deaf, because they cannot receive language aurally, are hindered in their expression of oral language. However, children with varying degrees of hearing losses are able to learn and communicate.

With amplification and auditory training, children who are hard of hearing can usually use their hearing to develop spoken language. They can and do talk. Some children who are deaf, with the benefit of little or no residual hearing, are able to develop speech reading (lip reading) and some speaking skills. Although some deaf people are very skilled at speech reading, others are not and skill level may vary because many speech sounds have identical mouth movements (such as *p* and *b*) and most only see 35 percent of what is said in conversation (Baker-Shenk & Cokely, 1980). The acquisition of clear, intelligible speech by the child born profoundly deaf is usually a laborious task. Both receptive and expressive language can be developed through the use of sign language. American Sign Language is its own language system that includes thousands of conceptual signs; it is not a word-for-word representation of the spoken English and is syntactically and semantically different. Offshoots of ASL were developed to help deaf people learn English but many deaf people believe that these systems were created to accommodate the hearing in teaching English to deaf and hard of hearing people. Other sign systems include Signing Exact English (SEE 2), Rochester Method, Cued Speech, Linguistics of Visual English (LOVE), Seeing Exact English (SEE 1), and Morphemic Sign System (Nover, 1995). Fingerspelling includes individual finger signs for each letter of the alphabet and numbers from 1 to 10 as shown in Figure 10.2.

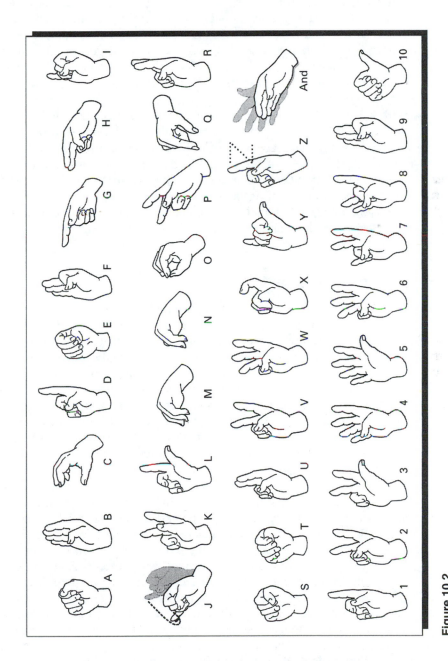

Figure 10.2
Finger Signs for the Alphabet and Numbers 1–10

Children Who Are Deaf Typically Do Not Have Cognitive Disabilities.   The measurement of intelligence has traditionally relied heavily on language, and language is precisely the area of greatest concern for the child with a serious hearing loss. Both professionals and laypersons have wrongly inferred that because persons who are deaf or hard of hearing evidence a spoken or aural language deficit there may also be an intellectual or cognitive deficit. A classic, broader conceptualization of intelligence includes considerations of nonverbal or performance aspects (Myklebust, 1964). Other theorists have addressed these aspects of intelligence as well (Gardner, 1983). With language factors accounted for, the intelligence of deaf and hard of hearing children approximates the norm for hearing children (McConnell, 1973; Wiley, 1971).

Observations of behavior of individuals who are profoundly deaf may also give the impression of retardation. A child who fails to respond to another's voice, fails to respond to very loud noises, demonstrates problems in balance, or produces unrecognizable vocalizations may mistakenly be judged as mentally retarded. These behaviors alone or in combination actually may indicate serious hearing problems. The alert observer should have the child checked for hearing loss.

INTERVENTIONS

Programs for deaf and hard of hearing children should include some or all of the following elements: (a) early identification, (b) parent counseling and participation, (c) concept development, (d) preschool education, (e) American Sign Language, (f) sign systems, (g) speech and auditory training, and (h) aspects of deaf culture.

Early identification of the child with a hearing loss is essential in order to initiate language and concept development both through visual communication such as American Sign Language and auditory training or learning to interpret meaning from sound. Gentile (1972) found that students of high school age who are deaf averaged fourth-grade level on a test of comprehension and averaged sixth-grade level on a test of computation. Early and intensive intervention in the area of language development is imperative if the deaf or hard of hearing child is to succeed in all academic areas. Assistance in providing concrete hearing and language experiences can serve to enrich the child's total fund of information, enhancing intellectual and social growth. Parents should participate directly in providing these experiences.

The development of basic social skills is a complex interaction between the individual with a hearing loss and the individuals in their environment (Hoemann & Briga, 1981). Thus, matters are further complicated because deaf children have a difficult time communicating their feelings of isolation, rejection, and frustration (Meadow, 1975). As a result the use of visuals such as sign language, posters with pictures of different emotional faces, or a picture dictionary can help facilitate understanding. Emphasis on inclusion can help foster healthy social and interpersonal relationships.

Children who are deaf and hard of hearing need activities that contribute to conceptual development. Skills should include comparisons of sizes, shapes, and colors of objects (Evelsizer, 1972). An understanding of these concepts will increase the opportunities for meaningful experiences in which there is variety, novelty, and occasion for selection. Such experiences can contribute to the development of divergent thinking and evaluation. Hearing loss most directly and generally affects two areas, divergent thinking and evaluation (Myklebust, 1964).

For a long time there has been great controversy over whether educators should rely strictly on oral language (oralism) or should use sign language when teaching children who are deaf. Unfortunately, the issue has not, as yet, been resolved. There has been a trend toward a combined use of written/oral English methods and sign language in a procedure identified as the *Bilingual/Bicultural* approach. Schools decide how and when to alternate the use of sign language only and oral methods only in the classroom.

In the past, combined use often was confused as Total Communication. In reality, *Total Communication* is a philosophy that encompasses all components of oral/auditory methods, sign systems, and ASL. In essence, Total Communication relies on any form or communication mode that facilitates mutual understanding between persons. Most proponents of Total Communication support the notion of establishing the program as early in a child's life as possible to establish and reinforce the basic communication pathways quickly.

In Deaf Education, teacher-training programs throughout the United States need to better prepare educators by including courses such as Deaf Culture and History, ASL studies, and a variety of literature on deaf issues. Educators need to learn how to add Deaf Studies information into the curriculum, use an educational interpreter, and help provide parents and caregivers with unbiased information on a range of topics to make informed decisions about their child's education. Educators should learn how to assist parents and caregivers in gaining specific skills on how to participate effectively in their child's IEP meetings (Hallan, 2002). Finally, in public or residential K–12 schools, ASL should be encouraged to promote literacy development. Efforts should be made to bring families of deaf children together with members of the local deaf community to work with school staff. Deaf staff members from a variety of cultural backgrounds should be viewed as equal team members (Hallan, 2002).

TRENDS AND ISSUES

Throughout history, deaf and hard of hearing people have faced many struggles in asserting their cognitive abilities because of the complexity of this "disability" with relation to the communicative nature that creates a disadvantage in an otherwise "hearing" society (U.S. Department of Education, 1992). However, in 1988 during the milestone Deaf President Now (DPN) protest, the Deaf community raised national awareness of identity, language, and culture of the Deaf. These days, various American Deaf communities are teaming up with international Deaf communities in an attempt to gain recognition and respect worldwide. Deaf people are rising up more than ever in leadership and professional roles to make social contributions in the mainstream (hearing) society (Prickett, 2002).

Since DPN, American Sign Language gained status as a foreign language in 1994 and is now offered at colleges and universities in 36 states (Jacobowitz, 1996). Thus, the utilization of ASL in education is on the rise with 22 states offering ASL at the elementary level, and 42 states at the secondary level (Jacobowitz, 1996). In 1999 a Modern Language Association survey found that enrollments in ASL classes rose from 4,000 in 1995 to 11,000 in 1998 (Freedman, 2002). As a result, it is imperative that all future teachers and/or professionals working with deaf and hard of hearing individuals be fluent in ASL as well as other sign systems in order to fully understand and relate to Deaf culture.

Educators of the deaf and hard of hearing not only need to learn about Deaf culture and become proficient in ASL, but they also need to be aware of technological advances. In addition to text telephone devices or TTY and closed captioning technology, deaf and hard of hearing people are reaping benefits from the use of computers, pagers, and personal digital assistants that incorporate programs such as e-mail and instant messaging. These devices are equivalent to the cell phones used by hearing people. Telecommunications Relay Services (TRS) offered by major phone companies have gone nationwide. TRS provides services for both deaf and hearing people as a way to communicate via the telephone. This particular service enables standard voice telephone users to talk to people who use a TTY and or vice versa. TRS uses operators called *communication assistants* to facilitate telephone calls between the two parties (U.S. Federal Communications Commission, 2003). Also video conferencing is becoming a popular medium. It can be used on a computer or a TV.

Finally, it is important to be knowledgeable about the latest and most contentious assistive hearing device, the cochlear implant, and its implications. Pros and cons are being voiced by both the medical community and the Deaf community. The question is, do parents have an ethical right to decide if their child should receive an implant? And if so, would these parents be sentencing their children to grow up in a netherworld without deaf or hearing roots? Ultimately, it appears likely that the cochlear implant is here to stay, but it is a huge undertaking for one to be responsible for providing accurate and complete information about every aspect of the process so that parents have a realistic understanding of what implants can and cannot achieve, and what the surgery and follow-up therapy entail (Byrd, 1999).

SUGGESTIONS FOR WORKING WITH DEAF AND HARD-OF-HEARING STUDENTS

Tips for communicating with a deaf person:

1. Face the person and maintain eye contact.
2. Be mindful of lighting and visual distractions.

3. Be sure mouth is in full view.
4. Speak slowly and clearly in a natural way.
5. Get person's attention by waving hands or tapping him or her on the shoulder.

Tips for the classroom:

1. Before class begins, determine optimal seating for communication and participation. Make sure that the student has full view of the interpreter, the teacher, and others in the classroom. You may want to consider placing desks in a circle or horseshoe formation.
2. Provide an outline of the lesson so that the student can follow along and take notes as needed.
3. During the lesson, check to be sure students are attending and following along.
4. Avoid standing in front of sunny windows and do not turn off all of the lights for video or overhead presentations.
5. Set up guidelines for acknowledging and recognizing participation from class members.
6. Use visual aids and demonstrations to teach new concepts.
7. Avoid talking while writing on the chalkboard or during video presentations.
8. Write homework assignments and reminders on the board and discuss with the students.

Use of interpreters:

1. Before class begins, introduce yourself to the interpreter prior to the lesson. Explain unique terminology, vocabulary, and/or concepts. Provide the interpreter with an outline of the lesson or daily activities and any handouts or written material that will be used by the students.
2. Determine optimal seating so that the student may participate in class discussion. As well, set up seating for the interpreter(s) next to or near the student so that the student may clearly see the interpreter and speaker. Ensure the lighting is optimal for interpreting so that the student can see the interpreter. For example, keep some of the lights on during video or overhead presentations.
3. Since interpreting occurs simultaneous to oral communication be sure to speak clearly in a natural way. Avoid distractions around your mouth so keep hands away from mouth, do not chew gum, and trim facial hair. Allow one person to speak at a time so that the interpreter may signal a speaker change and responses to the new speaker. Provide short breaks as needed (about every hour) so that the interpreter and student may rest, because interpreting can be very tiring.

PONDER THESE

1. Think of some methods you could use to determine the possibility of a hearing loss in young children.
2. Discuss the pros and cons of teaching communication skills to people who are deaf using the following methods:
   Oral only
   Manual communication (e.g., signing and fingerspelling, *not* including ASL)
   Bilingual/Bicultural approach
3. Investigate the impact of technology on the lives of deaf and hard of hearing individuals. Consider areas such as these:
   Use of telephones
   Computer technology
   Medical advances (e.g., cochlear implants)
4. List the major concerns that arise for a person with a profound hearing loss and list suggestions for integration in the following situations:
   Driving
   Staying at a hotel or motel
   Responding to someone knocking at the door
   Crossing the street
   Playing softball

INFORMATION/RESOURCES

1. American Society for Deaf Children
   P. O. Box 3355
   Gettysburg, PA 17325
   http://www.deafchildren.org
2. Captioned Media Program
   National Association for the Deaf
   1447 E. Main Street
   Spartansburg, SC 29307-2240
   http://www.cfv.org
3. National Association for the Deaf
   814 Thayer Avenue, Suite 250
   Silver Spring, MD 20910-4500
   http://www.nad.org
4. National Captioning Institute
   1900 Gallows Road, Suite 3000
   Vienna, VA 22182
   http://www.ncicap.org
5. National Deaf Education Network and Clearinghouse
   Gallaudet University
   800 Florida Avenue, NE
   Washington, DC 20002-3695
   http://clerccenter.gallaudet.edu/infotogo/index.html
6. Technology in Education Can Empower Deaf Students (TecEds)
   Gallaudet University
   800 Florida Avenue, NE
   Washington, DC 20002-3695
   http://clerccenter.gallaudet.edu/TecEds

REFERENCES

Baker-Shenk, C., & Cokely, D. (1980). *American Sign Language: A teacher's resource text on grammar and culture.* Washington, DC: Gallaudet University Press.

Byrd, T. (1999, Fall). Cochlear implants: Where do you stand? *Gallaudet Today,* pp.16–25.

Davis, H. (1970). Abnormal hearing and deafness. In H. Davis & S. R. Silverman (Eds.), *Hearing and deafness* (3rd ed., pp. 87–146). New York: Holt, Rinehart & Winston.

Easterbrooks, S. (1999). Improving practices for students with hearing impairments. *Exceptional Children, 65*(4), 537–554.

Evelsizer, R. L. (1972). Hearing impairment in the young child. In A. H. Adams (Ed.), *Threshold learning abilities: Diagnostic and instructional procedures for specific early learning disabilities.* Upper Saddle River, NJ: Prentice Hall.

Freedman, D. (2002, May 13). Enrollment in sign language classes swells. *The Oak Ridger.*

Retrieved January 9, 2003, from http://www. oakridger.com/stories/051302/stt_0513020026. html

Gardner, H. (1983). *Frames of mind.* New York: Basic Books.

Gentile, A. (1972). Academic achievement test results or a national testing program for hearing impaired students: 1971. *Annual Survey of Hearing Impaired Children and Youth.* Gallaudet College Office Demographic Studies, Ser. D, No. 9.

Hagemeyer, A. L. (2001). *The red notebook.* Silver Spring, MD: Library for Deaf Action.

Hallahan, D. P., & Kauffman, J. M. (2003). *Exceptional children: Introduction to special education* (9th ed.). Upper Saddle River, NJ: Merrill/Prentice Hall.

Hallan, M. (2002). Creating partnerships with families: In national forum educators and parents discuss roles, hammer out strategies. *Odyssey, 3*(1), 5–12.

Hoemann, J. W., & Briga, J. S. (1981). Hearing impairments. In J. M. Kauffman & D. P. Hallahan (Eds.), *Handbook of special education* (pp. 222–247). Upper Saddle River, NJ: Merrill/Prentice Hall.

Jacobowitz, L. (1996). President's message: State recognition of ASL as a foreign language. *American Sign Language Teachers Association Newsletter, 2*(1), 3.

Martin, F. N. (1994). *Introduction to audiology* (5th ed.). Upper Saddle River, NJ: Prentice Hall.

McConnell, F. (1973). Children with hearing disabilities. In L. M. Dunn (Ed.), *Exceptional children in the schools: Special education in transition* (2nd ed., pp. 351–410). New York: Holt, Rinehart & Winston.

McGee, T. M. (1968). Ototoxic antibiotics. *Volta Review, 70,* 667–671.

Meadow, K. P. (1968). Early manual communication in relation to the deaf child's intellectual, social, and communicative functioning. *American Annals of the Deaf, 113,* 29–41.

Meadow, K. P. (1975). Development of deaf children. In E. M. Hetherington (Ed.), *Review of child development research* (Vol. 5, pp. 441–508). Chicago: University of Chicago Press.

Myklebust, H. R. (1964). *The psychology of deafness: Sensory deprivation, learning and adjustment* (2nd ed.). New York: Grune & Stratton.

Northern, J. L., & Downs, M. P. (1974). *Hearing in children.* Baltimore: Williams and Wilkins.

Nover, S. M. (1995). Politics and language: American Sign Language and English in deaf education. In C. Lucas (Ed.), *The sociolinguistics of the Deaf communities* (pp. 109–163). Washington, DC: Gallaudet University.

Prickett, R. (2002, Fall). How it happened: The making of the Deaf Way II. *Gallaudet Today,* pp. 4–9.

Silverman, S. R., & Lane, H. S. (1970). Deaf children. In H. Davis and S. R. Silverman (Eds.), *Hearing and deafness* (3rd ed., pp. 433–482). New York: Holt, Rinehart & Winston.

U.S. Department of Education. (1989). *Eleventh annual report to Congress on the implementation of P. L. 94–142: The Education for All Handicapped Children Act.* Washington, DC: U.S. Government Printing Office.

U.S. Department of Education. (1992, October 30). Deaf students education services; policy guidance; notice. *Federal Register, 57*(211).

U.S. Federal Communications Commission. (2003). FCC consumer facts: Telecommunications Relay Services. Retrieved January 9, 2003, from http://www.fcc.gov/cgb/consumerfacts/trs.html

Vernon, M., & Koh, S. D. (1970). Early manual communication and deaf children's achievement. *American Annals of the Deaf, 115,* 527–536.

Wiley, J. A. (1971). A psychology of auditory impairment. In W. M. Cruickshank (Ed.), *Psychology of exceptional children and youth* (3rd ed., pp. 414–439). Upper Saddle River, NJ: Prentice Hall.

CHAPTER 11

Speech and Language Disorders

Our anecdotes to this point have depicted what it is like to work with people who are disabled. We have not attempted to convey directly what it is like to have a disability. Almost everyone has at some time or another experienced some embarrassment, guilt, frustration, anxiety, or pride stemming from verbal interaction with others. Few of us, however, have felt the overwhelming emotions that accompany severe difficulties in oral communication. Listening and talking are such ubiquitous social experiences that we tend to underestimate the handicap that can result from even minor speech deviations. We find it relatively easy to form an empathic relationship with an individual who has an obvious physical, emotional, or mental disorder, but we tend to feel that the individual with a speech disorder suffers no lasting penalty and could easily overcome the difficulty with a little determination. Consequently, we have chosen the following anecdotes to call your attention to the feelings and problems of children with speech and language disorders and their families.

My son, John, was always a delightful child. From the time he began to toddle around the house, his wonderful personality and intellect were apparent. It wasn't until he was approaching his second birthday that my wife and I became concerned. He rarely spoke. He followed directions and seemed to understand, but rarely tried to communicate, and when he did, it was in gibberish. Our family doctor told us "he's just a little slow in the development of oral language." But there was little improvement over time.

As John grew older and began to articulate clearly, the problem became more worrisome to us. When he spoke, his words were out of order, and his use of nouns and pronouns was, at best, inconsistent. Statements like "He's happy 'cause his am going" and "I'll maybe get go a new toy" were typical of his statements. After consulting with a speech clinician at a local university, the results of a language evaluation revealed that John had a language disorder. John had, in essence, learned a set of language rules that differed significantly from those of English. For John, the syntax and semantic rules of English either did not apply or were being modified in his utterances.

My wife and I were devastated. Something was wrong with our child, and we couldn't do anything about it. We began months of long, grueling language therapy with John, both in the speech clinic and through carryover at home.

Finally, John's language improved to the point that it was within "normal" limits. However, to this day he has reading problems (though his schoolwork in other areas is excellent). I can see his frustration, and I know how some teachers and students regard him. It hurts me so. They only see his problems. They'll never see beyond them to the wonderful person he really is.

I must be pretty tough because I'm not in the bug house. The constant experience of starting to say something and never having it come out when I want it to should have driven me crazy long ago. I can't even say my own name. Once in a while I get a little streak of easy speech and then wham, I'm plugged, tripped up, helpless, making silent mouth openings like a goldfish. It's like trying to play the piano with half the keys sticking.

I can't even get used to it because sometimes I can fear a word and out it pops; then again when I am expecting smooth speech and everything's going all right, boom I'm stuck. It sure's exasperating. (p. 72)[1]

Even when I was a little girl I remember being ashamed of my speech. And every time I opened my mouth I shamed my mother. I can't tell you how awful it felt. If I talked, I did wrong. It was that simple. I kept thinking I must be awful bad to have to talk like that. I remember praying to God and asking him to forgive me for whatever it was I must have done. I remember trying hard to remember what it was, and not being able to find it. (p. 61)[1]

The most wonderful thing about being able to pronounce my sounds now is that people aren't always saying "What? What's that?" I bet I've heard that fifty thousand times. Often they'd shout at me as though I were deaf and that usually made me talk worse. Or they'd answer "Yes" when that just didn't make sense. I still occasionally find myself getting set for these reactions and steeling myself against them and being surprised when other people just listen. (p. 72)[1]

After I came to high school from the country, everybody laughed at me whenever I tried to recite. After that I pretended to be dumb and always said "I don't know" when the teacher called on me. That's why I quit school. (p. 42)[1]

Therapist: *When you were stuck that time, what were your feelings?*
Subject: *I don't know. All, All mmmmmmmmmmmmixed up, I ggggguess.*
Therapist: *You probably felt helpless . . . sort of as though your mouth had frozen shut. . . .*
Subject: *And, and I cccccouldn't open it, Yeah.*
Therapist: *You couldn't open it. It was almost as though you had lost the ability to move a part of yourself when you wanted to. . . . Sure must be frustrating. . . .*
Subject: *Sssure is. BBBBBurns me up. I, I, I, jjjust hate mmmmm . . . Oh skip it. . . . I don't know.*
Therapist: *(Acceptingly) It almost makes you hate yourself when you get stuck like that.*
Subject: *Yeah, dih-dih-sigusted with mmmmmmyself and everything else . . .*
Therapist: *Some stutterers even find themselves hating the person they are talking to.*
Subject: *Yyyyeah, I,I,I,I, I wwwwwas huh-huh-huh-hating yyyyyyyyou just then.*
Therapist: *Uh huh. I know.*
Subject: *(Blurting it out) How, how come you know all these th-things? (pp. 384–385)[1]*

When I was 15, I participated with a group of five other boys in a stuttering therapy program. All of us in the group had a common problem—Mrs. Shinn, the lady who worked in our favorite ice cream parlor. We'd go into the store to order a strawberry cone and say, "I want a st-st-st-st-st- . . . ," and before we could finish the word she'd hand us a strawberry cone. Sometimes she'd even say, "Yeah, I know, strawberry." Well, that's pretty irritating to have someone think she can always predict what you're going to say. It's even worse when someone finishes a sentence for you. Much as we liked the ice cream she dished out, we all started to hate old Mrs. Shinn. So we thought of a way to teach her a lesson. One day we went into the ice cream parlor one after another. Each of us said the same thing. "I want a st-st-st-st-st- . . ." and just as Mrs. Shinn was about to hand us the strawberry cone we finished, " . . . st-st-st-chocolate cone." From that day on, she always let us finish our orders before she started to dip.[2]

BASIC CONCEPTS

Speech and language disorders are particularly complex problems. For this reason speech-language therapists typically receive rigorous training and are required to meet high professional standards. Correction of speech and language disorders is carried out in many different, often multidisciplinary settings. Therefore, in many universities, training programs for speech/language pathologists are located in departments other than special education, such as departments of speech pathology and audiology. Basic knowledge of speech and language disorders and their correction is important for all professionals working with persons who have disabilities, because many individuals with other primary handicaps, such as mental retardation and emotional disturbance, also experience difficulties in speech and language.

DEFINITIONAL PERSPECTIVE

Often the concepts of communication, language, and speech are confused. It is imperative for professionals and laypeople to employ the proper use of these terms. Hallahan and Kauffman (2003) aptly differentiate these concepts:

> *Speech and language are tools used for purposes of communication. Communication requires . . . sending . . . and receiving . . . meaningful messages. . . . Language is the communication of ideas through an arbitrary system of symbols that are used according to semantic and grammatical rules. . . . Speech is the behavior of forming and sequencing the sounds of oral language.* (p. 264)

We can consider speech as a part of oral language, in a subcategory of the more generic use of the term *language.* In this chapter, we will be most concerned with oral language—a system of communication incorporating spoken sounds.

---

[2]This anecdote was contributed by C. Lee Woods, Ph.D.

Unfortunately, the identification of a speech or language impairment can be a matter of subjective judgment. Just how much a language or speech pattern must differ from normal before it becomes a disorder often depends on characteristics of both the listener and the speaker. For instance, a mother having grown accustomed to her 9-year-old's unusual articulation may overlook the fact that the child's speech is unintelligible to his peers. Moreover, whether a speech difference is considered a disorder depends on the age of the speaker. That is, in a 3-year-old, faulty articulation is normal and certainly would not be thought of as a disorder, as it might be for an older child. Van Riper (1978) notes that abnormal speech is so different from normal speech that it (a) draws the listener's attention to itself rather than to what is being said and (b) interferes with communication, or (c) it produces distress in the speaker or the listener. Defective speech is conspicuous, unintelligible, or uncomfortable.

In spite of difficulties involved in precisely defining speech and language disorders, usable definitions have been developed by speech-language pathologists. Many professionals (Haynes and Pindzola, 1998; Hulit and Howard, 2002; McLean, 1978) note that the identification and classification of communication disorders, while not an easy task, is usually based on two comparisons:

> *Judgments of which children should be considered to have a communication disorder requiring special education or clinical programming are made from two basic comparisons. The first is a comparison of the child's language with the standard language form of the culture. The second is a comparison of the child's language with the language of other children at the same age level.* (McLean, 1978, p. 271)

PREVALENCE

It was reported by the U.S. Department of Education (2002) that 2.3 percent of the 2000–2001 school population was determined eligible for speech services. However, most authorities estimate that 5 percent of school-age students have some type of speech handicap. The estimated breakdown (of school-age population) of specific speech problems follows:

Phonological disorders	1 percent–3 percent
Voice disorders	1 percent–2 percent
Stuttering	Less than 1 percent

The prevalence of language disorders is difficult to estimate because there are no satisfactory figures for this impairment at present. The issue of determining a prevalence figure for language disorders becomes compounded by the significant overlap of language problems and learning disabilities.

ETIOLOGY

The cause of speech and language disorders may be either biological or functional. *Biological* etiologies involve known neurological deficits or structural malformations such as cleft palate, cleft lip, enlarged adenoids, hearing impairment, cerebral palsy, damage to various muscles that are used in articulation (dysarthria) or phonation, deformities of the vocal organs, and ear infections, to name a few.

Most disorders of speech and language, however, have no known biological cause and are, therefore, termed *functional* disorders. This implies that there is a definite functional loss of a certain ability, but it cannot be attributed to any organic cause. Functional disorders may include articulation and voice problems, stuttering, and specific language disabilities. Many theories, attempting to explain the etiology of various problems, have been offered, but no single explanation is generally accepted at this time.

CHARACTERISTICS

The American Speech and Hearing Association (1993) classifies communication disorders as either organic (physically based) or functional (environmentally based). However, to fully understand how language is disordered, we must know what constitutes normal language.

The development of language begins with the early cry of an infant and progresses through stages of differentiated crying, babbling, vocal play, single words, holophrastic speech (a single word representing a whole phrase or sentence), syntactical utterances, multiword expressions, and sentences. Recently, there has been some discussion of whether language comprehension precedes language production. The prevailing attitude seems to favor an interactive mechanism. That is, children progress through these stages in a predictable manner; however, this process is very complex and problems can occur. Because language acquisition is a very complex process, there are conflicting theories of language development. Individuals such as Chomsky, Skinner, Bloom, Nelson, and Bruner all have theories to explain the hows and whys of language development (Schiefelbusch & McCormick, 1981). Research does not yet conclusively support any single orientation; we must therefore await the further investigation of this complex phenomenon.

Language problems occur in the following areas: oral, written, and even gestural. However, our concern with the various aspects of oral language disabilities relates to Hull and Hull's (1973) description: "Disability in oral language occurs when an individual is unable to comprehend meaningful ideas which have been spoken or when he is unable to use spoken words to effectively express meaningful ideas" (p. 303). In other words, this individual is not effectively able to use the elemental symbols of oral language.

Naremore (1980) notes that in thinking about different types of language disorders one should keep in mind these three things: (a) the language and nonlanguage behaviors a child imitates, because a lot of language learning involves learning to imitate; (b) the language the child comprehends, because receptive language (understanding what is heard) is so important in early learning; and (c) the language the child uses spontaneously, because effective communication in natural situations is the ultimate goal of language remediation.

In addition to these three points, Naremore (1980) suggests four classes of disordered language. First, some children do not develop receptive and/or expressive language by the age of 3 years as most children (Bangs, 1982). The *absence of language* may be due to deafness, brain damage, mental retardation, or childhood psychosis. Regardless of the cause, the important thing is that the child shows no signs of understanding or being able to use language. These children need direct instruction in how to make speech sounds and say words. They also need to be given many opportunities to hear and use language. And these opportunities must be structured to teach the child how language is used for communication—to influence the environment for a desired result (for example, to get something the child wants).

A second class of language disorder is *qualitatively different language.* That is, the child may make speech sounds and even have an extensive vocabulary but not know how to use language to communicate effectively. Speech may be echolalic (parrot-like repetition of what is heard) or just not make sense or not accurately convey meaning. Such difficulties may have any number of causes, and often the causes are not really known in a specific case. Whatever the cause, a child with qualitatively different language needs remedial instruction in the *functions* of language—how it is used in social contexts (i.e., pragmatic language) and how it is related to thinking and behaving.

Delayed language, a third type of disorder, means that the child appears to be acquiring language by the normal processes and in the normal sequence, but at a significantly later age than most children. Finally, *interrupted language development*—the child has acquired language normally but loses it due, for example, to hearing impairment or brain damage—is another class of disorder. Again, the cause of the language disorder may or may not be known. Certainly, language instruction may be different for a hearing child than for one who is deaf. But, in any case, a remedial language training program must take into account what the child knows about, how the child talks about those things, and how the child communicates his wishes, intentions, demands, feelings, and so on (see Schiefelbusch & McCormick, 1981).

SPEECH IMPAIRMENT

"Speech is defective when it is ungrammatical, unintelligible, culturally or personally unsatisfactory, or abusive of the speech mechanism" (Perkins, 1971, p. 4). Remember that *unintelligible* and *unsatisfactory,* terms used in the preceding statement, are subjective descriptors. Just as beauty is in the eye of the beholder, defective speech can be in the ear of the listener. Speech can vary along numerous dimensions. Several that are the basis of classification of speech disorders include phonological disorders, voice disorders, and fluency problems. These classifications are not mutually exclusive because an individual may exhibit more than one type of speech problem.

Phonological Disorders

Phonology has to do with the way speech sounds are made (articulation). Phonological disorders consist of omissions (e.g., *tha* for *that*), substitutions (e.g., *thnake* for *snake*), and distortions (e.g., *s* produced by lateralized emission of air). Children with phonological difficulties are sometimes described as using "baby talk," being "tongue-tied," or not "talking plain." The causes of phonological difficulties include slow development, missing teeth, cleft palate or lip, neurological impairment, emotional problems, and faulty learning. In the vast majority of cases with which a speech/language pathologist works, the phonological problem is functional; that is, the etiology is unknown. It must be remembered that some children may not master all of the speech sounds until approximately 8 years of age. It is not uncommon or pathological for children between the ages of 5 and 8 to misarticulate some sounds and for children younger than 3 years of age to be unintelligible except to their parents. When evaluating a child's phonology, one must always keep in mind the child's overall developmental level.

Voice Disorders

Phonation or voice is the tonal or musical quality produced by vibration of the vocal folds. Voice disorders can affect pitch, loudness, and tonal quality, and cause the voice to have the sound of nasality and hoarseness (Perkins, 1980). More specifically, deviations along these dimensions may involve abuse of the larynx, interference with communication, or unpleasantness to the ear. The individual's voice may consistently be too high or low pitched, too loud or too soft, too monotone, or too breathy, harsh, or hoarse. These disorders of voice may be caused by malformation, injury or disease of the vocal folds, psychological factors, hearing loss, and so forth. Damage to the vocal folds can result from the person's persistent misuse of the voice, for example, through excessive screaming. It is also possible for voice disorders to arise from faulty learning.

Disorders of Speech Flow

The dimensions of speech flow include sequence, duration, rate, rhythm, and fluency (Perkins, 1980). Normal speech is perceived as relatively fluent or smooth flowing with various natural interruptions. All of us have experienced difficulties in speech fluency, usually when we try to speak too quickly or forget what we were saying in midsentence.

The most common problem associated with speech fluency is stuttering. Dysfluencies or disruptions in the flow of speech are one aspect of stuttering. Normal speech contains disruptions of rhythm or dysfluencies, but when these occur so frequently and severely that the listener's attention is drawn to them and they interfere with communication, the speaker may be considered to have a speech problem. The speech disruptions that characterize stuttering include repetitions or prolongations of sound, word, syllable, or speech posture, and/or avoidance and struggle behaviors. Stuttering has been classified into two types: (a) *primary*, involving the normal, dysfluent repetitions characteristic of a young child, and (b) *secondary*, referring to the more severe speech impairments that are compounded by the dysfluent nonspeech behaviors just noted.

Usually caused by a complex interaction of factors, stuttering involves social, emotional, and physiological reactions in both speaker and listener. Among the few facts about stuttering that we do know are the following:

1. Stuttering is a natural phenomenon of childhood. In learning speech and language, all children become dysfluent to some degree. Many children develop patterns of dysfluency that are transitory but do, nevertheless, cause their parents grave concern. In almost all cases, stuttering begins before adolescence, and, by late adolescence, approximately three fourths of children who stutter stop spontaneously. This phenomenon occurs independently of the assistance of speech/language pathologists or other professionals.

2. Most individuals who stutter have particular trouble with certain words or specific situations. For instance, speaking to strangers or talking on the phone may pose great difficulties, but reading aloud or singing is not affected.

3. Stuttering is more prevalent among boys than girls. Various studies have reported boy:girl ratios ranging from 3:1 to 8:1.

4. Stuttering runs in families. This may or may not be due to hereditary factors. One should remember that religious beliefs also run in families, but religion is not transmitted genetically.

5. There are numerous theories of stuttering, with none sufficient to explain all cases. Hereditary, psychoanalytical, organic, and learning theories have been proposed. It is also believed by some researchers that children become stutterers primarily because parents show exaggerated concern for the young child's normal dysfluencies ("diagnosogenic" theory).

6. Although a large number of treatment methods have been applied, none has been universally successful. Therapeutic efforts have included systematic desensitization, negative practice, ego building, psychotherapy, operant conditioning, voluntary control, modification of stuttering patterns, chemotherapy, surgery, hypnosis, and rhythmic speech. Although no universal "cure" has been found, it appears that some of the most successful treatments known to date are those based on learning principles.

MULTIPLE DISORDERS

Often speech and language disorders will be found together in an individual. Both problems often occur simultaneously under certain disabling conditions.

Disorders Associated with Hearing Impairment

If a child has a significant hearing impairment, speech may be characterized by voice disorders and articulation problems. This child is most likely to misarticulate unvoiced high-frequency sounds such as *s*, *f*, *p*, *t*, and *sh*. For this individual, the task of learning the sounds of language is severely impeded by the hearing difficulty. If the impairment is too severe, it may be necessary to use another language system such as signing.

Disorders Associated with Cerebral Palsy

The type of brain damage that results in cerebral palsy may make it difficult or impossible for the child to control the muscles necessary for proper phonation and articulation. The speech of such individuals may be characterized by fluctuating patterns of pitch, timing, intensity, and phonology. In addition, both cognitive and perceptual motor difficulties may inhibit the acquisition of language and speech. However, because of the considerable variance of this population, some individuals will display severe impairment, whereas others with milder forms of cerebral palsy will demonstrate normal speech and language abilities.

Disorders Associated with Cleft Palate or Cleft Lip

Cleft palate is a structural defect in the palate or roof of the mouth that may make it difficult or impossible for the individual to close off the nasal air passage, which is necessary for proper phonology. Speech associated with an unrepaired or inadequately repaired cleft palate is hypernasal; that is, too much air escapes through the nose as the person talks. Cleft lip (often inappropriately referred to as a "harelip") is a structural defect in the upper lip that, if unrepaired, may also result in defective articulation. Both cleft palate and cleft lip result from failure of the bone and/or soft tissue of the palate or lip to fuse during approximately the first trimester of pregnancy. Language facility in the young child may be hindered by the communication problems stemming from these physical disorders.

Disorders Associated with Mental Retardation, Emotional Disturbance, and Learning Disabilities

Children who are mentally retarded may exhibit speech problems and delays in language development. These individuals are more likely to develop greater speech problems than normal children of the same developmental age. It is also a fact that as the severity of the retardation increases, so does the probability that the individual will have significant speech and/or language problems. Children with severe emotional disturbance may display peculiar language patterns such as meaningless statements, parrot-like speech (echolalia), or frequent, inappropriate use of personal pronouns. Although the distinction between language disabilities and learning disabilities is not clearly demarcated, there is a strong relationship. Many professionals believe that language disorders may be the focal issue in regard to learning disabilities.

INTERVENTIONS

Speech therapists perform their services in a wide variety of settings, including elementary and secondary schools, speech and hearing clinics, residential facilities, and rehabilitation hospitals. As one might expect, schools serve the largest number of individuals needing intervention. However, only those students with the most severe communication disorders or multiple disabilities require more than pull-out services (Michael & Paul, 1991).

School speech and language programs are the most feasible means of providing services to children. Working together, teachers and speech/language specialists can identify and provide assistance to large numbers of children who otherwise might never be taken to a speech center. Unfortunately, because most school systems face chronic shortages of speech/language therapists, only those children with the most severe speech or language handicaps are typically served by them on a regular basis. However, most of these students have only mild associated disabilities or are solely speech/language disordered. Many students who are severely retarded and in need of speech/language therapy do not receive appropriate services. Many times the focus of intervention is on the primary disability (i.e., mental retardation) at the expense of the secondary disability. Some children with speech and language impairments may receive assistance from a learning disabilities specialist or resource teacher if the particular school is able to provide this type of service.

Teachers, then, play a vital role in assisting those children not seen regularly by the speech/language therapist. After a careful assessment of the child's speech, the specialist can recommend activities that the child can work on in the classroom. Only through the cooperative efforts of teacher and specialist can assistance be provided for all children with speech and language handicaps.

Speech/language intervention is a specific type of related service mentioned in the Individuals with Disabilities Education Act. Intervention currently focuses on the pragmatics or functionality of speech/language training, speech/language training in naturalistic settings, and instruction that focuses on the context or environment as it relates to speech/language. In combining these principles with behavioral procedures, interventions can emphasize (a) the development of speech/language skills peculiar to the current and future needs of the client, (b) the generalization of acquired speech/language to new environments, and (c) the enhancement of the client's motivation to communicate with others.

TRENDS AND ISSUES

We have outlined only major disorders of speech and language and the major etiological factors contributing to these conditions. A discussion of the other less common or more specific disorders and etiological factors is beyond the scope of this chapter. Moreover, within each of the broad categories we have outlined, wide variations are seen in degree of severity of the handicap. Additionally, an individual's speech may be disordered by more than one of the conditions already discussed. For more detailed treatment of speech and language impairments, see Hegde (2001); Nelson (1998); Owens, Metz, and Haas (2002); Shames and Anderson (2001); and Van Riper (1978).

Speech is one of an individual's most personal attributes. Certainly, as the anecdotes at the beginning of this chapter demonstrate, having a speech problem can be extremely embarrassing and painful. When people continually respond more to the sound than to the content of speech, a person's desire to communicate thoughts and feelings can be inhibited. Although children with speech disorders may choose a world of silence rather than face the disturbing reactions on a listener's face, they can, with help, overcome or learn to cope with their difficulties. At times, they can make light of their situation. Having a speech or language disorder, like having any other disability, does not exclude a child from the world of fun and humor.

SUGGESTIONS FOR WORKING WITH PEOPLE
WHO HAVE SPEECH/LANGUAGE DISORDERS

General:

1. Teachers, parents, and friends should be informed of what skills and/or behaviors the therapist is targeting so they can appropriately respond and reinforce them in educational settings, at home, or in the community.
2. Listen attentively and patiently when the person is talking. Give the person time.
3. If you do not understand what the individual said, explain what you did understand and ask for clarification of the rest.
4. Remember that the person with a speech/language impairment has trouble talking, not hearing; do not shout or yell.
5. Laugh with, but not at, the individual who has a speech/language impairment.

Working with Those Who Stutter:
1. Accept them as they are.
2. Look at and not away from them when they talk. Obvious uneasiness can make them uncomfortable.
3. Encourage but do not force them to talk.
4. Do not say things for them. That is, do not complete their words or statements when they get hung up.
5. Build their self-confidence by emphasizing their assets.
6. Encourage them to participate in group activities.
7. Create an environment in which these individuals can feel comfortable. Let them know that you are aware of but accept their problem.

PONDER THESE

1. We judge one another's speech to a large degree on the basis of what we are accustomed to hearing. Which, if any, of the following individuals would you judge to have defective speech? What specific characteristics of their speech distract you from the content of what they have to say?

   Jimmy Carter   Richard Lewis
   Mel Tillis   Jerry Van Dyke
   Stevie Nicks   Barbara Walters

2. Imagine that a parent comes to you with one of the following descriptions of a child's speech or language. What specific questions would you ask the parent to help you determine whether the child may in fact need the services of a speech/language specialist?

   "Now my little boy—he just don't talk plain so you can understand him."

   "Melinda stutters."

   "Fred sounds like he's talking through his nose."

   "I don't know what's the matter. She just hardly ever talks. I mean almost never! She doesn't say more than a couple of words in a day, and sometimes you can't even understand those."

INFORMATION/RESOURCES

1. American Speech-Language-Hearing Association
   1080 Rockville Pike
   Rockville, MD 20852
2. Trace Research and Development Center
   University of Wisconsin/Madison
   5151 Waisman Center
   1500 Highland Avenue
   Madison, WI 53705
3. Phonic Ear, Inc.
   3880 Cypress Drive
   Petaluma, CA 94954

4. Sentient Speech Systems Technology, Inc.
   2100 Wharton Street, Suite 630
   Pittsburgh, PA 15203
5. Innocomp
   33195 Wagon Wheel Drive
   Solon, OH 44139

Online Resources

American Speech-Language-Hearing Association
http://www.asha.org

Council for Exceptional Children/Division on
Communicative Disorders and Deafness
http://www.gsu.edu/~wwwdhh

REFERENCES

American Speech and Hearing Association. (1993). Definitions: Communicative disorders and variations. *ASHA, 35,* 40–41.

Bangs, T. E. (1982). *Language and learning disorders of the preacademic child with curriculum guide* (2nd ed.). Upper Saddle River, NJ: Prentice Hall.

Hallahan, D. P., & Kauffman, J. M. (2003). *Exceptional children: Introduction to special education* (9th ed.). Upper Saddle River, NJ: Merrill/Prentice Hall.

Haynes, W., & Pindzola, R. (1998). *Diagnosis and evaluation in speech pathology* (5th ed.). Needham Heights, MA: Allyn & Bacon.

Hedge, M. N. (2001). *Introduction to communicative disorders* (3rd ed.). Austin, TX: PRO-ED.

Hulit, L. M., & Howard, M. R. (2002). *Born to talk: An introduction to speech and language development* (3rd ed.). Needham Heights, MA: Allyn & Bacon.

Hull, F. M., & Hull, M. E. (1973). Children with oral communication disabilities. In L. M. Dunn (Ed.), *Exceptional children in the schools* (2nd ed., pp. 299–348). New York: Holt, Rinehart & Winston.

McLean, J. E. (1978). Language structure and communication disorders. In M. G. Haring (Ed.), *Behavior of exceptional children* (2nd ed., pp. 253–288). Upper Saddle River, NJ: Merrill/Prentice Hall.

Michael, M. G., & Paul, P. V. (1991). Early intervention for infants with deaf-blindness. *Exceptional Children, 57*(3), 200–210.

Naremore, R. C. (1980). Language disorders. In T. J. Hixon, L. D. Shriberg, & J. H. Saxman (Eds.), *Introduction to communication disorders.* Upper Saddle River, NJ: Prentice Hall.

Nelson, N. W. (1998). *Childhood language disorders in context: Infancy through adolescence* (2nd ed.). Boston: Allyn & Bacon.

Owens, R. E., Metz, D. E., & Haas, A. (2002). *Introduction to communication disorders: A life span perspective* (2nd ed.). Boston: Allyn & Bacon.

Perkins, W. H. (1971). *Speech pathology: An applied behavioral science.* St. Louis: Mosby.

Perkins, W. H. (1980). Disorders of speech flow. In T. J. Hixon, L. D. Shriberg, & J. H. Saxman (Eds.), *Introduction to communication disorders.* Upper Saddle River, NJ: Prentice Hall.

Shames, G. H., & Anderson, N. B., (2001). *Human communication disorders: An introduction* (6th ed.). Boston: Allyn & Bacon.

U.S. Department of Education. (2002). *Twenty-third annual report to Congress on the implementation of the Individuals with Disabilities Education Act.* Washington, DC: Author.

Van Riper, C. (1978). *Speech correction: Principles and methods* (6th ed.). Upper Saddle River, NJ: Prentice Hall.

PART III

Other Exceptional Areas

CHAPTER 12

Giftedness

I was standing at the front of the room explaining how the earth revolves and how, because of its huge size, it is difficult for us to realize that it is actually round. All of a sudden Spencer blurted out, "The earth isn't round."

I curtly replied, "Ha, do you think it's flat?"

He matter-of-factly said, "No, it's a truncated sphere."

I quickly changed the subject. While the children were at recess I had a chance to grab a soft drink in the teacher's lounge. While sipping my drink, I looked up the word "truncated" in the dictionary. I'm still not sure if he was right, but it sounded good; so good that I wasn't going to make an issue of it. Spencer said the darndest things.

At 4 Ellie was reading on a third-grade level. At 5 she could complete long arithmetic problems in her head. At 6 she played sonatinas on the piano. At 7 she said, "At Sunday school they told us that God created all the things in the world. I already knew that, so I didn't learn anything new. What I'm anxious to know is how did he make everything. Do you know what I mean? When are they going to teach me how he created all these things?"

Not long ago, I was invited to go on a "reef walk" with a class of gifted third and fourth graders. It was a very educational experience.

While we were wading in shallow water, we came upon a familiar marine organism commonly called a feather duster (tube worm). Forgetting that these students had vocabularies well advanced of their nongifted age peers, I was ready to say something like, "Look how that thing hangs on the rock."

Before I could get my highly descriptive statement out, Eddie, who always amazes us with his comments, offered the following: "Notice how securely anchored the organism is to the stationary coral."

All I could reply was: "Yes, I did."

It was explained quite clearly to his father that Albert would never make a success of anything, and when Albert was expelled from the "gymnasium" he was emphatically told, "Your presence in the class is disruptive and affects the other students." According to Clark (1971, p. 12) Albert's last name was Einstein.

Barlow (1952), quoting from the mid-19th-century *Chamber's Journal*, reported the arithmetical examination given to Truman Stafford, a child prodigy. The examination was given by the Rev. H. W. Adams when Truman was 10 years old.

I had only to read the sum to him once. . . . Let this fact be remembered in connection with some of the long and blind sums I shall hereafter name, and see if it does not show his amazing power of conception and comprehension. The questions given him became continually harder. What number is that which, being divided by the product of its digits, the quotient is 3; and if 18 be added, the digits will be inverted? He flew out of his chair, whirled around, rolled up his eyes and said in about a minute, 24. Multiply in your head 365,365,365,365,365,365 by 365,365,365,365,365,365. He flew around the room like a top, pulled his pantaloons over the tops of his boots, bit his hands, rolled his eyes in their sockets, sometimes smiling and talking, and then seeming to be in an agony, until, in not more than one minute said he, 133,491,850,208,566,925,016,658,299,951,583,225! (p. 43)

A great print ad, related to providing more challenging academic courses for students, appeared not long ago in a magazine. It pictured three elementary-aged students located in the operating room of a hospital and outfitted in surgical gear. The main ad line was: "Joey, Katie, and Todd will be performing your bypass." The message that is so poignantly made is, do we want our young, talented kids, who will eventually be treating us and our loved ones in life and death matters, to be trained as best as they possibly can be? The answer to this question is profound and at the core of gifted education.

Mr. Palcuzzi, principal of the Jefferson Elementary School, once got tired of hearing objections to special provisions for gifted children, so he decided to spice an otherwise mild PTA meeting with his proposal for the gifted. The elements of the Palcuzzi program were as follows:

1. Children should be grouped by ability.
2. Part of the school day should be given over to special instruction.
3. Talented students should be allowed time to share their talents with children of other schools in the area or even of other schools throughout the state. (The school, that is, taxpayers, will pay the transportation costs.)
4. A child should be advanced according to his talents, rather than according to his age.
5. These children should have special teachers, specially trained and highly salaried.

As might be expected, the "Palcuzzi program" was subjected to a barrage of criticism:

❏ "What about the youngster who isn't able to fit into the special group; won't his ego be damaged?"
❏ "How about the special cost; how could you justify transportation costs that would have to be paid by moving a special group of students from one school to another?"
❏ "Mightn't we be endangering the child by having him interact with children who are much more mature than he is?"
❏ "Wouldn't the other teachers complain if we gave more money to the instructors of this group?"

After listening for 10 or 15 minutes, Mr. Palcuzzi dropped his bomb! He said that he wasn't describing a new program for the intellectually gifted, but a program the school system had been enthusiastically supporting for a number of years—the program for gifted basketball players! Gallagher (1975) refers to this as the "Palcuzzi ploy." (p. 83)

The Palcuzzi ploy illustrates the very real problem of selling the general public on committing to the development (i.e., funding) of more appropriate educational programs for the gifted. There has been a tendency to view *equal* education for all as being the *same* educational practices for all, even though a major objective of public school education should be to provide programs that will allow all individuals to develop their potential. However, we are aware that "appropriate education" for students with disabilities means services that provide educational benefit to the student—not maximum benefit. When students reach a certain criterion of excellence, we tend to say, "Enough is enough! You only need to learn so much and we don't need a bunch of intellectual elitists around anyway."

Albert Einstein was bored in school and maintained a below-average to mediocre school record. Thomas Edison, at the age of 7, was at the bottom of his class, His mother got so upset with the school that she pulled him out of class and taught him at home. He was never again admitted to a public school. Stories like these tend to confirm the popular belief that persons who are gifted can and will learn on their own in spite of problematic school experiences.

Students who are gifted are generally perceived as being capable of shifting for themselves. In fact, many people feel that they will learn even under the most adverse learning conditions. The fact is that these students possess a unique array of learning characteristics that are best utilized through nontraditional teaching techniques. In other words, the learning and thinking of gifted pupils are best facilitated through a *special* education. The point is that we need to provide bright, talented, and creative students an appropriate education that ultimately should pay great dividends to society in general and, in many cases, to us individually (see earlier vignette on "Joey, Katie, and Todd").

For some gifted students, outcomes are not so good. For instance, we have to be concerned about the gifted children who lose interest in school because they are bored and unchallenged or the gifted students who lack the opportunities to achieve their potential. What about Dorothy J., a middle-aged Cahuilla Indian woman? In spite of Dorothy's fear of teachers and lack of knowledge of English, she completed high school. As reported by Martinson (1973), "She is co-author, with university professors, of several books in linguistics, ethnobotany, and music, and has served as a university lecturer in both the United States and abroad. Meanwhile, because she lacks formal higher education, she earns a living on an assembly line in a factory near her reservation" (p. 205).

BASIC CONCEPTS

Terminology

As is the case with most of the topics covered in this book, the terminology used to describe individuals who are gifted varies across settings and professionals. In fact, there is considerable disagreement about which terms should be used to describe giftedness. The most commonly used term is *gifted* and some professionals use this term to refer to the heterogeneous spectrum of students with exceptional abilities (Smith, Polloway, Patton, & Dowdy, 2004), as is done in this chapter. Others, however, reserve the term *gifted* to refer only to those individuals with high levels of intelligence.

Other terms such as *talented* and *creative* are also used on a common basis. The term *talented* is most often in reference to individuals who demonstrate specific talents in areas such as art, music, dance, drama, interpersonal relationships, and athletics. The term *creative* is typically used to describe individuals who display innovative and novel aspects in their thinking or action.

Definitional Perspectives

It would seem that there are as many definitions of the gifted as there are authorities in the field. Much discussion has focused on whether high IQ alone should define giftedness or whether other characteristics like high creativity, achievement, motivation, or special talents (see above) should be considered. The conversation about definition continues to this day.

Specific definitions of giftedness have changed over the years. Early definitions relied almost exclusively on IQ. Contemporary definitions typically refer to creativity, motivation, and/or exceptional performance in some culturally valued activity as well. All definitions state that gifted students are clearly superior in some ability area to most others of the same age and setting. How far superior they should be, who should be the comparison group for judging superiority, and in what specific ways they should be superior have become, and remain, the debatable issues in defining giftedness.

Federal Definition.   The first federal definition that was used widely in the United States for many years was first submitted to Congress in 1972. The most current definition, promoted by the U.S. Department of Education, is from the Jacob K. Javits Gifted and Talented Education Act of 1988 (reauthorized in 1994) and is as follows:

> *Children and youth with outstanding talent perform or show the potential for performing at remarkably high levels of accomplishment when compared with others of their age, experience, or environment. These children and youth exhibit high performance capability in intellectual, creative, and/or artistic areas, possess an unusual leadership capacity, or excel in specific academic fields. They require services or activities not ordinarily provided by schools. Outstanding talents are present in children and youth from all cultural groups, across all economic strata, and in all areas of human endeavor.* (U.S. Department of Education, 1993, p. 3)

This federal definition is a helpful guide for addressing the needs of students who are gifted. It also includes components that are important considerations in serving this population. For instance, an important element of the definition is the emphasis that children and youth who come from diverse backgrounds are gifted. However, the definition may be misleading in some respects. No one has devised a technically adequate measure to determine potential abilities in certain areas such as leadership ability. And while the federal definition gives the impression that there are many *independent* features of giftedness, in reality many of the characteristics listed (e.g., intellectual, creative, and excellence in specific academic fields) are highly correlated. It is also noteworthy to point out that the psychomotor domain is absent from the definition. It was felt that this area is addressed sufficiently through other programs such as athletics.

What also needs to be pointed out, however, is that the law from which the federal definition derives does not mandate gifted education. Unlike IDEA, which does mandate an appropriate education for students with disabilities, the Javits legislation serves only as a guide for services, as noted earlier. As a result, in many locations throughout the United States, few, if any, services may exist for this population.

Other Conceptualizations.   A number of different conceptualizations of giftedness have emerged over the years. Three of the more popular and better received conceptualizations are discussed next. They include Renzulli's "three-ring" conception of giftedness, Sternberg's "triarchic theory" of intelligence, and Gardner's theory of "multiple intelligences."

Renzulli and Reis (1997) have suggested that giftedness should be conceptualized in a multifaceted way. They suggested that gifted individuals should demonstrate or show potential in the following areas:

1. High ability (includes intelligence)
2. High creativity (implies the development and application of innovative ideas)
3. High task commitment (related to high degree of motivation and diligence)

Another popular theory of intellectual giftedness has been developed by Sternberg (1997). His theory includes three types of abilities: analytic giftedness (i.e., ability to dissect a problem and understand its parts), synthetic giftedness (i.e., insightful, intuitive creative, or adept at coping with relatively novel situations), and practical giftedness (i.e., ability to apply aspects of analytical and synthetic strengths to everyday situations). All individuals demonstrate some blend of these three abilities. However, gifted individuals show high ability in one or more of these areas.

Gardner and colleagues (Gardner, 1983; Gardner & Hatch, 1989) have proposed the concept of "multiple intelligences." He and his colleagues originally identified seven different areas in which one can demonstrate specific degrees of ability. In recent years, more areas have been added to the theoretical schemata. The different intelligences, examples of occupations that might relate to each area, and a

Table 12.1
Multiple Intelligences

Intelligence	End States	Core Components
Logical-mathematical	Scientist Mathematician	Sensitivity to, and capacity to discern, logical or numerical patterns; ability to handle long chains of reasoning
Linguistic	Poet Journalist	Sensitivity to the sounds, rhythms, and meanings of words; sensitivity to the different functions of language
Musical	Composer Violinist	Abilities to produce and appreciate rhythm, pitch, and timbre; appreciation of the forms of musical expressiveness
Spatial	Navigator Sculptor	Capacities to perceive the visual–spatial world accurately and to transform one's initial perceptions
Bodily-kinesthetic	Dancer Athlete	Abilities to control one's body movements and to handle objects skillfully
Interpersonal	Therapist Salesperson	Capacities to discern and respond appropriately to the moods, temperaments, motivations, and desires of other people
Intrapersonal	Person with detailed, accurate self-knowledge	Access to one's own feelings and the ability to discriminate among them and draw upon them to guide behavior; knowledge of one's own strengths, weaknesses, desires, and intelligences
Naturalistic	Naturalist Park ranger	Affinity and appreciation for the wonders of nature

short description of the intelligence are presented in Table 12.1. Although these different intelligences have not yet been empirically validated, they do provide a foundation for looking at individuals in a more expansive way by equally distributing the importance of different types of abilities.

A conceptualization of giftedness that combines Renzulli's ideas with those of Gardner's is depicted in Figure 12.1. It acknowledges the different types of intelligence (Gardner) and provides a mechanism for considering giftedness in any of the areas by requiring that a person display certain features or dimensions (Renzulli's "above-average ability," "creativity," and "task commitment"). This conceptualization clarifies the connection between giftedness and creativity by suggesting that the development and application of innovative ideas are part of any type of giftedness.

Prevalence

Students who are gifted continue to be an underidentified and underserved group, for whom there is no federal mandate to identify and provide services.

Type of Giftedness	Above average ability	Dimensions Creativity	Task commitment
Logical-mathematical			
Linguistic			
Musical			
Spatial			
Bodily-kinesthetic			
Interpersonal			
Intrapersonal			
Naturalistic			

Figure 12.1
Conceptualization of Giftedness

Many students are not identified because of ineffective assessment procedures as well as an unawareness on the part of teachers and parents of what constitutes giftedness. Many individuals such as female students, students who are under-achieving, students with disabilities, and students from diverse backgrounds have traditionally been underidentified. For those students who are identified, their programs may not be comprehensive and sometimes not suited to their unique needs.

The number of students or individuals in the general population who are gifted is unknown. It is logical to conclude that prevalence figures will be influenced by how giftedness is defined, how it is measured, and who is assessed. Clark (2002) has noted that gifted students make up approximately 5 percent of the school-age population. The percentage of students identified and served varies greatly by state, however, with some states reportedly identifying more than 10 percent of their student population as being gifted and other states reporting less than 3 percent (Council of State Directors of Programs for the Gifted, 2000).

Etiology—Origins of Selected Types of Giftedness

Galton's (1869) classic contribution to the quantitative psychological study of gift-edness touched off the nature–nurture controversy. His examination of adult geniuses lent support to the argument for a hereditary cause. In the years after his study, environmental factors were emphasized by the majority of authorities in the field of giftedness as contributing to being gifted. However, it was observed that gifted individuals walked, talked, and read much earlier than normally developing peers and such early acceleration in behavioral development was difficult to attribute primarily to environmental events. Yet it was also observed that the environments in which the majority of the gifted developed were unquestionably wholesome and stimulating.

Because the nature–nurture controversy became so complex and conjured up so many emotional overtones, a pragmatic resolution evolved:

> . . . in the relationship between genetics and environment, genetics sets boundary lines of intellectual performance—an upper limit and lower limit—that an individual will be able to achieve. Whether the individual is near the top of that boundary line or near the bottom is dependent on his or her environmental circumstances. (Gallagher & Gallagher, 1994, p. 283)

Although the logic of this approach seems irrefutable, Jensen (1966, 1969) insisted that genes and prenatal development account for 80 percent of the variance in intelligence and that environment accounts for only 20 percent of the variance. Citing research studies, growth figures, and models of intelligence, Jensen presented a convincing case. Torrance (1971) summarizes Jensen's position as follows:

> He especially questioned the idea that IQ differences are almost entirely a result of environmental differences and the cultural bias of intelligence tests. As in his earlier papers, he argued that environmental factors are less important in determining IQ than genetic factors. After examining the recent research concerning compensatory educational programs for young children, Jensen concluded that extreme environmental deprivation can keep a child from performing up to his genetic potential, but an enriched educational program cannot push the child above the potential. Jensen argues, however, that there are other mental abilities not included in intelligence tests that might be capitalized upon in educational programs. He believes that current educational attempts to boost IQ have been misdirected, and he advocates the development of educational methods that are based on other mental abilities besides IQ. (p. 550)

Early childhood studies have established that environmental factors can have a significant influence on intelligence and school success (Schweinhart & Weikart, 1985). Just how much of a part environmental versus genetic factors play in determining functional intelligence has yet to be established. While researchers and educators debate the question of how much the environment affects intelligence, a growing number of parents currently are doing their best to create "superbabies." Glenn Doman (1984) in *How to Multiply Your Baby's Intelligence* tells parents that high and low intelligence are products of the environment and that to produce superior intellectual abilities in their children, parents should present stimulating learning activities from birth onward.

David Elkind (1981), in reaction to the drive for early development of abilities, warns parents that too much early pressure to learn can create depression in young children. Certainly both educators and parents continue to await clarification on how much early stimulation and skill training are appropriate in developing children's full capacity for superior functioning and emotional well-being.

CHARACTERISTICS

Individuals who are gifted may display a wide variety of specific interests, aptitudes, knowledge, and skills. When examining lists of possible characteristics, we run the risk of overgeneralizing that all students who are gifted show evidence of these features. Nevertheless, some distinguishable characteristics are noticeable in many students so identified.

Terman's Study

In describing gifted persons, however they are defined, mention must be made of Terman's monumental contribution, collectively know as the *Genetic Studies of Genius* (Sears, 1978; Terman, 1925; Terman & Oden, 1947, 1959; Tomlinson-Keasey & Little, 1990). Terman actually devoted his life to the study of 1,528 gifted (high-IQ) individuals, following them for 35 years from 1920 until his death in 1956. This five-volume study continues to this day. The study is noted not only for its large sample size and longitudinal contribution but also for its consistent accuracy. The findings of Terman's investigation have been confirmed and reconfirmed.

Terman's study counteracts the stereotypic concept that gifted individuals are physically weak, are small in stature, wear glasses, read all the time, are not interesting to be around, and are "bookworms." Terman's findings indicate not only that the gifted are superior in intellect but also that they are physically, socially, emotionally, and morally advanced.

Terman's gifted subjects were reported to be taller, stronger, and heavier than nongifted children. They walked earlier and had a lower incidence of sensory defects, malnutrition, and poor posture. They came from above-average to high-income homes, and their parents were well educated. When compared with the general population, they had a low incidence of delinquency, mental illness, and alcoholism. These individuals seemed to be more happily married, to have fewer divorces, and to have fewer offspring. Of more than 1,500 offspring, there is a reported mean IQ of 132, with only 2 percent falling below 100 and 33⅓ percent scoring over 140. After studying Terman's classic work, you cannot help but wonder what causes giftedness.

On the other hand, as Turnbull, Turnbull, Schank, Smith, and Leal (2002) point out, Terman's work also led to some misconceptions. First, he equated genius with IQ, thus excluding other areas such as artistic ability. Second, Terman stressed the strong association of genius and genetics, thus precluding the fact that some variability in intelligence can occur due to psychosocial factors and other life-related opportunities.

Contemporary Perspective

We enter a word of caution here—gifted children are not necessarily superchildren (the new stereotype)—however, highly gifted individuals do exist. Individuals may vary from the generally superior description one gets from Terman's studies. Some gifted children are physically or emotionally labile.

Clark (2002) has developed a list of characteristics (as shown in Table 12.2) that individuals who are gifted may display. These characteristics are divided into four domains: cognitive, affective, physical or sensing, and intuitive. An interesting phenomenon that sometimes occurs is the paradoxical negative effect of seemingly desirable behaviors displayed by gifted students. For instance, extreme curiosity about a topic being covered in class can sometimes be interpreted as annoying or disruptive by a teacher or fellow students. Quick answers or certainty that they are right may be misconstrued as brash arrogance. Many of the characteristics highlighted in Table 12.2 can be misperceived as problem behavior for students who are gifted.

Table 12.2
Differentiating Characteristics of the Gifted

Domain	Characteristic
Cognitive function	• Extraordinary quantity of information; unusual retentiveness • Advanced comprehension • Unusual varied interests and curiosity • High level of language development • High level of verbal ability • Unusual capacity for processing information • Accelerated pace of thought processes • Flexible thought processes • Comprehensive synthesis • Early ability to delay closure • Heightened capacity for seeing unusual and diverse relationships, integration of ideas, and disciplines • Ability to generate original ideas and solutions • Early differential patterns for thought processing (e.g., thinking in alternatives; abstract terms; sensing consequences; making generalizations; visual thinking; use of metaphors and analogies) • Early ability to use and form conceptual frameworks • An evaluative approach toward oneself and others • Unusual intensity; persistent goal-directed behavior

Domain	Characteristic
Affective function	• Large accumulation of information about emotions that have not been brought to awareness • Unusual sensitivity to the expectations and feelings of others • Keen sense of humor—may be gentle or hostile • Heightened self-awareness, accompanied by feelings of being different • Idealism and a sense of justice, which appear at an early age • Earlier development of an inner locus of control and satisfaction • Unusual emotional depth and intensity • High expectations of self and others, often leading to high levels of frustration with self, others, and situations; perfectionism • Strong need for consistency between abstract values and personal actions • Advanced levels of moral judgment • Strongly motivated by self-actualization needs • Advanced cognitive and affective capacity for conceptualizing and solving societal problems • Leadership ability • Solutions to social and environmental problems • Involvement with the metaneeds of society (e.g., injustice, beauty, truth)
Physical/sensing function	• Unusual quantity of input from the environment through a heightened sensory awareness • Unusual discrepancy between physical and intellectual development • Low tolerance for the lag between their standards and their athletic skills • Cartesian split—can include neglect of physical well-being and avoidance of physical activity
Intuitive function	• Early involvement and concern for intuitive knowing and metaphysical ideas and phenomena • Open to experiences in this area; will experiment with psychic and metaphysical phenomenona • Creativity approach in all areas of endeavor • Ability to predict; interest in future

From *Growing Up Gifted,* 6th ed., by Barbara Clark, © 2002. Reprinted by permission of Pearson Education, Inc., Upper Saddle River, NJ.

Some Thoughts About Creativity

Because a low tolerance for nonconformity exists in our society, creativity may often be discouraged. Torrance (1965) attempted to accelerate creativeness in children by offering them $2 prizes for stories that were interesting, exciting, and unusual. He found that children would produce such stories when reinforced for doing so. By using reinforcement techniques, other researchers too have found that creativity in story writing, easel painting, block building, and selection of word combinations can be increased (Baer, Rowbury, & Goetz, 1976; Brigham, Graubard, & Stans, 1972; Glover & Gary, 1976; Goetz & Salmonson, 1972).

Torrance and others have demonstrated that creative thinking abilities need to be energized and guided and that the earlier this is done the better. Unfortunately, creativity is not being identified by conventional methods of measurement and evaluation.

Highly Gifted Individuals

Clark (2002) distinguishes among students who would be considered typical or moderately gifted and those who are *highly gifted* and those who are *exceptionally gifted.* According to Clark, highly gifted students "tend to evidence more energy than gifted individuals; they think faster and are more intent and focused on their interests and they exhibit a higher degree of ability in most of the traits . . . identified with giftedness" (p. 63). Clark describes exceptionally gifted as those who "seem to have different value structures . . . tend to be more isolated by choice and more invested in concerns of a meta-nature (e.g., universal problems) . . . seldom seek popularity or social acclaim" (p. 63).

Both highly gifted and exceptionally gifted students pose significant challenges to educators in meeting their needs within the general education classroom. For example, the media will from time to time cover stories of exceptionally gifted children who graduate high school at age 6, graduate from college at age 10, are in graduate school at age 11 or 12, and so on. Note that individuals who are highly or exceptionally gifted may be particularly prone to difficulties in social adjustment. This can occur because their advanced abilities are so *exceedingly* rare among persons their age (see Hollingworth, 1942).

INTERVENTIONS

This section addresses three important intervention issues: identification, placement, and programmatic options.

Identification

Teachers play an important role in the identification of students who are gifted, because they are often the ones who recognize that a person is gifted and initiate the confirmation process. Certain types of characteristics and behaviors (refer to Table 12.2) might suggest that a student is gifted, thus requiring a more in-depth assessment.

Once a student is nominated by a teacher to be considered for gifted programming, other information is typically gathered to determine eligibility. Sources of information can include formal tests; informal assessments; interviews with teachers, parents, and peers; and actual student products including portfolios. The important point is that many sources of information should be used in determining whether a student is gifted or not.

Although it might be said that identifying gifted students has been often over-looked in education, this is definitely the case with certain groups of children. As mentioned previously, four different groups of students are typically underrepre-sented in gifted education, including children and youth from diverse backgrounds, females, those with disabilities, or those who are underachieving. There are gifted learners in all of these groups, and efforts must be undertaken to identify them.

Placement

Although students with disabilities can generate concern in others in relation to addressing their needs, students who are gifted are usually left to fend for them-selves in the general classroom with their chronological peers. In schools today, students who are gifted are most likely to spend the greater part of their instruc-tional day in a general education classroom setting with some differential program-ming available for part of the day. For this reason it is critical that general educa-tors become more knowledgeable of, skilled at, and comfortable with teaching students who are gifted. Certain school systems will have a continuum of educa-tional arrangements available to students who are gifted. A sampling of some of the educational settings that might be utilized is illustrated in Figure 12.2.

Students who are gifted may be capable of learning at such a high level of cognition and fast rate of acquisition that traditional instruction for students of their age is often not meeting their needs and is considered boring, tedious, and redundant. It is no wonder why many case histories of very bright individuals reveal that at some time in their lives they experienced difficulties in school. Kirk (1972) reported that Norbert Wiener, one of the great men in cybernetics, read *Alice in Wonderland* and *The Arabian Nights* by age 4 but was refused admission to school because he was not old enough. At age 7, he was placed in the third grade. At age 18, he received his Ph.D. in mathematics.

Even though the general education setting is an important setting in which to address the needs of students who are gifted, it "should not, cannot, and must not be the *only* setting in which appropriate services are provided" (Maker, 1993, p. 4). These students need programming that is different "in depth, scope, pace,

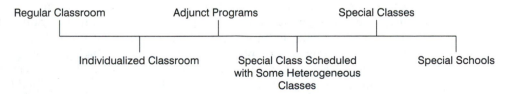

Figure 12.2
Options for Providing Services to Gifted Students
Source: Adapted from *Growing Up Gifted Developing the Potential of Children at Home and at School,* 6th ed. by B. Clark, 2002. Reprinted by permission of Pearson Education, Upper Saddle River, N.J.

self-directedness of expectations" (Lopez & MacKenzie, 1993, p. 288) that can only be offered in other settings.

Programming Options

The logic of special education services for the gifted is based on the following assumptions and observed facts, which were first noted by Virgil Ward (1962) many years ago:

❏ Gifted children as a group differ from others in learning ability; they learn faster and remember more, and they tend to think more deeply with and about what they learn.
❏ As adults, gifted persons tend to remain similarly advanced beyond the average and tend to assume distinctive social roles as leaders in the reconstruction and advancement of whatever lines of activity they pursue.
❏ The regular school curriculum only barely approximates the demands of either the greater learning capacity or the anticipated social roles of gifted persons.
❏ An educational program *can* be devised that *does* more adequately meet these basic demands, and which on the whole, being uniquely suited to the gifted, is both unnecessary for and not capable of being accomplished by students of lesser ability.
❏ Differential educational provisions for the gifted promise to discover more gifted persons, to improve their education, and to launch them earlier into their chosen careers so that society, as well as the persons themselves, may enjoy longer the fruits of their productive and creative labors (p. 22).

Ward's points, though written four decades ago, are hard to argue against; nearly all current educational programs for students who are gifted are built around most or all of his assumptions.

A number of specific program options and practices can be identified in the literature, but we will discuss only three in this section: acceleration, enrichment, and ability grouping.

Acceleration.   By this means the student is introduced to content, concepts, and educational experiences sooner than is done with other students of the same age. There are many types of accelerative practices, as identified by Southern and Jones (1991) and depicted in Table 12.3, some of which are utilized at certain levels of schooling (e.g., advanced placement courses at the high school level). Research seems clearly to support acceleration, but programs of this type can be met with criticism and disfavor.

Although administrative arrangements for handling any student—disabled, normal, or gifted—assist or interfere with instruction, the major educational concerns focus on what goes on in the classroom. No administrative manipulation of environmental variables can *assure* learning. This is not to minimize the importance of administrative approaches, but it is commonly recognized that although

Table 12.3
Range and Types of Accelerative Options

1. Early entrance to kindergarten or first grade	The student is admitted to school prior to the age specified by the district for normal entry to kindergarten or first grade.
2. Grade skipping	The student is moved ahead of normal grade placement. This may be done during an academic year (placing a third-grader directly into fourth grade), or at year end (promoting a third-grader to fifth grade).
3. Continuous progress	The student is given material deemed appropriate for current achievements as the student becomes ready.
4. Self-paced instruction	The student is presented with materials that allow him or her to proceed at a self-selected pace. Responsibility for selection of pacing is the student's.
5. Subject matter acceleration	The student is placed for a part of a day with students at more advanced grade levels for one or more subjects without being assigned to a higher grade (e.g., a fifth-grader going to sixth grade for science instruction).
6. Combined classes	The student is placed in classes where two or more grade levels are combined (e.g., third- and fourth-grade split rooms). The arrangement can be used to allow younger children to interact with older ones academically and socially.
7. Curriculum compacting	The student is given reduced amounts of introductory activities, drill review, and so on. The time saved may be used to move faster through the curriculum.
8. Telescoping curriculum	The student spends less time than normal in a course of study (e.g., completing a one-year course in one semester, or finishing junior high school in two years rather than three).
9. Mentorships	The student is exposed to a mentor who provides advanced training and experiences in a content area.
10. Extracurricular programs	The student is enrolled in course work or summer programs that confer advanced instruction and/or credit for study (e.g., fast-paced language or math courses offered by universities).
11. Concurrent enrollment	The student is taking a course at one level and receiving credit for successful completion of a parallel course at a higher level (e.g., taking algebra at the junior high level and receiving credit for high school algebra as well as junior high math credits upon successful completion).
12. Advanced placement	The student takes a course in high school that prepares him or her for taking an examination that can confer college credit for satisfactory performances.
13. Credit by examination	The student receives credit (at high school or college level) upon successful completion of an examination.
14. Correspondence courses	The student takes high school or college courses by mail (or, more recently, through video and audio presentations).
15. Early entrance into junior high, high school, or college	The student is admitted with full standing to an advanced level of instruction (at least one year early).

Source: Reprinted by permission of the publisher from Southern, W. T., & Jones, E.D., *The Academic Acceleration of Gifted Children,* (New York: Teachers College Press, © by Clara Hemphill. All rights reserved.), Figure 1.1.

appropriate facilities, materials, and wholesome environmental conditions are necessary, these important facets are no substitute for a conscientious, sensitive, skillful, and competent teacher.

Enrichment.   This approach uses techniques that provide topics, skill development, materials, or experiences that extend the depth of coverage beyond that typically presented in the existing curriculum. This practice is commonly used in general education settings where it may be the easiest type of intervention to implement for students who are gifted. Enrichment activities are sometimes categorized as horizontal or vertical. *Horizontal enrichment* refers to providing *more* educational experiences at the same level of difficulty, whereas *vertical enrichment* refers to providing higher level activities of increasing complexity. This latter type of enrichment activity might more properly be considered a type of acceleration technique (Southern & Jones, 1991).

Renzulli (1977) observed that much of what passes as enrichment (i.e., the horizontal variety) is actually a waste of gifted students' time. He has proposed a three-stage model for enrichment activities. Two levels of enrichment (general exploratory activities and group exercises to increase creativity, affective awareness, and problem-solving skills) are appropriate for *all* children, including the gifted. But a third type, individual and small-group investigations of real-life problems, is particularly suited for students who are gifted. In this kind of enrichment, the child actually carries out an experiment or project as a chemist, politician, writer, meteorologist, or what have you. The child *becomes* a professional or artisan, working like an adult counterpart and producing valuable information or creating a valuable product.

A slightly different way to think about students who are gifted is that they may only display the dimensions of giftedness some of the time (i.e., they may not always meet the dimensions described in Figure 12.1) or only in some specific area (not in others). This idea has led Renzulli, Reis, and Smith (1981) to propose a "revolving door" plan for enrichment. This plan means children will be phased in and out of the special third level of enrichment (the real-life investigations or projects) as they demonstrate their ability and interest by producing something valuable. If and when a "gifted" student does not display the motivation, creativity, or knowledge to pursue a particular project at this level, then he or she returns to the general education classroom activities and another child who meets the necessary criteria for the project is included in the special enrichment.

Ability Grouping.   In this method, those who are gifted are separated into more homogeneous groupings for at least part of the instructional day (VanTassel-Baska, 1989). One example of this technique is cluster grouping, a practice that allows students with similar interests and enthusiasm to explore topics from different perspectives and to stimulate the creative thinking of others in the group.

The benefits of such grouping warrant continued consideration of such an approach. However, Getzels and Dillon (1973), in quoting Gold, warn, "Grouping apparently is a helpful but not automatically effective instructional adjustment; achievement seems to improve only when grouping is accompanied by a differentiation in teacher quality, curriculum, guidance and method" (p. 716).

As the "Palcuzzi ploy" illustrates (see the vignette at the beginning of this chapter), American schools support ability grouping in athletics but seem to be less supportive of such grouping in academics. Legal action in the 1960s and 1970s tended to eliminate special "tracking" or ability grouping on the grounds that it is a discriminatory practice. The feeling of many Americans seems to be that equality should be the overriding concern in public education. But, as Gallagher and Weiss (1979) noted, "society's notion of 'equality' tends to be destructive of giftedness in elementary and secondary school" (p. 2). It seems likely that public schools will maintain an emphasis on inclusion and heterogeneous grouping—for both students who have disabilities and those who are gifted. The practice of special grouping will be found most often in private schools where the policy of equality is handled differently.

TRENDS AND ISSUES

A number of trends and issues exist in relation to individuals who are gifted, three of which are addressed in this section: inclusion, special populations of gifted individuals, and career development.

Inclusion

An interesting paradox exists in relation to the concept of inclusion. This concept has been a leading issue in the field of special education for students with disabilities and has been promoted extensively as reflected throughout this book. However, on the other hand, many professionals in the field of gifted education argue strongly against having students who are gifted placed in inclusive settings, promoting instead that differential programming provided in separate settings is more beneficial.

The fact, however, is that most students who are gifted will spend the greater part of their school careers in inclusive settings. Some professionals, even though they favor differential approaches to programming, recognize that individuals who are gifted must learn to work, socialize, and exist with others who do not share their abilities and interests.

Special Populations

Females. Historically, females who were gifted were overlooked—identified less often and, as a result, not provided with programs that served them as well as possible. In recent times, the needs of gifted females have received more attention. Reis (2001) discussed some of the barriers that gifted girls and women still face. She generated a list of general recommendations for teachers to use to assist gifted

Table 12.4
Recommendations for Girls and Women

Teachers should:
- Provide equitable treatment in a nonstereotyped environment and in particular, provide encouragement.
- Reduce sexism in classrooms and create an avenue for girls to report and discuss examples of stereotyping in schools.
- Help creative, talented females appreciate and understand healthy competition.
- Group gifted females homogeneously in math/science or within cluster groups of high-ability students in heterogeneous groups.
- Encourage creativity in girls.
- Use problem solving in assignments and reduce the use of timed tests and timed assignments within class periods; rather, provide options for untimed work within a reasonable time frame.
- Expose girls to other creative, gifted females through direct and curricular experiences—field trips, guest speakers, seminars, role models, books, videotapes, articles, movies.
- Provide educational interventions compatible with cognitive development and styles of learning (i.e., independent study projects, small group learning opportunities, and so forth) and use a variety of authentic assessment tools such as projects and learning centers instead of just using tests.
- Establish equity in classroom interactions.
- Provide multiple opportunities for creative expression in multiple modalities.

Source: From "External Barriers Experienced by Gifted and Talented Girls and Women," by S. M. Reis, 2001, *Gifted Child Today, 24*(4), pp. 33–34. Copyright © 2001 by Prufrock Press. Reprinted by permission.

girls in dealing with the external barriers that inhibit their talent development (see Table 12.4).

Culturally/Linguistically Different.   As has been pointed out, cultural and linguistic diversity remains an area of concern in the education of gifted students. Too few students who are culturally and/or linguistically different from the majority of their peers are identified and served through programs for gifted students. "Culturally diverse children have much talent, creativity, and intelligence. Manifestations of these characteristics may be different and thus require not only different tools for measuring these strengths, but also different eyes from which to see them" (Plummer, 1995, p. 290). Teachers should look for certain behaviors associated with giftedness in children who are culturally different. Some of these features include the following (Torrance, 1971):

❏ Ability to express feelings and emotions
❏ Enjoyment of and ability in visual arts, creative movement, and music
❏ Expressiveness of gestures, body language, and so on
❏ Richness of imagery in informal language
❏ Originality of ideas in problem solving

Programming for gifted students from diverse backgrounds often has not been sensitive to their needs. As Plummer (1995) notes, few programs have the resources (i.e., personnel, materials) available to tap the interests and strengths of these students. Often the general education teacher needs such supports to address these students' educational needs in inclusive settings. The threefold challenge for teachers is (a) to respect ethnic and cultural differences of students from diverse backgrounds, (b) to integrate diverse cultural topics into the curriculum, and (c) to differentiate instruction so as to challenge the gifted students.

Twice Exceptional.   The term *twice exceptional* is becoming more popular in the professional literature and popular media. It refers to those students who are gifted and also have some type of disability. This population poses some fascinating challenges to educators, because they possess both superior abilities in some area(s) as well as significant difficulties in some other area(s).

Developing effective programs for this population has been extremely difficult for public schools due to the very unique needs of this group of students. As a result, a number of private schools throughout the country have designed programs to address the needs of select twice exceptional populations. Most of these schools have been set up to teach students who are gifted and also have a learning disability, dyslexia, or attention deficit hyperactivity disorder.

Underachievers.   One group of gifted students that is of particular note includes those who are underachieving. These students, by their very nature of not performing up to their capabilities, defy detection. This group might be the most difficult to recognize within the context of the school setting. Two of the factors that comprise Renzulli's model of giftedness, high ability and high task commitment, may be nearly impossible to identify in these students. As a result, it takes a very astute teacher to detect underachieving gifted students who are flying under the cover.

Career Development

Gifted and talented students need to learn about possible career choices that await them. They may need to do so at an earlier time than other students because they may participate in accelerated programs that necessitate early decisions about career direction. Students should learn about various career options, the dynamics of different disciplines, and the training required to work in a given discipline.

One way to do this is to ensure that gifted students have access to mentor programs, a type of accelerative practice, where students spend time with adults who are engaged in professional activities that interest them. Another technique is to integrate the study of careers into the existing curriculum by discussing various careers as they relate to curricular topics covered or to engage the students in some activities associated with different careers.

Career counseling and guidance are essential. Because of their multiple exceptional abilities and wide range of interests, some gifted students have a difficult time making career choices or narrowing down mentorship possibilities. These students should spend some time with counselors or teachers who can help them make these choices and other important postsecondary decisions.

The notion of transition planning, as introduced in chapter 2 and further discussed in chapter 14, is a worthwhile idea for this population. Helping students to identify areas of strength and need can be accomplished at an earlier date than is done with students with disabilities. Moreover, gifted students can take a very active role in planning their futures.

FINAL THOUGHTS

Individuals who are gifted are very bright, yet they too need attention and selected support, and their learning and thinking can most certainly be inhibited or suppressed. If we are to do what we say *should* be done, that is, develop each individual to her optimum or maximum potential, then we must take another look at our educational services for students who are gifted.

Not only is differential instruction important to gifted individuals themselves, it is essential for society. We are living in a world that becomes more complex every day. Conflict, violence, drugs, alcoholism, overpopulation, and pollution are problems that threaten our very survival. How can these problems be resolved now and in the future? It is extremely likely that we will turn to the Joeys, Katies, and Todds—today's gifted students—and hope they will come up with some answers. Should we not provide these future leaders, scientists, health providers with the best possible preparation?

In the 1950s, during the era of *Sputnik,* the nation turned to gifted individuals for solutions to problems in the physical sciences (e.g., space exploration). The public at that time supported differential educational programs for gifted students, especially those in science and engineering. Unfortunately, the programs were short lived, because the United States quickly caught up in the space race. At present, it is the social sciences that need a booster shot. We should now begin to train and entice our gifted individuals into the area of social science exploration.

Maslow's (1971) analogy of how tall our species can grow and how fast we can run brings the value and importance of those who are gifted into meaningful perspective:

> *If we want to answer the question how tall can the human species grow, then obviously it is well to pick out the ones who are already tallest and study them. If we want to know how fast a human being can run, then it is no use to average out the speed of a "good sample" of the population, it is far better to collect Olympic gold-medal winners and see how well they can do. If we want to know the possibilities for spiritual growth, value growth, or moral development in human beings, then I maintain that we can learn most by studying our most moral, ethical, or saintly people.*
>
> *On the whole I think it is fair to say that human history is a record of the ways in which human nature has been sold short. The highest possibilities of human*

nature have practically always been underrated. Even when "good specimens," the saints and sages and great leaders of history, have been available for study, the temptation too often has been to consider them not human but supernaturally endowed (p. 12)

As we begin to think about gifted individuals as a human resource to solve society's problems, we must be aware that we have no right to harness their intellectual talents at the cost of their basic freedoms. Getzels (1957) reminds us that there comes a time when we must look at the gifted as people and not be compelled to figure out how we can get the most out of them. Hopefully, if they are properly treated in our educational settings, gifted people will find gratification as well as intriguing challenges in all learning.

SUGGESTIONS FOR WORKING WITH PEOPLE WHO ARE GIFTED

- ❑ In helping an underachieving student become motivated, present ideas and tasks in terms of the needs and interests of the child.
- ❑ Help individuals set realistic goals.
- ❑ Give students choices in deciding learning goals and activities. Choices give the student an opportunity to develop self-esteem and a sense of competency.
- ❑ Do not expect perfection. Gifted individuals need to know that mistakes are a natural part of growing and learning.
- ❑ Provide extra activities and experiences for students who are gifted, but be thoughtful about scheduling. Be sure the gifted student does not become overscheduled.
- ❑ Be sure the gifted student and the other children in her class or neighborhood understand that she is more like them than different. Like everyone else, the gifted child sometimes has feelings of fear and inadequacy, a huge need for love and acceptance, and the desire to play and have fun.
- ❑ Be sure that educational experiences challenge the student and awaken her interest in learning. Watch for signs of boredom. Gifted children need schools to be exciting, not places where they must sit through long hours of learning activities below their level.
- ❑ Provide opportunities for creative problem solving.
- ❑ Avoid comparisons of the gifted child and youth with others, particularly siblings.
- ❑ Help the gifted person develop a respectful attitude toward the feelings, skills, and abilities of her nongifted peers.
- ❑ Help the gifted student develop leadership skills.
- ❑ Appreciate the gifted student simply for being a fine human being. Communicate that you like the individual, not just because of her superior ability, but because she is just a good person and a delight to spend time with.

PONDER THESE

1. By what criteria could the following individuals be judged to be gifted?

Thomas Jefferson	Yo Yo Ma
Jesse Jackson	John Grisham
Tom Hanks	Lance Armstrong
Spike Lee	Shakira
Bill Gates	Mother Teresa

2. Is it possible to become nationally known—a household word—without being gifted?

3. Read some accounts, factual or fictional, of giftedness (e.g., *The Child Buyer* by Lewis Hersey or *Mental Prodigies* by Fred Barlow). How would you handle the children described if they were in a regular public school class?

4. Plan a hypothetical educational program to make children gifted. Would the opposite of your program make children retarded?

REFERENCES

Baer, D. M., Rowbury, T. G., & Goetz, E. M. (1976). Behavioral traps in the preschool: A proposal for research. In A. D. Pick (Ed.), *Minnesota symposia on child psychology* (Vol. 10, pp. 3–27), Minneapolis: University of Minnesota.

Barlow, F. (1952). *Mental prodigies.* New York: Greenwood.

Brigham, T. A., Graubard, P. S., & Stans, A. (1972). Analysis of effects of sequential reinforcement contingencies on aspects of composition. *Journal of Applied Behavior Analysis, 5,* 421–427.

Clark, B. (2002). *Growing up gifted: Developing the potential of children at home and at school* (6th ed.). Upper Saddle River, NJ: Merrill/Prentice Hall.

Clark, R. W. (1971). *Einstein: The life and times.* New York: World.

Council of State Directors of Programs for the Gifted. (2000). *The 1998–1999 state of the states gifted and talented education report.* Denver, CO: Author.

Doman, G. (1984). *How to multiply your baby's intelligence.* New York: Doubleday.

Elkind, D. (1981). *The hurried child.* Reading, MA: Addison-Wesley.

Gallagher, J. J. (1975). *Teaching the gifted child* (2nd ed.). Boston: Allyn & Bacon.

Gallagher, J. J., & Gallagher, S. A. (1994). *Teaching the gifted child.* Boston: Allyn & Bacon.

Gallagher, J. J., & Weiss, P. (1979). *The education of gifted and talented students. A history and prospectus.* Washington, DC: Council for Basic Education.

Galton, F. (1869). *Hereditary genius: An inquiry into its laws and consequences.* London: Macmillan.

Gardner, H. (1983). *Frames of mind: The theory of multiple intelligences.* New York: Basic Books.

Gardner, H., & Hatch, T. (1989). Multiple intelligences go to school: Educational implications of the theory of multiple intelligences. *Educational Researcher, 18*(8), 4–9.

Getzels, J. W. (1957). Social values and individual motives: The dilemma of the gifted. *School Review, 65,* 60–63.

Getzels, J. W., & Dillon, J. T. (1973). The nature of giftedness and the education of the gifted. In R. M. W. Travers (Ed.), *Second handbook of research on teaching.* Chicago: Rand McNally.

Glover, J., & Gary, A. L. (1976). Procedures to increase some aspects of creativity. *Journal of Applied Behavior Analysis, 9,* 79–84.

Goetz, E. M., & Salmonson, M. M. (1972). The effect of general and descriptive reinforcement on "creativity" in easel painting. In G. Semb (Ed.), *Behavioral analysis in education—*

1972. Lawrence: University of Kansas Department of Human Development.

Hollingworth, L. S. (1942). *Children above 180 IQ, Stanford-Binet: Origin and development.* Yonkers-on-Hudson, NY: World Book.

Jensen, A. R. (1966). Verbal mediation and educational potential. *Psychology in the Schools, 3,* 99–109.

Jensen, A. R. (1969). How much can we boost IQ and scholastic achievement? *Harvard Educational Review, 39,* 1–119.

Kirk, S. A. (1972). *Educating exceptional children* (rev. ed.). Boston: Houghton Mifflin.

Lopez, R., & MacKenzie, J. (1993). A learning center approach to individualized instruction for gifted students. In C. J. Maker (Ed.), *Critical issues in gifted education: Vol. 3. Programs for the gifted in regular classrooms* (pp. 282–295). Austin, TX: PRO-ED.

Maker, C. J. (Ed.). (1993). *Critical issues in gifted education: Vol. 3. Programs for the gifted in regular classrooms.* Austin, TX: PRO-ED.

Martinson, R. A. (1973). Children with superior cognitive abilities. In L. M. Dunn (Ed.), *Exceptional children in the schools* (2nd ed., pp. 191–241). New York: Holt, Rinehart & Winston.

Maslow, A. H. (1971). *The farther reaches of human nature.* New York: Viking.

Plummer, D. L. (1995). Serving the needs of gifted children from a multicultural perspective. In J. L. Genshaft, M. Bireley, & C. L. Hollinger (Eds.), *Serving gifted and talented students: A resource for school personnel* (pp. 285–300). Austin, TX: PRO-ED.

Reis, S. (2001). External barriers experienced by gifted and talented girls. *Gifted Children Today, 24,* 31–36.

Renzulli, J. S. (1977). *The enrichment triad model: A guide for developing defensible programs for the gifted and talented.* Wethersfield, CT: Creative Learning.

Renzulli, J. S., & Reis, S. M. (1997). The schoolwide enrichment model: New directions for developing high-end learning. In N. Colangelo & G. A. Davis (Eds.), *Handbook of gifted education* (2nd ed., pp. 136–154). Boston: Allyn & Bacon.

Renzulli, J. S., Reis, S. M., & Smith, L. H. (1981). *The revolving door identification model.* Mansfield Center, CT: Creative Learning.

Schweinhart, L. J., & Weikart, D. P. (1985). Evidence that good early childhood programs work. *Phi Delta Kappan, 66,* 545–551.

Sears, P. S. (1978). The Terman genetic studies of genius, 1922–1972. In A. H. Passow (Ed.), *The gifted and talented: Their education and development* (Vol. 78, pp. 75–96). Chicago: University of Chicago Press.

Smith, T. E. C., Polloway, E. A., Patton, J. R., & Dowdy, C. A. (2004). *Teaching students with special needs in inclusive settings* (4th ed.). Boston: Allyn & Bacon.

Southern, W. T., & Jones, E. D. (1991). *Academic acceleration of gifted children.* New York: Teachers College Press.

Sternberg, R. J. (1997). A triarchic view of giftedness: Theory and practice. In N. Colangelo & G. A. Davis (Eds.), *Handbook of gifted education* (2nd ed., pp. 43–53). Boston: Allyn & Bacon.

Terman, L. M. (1925). Mental and physical traits of a thousand gifted children. *Genetic studies of genius* (Vol. 1). Palo Alto, CA: Stanford University.

Terman, L. M., & Oden, M. H. (1947). The gifted child grows up. *Genetic studies of genius* (Vol. 4). Palo Alto, CA: Stanford University.

Terman, L. M., & Oden, M. H. (1959). The gifted group at mid-life. *Genetic studies of genius* (Vol. 5). Palo Alto, CA: Stanford University.

Tomlinson-Keasey, C., & Little, T. D. (1990). Predicting educational attainment, occupational achievement, intellectual skill, and personal adjustment among gifted men and women. *Journal of Educational Psychology, 82,* 442–455.

Torrance, E. P. (1971). Psychology of gifted children and youth. In W. M. Cruickshank (Ed.),

Psychology of exceptional children and youth (3rd ed., pp. 528–564). Upper Saddle River, NJ: Prentice Hall.

Turnbull, R., Turnbull, A., Schank, M., Smith, S., & Leal, D. (2002). *Exceptional lives: Special education in today's schools* (3rd ed.). Upper Saddle River, NJ: Merrill/Prentice Hall.

U.S. Department of Education. (1993). *National excellence: A case for developing America's talent.* Washington, DC: U.S. Department of Education, Office of Educational Research and Development.

VanTassel-Baska, J. (1989). Appropriate curriculum for gifted learners. *Educational Leadership,* pp. 13–15.

Ward, V. S. (Ed.). (1962). *The gifted student: A manual for program improvement.* Charlottesville, VA: Southern Regional Educational Board.

CHAPTER 13

Children and Youth Placed at Risk

Wilson, a 6-year-old European American boy, is considered to be a child placed at risk because he was born to HIV-positive parents. Although his mother has full-blown AIDS, she is able to care for Wilson most of the time. His father died at the beginning of his first-grade school year. Neither parent had been able to work for several years, so the family has existed on disability, Social Security, and social welfare programs such as food stamps. Wilson is HIV negative and spends much of his free time with his maternal grandmother, who plans to care for him if his mother becomes incapacitated or dies.

Wilson enjoys school. He is eager to participate in class activities and works hard to please his teacher. He likes to do art projects and he communicates very effectively with adults. He has difficulty getting along with other children, and his peers who live in his neighborhood make comments about his parents having AIDS, to which he reacts very defensively. He once reacted with aggression, and was suspended for 3 days for physically fighting another student. Since the death of his father, Wilson has been distracted during story time and has had difficulty separating from his teacher during recess and lunch. Although he began the year with prereading skills and a natural curiosity about books, he rarely wants to read aloud or independently. Recently, he has begun to cry when he is frustrated or unable to exercise his will, and some of his peers have teased him about "acting like a baby."

Although Wilson has many strengths, he has challenges related to the significant loss he experienced when his father died, as well as the financial difficulties the family has experienced over time. The family lives in subsidized housing, which is located in a high-crime, urban area in a large, southeastern city. From time to time, the family has no telephone service, nor do they own a car. Although his mother is able to help with homework, she is sometimes too sick to provide sustained assistance or attention and is frequently unable to attend parent conferences and school functions.

Wilson's teacher understands some of the difficulties he is experiencing. Many of the children he teaches are from low-income families who struggle for daily living resources. He does not know much about HIV/AIDS or childhood grieving. He communicates with Wilson's mom via a home–school notebook and together they developed a plan to help Wilson stay on track during this difficult time.

1. The teacher will work with the school counselor and parent to determine a behavior intervention plan to address Wilson's aggression and bouts of crying.
2. Wilson will be placed on a waiting list for a mentor who will spend time with him outside of school, involve him in recreational activities, and help him with his homework.
3. The teacher will provide his mother with an application for group counseling for children who are experiencing loss and grieving at the local hospice center.
4. Wilson's grandmother will volunteer once a month as the classroom story time guest reader. A PTA volunteer will provide transportation.
5. Wilson's mother will contact the local AIDS service organization for information and enrollment in a play group for children who experience loss as a result of AIDS.

6. The teacher will also contact the local AIDS service organization to learn more about the disease and its impact on families.

7. The teacher will plan a mini-lesson on AIDS during the unit on health care. He will use children's literature to help the students understand facts and myths about the disease.

8. Teacher and parent will continue to use the notebook for communication.

What does the term *at risk* really mean? Which students are described as students at risk? What are the implications for academic success or failure for children described as being at risk? These questions are at the heart of the controversy regarding defining and using the term *at risk*. Currently, the term itself can be found in legislation and policy reports, books, journal articles, Web sites, and in the names of educational policy and research institutes. The term is in the vernacular of most educators. Yet many scholars, researchers, and practitioners disagree on the meaning and use of the term. In this chapter we review definitions of the at-risk label and the implications of its widespread use. We also highlight specific interventions that have been effective for students traditionally thought of as students at risk for educational failure.

BASIC CONCEPTS

At Risk Defined

In the field of education, a very broad definition of a child at risk is one whose characteristics or contextual variables increase the likelihood that educational outcomes (i.e., academic achievement, diploma attainment) will not be the same as those for children who are not considered to be at risk (Keogh, 2000). Discussion of exactly which variables (related to child, family, school, community, or society) can be complex because risk factors can be weakened or eliminated by protective factors. For example, a child who is poor (a risk factor) may achieve academic success if the school she attends maintains a safe environment, a stable teaching staff, and adequate materials for learning (all protective factors).

According to Valencia and Solórzano (1997), the term *at risk* has been used in educational research, policy, and practice since the 1980s. Originally the term was used to make the point that individual control of school success and failure was limited and that environmental factors (e.g., impoverished conditions of urban school settings) exerted influence on school-related experiences and outcomes. Increasingly, however, the term has been used to describe person-centered reasons for failure (Valencia & Solórzano, 1997). As such, use of the term *at risk* is considered problematic because it is generally used to describe student or family characteristics that have been associated with school failure, oversimplifying the complex nature of outside factors that influence student achievement.

Additionally, the usefulness of the term *at risk* has been further limited by overuse. The precise reason that children are described as being at risk is lost. Does socioeconomic status or ethnic identity indicate automatic success or failure? Many examples of students of color, as well as students living in poverty, illustrate that these factors can be associated with either success or failure, although the latter is more frequently explored in research. Conceptualizing student success and failure as a result of the complex interaction of societal and systemic variables and student and family characteristics is more productive.

Swadener and Lubeck (1995) summarize the problematic nature of the *at risk* label:

❏ Focus is on the deprivation or repression of students and families, leading people to utilize deficit models of thinking.
❏ Issues of power, race, and class that are omnipresent in educational settings are downplayed.
❏ Implications that students at risk are victims of circumstance with little chance for self-determination or positive outcomes are promulgated.
❏ A political buzzword, the term evokes opinions and stereotypical images that lack true or useful meaning.
❏ Strength-based approaches are overshadowed and factors leading to the academic success of groups of students are de-emphasized.

A New Paradigm

In response to some of the issues raised by the term *at risk,* many educators opt for the term *children placed at risk* in an effort to move away from locating the source of student failure within the students themselves and focus instead on proactive, successful characteristics of school and system programs that serve diverse youth (i.e., children living in poverty and urban areas, children of color, English language learners) with high levels of efficacy.

The Center for Research on the Education of Students Placed at Risk (CRESPAR) is a collaborative effort between Howard University and Johns Hopkins University. The mission of this research institute explains the philosophy behind the revised term *children placed at risk:*

> *The philosophy . . . is that students are not inherently at risk but rather are placed at risk of educational failure by many adverse practices and situations. . . . It is clear that there is no single overriding reason why students fail, thus educators should be about the business of identifying and utilizing multiple determinants of success simultaneously. CRESPAR's projects aim in various ways to discern and document the differing determinants of success for students placed at risk.* (CRESPAR, 2001).

In the Leave No Child Behind Act of 2001 (LNCB), President George W. Bush and the U.S. Congress acknowledged that membership in certain racial, ethnic, economic, ability, and/or native language groups was a factor in educational attainment. This act, which is the most recent reauthorization of the Elementary and Secondary Education Act of 1965 to date, emphasizes accountability of schools, measured primarily by standardized curriculum and testing, to demonstrate educational attainment of all children regardless of group membership or risk factor. Schools cannot explain the failure of groups of students by referring to them as *at risk*.

The revised term, *children placed at risk,* emphasizes the active roles educators must take to make sure that schools find effective ways to educate students who have traditionally been described as at risk, rather than assign a risk category that becomes part of the child's identity. The idea is to capitalize on students' strengths, so that all students can experience maximum educational achievement. This is of key importance to the well-being of our society as a whole. Many groups of children who have been labeled at risk are members of the fastest growing groups of U.S. society and represent future human capital. For example, Latino youth have the highest high school dropout rate over any other ethnic group (see Figure 13.3 later in this chapter), and demographic studies show that Latinos are the fastest growing subgroup of the U.S. school-aged population. To ensure that these children do attain educational success equal to that of their peers, educators must recognize the strengths and resources Latino youth bring to their educational settings and also minimize obstacles to their educational attainment.

Identifying exactly which groups of children are placed at risk of educational failure varies. Groups of students who have traditionally been placed at risk for educational failure include children from economically disadvantaged backgrounds (Smith, Polloway, Patton, & Dowdy, 2004), children attending urban schools (Citizen's Commission on Civil Rights, 1999; Rashid, 2000), and children from racially and ethnically diverse backgrounds (Winzer & Mazurek, 1998). Other risk factors have been identified: single-parent households, loss of parent or sibling, child abuse, drug and alcohol abuse, teen pregnancy, and delinquency (Smith et al., 2004). Last, the presence of a disability, in particular a cognitive or emotional disability, is associated with lower rates of college enrollment and full-time employment (Blackorby & Wagner, 1996). Additional factors typically associated with risk for educational failure include living in poverty (Keogh, 2000), learning English as a second language or bilingualism (Baca & Cervantes, 1998; National Research Council, 2002), and involvement in the court system (Smith et al., 2004). Membership in any of these groups is rarely succinct, and interaction among them often means that membership in one group increases the likelihood of membership in another group. For example, students of color are more likely than their European American peers to attend impoverished, urban schools.

As the paradigm continues to shift to the idea that all children can reach their potential regardless of risk factor, scholars and educators have collected evidence and explored theories that identify effective educational practices for students placed at risk. (For examples, see studies presented by the Center for Research of Education, Diversity, and Excellence at http://www.crede.ucsc.edu/index.html)

Making connections between the unique needs and strengths of students who have been labeled at risk and programs that increase their academic achievement is an important step toward erasing educational inequities that currently exist.

In this chapter, the unique needs of the largest groups of children placed at risk and effective programming for these groups are discussed. Risk factors associated with disabilities, as well as effective interventions for students with disabilities, will not be a focal point here, because they are discussed at length in other chapters throughout this text.

CHILDREN AND YOUTH LIVING IN POVERTY

The relationship between poverty and school failure has been recognized for decades. Poverty can impact the physical development of infants and children (e.g., exposing them to environmental hazards). For example, low birth weight and premature deliveries have been associated with certain disabilities (Winzer & Mazurek, 1998) and both occur more commonly when the infant is born to poor parents. Lead poisoning, another example, is associated with learning and cognitive disabilities and is far more common among poor children than children in middle- or high-income brackets (National Council for Research, 2002). This is significant because outcomes (i.e., high school graduation rates and employment) tend to be lower for students with disabilities.

In addition to the relationship between poverty and disability, being poor has been associated with a lack of resources such as food, housing, and health care and a myriad of social problems including crime, drug and alcohol abuse, child abuse, and neglect. Each of these conditions has the potential to act as an obstacle to students' academic achievement. Although poverty has not been established as a cause of school failure, a discernible relationship exists, as is illustrated by dropout data. In fact, high school students from the poorest 20 percent of all family incomes were six times as likely as their peers from the richest 20 percent of family incomes to drop out of high school (Kaufman, Alt, & Chapman, 2001).

Communities, schools, and teachers respond to children and youth living in poverty in a variety of ways that seem to be effective. Schools and systems are supported by federal support, included in Title I of LNCB, which must go directly to support the education of impoverished youth. Title I is the allocation of federal funds to the education of children living in poverty. However, the success of the implementation of Title I funding, available since 1965, is controversial because its primary goal, narrowing the achievement gap between low-income students and their more advantaged peers, has not been met (Borman, 2000). Currently, Title I funding is comprised of $8 billion federal dollars per year, distributed among 50,000 schools and 10.5 million students (Citizen's Commission on Civil Rights, 1999). Other programs include grant funding and social service coordination to ensure that children's daily living needs are being met.

Most teachers and administrators have no firsthand experience of living in poverty. For school personnel, specific efforts to meet the needs of students living in poverty may include the following (adapted from Smith et al., 2001, pp. 358–359):

1. Increase an understanding of how poverty impacts the lives of students.
2. Avoid judging financial decisions of low-income families.
3. Avoid making all students aware of the economic situations of others.
4. Act as a liaison or contact person for social service providers.
5. Utilize school resources to provide specific necessities (e.g., school supplies).
6. Accommodate the work schedules of parents who work multiple jobs and overtime.
7. Utilize alternative modes of home–school communication when telephones are unavailable.

CHILDREN AND YOUTH ATTENDING URBAN SCHOOLS

Urban schools are often situated in low-income, high-crime areas of large cities and have historically been associated with the phenomena of underachievement of poor, urban youth, many of whom are children of color. In fact, although African American children represent 15 percent of the school-aged population, they represent 63 percent of the population living in the nation's poorest neighborhoods in 75 U.S. cities (Citizen's Commission on Civil Rights, 1999).

Urban school reform is the subject of much scholarly research, legislative and policy design and implementation, and popular attention. Often children who attend these schools are placed at risk for educational failure. The Citizen's Commission on Civil Rights (1999), a bipartisan organization that monitors federal programs including Title I, makes this point:

> There is much evidence that all children can learn and that the public schools serving minority and poor children can be successful in educating students to high standards. What is missing is a major commitment on the part of educators and public officials at all levels—federal, state, and local—to make educational opportunity for poor children a priority, to provide sufficient resources and deploy them effectively, to insist on high academic standards, and to hold all schools and school districts accountable for results.

So which urban education reforms have been proven effective? The answer to this question is hotly debated and full of complexities. Educational change for urban schools surely requires educators to adopt attitudes and conceptual frameworks that promote success for children placed at risk (Rashid, 2000). The conceptualization of "schools as community," which capitalizes on the relationships among educators, students, parents, and other community members, has been met with favorable response (Sergiovanni, 1994).

Of late, however, the political zeitgeist is accountability testing and standards-based curricula. Whether the accountability movement hinders or helps urban schools close achievement gaps remains to be seen. Early indicators show mixed results (Skrla, Scheurich, & Johnson, 2001). Some policy makers and scholars argue that accountability testing forces educators to take an interest in the progress of children typically placed at risk. Others argue that the tests are too "high stakes" and that the emphasis on standardized test results as a sole measure of achievement can have deleterious effects on both students and teachers. Regardless, accountability measures are part of current educational legislation such as LNCB, which is tied to funding for schools and, as such, are likely to be implemented for some time to come.

RACIAL AND ETHNICALLY DIVERSE CHILDREN AND YOUTH

Educational achievement for students who are members of certain racial and ethnic groups in the United States has been an ongoing struggle since before desegregation. Particularly, the achievement rates of African Americans, Latinos, and Native Americans have not been comparable to the achievement rates of Asian American and European American children. Although much debate has taken place regarding the nature of this struggle, researchers generally agree that educational conditions (e.g., urban schools with high numbers of uncertified teachers) pose larger obstacles to student achievement than do student characteristics (Valencia & Solórzano, 1997).

Large achievement gaps are seen when the achievement trends of African American and Latino children are compared to those of European American students. Figures 13.1 and 13.2 illustrate the extent to which proficiency test scores in reading and mathematics vary according to race (Leave No Child Behind, 2001). The dropout rate (Figure 13.3) also varies according to race (National Center for Education Statistics, 1999). Important to note, however, is that information in each of these figures is not broken down by socioeconomic backgrounds. In other words, this information is limited because we cannot determine what factors, *other than race/ethnicity* (e.g., poverty), are impacting academic achievement.

Students of color continue to be disproportionately represented in special education programs, an indicator that all students do not have equal access to all educational programs in either special or regular education. Of particular concern is the overrepresentation of African Americans and Latinos in categories of disabilities (i.e., mental retardation and emotional disturbance) that lack organic causes (National Research Council, 2002). Similarly, African Americans and Latinos are underrepresented in gifted and talented programs. For Asian American students, these phenomena are the opposite: underrepresentation in disability categories and overrepresentation in gifted education programs.

Figure 13.1

Percentage of Fourth-Grade Students
Proficient in Reading

Source: From Leave No Child Behind Act, 2001.
Retrieved July 21, 2002, from the U.S. Department of Education Web site: http://www.
ed.gov/legislation/ESEA02

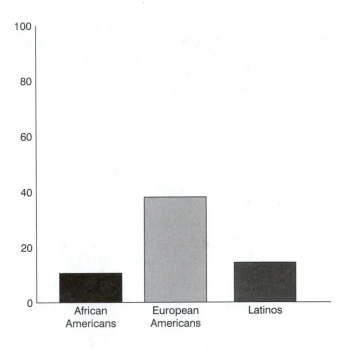

Figure 13.2

Percentage of Fourth-Grade Students
Proficient in Math

Source: From Leave No Child Behind Act, 2001.
Retrieved July 21, 2002, from the U.S. Department of Education Web site: http://www.
ed.gov/legislation/ESEA02

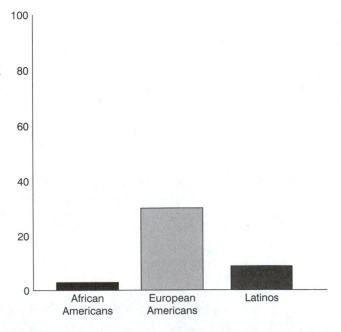

Figure 13.3

Percentage of U.S. High School Dropouts by Race/Ethnicity in 1998*

*Total U.S. dropout rate was 11.8%

Source: From *Dropout and Completion Measures,* by National Center for Education Statistics, 1999. (See reference list.)

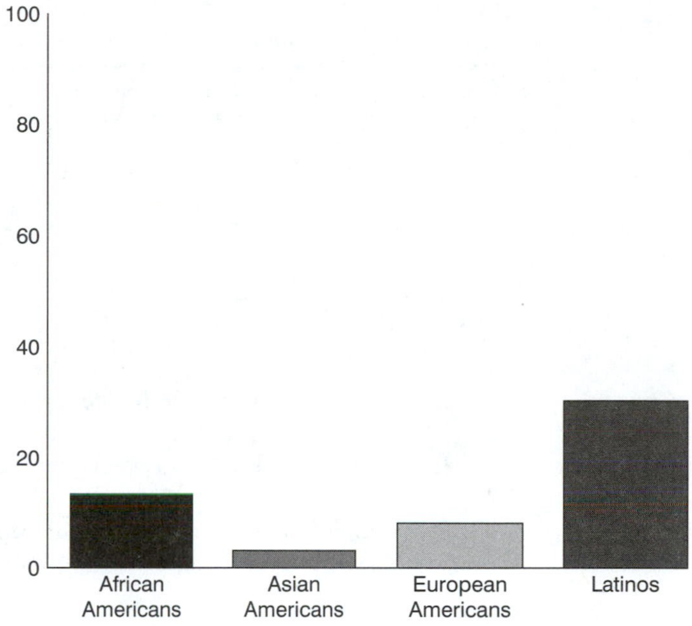

Principles of multicultural education have been designed to address the changing demands of the nation's diverse school-aged population. Currently, children of color comprise 35 percent of the nation's student body. Estimates for population growth vary, but most sources agree that this population will comprise a majority in the first half of this century. Currently, culturally responsive pedagogy is one response to addressing educational concerns regarding diversity (Harry, Kalyanpur, & Day, 1999; Ladson-Billings, 2001). Although the nation's student body is becoming increasingly diverse, the majority of teachers in the United States continues to be European Americans (87 percent) (Sleeter, 2001). Many teachers do not have experiences living in racially and ethnically diverse communities, or living in areas of extreme poverty and high crime, and as a result may harbor assumptions and stereotypes about the racially and ethnically diverse students they teach. Increasing teacher awareness of diversity issues has the potential to increase teachers' abilities to effectively teach culturally and linguistically diverse groups of students (National Research Council, 2002).

Teaching is thought to be most productive for all students when done in a way that responds to the diverse cultural backgrounds children bring to school, as is conceptualized in the tenets of multicultural pedagogy (Banks, 1995, p. 393):

1. Teachers integrate examples and materials from a variety of cultures into their curriculum.
2. Teachers help students understand how all knowledge maintains perspective and cultural assumptions.

Table 13.1
Steps to Developing Cultural Reciprocity

Step 1	Identify cultural values embedded in teacher interpretations of student difficulties or recommendations for services.
Step 2	Determine whether these values match the family's and how the family's values differ.
Step 3	Acknowledge cultural differences and explain the cultural basis of the teacher perspectives.
Step 4	Through collaboration, find common ground between teacher recommendations and family values.

Source: Building Cultural Reciprocity with Families (pp. 7–11), by B. Harry, M. Kalyanpur, and M. Day, 1999, Baltimore: Paul H. Brookes Publishing Co.

3. Teachers engage in "prejudice reduction" and facilitate attitudinal change that prioritizes equity.
4. Teachers employ "equity pedagogy" and support the development and academic achievement of culturally and linguistically diverse children.
5. All members of the educational community visualize the school as part of a social system and support change that promotes educational equity.

Application of the principles of multicultural education to special education may help teachers more effectively implement special education programs (Harry et al., 1999). Increasing teachers' ability to recognize cultural assumptions that underlie their own value systems, as well as the value systems of the families with whom they interact, can improve teachers' attitudes and skill levels as they work with diverse populations. One way to help teachers develop attitudes and skills that increase their effectiveness in the area of diversity is called *developing cultural reciprocity* (Harry et al., 1999). Table 13.1 outlines the steps teachers must take to increase their ability to effectively collaborate with diverse students and families.

ENGLISH LANGUAGE LEARNERS AND IMMIGRANT AND MIGRANT CHILDREN AND YOUTH

Although the educational rights of English language learners (ELLs; also called LEP for limited English proficient) have been protected under civil rights legislation since the mid-1960s, these children are placed at risk because they have not, as a whole, been granted the quality education they have been guaranteed (Baca & Cervantes, 1998). Many of these children come from families who are poor, underscoring the relationship between access to adequate education programs and socioeconomic status. Similar problems, such as increased dropout rates and low scores on standardized tests, have been reported for ELLs and students who are new to the United States.

Improving bilingual and immigrant education is essential to providing equitable educational opportunities to all students. The number of students who are learning English as a second language exceeds 3.5 million (LNCB, 2001). Students whose first language is Spanish comprise the largest group (75 percent) of ELLs (Baca & Cervantes, 1998). Among all ELLs, however, great diversity exists in terms of language proficiency, literacy skills, and academic preparedness. Similarly, great variation exists in the types of educational programs that address bilingual and ELL students' needs. Some programs are bilingual, where instruction and content is delivered in two languages; some programs are English only and are called *immersion programs;* others, the English as a Second Language (ESL) program, focus on the acquisition of English; still others are comprised of combined approaches. Additionally, bilingual special education programs are designed to meet the needs of ELLs with disabilities. Detailed descriptions of such programs are beyond the scope of this chapter.

Currently, heated controversy surrounds the discussion regarding effective programming for ELLs. For proponents of bilingual education, the overarching program goal is not assimilation (Baca & Cervantes, 1998). This means that students learn the cultural protocols of U.S. society without losing their own cultural heritage. In fact, students should be able to maintain their home language as well as develop English proficiency. The benefits of bilingual instruction, including positive impact on students' cognitive development, language arts skills, attitude, and self-concept (Baca & Cervantes, 1998), have been established through empirical research that supports the significant and positive effects of bilingual instruction (August & Hakuta, 1997).

Recent U.S. educational policy at both the federal and state levels, however, has been shifting the emphasis from bilingual to English-only instruction; hence the name change of the National Clearinghouse for Bilingual Education to the National Clearinghouse for English Language Acquisition during President George W. Bush's administration. In states such as California and Arizona, English-only laws have been passed, as well as laws that prevent children of undocumented workers from attending U.S. public schools. (For complete references to bilingual education policy and legislation, see the National Association for Bilingual Education at http://www.nabe.org.) Additionally, in the LNCB, the push has shifted from bilingual education to English-only instruction. Proponents of these policies criticize bilingual education for what they see as inefficient transition from students' native languages to English. While this debate continues, expert scholars in the field of bilingual education have called for additional research to determine which instructional components most effectively address the various needs of language communities in schools, whether they are classes in Texas for Spanish-dominant children with varied exposure to English or classes in New Jersey for new immigrant children who speak a variety of native languages.

In addition to language considerations, children of migrant workers have unique considerations for accessing appropriate education. High mobility and low access to health care and other daily living resources complicate migrant children's efforts to be successful in school. Like other populations placed at risk, migrant children have high dropout rates and low academic achievement. Some migrant workers have documentation of their citizenship status while others do not; however, in most states, this is not an issue because children are eligible for public school education regardless of their parents' immigration status. At times, the economic situations of migrant families force the need to attend school to compete with the need to work alongside parents. Although relatively few studies have tested the effectiveness of interventions designed to help this population, existing work in this area strongly supports efforts of schools to increase school–home collaboration. For example, schools that have been successful in meeting the needs of migrant children can be characterized as schools where staff and faculty are aware of the demands of migrant life and whose programs provide a range of services (e.g., coordination with social service agencies, availability of adult learning opportunities such as ESL classes) (López, Scribner, & Mahitivanichcha, 2001).

CHILDREN AND YOUTH INVOLVED IN THE U.S. LEGAL SYSTEM

Family Law

Children can be involved in the U.S. legal system in a variety of ways. If children have been abused or neglected, they may be involved in the legal court system or with social service organizations, such as departments of child welfare and child protective services, which monitor such cases. Children who are placed in foster care also have experiences with family law. Children of divorce, usually to a much lesser extent, may also be involved in the legal system in cases of child custody disputes.

The number of cases of child abuse and neglect continues to increase (Sedlak & Broadhurst, 1996). In 1999, the National Center on Child Abuse Prevention Research conducted a national survey of reported cases of neglect and abuse (Peddle & Wang, 2001). Suspected cases for child maltreatment were reported at a national rate of 46 per 1,000 children. Of the 46 per 1,000 cases of suspected abuse or neglect, 15 of 1,000 were confirmed. Of the confirmed cases, 46 percent were cases of neglect, 18 percent were cases of physical abuse, 9 percent were cases of sexual abuse, and 4 percent were cases of emotional abuse/domestic violence. The remaining 23 percent were cases of other forms of abuse, such as a combination of neglect and abuse, threat of harm, and abandonment.

Children and youth and/or their family's involvement with the police and justice system have the potential to negatively impact children's education. Specifically, children in crisis situations may feel anxious, withdrawn, or depressed (Smith et al., 2004). These emotions may manifest in age-inappropriate behavior, sleep or eating disorders, and self-destructive behaviors. Schools must be ready to report suspected cases of abuse. National hotlines are available for reporting cases of suspected abuse: Childhelp USA sponsors one such hotline, the National Child Abuse

Hotline at 1-800-4-A-CHILD. In addition to reporting suspected cases, schools can help prevent child abuse by strengthening school–home connections and facilitating family access to needed supports (U.S. Department of Health and Human Services, 2002).

Juvenile Delinquency

In addition to family law, children themselves, more commonly during adolescence than during childhood, can be involved in the juvenile justice system. Gang activity, truancy, drug and alcohol use and abuse, violence, and theft are common acts that result in the involvement of adolescents in the U.S. juvenile justice system. The presence of emotional and behavioral disorders is commonly associated with delinquent behavior (Beymer & Huchinson, 2002), but children with documented disabilities are not the only ones who break laws. Although reasons for illegal activity committed by adolescents are multifaceted, traditional risk factors have been poverty, poor self-concept, low academic achievement, lack of social relationships, and lack of parental support and parental skill. Using these risk factors to predict juvenile delinquency, however, is an example of using a deficit model to understand delinquent behavior and, therefore, has only limited applicability.

> The risk perspective depicts the youth offender on a trajectory of criminality, addiction, and dependency. Although repeated delinquency can lead to career paths in criminal activity . . . many individuals raised in adverse circumstances, with early criminal records, have . . . developed into productive, well-adjusted adults. (Carr & Vandiver, 2001, p. 410)

Issues of gender do complicate the study of juveniles who are involved with the justice system; typically males have been associated with delinquency more often than females. In at least one study, however, the contrast between female and male unlawful behavior seems to be one of severity rather than frequency of infractions. For example, childhood exposure to spousal and child abuse has been long thought to be a predictor of later criminal activity on the part of the child. Herrera and McCloskey (2001) found that referral rates of juvenile offenders did not vary by gender among study participants who had been exposed to family abuse. Rather, these researchers found that male adolescents were more likely to have committed property, felony, and violent offenses, while females were referred for running away and petty theft.

The educational needs of children who are processed through the legal system can be substantial. If punishment occurs in the form of incarceration, the transition between jail and classroom can be difficult. For children in special education, federal laws mandate that no break in services can occur; therefore, special education services must be provided in any alternative setting, including detention or jail. Although recent incidents of school violence have caused schools to develop strict punitive guidelines, strengthening the school–community connection and taking proactive measures to prevent school failure for students involved in the legal system are considered preferred educational practices (Karp & Breslin, 2001).

ISSUES AND TRENDS

The emphasis in this chapter has been on the understanding that educators are empowered to make choices that facilitate student success. The overarching issues and trends that are defining how educational research and practice address the needs of students placed at risk include the following:

❑ Teachers should acknowledge that groups traditionally placed at risk have less to do with personal characteristics, and more to do with the interaction between personal, community, and societal variables requiring educators to be critical thinkers and question the status quo.
❑ High expectations must be maintained for all students, including those placed at risk.
❑ Strength-based approaches that rely on the resources children *do* have, rather than on ones they do not have, help focus attention on how students can pass instead of how students will fail.
❑ Schools are integral parts of the communities in which they are situated and, as such, have the potential to positively impact students' lives by responding to the unique strengths and needs of the community and increasing the opportunities for genuine collaboration between school and home.

FINAL THOUGHTS

Understanding the terms *at risk* or *children placed at risk* requires information on a wide set of individual, family, school, community, and society characteristics. No attempt was made here to describe every possible risk factor or variable that may predict school failure, for such rules are not steadfast, and we know from studies of resiliency and success that many students and families succeed despite insufficient economic resources and other hardships. Similarly, individual teachers, school programs, and local districts have been successful at providing appropriate education and opportunities for academic success regardless of shoestring budgets, high-crime locations, and large enrollments of students placed at risk.

PONDER THESE

1. John Dewey, forefather of the U.S. education system, once said, "The best education is the best education for all." What are the implications of this statement in the 21st century?
2. Identify three ways in which teachers can address societal inequities that contribute to the educational failure of students placed at risk.
3. Agree or disagree: Teachers are agents of social justice and change.

ONLINE RESOURCES

National Center for Children in Poverty
http://www.nccp.org/

National Institute for Urban School Development
http://www.edc.org/urban/index.htm

Southern Poverty Law Center
http://www.splcenter.org/teachingtolerance/tt-index.html

National Association for Bilingual Education
http://www.nabe.org/

National Clearinghouse for English Language Instruction and Acquisition
http://www.ncbe.gwu.edu

U.S. Department of Health and Human Services
http://www.acf.hhs.gov/programs/cb/

U.S. Office of Juvenile Justice
http://ojjdp.ncjrs.org/

REFERENCES

August, D., & Hakuta, K. (Eds.). (1997). *Improving schooling for language-minority children: A research agenda*. Washington, DC: National Academy Press.

Baca, L. M., & Cervantes, H. T. (1998). *The bilingual special education interface* (3rd ed.). Upper Saddle River, NJ: Merrill/Prentice Hall.

Banks, J. (1995). Multicultural education and curriculum transformation. *Journal of Negro Education, 67,* 390–400.

Beymer, J. K., & Hutchinson, R. L. (2002). Profile of problem children from a rural county in Indiana. *Adolescence, 37,* 183–208.

Blackorby, J., & Wagner, M. (1996). Longitudinal postschool outcomes of youth with disabilities: Findings from the National Longitudinal Transition Study. *Exceptional Children, 62,* 399–413.

Borman, G. D. (2000). Title I: The evolving research base. *Journal of Education for Students Placed at Risk, 5*(1–2), 27–45.

Carr, M. B., & Vandiver, T. A. (2001). Risk and protective factors among youth offenders. *Adolescence, 36,* 409–426.

Citizen's Commission on Civil Rights. (1999). *Title I in midstream: The fight to improve schools for poor kids*. Washington, DC: Author.

CRESPAR. (2001). *Mission statement*. Retrieved November 20, 2002, from http://crespar.law.howard.edu/themission.html

Harry, B., Kalyanpur, M., & Day, M. (1999). *Building cultural reciprocity with families*. Baltimore: Paul H. Brookes.

Herrera, V. M., & McCloskey, L. A. (2001). Gender differences in the risk for delinquency among youth exposed to family violence. *Child Abuse & Neglect, 25,* 1037–1051.

Karp, D. L., & Breslin, B. (2001). Restorative justice in school communities. *Youth & Society, 33,* 249–272.

Kaufman, P., Alt, M. N., & Chapman, C. D. (2001). Drop-out rates in the United States: 2000. *Education Statistics Quarterly, 3*(4), 41–44.

Keogh, B. K. (2000). Risk, families, and schools. *Focus on Exceptional Children, 33*(4), 1–17.

Ladson-Billings, G. (2001). *Crossing over to Canaan*. San Francisco: Jossey-Bass.

Leave No Child Behind Act. Retrieved July 21, 2002, from http://www.ed.gov/legislation/ESEA02/

López, G. R., Scribner, J. D., & Mahitivanichcha, K. (2001). Redefining parental involvement: Lessons from high-performing migrant-impacted schools. *American Educational Research Journal, 38,* 253–288.

National Center for Education Statistics. (1999). Dropout and completion measures. Retrieved August 22, 2001, from http://nces.ed.gov/quicktables/Detail.asp?SrchKeyWord=dropouts&Key=266&optSearch=exact&quarter=&topic=All&survey=All&sortby=

National Research Council. (2002). *Minority students in gifted and special education.* Washington, DC: National Academy Press.

Peddle, N., & Wang, C. T. (2001). *Current trends in child abuse prevention, reportings, and fatalities: 1999 50 state survey.* Chicago: Prevent Child Abuse America.

Rashid, H. M. (2000). Professional development and the urban educator: Strategies for promoting school as community. *Contemporary Education, 71,* 256–260.

Sedlak, A. J., & Broadhurst, D. D. (1996). *Executive summary of the third national incidence study of child abuse and neglect.* U.S. Department of Health and Human Services, National Center on Child Abuse and Neglect.

Sergiovanni, T. (1994). *Building communities in schools.* San Francisco: Jossey-Bass.

Skrla, L., Scheurich, J. J., & Johnson, J. F. (2001). Toward a new consensus on high academic achievement for all students. *Education and Urban Society, 33,* 227–234.

Sleeter, C. E. (2001). Preparing teachers for culturally diverse schools: Research and the overwhelming presence of whiteness. *Journal of Teacher Education, 52,* 94–106.

Smith, T. E. C., Polloway, E. A., Patton, J, R., & Dowdy, C. A. (2004). *Teaching students with special needs in inclusive settings* (4th ed.). Boston: Allyn & Bacon.

Swadener, B. B., & Lubeck, S. (1995). *Children and families 'at promise': Deconstructing the discourse of risk.* Albany: State University of New York Press.

U.S. Department of Health and Human Services. (2002). *Child abuse prevention.* Retrieved November 1, 2002, from http://www.calib.com/nccanch/prevention/overview/prevention.cfm

Valencia, R. R., & Solórzano, D. G. (1997). Contemporary deficit thinking. In R. R. Valencia (Ed.), *Evolution of deficit thinking* (pp. 160–211). London: Palmer Press.

Winzer, M. A., & Mazurek, K. (1998). *Special education in multicultural contexts.* Upper Saddle River, NJ: Merrill/Prentice Hall.

PART IV

Exceptional Perspectives

CHAPTER **14**

Life-Span Services

Darrell was the kind of preschooler every teacher dreads having in the class—a 4-year-old public nuisance. Unable (or unwilling) to follow the simplest directions, he could usually be found poking an innocent classmate or doing his best in any number of ways to disrupt my Head Start class. But Darrell was not incapable of showing affection. I cannot easily forget the day he interrupted his finger painting to "lovingly" hug me and run his paint-covered fingers through my hair. I thought I caught a devilish gleam in his eye when he released his grip, but I quickly dismissed it. Darrell had long been tagged mentally retarded, and his misbehavior, we all knew, was due to his mental disability. Thus, Darrell was forgiven for this and other equally trying acts in the classroom.

It was George Washington's birthday, and I stood the class in a circle and put on a favorite record, "Chopping Down the Cherry Tree." The record was ideal for gross motor development. I instructed the children to swing their arms rhythmically to the "chop" of the music as if they were all little Georges chopping away at the proverbial cherry tree. The children loved it. Everyone swung his imaginary ax with the greatest enthusiasm, everyone of course except "dumb" Darrell, who just stood there with his arms straight out in front of him, hands clasped together making a huge fist. Patiently, I attempted to teach Darrell the act of chopping. But even after much demonstrating and coaxing, he stubbornly refused to change his original position and continued to stand motionless with his "ax" extended. Close to the end of my patience, I cried, "Darrell, why won't you chop with your ax like the rest of us?"

His reply shocked me into reassessing Darrell's mental retardation label: "I don't need to chop. Can't you see I have a power saw!"[1]

Richard was a blond, blue-eyed 6-year-old who had been living in a residential school for emotionally disturbed children for 3 years. On weekends he went home with his family. He was diagnosed as autistic and displayed many of the typical behaviors of children so labeled. Although he was quick to complain with high-pitched squeals, he never spoke and showed no emotion when people talked to him. He avoided eye contact with teachers, staff, or other children, preferring to isolate himself in a corner whenever he could. He liked to hold a toy truck upside down so that he could push its wheels and intently watch them spin. In the hope that some day Richard could learn to make letters and write his name, the staff had spent every school day reinforcing Richard for going to the table and making an approximation of a circle or a triangle, prerequisite skills for writing words. After so many days, weeks, and months of no improvement, the staff became discouraged and feared that Richard would never learn to make shapes, not to mention write his name. It was on one of these days that Richard left his corner, stepped up to the chalkboard, on which he had never written, and in perfect letters wrote, "PANTRY PRIDE." Never having written a letter before, he produced the name of the grocery store where his mother shopped. We were shocked and overjoyed, but our hearts sank when Richard returned to his corner and refused to produce another word. Yet Richard had stepped out of his usual behavior to show us his capacity for learning if

[1] This anecdote was contributed by Ms. Roxana G. Davison.

only for a few minutes. We were then in a much better position to plan appropriate learning experiences.

Placed in a strange environment, the one thing that preschoolers are not is predictable. Thus, I prepared myself for the worst when I took my Head Start class of 30 inner-city 4-year-olds to the famous Bronx Zoo. How could I expect them to be orderly and restrained? Flashing through my mind were frightful fantasies of Freddy taking a bath with the walruses or Linda slipping through the bars to pet the leopards. To my great surprise, the children were very well behaved despite their obvious excitement at viewing the many wild animals that had previously only been magazine pictures. My major problem in controlling the children occurred quite unexpectedly as we rounded a corner and faced a large square of lush green grass bearing several "Keep off the grass" signs. After having survived elephant pens and monkey cages, I was hardly concerned about a grassy plot of ground. I was, in fact, stunned when almost every child bolted from our orderly little procession and tumbled onto the grass screaming with delight. It took me several seconds to realize that these inner-city children were growing up playing on concrete sidewalks and black asphalt streets covered with broken glass. That simple plot of green grass gave them their greatest thrill of our entire zoo trip.

Craig was the precocious one of the group. I was continually in awe of his insight and his eagerness to solve the mysteries of his world. Of course, there were a few times when even Craig put two and two together and came up with five.

Craig's mother, a divorcee, was dating an obstetrician. Like so many preschoolers, Craig kept his teachers and classmates well informed about his mother's personal life by frequently making announcements such as, "My mother dates a doctor named Phil, and he delivers real babies."

One day as we were out for a drive, Craig shouted, "Oh, look! There's Dr. Phil's house!" Pointing to a van parked in front of the house, he said, "There's his truck too!"

Since I was acquainted with Dr. Phil and knew that he owned no truck, I said gently, "No, Craig, that truck doesn't belong to Dr. Phil."

Looking me squarely in the eyes, he impatiently retorted, "Well, I bet it is too his truck. He must have a truck because Mommy says he delivers babies!"

Sometimes what seems like success may be just the opposite. For instance, Gary, a high school student, was involved in our "transition" project. This program attempts to help prepare students for various roles they must assume after formal schooling is over. At first glance, Gary looked like a success story. Not only did he complete high school but he also began taking courses at one of the local community colleges. Things were going so well for him that he qualified for and received financial aid from the school. Here was a textbook example of how the transition process could work successfully. Unfortunately, this story turns a bit sour. Although Gary was fortunate enough to get financial assistance, he did not know how to handle this monetary windfall. As soon as he received his check, he left school and has not been seen since. Is this a case of being successful too quickly?

A high school girl was seeking competitive employment. What happened to her during one particular interview illustrates that general job-seeking skills can be more important than highly refined vocational skills.

This girl went to interview at a local fish cannery. She had been trained very well in the specific vocational skills needed for this job, exceeding the skill level as determined by industry standards. She was accompanied on this interview by one of her trainers. However, she picked her nose during the entire interview. Of course, she didn't get the job. Her lack of personal hygiene negated any advantage she might have had over less qualified competitors. And when you think about it, it was good that she played her hand too soon, especially if you eat canned fish.

Phyllis has been a maid at the Ramada Inn since graduating from her high school program for people with severe disabilities. In 5 years, she had never missed a day of work or been late. Her supervisor often said, "I wish I had 20 others just like her!" Once, during her first year of work, he happened to pass the break room just as it was time for the maids to return to work. Five or six of the maids had apparently decided to extend their 15-minute coffee break. However, Phyllis quickly told them, "Break's over. It's time to work." Her supervisor simply said, "She gives a good day's work for a fair wage. I wish everybody was like that."

Kevin, who is blind, went to the movies with a group of friends one evening. The person selling tickets became perplexed when Kevin stepped up to the window. The ticket person asked Kevin if he could see and the answer given was "No." As there was no recollection of ever issuing a ticket to a blind person, the employee thought carefully about what to do. There was a long line, the ticketer was under pressure, and realized that a decision had to be made. Without any further hesitation, he told Kevin that he would charge him half price as Kevin was only going to hear the movie. Kevin readily accepted this offer and later confided that he'd take this deal anytime.

Usually, we only conceive of people with disabilities as school-aged children. We seldom look at a 7-year-old child with Down's syndrome and see him as eventually becoming a 50-year-old adult with a disability. This lack of vision on our part often causes us to concentrate our effort on developing academically related skills in individuals with disabilities. People do not "become" disabled upon school entry and cease to be disabled following their departure from our educational institutions. Interventions focused on developing practical, functional skills at all developmental levels are a critical part of special education. A life-span approach, from infancy through adulthood, must form the foundation of our profession. This chapter examines the areas of early childhood special education and adolescent/adult services and their relationship to facilitating and enhancing a high quality of life for persons with disabilities.

EARLY CHILDHOOD/BASIC CONCEPTS

Rationale for Early Childhood Education

Early scholars such as Montessori, Froebel, and Hall first directed attention toward early childhood as important foundation years for learning. A widespread interest in early childhood education, however, did not develop until the 1960s when psychological research began to reveal that the early years are indeed most critical for a child's future development.

Research findings suggested that the rate of learning roughly parallels a child's physical growth. It appears that learning occurs quite rapidly in the first 2 years, slightly less rapidly for the next 4, and then begins to level off to a lower and gradually decreasing rate. In fact, some assert that 50 percent of a child's total intellectual capacity has been developed by age 4, and 80 percent by age 8. Skeels's (1966) classic study of orphanage children dramatically demonstrated that modifying the environment during the early formative years can greatly improve a child's capacity for intellectual and social development at a later age.

Further, Schweinhart and Weikart (1985) reviewed seven longitudinal studies of the effects of early education on children living in poverty and found that every comparison of scholastic placement was favorable to the group that had received early childhood education. Moreover, avoiding later placement in special education programs emerged as one of the major financial benefits of preschool education (Howard, Williams, Port, & Lepper, 2001; Peterson, 1987).

Today, a sound foundation during the early childhood years is considered essential for subsequent success in school (Blackbourn, 1988; Blasco, 2001). In fact, Burton White's (1975) research at Harvard University's Pre-School Project led him to conclude that the period that begins at 8 months and ends at 3 years is a period of primary importance to the development of human intelligence and social skill. White insists that "to begin to look at a child's educational development when he is 2 years of age is already much too late" (p. 4). The need for thoughtful and rich early stimulation is critical for all children, particularly for those children with physical, emotional, mental, or social handicaps (Hayden, 1979). McDaniels (1977) argues that we cannot wait until age 6, or even age 3, to begin our interventions with young children. Programs for some young exceptional children should begin not long after birth.

This position entails the incorporation of the entire family into the intervention model. Indeed, the family as a system must become the focus of all intervention (Foster, Berger, & McClean, 1981; Turnbull & Turnbull, 1986; Winton &

Turnbull, 1981). Such a perspective emphasizes not only the uniqueness of each individual child, but the uniqueness of each specific family. Turnbull, Summers, and Brotherson (1984) outline a framework for understanding the family as a system made up of (a) family resources, (b) family interactions, (c) family functions, and (d) family life cycle.

Nagera (1975) warns that poorly conceived school-based centers for infants and toddlers may do more harm than good. During the 1970s, educators learned that parents play a critical role in facilitating development. Today's educators recognize that well-conceived programs involve parents in the teaching of their young children (Anastasiow, 1981). In particular, home- and center-based parent training can greatly change the young exceptional child's chances for developing to his or her full potential (Sandler, Coren, & Thurman, 1983; Shearer & Shearer, 1972; Sontag, 1977).

Legislative action, specifically Public Law 94–142, has mandated programs for all children with disabilities between the ages of 3 and 21. As a result of this significant law, the area of early childhood education has moved into the spotlight of attention. The guarantees of this law ensure parental participation, protection of rights, written notification of any placement changes, teacher training efforts, and incentive funding to the states. Efforts to locate and identify preschool-age children with disabilities (commonly referred to as *child find*) have been conducted nationwide. A U.S. Department of Education (1984) report to Congress argues that early intervention with children who have disabilities results in significant decreases in services required later. In those cases where early intervention eliminates or reduces the services otherwise needed when the child enters school, notable cost savings are realized.

Although the states were mandated under PL 94–142 to provide services to all students (aged 3 to 21 years) with disabilities, less than half of the states actually initiated services for the full 3- to 5-year age range. This was due to the limited mandate of PL 94–142 with respect to early childhood special education. This legislation mandated early intervention for young children (under age 3 years) with disabilities only if such services existed for nondisabled children under 3 years. However, Public Law 99–457, *The Education of the Handicapped Amendments of 1986,* extended the age range downward for children with disabilities to birth.

Definitional Perspective

Early childhood education was traditionally conceived of as the group learning experiences provided for children from the ages of 3 to 8. Thus, programs for early childhood education encompassed nursery schools, kindergartens, and primary grades. The growing realization, however, that infancy and toddlerhood are critical years for later social and intellectual development has largely accounted for the current notion that early childhood education embraces programs for all children under 9 years of age. This notion has been reflected and put into application through PL 99–457 and its emphasis on families and children in the birth to 3 years of age range. Quite logically, a significant proportion of educational and psychological research is now focused on the infant and toddler years and on parental involvement.

Early childhood special education programs are, by necessity, noncategorical in nature. Only a small percentage of those children who eventually make up the special education population in the public schools have identifiable disabilities during the early stages of development. Indeed, it is often the demands of the traditional classroom that make a student's disability apparent. Therefore, professionals in early childhood special education must focus primarily on those factors that place an individual child "at risk" for developing a disability. As a result, students served by early childhood special education programs generally have no categorical label but are often identified as developmentally delayed.

Early childhood education relies on the continued execution of various important dimensions: (a) early identification, (b) continuous assessment, (c) appropriate curricula, (d) effective teaching procedures, (e) parental involvement, and (f) multidisciplinary interaction. The omission of any of these dimensions in any early childhood program is detrimental to the education of children with disabilities. The curriculum for a young child who has a disability is generally determined by the child's strengths and delays in seven areas of development: self-help skills, gross motor development, fine motor development, communication skills, perceptual development, conceptual development, and social-emotional development.

Prevalence

Figures on the number of school-age children who have disabilities and who are receiving special education and related services are available from the federal government. The *Twenty-third Annual Report to Congress on the Implementation of the Individuals with Disabilities Act* (U.S. Department of Education, 2002), listed 829,330 children between the ages of birth and 5 years as receiving special education services. In 1976, the National Advisory Committee on the Handicapped reported that in the United States, approximately 1,187,000 preschool children displayed physical, emotional, or mental disabilities. Haring and McCormick (1990) note that, of the approximately 3.4 million infants born in this country each year, about 7 percent have congenital abnormalities that will be identified prior to their becoming school age. To this group, other preschool children who are "at risk" for eventual school problems could be added. This group includes those children who are abused, malnourished, homeless, and/or live in poverty.

Of those children identifiable as needing special services, many are multiply disabled, having secondary deficits accompanying their major disability. Most of the young exceptional children do not fit neatly into the traditional special education categories. Many of the milder disabilities (e.g., mild retardation, learning disabilities) may not be evident until a child is of school age. Many of these children may be considered "at risk" for potential future school failure. They should be provided with services in various early intervention programs that do not specifically identify them as "disabled."

Some states have designated special categorical distinctions for preschool-age children with disabilities. Terms such as *learning impaired* may be used with this population until these children reach school age. Then a reevaluation would be conducted and the children would be either declassified or reclassified. Unfortunately, some infants and preschoolers with disabilities are not receiving the educational experiences necessary to ensure continued progress and later successful school adjustment.

Etiology

The causes of disabilities in young children can be divided into five major categories: (a) genetic, (b) prenatal, (c) perinatal, (d) postnatal, and (e) environmental. Although a child's difficulty often results from a complex interaction of two or more factors, most educators focus attention on remediation rather than search for causes. However, remediation can sometimes be facilitated when etiological, or causative, factors are understood.

Genetic difficulties include biochemical disorders, such as galactosemia and phenylketonuria (PKU), and such chromosomal abnormalities as Down's syndrome. Today both PKU and galactosemia can be detected by urine tests, and, if found early enough, the harmful effects can be controlled by putting the infant on special diets. Some *prenatal* conditions frequently associated with childhood disabilities are (a) anoxia (i.e., premature separation of the placenta), severe anemia, or a heart condition of the mother; (b) Rh factor incompatibility; and (c) rubella contracted by the mother during the first trimester of pregnancy. Birth injuries, asphyxia, and prematurity are among the *perinatal* conditions that may affect the child during or immediately preceding birth. During infancy and early childhood, disabling conditions can result from malnutrition, accidental physical trauma (especially to the brain), child abuse/neglect, and diseases and infections such as encephalitis, meningitis, and chronic otitis media. Finally, it appears that a great proportion of the children suffering from school learning difficulties have simply not received the necessary experiential and cultural prerequisites such as social and educational stimulation.

Obviously, the early medical, nutritional, social, and educational needs of children must be satisfied in order to maximize their opportunities for healthy development. And it is equally true that the sooner an etiological factor is arrested or ameliorated, the less profound will be its debilitating effects. Unfortunately, early delivery of services, which may be of great importance to some young children and their families, is frequently difficult. Not only are funds and services limited but also the identification of children with less severe but potentially disabling conditions is no easy task.

Characteristics

Language Development.   That language and intellectual competence are closely intertwined is becoming increasingly obvious. Often accompanying immature language are such immature thought processes as delayed discrimination and reasoning skills. Indeed, severe language delay or inadequacy is the most significant single behavioral sign indicating a young child's need for special help in order to succeed in school.

Socialization depends on experiences with language and communication. The ability to abstract the essence of experiences and the urge and power to express complex thoughts and feelings are uniquely human. Although animals may respond to symbols for specific things, such as a dog knowing he is going for a walk when he sees his leash, only people can generalize from their experiences and share an analysis and synthesis of their ideas with others. From infancy on, human learning is dependent on the acquisition of the communication code of that culture.

The very young child faces the task of learning to understand the world's confusing happenings. Understanding is restricted to the immediate and concrete during early childhood. Concomitant with the development of language skills, the child gradually begins to deal with abstractions, and begins to use symbolization in more complex ways.

Unfortunately, as all educators know, the path leading from simple and concrete communication to the complex and abstract variety of understanding is a treacherous one that can be followed only if the child is afforded appropriate environmental experiences. A rich and stimulating language environment during the early childhood years is required to develop the verbal and intellectual skills essential for later school success (Hart and Risley, 1999; Hulit and Howard, 2002; Owens, 2002; Vygotsky, 1978). Moreover, to develop intellect and expressive skills, a child must be provided with stimulating sensory and social experiences that involve the child emotionally and help create a need for communication. Clearly, insufficient and unsatisfying experiences with the social and physical worlds can hamper the drive to talk and question. They may eventually reduce the child's motivation and create language and thought patterns that cause school failure.

The language patterns of many children from lower socioeconomic levels are a source of considerable concern to linguists, psychologists, and educators. The language of lower-class children often differs significantly from the standard English spoken by middle-class children and expected by teachers within the public schools. Bereiter and Engelmann (1966) go so far as to equate cultural deprivation with language deprivation, insisting that for lower-class children to succeed in school, they must learn the middle-class language of the school system. Similarly, Bloom, Davis, and Hess (1965) treat the speech of lower-class children in terms of "language deficit." They maintain that the language and future learning of lower-class children are inhibited because their parents are less likely to provide the quantity and quality of verbal "corrective feedback" found in typical middle-class environments. Unfortunately, viewing a child from a language-deficit perspective suggests that the child is deprived of a structurally systematic and functionally adequate language. Further, it suggests that the lower-class child is generally deprived of culturalization when, in fact, the deprivation may relate only to middle-class culture. Hence, perceiving the lower-class child as having "language differences" rather than "language deficiencies" is preferable (Baratz, 1969).

Whether viewed as different or deficient, the language used by lower-class children in their homes frequently varies considerably from that used in school. Hess and Shipman (1967) conducted class-related research that found language learning and intellectual growth to be by-products of the verbal interaction between mother and child. Their research revealed that middle-class mothers most often employed a democratic type of control, used expanded sentences, and provided labels for objects. Most lower-class mothers, on the other hand, used an imperative type of control, spoke in a restricted form of language, and failed to provide their children with labels for objects. Although language style does vary within lower socioeconomic groups, lower-class children typically develop a mode of communication, perhaps adequate at home, which nonetheless may not be sufficient for progress in school.

Language difficulties, however, are not unique to lower-class youngsters. Many middle- and upper-class parents fail to provide their children with a language environment conducive to later school success. Moreover, language disabilities result not only from faulty learning but often from emotional disturbance, hearing impairment, central nervous system dysfunction, and mental retardation, none of which knows social class distinctions.

INTERVENTIONS

Head Start

Because large numbers of children within the lower class have experienced school difficulties, the nation's first comprehensive effort to provide prerequisite educational opportunities focused on economically disadvantaged children. Within this population were found the highest incidences of language differences as well as all other types of disabilities. The first nationwide program specifically designed for children likely to experience later educational difficulties was Project Head Start. Head Start programs began with the hope of providing not only rich language environments but also a wide range of health, nutritional, and educational experiences for economically disadvantaged preschoolers.

The commencement of Project Head Start in the spring of 1965 engendered hope in some circles of one day significantly reducing personal failure and poverty in society. Born under the auspices of the Office of Economic Opportunity, Project Head Start authorized the organization and establishment of 6-week summer programs for children whose family income fell below the poverty level set by Congress. Geared to the early childhood years, the program attempted to provide whatever environmental supplements were needed to prevent failure in the elementary grades. Following the first summer's operation, Head Start programs for the full academic year were initiated. Although the personnel of early Head Start centers were free to determine specific objectives and their means of achievement, greater levels of program specificity were gradually introduced. And because of abundant differences in beliefs among centers as to the needs of children, substantial variation in programs developed. The creators of some programs emphasized development of social skills, whereas others concentrated on the development of good health and dietary habits. Many programs resembled a traditional nursery school, but others emphasized intensive directive instruction in language, reading-readiness skills, science, and math. Thus, Head Start was in effect many different programs with centers varying widely in terms of what and how they taught.

One of the most innovative and exciting aspects of Project Head Start was its concept of parent involvement. Active parents can add continuity to the child's home and school experiences while also encouraging at-home practice of the cognitive skills disadvantaged children may lack. In addition, a parent's active contribution to the child's education often engenders new feelings of adequacy and self-worth in the parent that, in turn, may enhance affectional relationships in the home (Evans, 1971). However, while federal Head Start officials encouraged parent participation, they failed to adequately specify how parents were to be involved; and there was substantial variation from center to center.

The nationwide interest in early childhood education and the exciting possibilities presented by Project Head Start appear in retrospect to have generated some unfortunate side effects. Amid the excitement, child development experts failed to caution the nation that a 6-week summer session or even a full-year program prior to school entrance would provide only a beginning in meeting the educational needs of young children. And specialists did not adequately inform the public that the scientific study of child development, in its infancy, could provide only a few clues about the necessary social and educational experiences required for optimal development of young children. Moreover, at the time, educators had not fully recognized the critical influence of the years from birth to age 3 and had not included infants and toddlers in the project. Thus, expectations of success for Head Start ran unrealistically high.

Although significant increases on cognitive measures were found, especially from those children from the southeastern geographical region and from large urban areas (Caldwell, 1972; Payne, Mercer, Payne, & Davison, 1973), the effects of the Head Start experience appeared to wash out as children entered school.

Some time after the initiation of Head Start, the nation's attitude toward early intervention became perceptibly more skeptical, and disillusionment displaced the former climate of optimism. Although Head Start had doubtlessly helped many young children overcome classroom difficulties, it failed to realize its promise of healing the nation's educational ills. Unfortunately, Head Start as initially conceived did not include many important aspects of educational planning more clearly understood by today's educators.

Educators now know that unless the content of a program is carefully defined, a preschool is just another place for a child to be (Schweinhart, Berrueta-

Clement, Barnett, Epstein, & Weikart, 1985). Current Head Start programs have improved their content and are proving to have significant short- and long-term positive effects on low-income children (Schweinhart & Weikart, 1985). Today the federal government invests about a billion and a half dollars annually in such early childhood programs.

After the need for early educational experiences for children with disabilities received wide recognition in the late 1960s, Head Start legislation was amended to require that at least 10 percent of the enrollment opportunities in each state be made available to these children. Although the available spaces do not begin to equal the number of young children with disabilities, today many exceptional preschoolers are participating in this program.

Follow Through

In many primary schools throughout the nation, Project Follow Through has been implemented as a means of sustaining early gains produced by Head Start experiences. Authorized in 1968 under the Office of Economic Opportunity, the programs provide continued educational enrichment for primary-grade children formerly enrolled in Head Start classes. Clearly, all special services for young children have the greatest chance for lasting success when continued assistance is provided in the elementary grades.

Originally conceived as an extension of Head Start, Follow Through changed its focus as time progressed. The Office of Education altered it so that it was described as a "planned variation experiment." House, Glass, McLean, and Walker (1978) critiqued a report on early intervention that compared the data collected on various features of 13 early intervention models. The authors concluded that the existence of substantial intersite variation across programs was indeed accurate, while the superiority of the "basic skills" type of model was not substantiated. In their article, they present a number of arguments that challenge the second conclusion. House and his colleagues stress the very intricate dynamics of Project Follow Through and the lack of definitive answers:

> *The truth about Follow Through is complex. No simple answer to the problem of educating disadvantaged students has been found. . . . Unique features of the local settings had more effect on test scores than did the models. This does not mean that federal programs are useless or inappropriate for pursuing national objectives; however, many of the most significant factors affecting educational achievement lie outside the control of federal officials.* (p. 156)

Project RUN

Project RUN (Reach Us Now) is an early intervention program that focuses on the needs of children with disabilities (birth to 3 years of age) and their families. This program, which is funded and operated by the Mississippi Department of Mental

Health, primarily serves children with severe to moderate disabilities. The program incorporates both the center-based and the home-based service delivery approaches, a parent training component, and multidisciplinary assessment/intervention. Project RUN emphasizes developmentally appropriate intervention, basic skill instruction, sensory stimulation, assistive technology, physical/occupational therapy, and facilitative parent–child interactions in its approach. The project serves persons in the 23 primarily rural counties of North Mississippi.

Project RUN also focuses on connecting parents and their children with disabilities with appropriate local services and assisting in the transition of the children into special education programs offered by their local school districts. Approximately 83 percent of those students served by Project RUN make a successful transition to public school programs.

TRENDS AND ISSUES

Recent Federal Initiatives Supporting Preschool Programs

Four federal initiatives—Education for All Handicapped Children Act–B (EHA-B), the Preschool Incentive Grant Program, the State Implementation Grant Program, and the Handicapped Children's Early Education Program (HCEEP)—have played a critical role in encouraging preschool programs. The U.S. Department of Education (1984) reports that the number of states choosing to participate in these preschool programs has more than doubled since fiscal year 1978. It also reports that the accomplishments of the HCEEP, better known as the First Chance Network, are greater and more varied than those of any other documented education program.

In 1986, PL 99–457 was signed. This legislation was designed to amend and expand the mandate of PL 94–142, thus extending the rights and protections of PL 94–142 to all young children with disabilities who are 3 to 5 years of age. States applying for funds under PL 94–142 must provide assurances that all children with disabilities who are 3 through 5 years old are receiving a free, appropriate education at public expense. In addition, PL 99–457 provides for a state grant program addressing the needs of infants and toddlers (i.e., birth to 3 years of age) with disabilities through early intervention. Parent/family support, resource centers, and the development of individual family service plans (IFSPs), which are similar in concept to individualized education plans (IEPs), are required under PL 99–457.

Furthermore, the law mandates interagency agreements to meet the needs of the target population. Social service agencies must now work cooperatively with educational agencies to serve children with disabilities and their families. A legal basis now exists for early intervention services to all young children who have disabilities. States now have the opportunity to provide appropriate service delivery to persons with disabilities during the most critical stage of their development, birth through 5 years of age.

Educational Strategies

Today, a variety of intervention strategies are used as evidenced by the various models in the Follow Through Project. The Follow Through Project classifies their various orientations into three main categories (Stebbins, St. Pierre, Proper, Anderson, & Cerva, 1977, pp. 131–132):

1. *Basic skills:* These models focus first on the elementary skills of vocabulary, arithmetic computation, spelling, and language.
2. *Cognitive-conceptual:* These models emphasize the more complex "learning-to-learn" and problem-solving skills.
3. *Affective-cognitive:* These models focus primarily on self-concept and attitudes toward learning, and secondarily on "learning-to-learn" skills.

Underlying each of these orientations is a theoretical foundation derived from years of psychological research. Although a full discussion of these orientations currently in use is beyond the scope of this book, we can presently state that more research is needed before establishing the superiority of any specific orientation.

Parent Involvement

In past years the advice given to parents of exceptional children by physicians, teachers, and psychologists was often ill founded: "Just wait and see what happens. He'll probably grow out of it." Instead, difficulties were compounded and the children fell further and further behind their nondisabled peers.

Clearly, the efforts to educate parents and to involve them in the total educational program of their child are warranted. The impact of parental (or primary caregiver) behavior is so profound that it not only greatly influences intelligence (Blasco, 2001; Garber & Heber, 1973; White, 1975), but it also affects the rate of neuromotor attainments such as sitting, crawling, and walking (Anastasiow, 1981; Bowe, 2000; Kearsley, 1979). Furthermore, not only does the parent affect the child, but the presence of a child with a disability can have a powerful influence on parents. As Hayden (1978) points out: "Having a handicapped child can be a traumatic experience for parents, not only when they first learn of the child's disability but throughout the child's growing years" (p. 42).

Although some parents are quick to recognize when something is wrong with their child, some parents have difficulty accepting the reality of their child's disability. Such reality avoidance often prevents the child with a disability from receiving professional attention in the early years when remediation could be advantageous. And this unfortunate fact underscores the importance of the teacher's role in identifying disabilities.

The amendments to the Education for all Handicapped Children Act (PL 99–457) assure parental involvement and that efforts to get them involved through the development of IFSPs are under way. Although some disabling conditions are immediately obvious, others are more subtle and difficult to detect. Developmental lags or deviations in children are frequently overlooked because parents lack basic knowledge concerning child development and have little opportunity to compare their child's development with that of others (Allen, Rieke, Dmitriev, & Hayden, 1972). Moreover, even those few parents who can quickly detect minor disabilities in other children can be oblivious to their own child's slight limp, speech delay, or vision impairment. Understandably, many parents find it difficult to admit that their child has a disability.

Identification

Teachers should proceed with considerable caution, however, in their efforts to avail children with disabilities of needed services. Their job should be simply to observe the children carefully and alert parents that additional help *may* be needed. Teachers must remember that they are not in a position to render a definitive medical diagnosis of a disorder.

Before causing parents needless alarm, teachers should recognize that whether or not a particular developmental skill is appropriate may depend on the community in which the child lives. Personal judgments of disability may be subject to cultural or educational bias. Branding a child as disabled can have devastating effects on his or her self-esteem, and the label may well become a self-fulfilling prophecy. Stated differently, low expectations can encourage low performance.

Clearly, it is within the teacher's proper role to observe children carefully and to obtain professional assistance in interpreting behavioral signs. Appropriate parental warnings and referrals for further diagnosis should be made only after the teacher systematically records observations of the child's behavior. All early childhood teachers should familiarize themselves with developmental, age-appropriate behaviors and with potentially troublesome behaviors in young children. Teachers should keep in mind that even among "normal" children vast differences abound in the physical, social, and intellectual growth rates of individuals. Only those children who after careful observation appear well behind their peers in some basic facet of development will need to be referred for further diagnosis and special services. (For lists of specific behaviors indicative of potential problems, see Hanson & Lynch, 1995; Krajicek, Hertzberg, Saudall, & Anastasiow, 2003)

In addition to the teacher's identification of students who need special services, there is now a trend toward the early identification of infants with disabilities. With our present knowledge, approximately 6.8 percent of children with disabilities can be identified at birth or very shortly thereafter. Pediatricians, then, are in the best position to identify infants and toddlers who have disabilities, and, if appropriately trained, they can communicate helpful suggestions to parents. Major efforts are currently being made to educate physicians in normal and exceptional child development (Guralnick, Richardson, & Heiser, 1982). Techniques for postnatal evaluation are presently available. To be useful, or perhaps justified, this early identification must be followed up with the appropriate commensurate services.

Presently, only a few of these services are available to neonates with disabilities. However, along with increasing research in this area emphasizing the importance of the child's first 3 years of life, appropriate services are being developed as well.

Prevention

Early identification and intervention sometimes become a vehicle for preventing or inhibiting the further development of disabling conditions. If services for the child and the parents can be provided at a very early point in the infant's development, many major problems can be avoided at a later time. However, the prevention of severe problems also depends on the continued improvement of medical and health services and on the ability to improve environmental factors (e.g., proper nutrition, adequate medical care, and healthy living conditions).

Conclusion

Early childhood programs are here to stay. Research has clearly documented their importance. We have no substantial evidence, however, to indicate that any one teaching approach is superior in every situation and with every child. We do know that some exceptional children require positive reinforcement and direct instruction before they begin to manipulate and meaningfully interact with the physical environment. On the other hand, many young children clearly respond to directive teaching with greater enthusiasm and more correct responses if first given the opportunity to manipulate concrete objects. The likelihood is that the optimum development of the young child with disabilities is best fostered in an environment that provides ample opportunity for self-directed exploration supplemented by directive instruction in areas of the child's greatest need. Parent involvement can maximize training efforts.

The study of human behavior is still in its infancy. Seventy years ago, Freud and Watson were only beginning their studies on the nature of behavior and learning. The real impetus for early childhood education began as late as the 1960s, and the importance of the first 3 years is just beginning to be widely recognized.

We have learned much in a very short time. Yet, we are still falling far short in meeting the needs of our young children with disabilities. However, with continued progress in our commitment to educational programming and research, the future for young exceptional children is full of promise.

ADOLESCENTS AND ADULTS WITH DISABILITIES/BASIC CONCEPTS

With the original passage of PL 94–142, much attention was directed toward providing appropriate education to students in need of such intervention. The thrust of these efforts was centered on the younger school-age population even though this legislation mandated that concern be given to all individuals between the ages of 3 and 21. Parent groups were very concerned with this younger population as well. As a result, great changes were occurring in educating these children. Unfortunately, the needs of older students were overlooked to a great extent (Blackorby & Wagner, 1996; Sherbenou & Holub, 1982). It was not until the passage of Public Law 98–199, the *1983 Amendments to the Individuals With Disabilities Education Act,* that Congress authorized funding for secondary education and transition services for youth with disabilities.

More recently, increasing professional attention and action has been directed toward the needs of exceptional youth and adults. Some of this interest has been buttressed by the fact that the children to whom much attention was given over 20 years ago are now grown up. Additional motivation has been provided by the realization that many students with disabilities do not outgrow their problems. Years of frustration with a difficult and often unrewarding educational experience have taken their toll on far too many individuals.

As the termination of formal schooling approaches for youth with disabilities, parents, teachers, support personnel, administrators, school board members, and the community at large become concerned about what lies ahead. The adult outcome data that have emerged during the last few years paint a less than optimistic picture for many individuals with disabilities (Frank & Sitlington, 2000; Trupin, Sebesta, Yelin, & LaPlante, 1997).

What are the life choices for most exceptional youth as they prepare to exit lower education? The major options are as follows:

❏ Employment (full-time or part-time; supported or nonsupported)
❏ Further education or training (2- and 4-year colleges/universities, technical schools, trade schools, adult education)
❏ Military service
❏ Volunteer work (community-based service, Peace Corps, etc.)
❏ "Domestic engineering" (househusband/wife)
❏ Absence of gainful employment or purposeful activity

This section highlights many of the critical variables related to making a successful transition from adolescence to adulthood. Most of the discussion focuses on those exceptional adolescents and adults who have disabilities; nevertheless, the issues and needs of gifted individuals will also be highlighted. We have also made an arbitrary distinction between individuals with milder forms of disability and those with more severe types of disability. This has been done for the sake of making the discussion clearer, because some specific issues for these two groups are significantly different.

Characteristics of and Interventions for Adolescents

Nature of Adolescence.   Although trying to define adolescence in a universally accepted fashion is not easy, this stage of life is clearly very important. It is in itself a transitional phase of moving from childhood to adulthood. It is a difficult time for everyone and may even be more trying for youth who have disabilities. Smith, Price, and Marsh (1986) have summarized the major tasks of adolescence documented in the literature:

❑ Creation of a sense of sexuality as part of a personal identity
❑ Development of confidence in social interactions
❑ Infusion of social values into a personal code of behavior
❑ Acceptance of biological changes
❑ Attainment of a sense of emotional independence
❑ Contemplation of vocational interests
❑ Identification of personal talents and interests
❑ Awareness of personal weaknesses and strengths
❑ Development of sexual interests with nonfamily members
❑ Development of peer relationships
❑ Completion of formal educational activities
❑ Preparation for marriage, parenting, and adult relationships (p. 212)

The relevance of some of these tasks for adolescents with disabilities will vary according to their level of functioning.

Special Concerns of Adolescence. In addition to the normal challenges the typical adolescent has to face, other at-risk conditions must also be considered. The exact relationship of these potential problem areas to exceptionality is not clearly understood; however, we do know that exceptional youth are just as susceptible to and may be more at risk. The statistics that correspond with these areas are staggering and sobering. Although we will simply list the areas of concern here, the reader is encouraged to examine them more closely. Professionals who work with adolescents must be familiar with these areas:

❑ Substance abuse (drugs and alcohol)
❑ Teenage pregnancy
❑ Teenage suicide
❑ Runaways/homelessness
❑ Dropping out of school
❑ Juvenile delinquency

These are problems to which teenagers are constantly being exposed and with which they must contend. These issues cannot be ignored, because they will not go away. In today's society, we have to find ways to help adolescents deal with the complexities of life and to let them understand that others care about them.

Curricular Needs. Adolescents with mild disabilities include those individuals whose educational needs should allow them to be included in general education to a great degree. Categorically, this population often includes individuals with learning disabilities, mild behavior problems, and mild mental retardation. Some of the major issues affecting this population are described in the following paragraphs.

Caution must be exercised when presenting a list of general characteristics; however, it is instructive to provide a school-based perspective of the needs of this group of students. The following characteristics can be found in many students at the secondary level:

❏ Low achieving—typically demonstrated in reading, written expression, and math
❏ Plateau of basic skill development
❏ Deficiencies in the study skills area (e.g., note taking, test taking, time management, and using reference materials)
❏ Ineffective use of strategic behaviors necessary for academic success
❏ Social skills deficits
❏ At risk for dropping out

The last characteristic is worth exploring in more detail. The exit data for students who are mentally retarded or learning disabled or who have emotional/behavioral disorders (the current terminology used in IDEA) are presented in Table 14.1 (U.S. Department of Education, 2002). These data, based on the 2000–2001 school year, are cause for alarm, especially if one accepts the derived figures for what is likely to be the "real dropout" rate. The clear message sent by these data is that significant numbers of students are not finding the school experience to be worth staying around for.

For those students who are in school, some professionals argue that they are not being adequately prepared to deal with the demands of adulthood when one considers what those demands are and how many of them are addressed in school.

Table 14.1
Exit Data for Students Who Are Mentally Retarded,
Learning Disabled, and Behaviorally/Emotionally
Disordered, 2000–2001.

Exit Basis	Select Groups		
	LD	ED	MR
Diploma	48.6%	27.1%	29.1%
Certificate	10.2	6.3	37.7
Age-out	0.6	1.1	6.3
Dropout	19.8	36.2	17.6
Unknown exit	17.3	29.4	10.5
"Real" dropout rate	37.1	65.6	28.1

Source: From *Twenty-third Annual Report to Congress on the Implementation of the Individuals with Disabilities Education Act,* by U.S. Department of Education, 2002, Washington, DC: Author.

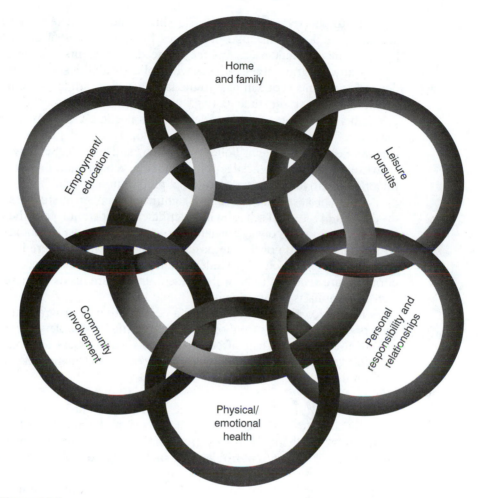

Figure 14.1

Domains of Adulthood

Source: From *Life Skills Instruction for All Students with Special Needs* (p. 13), by M. E. Cronin and
J. R. Patton, 1993, Austin, TX: PRO-ED.

All of the demands of adult living can be categorized into six arbitrary domains of
adulthood, as illustrated in Figure 14.1. Even at this macro level, it is obvious that
some important areas related to dealing with adulthood successfully are not
directly taught to most students.

The dominant types of programming available to students with mild disabilities can be categorized into four major areas (Smith, Polloway, Patton, & Dowdy,
2004): academic content mastery (i.e., teaching general education content), remedial (basic skills, social skills training), maintenance (learning strategies, tutorial),
and adult outcomes (vocational, life skills). To this day, much attention is still

devoted to the remediation of basic skills, and too little attention is given to preparing students with mild disabilities for the realities of adult life. A balance between the academic needs and the life needs of students is lacking.

Many programs for students with mild disabilities still have a strong academic focus. This is due in part to the fact that some students are in diploma track programs. For certain students (e.g., those for whom postsecondary education is a possibility), a strong academic orientation is needed. Others who are less capable may benefit from continued efforts to develop basic skills and remediate deficiencies, as Polloway, Epstein, Polloway, Patton, and Ball (1986) have demonstrated. However, any focus on academics, whether developmental or remedial, should be integrated with life skills and vocational preparation as well.

Many professionals feel that a significant number of students who have mild disabilities exit formal school with insufficient preparation for "the life after." This fact becomes more poignant when one realizes that most secondary-level students with disabilities do not pursue postsecondary education. There is a great need for comprehensive curricula for students with disabilities at the secondary level. Such curricula are sensitive to both the present and future needs of these students, with a strong emphasis on functionality.

Most secondary programs offer a combination of programmatic orientations, thus preparing students for a range of possibilities. Exemplary secondary programs can be identified by their attempts to realistically assess and match a student's interests, preferences, and abilities to the requisite demands of likely subsequent environments.

Youth With More Severe Disabilities. The population referred to as more severely disabled can best be characterized as having "substantial functional limitations." Individuals in this group may have mental, physical, and/or other emotional and behavioral problems of such a degree and nature that they require extensive supports.

According to Wehmeyer and Patton (2000), the most important curricular issue for this group is the need to teach basic daily living skills (e.g., self-care, communication, "functional" academics, socialization, leisure/recreational skills) and to provide appropriate vocational training. To be successful, practitioners need to (a) use a variety of training procedures, (b) provide instruction in community-based settings, (c) maintain skill acquisition by employing naturally occurring events, and (d) program for generalization of skills.

Low-Incidence Conditions. Youth with low-incidence conditions include adolescents with vision, hearing, or certain types of physical/health problems. For this group, the major issues center on preparing them for postsecondary education and/or to function independently as adults. Specific training in the use of various assistive technology (both low and high tech) may be required. One of the most sensitive areas that needs careful attention is the acceptance of these individuals by others. We know how important peer acceptance is at this level of development, and for this reason, special effort might be required to ensure that adolescents with vision, hearing, or physical disabilities are accepted as part of inclusive school settings.

Giftedness. It is a tragic oversight to think that gifted adolescents do not have special needs in terms of intervention. It has been said that the needs of this group may be just as unique and important as those of adolescents with mental retardation. Students who excel in specified ways (see chapter 12 for a breakdown of the different distinctions of giftedness) typically require unique forms of career development that match their diverse and accelerated needs. This group also requires programs that allow them to discover who they are (i.e., programs that emphasize self-examination) (Fleming, 1985). Gifted students can also benefit from well-designed and quality counseling services. The importance of this need is underscored by the amount of recent professional attention being given to this area.

Transition from School to Community Living

The need to better bridge the transition from school to community living has enjoyed a wave of interest and activity in recent years. In 1984 the Office of Special Education and Rehabilitative Services identified this topic as a national priority (Will, 1984) and funded a number of major transition projects. This early attention to the transition needs of students was initiated by concern about what was happening to students who had been served by special education during their school careers after they exited the school system. This need to better prepare young adults with disabilities for various subsequent environments and to assist them in being placed in such was also recognized by local education agency personnel and professionals in the field of special education, as well as by the parents of these youth.

The *1997 Amendments to the Individuals With Disabilities Education Act* provides a federal mandate for transition services that must be implemented for all students with disabilities reaching 14 years of age. It defines transition services as a coordinated set of activities for a student, designed within an outcome-oriented process, which promotes movement from school to postschool activities, including postsecondary education, vocational training, integrated employment (including supported employment), continuing and adult education, adult services, independent living, or community participation.

The coordinated set of activities must be based on the individual student's needs, taking into account the student's preferences and interests, and must include instruction, community experiences, the development of employment and other postschool objectives, and, if appropriate, acquisition of daily living skills and functional vocational evaluation.

The concept of transition links the two themes of adolescence and adulthood and involves three distinct phases: assessment, planning, and action. It is an important part of the overall nature of preparing individuals for adulthood, as presented

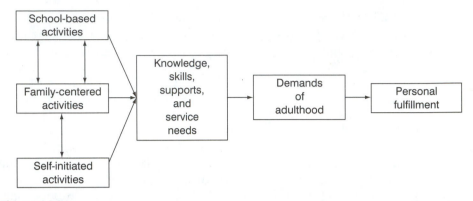

Figure 14.2
Preparing Students for Adulthood
Source: From *Transition From School to Young Adulthood* by J. R. Patton and C. Dunn, 1998, Austin, TX: PRO-ED.

in Figure 14.2. As pointed out in this figure, a person's quality of life is a function of being personally fulfilled, which comes from being able to deal with the demands of adulthood successfully. (This idea is a variation of the concept of quality of life proposed by Halpern, 1993.) Those who deal successfully with the demands of adulthood typically possess usable knowledge and requisite skills and/or have necessary supports and services in place. This competence and support are achieved through exposure to appropriate transition education (i.e., comprehensive curricula, as defined earlier) and transition planning. Note that families often contribute considerably to what is being referred to as *transition education.* The essence of the transition planning process is when school-based personnel, the family, and the student work together to determine transitional needs and a plan of action.

The prospect of youth with disabilities adjusting successfully to life after high school depends greatly on various personal factors (e.g., knowledge and skills) and other community supports (e.g., social workers, vocational rehabilitation counselors, postsecondary education staff, various adult service providers, and other community agencies). Certain students with disabilities may not need any specialized supports in adjusting to adult life; however, for those who do, school-based personnel must take the lead in assisting the student and the family in linking with needed services.

If transitional planning is to be effective, a number of concerns must be addressed within all phases of the process. We must ensure that (a) transitional needs of students are addressed through curricula; (b) students' interests, preferences, and transitional needs are assessed adequately; (c) transition plans are comprehensive (i.e., not focused only on employment goals); and (d) linkage activities are continually enhanced. This whole process must be guided by the overriding goal of preparing young adults with disabilities to deal successfully with the complexities of adulthood that await them.

Adulthood

In recent years, much effort has been directed toward the inclusion of all types of exceptional individuals into the mainstream of everyday life. For many, this has not been too difficult; for others—especially those who are more severely disabled—it has been a challenge.

The landmark legislation, the Americans with Disabilities Act, now provides civil rights protections to this group. The scope of the law applies to public or private employment, transportation, accommodations, and telecommunications. Fundamentally, it prohibits discrimination against persons with disabilities. Its intent is wonderful and welcomed; its actual implementation and effects await the test of time.

The demands placed on adults are many. As pointed out earlier in this chapter, a young adult needs to be competent in a number of skill areas to deal adequately with community living. However, certain demands change over time and individuals must be able to adapt to these changes. For this reason, it might be necessary to examine the experiences of exceptional adults throughout their life span.

Even though a model for conceptualizing successful community adjustment (see Figure 14.2) has been proposed, the concept remains elusive. Even within the current professional excitement related to "transition," no uniformity exists as to what successful outcomes actually are. Adjustment variables that are typically studied, and that imply what researchers think are important, relate to living environments, employment, monetary status and management, marriage and children, sexuality issues, infrequency of antisocial behaviors, and use of leisure time. Although some consensus may be found to support the importance of most of these variables, we cannot help but be concerned about the value judgments implicit in some of them. For instance, people are no longer suspicious of any person or group that prefers a single lifestyle to being married and having children. Our responsibility is to help exceptional adults achieve to the best of their abilities and to accomplish what they want, not what we think that they want.

A cycle of frustration can arise for some individuals who are disabled, as described in the following scenario:

> *Having a job, a sweetheart or spouse, a room or home of their own, and personal possessions have become the hallmark of normalcy for many . . . persons and their major goal. Yet, even when these have been acquired, individuals may still feel that they risk exposure through daily blunders or failures, and remain caught in a whirlwind of stress—coping with frustrations of what they are, struggling to be what they are not.* (Beirne-Smith, Ittenbach, & Patton, 1998, p. 406)

Although we still lack precision in defining the specifics of community adjustment, we can refer back to Figure 14.2. This figure underscores the importance of

(a) the knowledge and skills of the individual, (b) the supports and services that are needed, and (c) the demands placed on the person to live and function adequately within the community setting—some of these demands are common to all adults, whereas others are specific to a given person or setting.

For the purposes of this section, we consider the term *exceptional adults* to apply to people with characteristics that make them uniquely different and with needs that usually require special attention. In general, adults with disabilities can be described as manifesting significant functional limitations interfering with major life activities. Many exceptional adolescents might not necessarily become exceptional adults.

Characteristics of and Interventions for Adults with Disabilities

As mentioned earlier, when discussing characteristics, there is always a danger of overgeneralization. Thus, do not think that each of the findings listed in the following paragraphs will apply to every adult with a disability. Table 14.2 provides some data on adults with disabilities.

According to Blackorby and Wagner (1996), the unemployment rate for youth with disabilities is 46 percent; for adults with disabilities, it is 36.5%. This is understandable considering that the rate of those students with disabilities who earn a high school diploma is around 25 percent.

Key Features of Community Living.   Where do adults who have disabilities work and live? What do they do with their time? How well do they get along in the community? To a great extent, the answers to these questions depend on the abilities of the individual, the availability of appropriate individual supports and community services, and community attitudes and behaviors. This section of the chapter describes some important dimensions related to living in the community.

Employment.   For those who are employed, a number of options are possible. Many adults with disabilities are engaged in competitive employment and receive typical wages. Some people with disabilities have earned advanced graduate degrees and have become leaders in their fields. However, for most adults with disabilities who have been competitively employed, jobs are likely to be unskilled or semiskilled. Another option is supported employment. This is a type of competitive employment in which an individual acquires the essential vocational skills of a job while at the job site and under the supervision of a job coach or employment specialist. This particular employment option has been very successful and is being used throughout the country to gain employment for individuals with a wide range of abilities. A sheltered employment setting remains another employment option, although its attractiveness has waned dramatically during the course of the last few years with the advent of the supported employment model.

Table 14.2
Data on Adults with Disabilities

Who are the 48.9 Million Persons with Disabilities?		
• under 15		6%
• between age 15–64		60%
• between age 21–64		56%
• 65 and over		34%
• men		22.9 million
• women		26.0 million
• people with severe disabilities		24.1 million
• men		9.9 million
• women		14.2 million

Race and Ethnic Groups age 15–64

• Blacks	4.1 million
• Asian and Pacific Islanders	515,000
• People of Hispanic origin	2.4 million
• Whites not of Hispanic origin	22.6 million
• American Indian, Eskimo, or Aleut	285,000

What Is the Employment Status?
Employed Persons Age 21 to 64

• total	108.7 million
• people with disabilities	14.3 million
• men	7.9 million
• women	6.4 million
• of 14.3 million people with disabilities, those with severe disability	2.9 million
• men	1.3 million
• women	1.6 million

What Are the Leading Causes of Disability and Their Impact?
Over 27 million individuals age 15 and over reported having a limitation in a physical or daily living activity, causing a disability. Following are the leading causes

• arthritis/rheumatism	7.2 million
• back spinal problems	5.7 million
• heart trouble	4.6 million
• lung/respiratory trouble	2.8 million
• high blood pressure	2.2 million
• stiffness or deformity of the foot, leg, arm, or hand	2.0 million
• diabetes	1.6 million

Those Individuals Age 15 and Over Reported the Following

• used a wheelchair	1.5 million
• women	919,000
• men	575,000
• used a cane, walker, or crutches for six months or longer	4.0 million
• even when wearing corrective lenses, had difficulty seeing words or letters in ordinary newsprint	8.1 million
• even when wearing corrective lenses, could not see the words or letters in newsprint at all	1.6 million
• had difficulty hearing a normal conversation with another person	10.0 million
• could not hear what is said in a normal conversation	924,000

Source: From *Population Profile of the United States, 1995,* by U.S. Department of Commerce, 1995, Washington, DC: Author.

Living Arrangements. A great number of adults who have disabilities live very much like anyone else—with their parents, relatives, nonrelated persons, or alone. As with all of us, living arrangements are determined to a great extent by income level and financial status. For many adults with disabilities, low levels of income limit the choices of where they can live. Consequently, we are reminded of the axiom that states "Where one lives greatly determines how one lives."

The continuum of living arrangements for adults with more severe disabilities includes the following:

1. *Apartment programs:* independent, residential, or cluster arrangements
2. *Protected settings:* care, boarding, or companion homes
3. *Group homes:* family-like setting within a residential neighborhood
4. *ICF-MR programs* (Intermediate Care Facilities for the Mentally Retarded): settings that provide 24-hour care (nursing, medical support, therapy, and training)
5. *Institutions:* residential facilities that tend to have individuals with the most severe handicaps

There has been a strong movement to establish living environments in the community for all adults with severe disabilities. Many arrangements involve the concept of supportive living. Although this trend is in evidence, the availability of community residences is limited in some locations, and the quality of services varies greatly.

Leisure and Recreation. As indicated in Figure 14.1, a major domain of adulthood is leisure pursuits. Adults with disabilities need leisure activities as much as anyone else to enhance their lives. Unfortunately, many remain outside the mainstream of community life with regard to recreational activities and leisure pursuits, due to the nature of their disabilities and/or the inaccessibility of various community programs. A lack of community funds, trained personnel, and community awareness of the needs of adults with disabilities have also contributed to this situation. However, therapeutic recreational programs designed for special populations do exist in many locales. And more attention has been given to the need to teach leisure skill activities while in school, as well as in continuing education.

Mobility. Traveling about within one's environment provides the opportunities to develop awareness of other people and places, facilitates a sense of personal control over the environment, and is something most adults do. This aspect of community living is problematic for many adults with disabilities. In the past, public transportation systems have often been inaccessible or inefficient. With the passage of the Americans with Disabilities Act, these past oversights and discriminatory practices are now illegal.

TRENDS AND ISSUES

For adults with various forms of disability, other issues are very important. Each of these issues influences their inclusion into society and their quality of life. These are issues that all persons must address in the course of their lives.

Continuing Education

As we all are finding these days, there is a real need to be lifelong learners. Adults who have disabilities—perhaps more than nondisabled adults—require systematic efforts to assure their skills match the changing demands placed on them. As society gets technologically more complex, a great need for some form of continual updating is warranted.

Friendship

As reflected in Figure 14.1, relationships are a very important part of adulthood. They provide a sense of belonging, a feeling of being accepted, and an attitude of personal worth. A significant number of adults with disabilities are often denied opportunities to form relationships, perhaps due to their isolation or lack of appropriate interpersonal skills.

Sexuality

The areas of sexuality, marriage, and parenthood are of great concern for many adults with disabilities. These related topics can be controversial (e.g., persons who are mentally retarded as parents) or involve unique problems for individuals with physical disabilities. Nevertheless, there is a verifiable need to deal with the topic of sexuality.

Old Age

Far too little professional attention has been directed toward the needs of people with disabilities as they age. However, interest has developed concerning the needs of those who are elderly in general. We know that as people age, they naturally acquire various disabilities (e.g., visual, hearing, and other health problems). As a result, persons who were never considered disabled become so, thus having more in common with their peers with long-term disabilities.

FINAL THOUGHTS

It is clear that we must broaden our interests and professional efforts to take notice of older disabled populations. Although many persons with disabilities will not need any or possibly very few supports in adulthood, others may require more intensive and ongoing supports. If we want to maximize the probability of a successful transition from adolescence into adulthood or from school to community living, then we need to do a better job of preparing individuals with disabilities for such. To help accomplish this, we must recognize the major demands they will face as adults, appreciate the complex nature of these problems, and assure that they acquire the knowledge and skills to deal with these demands or be linked with supports and services to assist them in doing so.

SUGGESTIONS FOR WORKING WITH YOUNG CHILDREN, ADOLESCENTS, AND ADULTS WITH DISABILITIES

Children:

1. Be familiar with milestones for normal development, and focus instructional activities around the delays of the child with disabilities. Help the child enjoy and appreciate his or her strengths.
2. Don't waste time teaching unnecessary skills. Focus on those skills that the child must have to succeed in school and in his or her social world.
3. Break down learning tasks so that the child proceeds one step at a time.
4. High expectations that the child can take the next developmental step are critical to his or her willingness to try.
5. Spend some time helping parents learn teaching principles such as goal setting, breaking down tasks, and so on. Parents can then support your educational program at home.
6. Ask parents about the most time-consuming and frustrating parts of their time with the child. Help parents set up at-home programs for the areas where they would like to see their child's behavior change. Frequent problem areas are bath taking, dressing, eating, discipline, bedtime routine, and success with neighborhood children.
7. Preschool children with disabilities need a good, sound educational program where time is not wasted on nonessential learning tasks. They also need a warm, loving connection with the teacher and an abundance of affirmation.
8. Low teacher–child ratios can enhance the progress toward learning goals.

Adolescents:

1. Consider likely postsecondary settings when deciding which curricular orientation to follow.
2. Educators should be prepared to spend as much time counseling as teaching students.
3. Ensure that transitional planning occurs; involve parents as much as possible. Be sensitive to family values.
4. Know what postsecondary services and agencies exist and how they can be accessed.
5. Be perceptive of subtle "at-risk" signs (e.g., depression) that can have tragic consequences.
6. Encourage young people with disabilities to get involved in extracurricular activities.

Adults:

1. In general, be aware of the individual's life situation and personal preferences and interests.
2. Realize that exceptional persons need to be lifelong learners, and as a result, provide mechanisms for giving them the necessary skills and knowledge to deal with an ever-changing, complex society.
3. For adults with more severe disabilities, provide inclusive situations (e.g., living arrangements, work settings) where they are welcomed as contributing members.

PONDER THESE

1. Suppose you suspect that a child in your preschool group has a language deficiency. What would be the advantages and disadvantages of alerting the child's parents to this possible difficulty?
2. Read the following list of problem behaviors exhibited by a 6-year-old child with whom you work, and determine which of the behaviors you would work on first and why, and how you would go about changing these behaviors:
   Antisocial behavior (kicking, hitting, scratching, spitting on others)
   Severe language and speech disorders (poor articulation, poverty of expression)
   Lack of independent play skills (cannot play alone with toys)
   Lack of appropriate self-help skills (cannot feed herself or himself without spilling or dress herself or himself without help)
3. Consider what a "learning disability" is in a preschool youngster. How can it be manifested and identified?
4. Identify some specific concerns associated with the following areas that might put a preschool-age child at risk for future school failure:
   Medical factors
   Environmental factors
   Cultural factors
5. What are the advantages and disadvantages of each of the following program orientations as the sole thrust of a secondary-level special education curriculum?
   Academic
   Functional/life skills
   Vocational
6. What are some major life demands that are associated with the adult domains presented in Figure 14.1?
7. What are the advantages and disadvantages of technological advances for people with disabilities?
8. How would you react if you found out that a group home for adults with mental retardation was going to be established next door to your house? What concerns would you have? Are they justified?

ONLINE RESOURCES

Schiefelbusch Institute for Lifespan Studies
http://www.lsi.ku.edu

National Center for Secondary Education and Transition
http://www.ici.umn.edu/ncset

Beach Center on Disability
http://www.beachcenter.org

Council for Exceptional Children/Division on Early Childhood
http://www.dec-sped.org

Council for Exceptional Children/Division on Career Development and Transition
http://www.dcdt.org

REFERENCES

Anastasiow, N. J. (1981). Early childhood education for the handicapped in the 1980's: Recommendations. *Exceptional Children, 47,* 276–282.

Baratz, J. (1969). Linguistic and cultural factors in teaching reading to ghetto children. *Elementary English, 46,* 199–203.

Beirne-Smith, M., Patton, J. R., & Ittenbach, R. (1998). *Mental retardation* (5th ed.). Upper Saddle River, NJ: Merrill/Prentice Hall.

Bereiter, C., & Engelmann, S. (1966). *Teaching disadvantaged children in the preschool.* Upper Saddle River, NJ: Merrill/Prentice Hall.

Blackbourn, J. M. (1988). Varying preschool arrangements and self-concepts of educable mentally retarded children in first grade. *Perceptual and Motor Skills, 66,* 1013–1014.

Blackorby, J., & Wagner, M. (1996). Longitudinal postschool outcomes of youth with disabilities: Findings from the National Longitudinal Transition Study. *Exceptional Children, 62,* 399–413.

Blasco, P. M. (2001). *Early intervention services for infants, toddlers, and their families.* Needham Heights, MA: Allyn & Bacon.

Bloom, B., Davis, A., & Hess, R. (1965). *Compensatory education for cultural deprivation.* New York: Holt, Rinehart & Winston.

Bowe, F. G. (2000). *Birth to five: Early childhood special education.* Albany, NY: Delmar.

Caldwell, B. M. (1972). Consolidating our gains in early childhood. *Educational Horizons, 50,* 56–62.

Evans, E. D. (1971). *Contemporary influences in early childhood education.* New York: Holt, Rinehart & Winston.

Fleming, E. S. (1985). Career preparation. In R. H. Swassing (Ed.), *Teaching gifted children and adolescents* (pp. 340–374). Upper Saddle River, NJ: Merrill/Prentice Hall.

Foster, M., Berger, M., & McClean, M. (1981). Rethinking a good idea: A reassessment of parent involvement. *Topics in Early Childhood Special Education, 1*(3), 55–56.

Frank, A. R., & Sitlington, P. L. (2000). Young adults with mental disabilities—does transition planning make a difference? *Education and Training in Mental Retardation and Developmental Disabilities, 35,* 119–134.

Garber, H., & Heber, R. F. (1973). *The Milwaukee Project: Early intervention as a technique to prevent mental retardation* (Technical paper). Storrs: University of Connecticut.

Guralnick, M. J., Richardson, H. B., Jr., & Heiser, K. E. (1982). A curriculum in handicapping conditions for pediatric residents. *Exceptional Children, 48,* 338–346.

Halpern, A. S. (1993). Quality of life as a conceptual framework for evaluating transition outcomes. *Exceptional Children, 59,* 486–498.

Hanson, M. J., & Lynch, E. W. (1995). *Early intervention: Implementing child and family services for infants and toddlers who are at risk or disabled.* Austin, TX: PRO-ED.

Haring, N. G., & McCormick, L. (1990). *Exceptional children and youth* (5th ed.). Upper Saddle River, NJ: Merrill/Prentice Hall.

Hart, B., & Risley, T. R. (1999). *The social world of children learning to talk.* Baltimore: Paul H. Brookes.

Hayden, A. H. (1978). Special education for young children. In N. G. Haring (Ed.), *Behavior of exceptional children* (2nd. ed., pp. 29–43). Upper Saddle River, NJ: Merrill/Prentice Hall.

Hayden, A. H. (1979). Handicapped children, birth to age 3. *Exceptional Children, 45,* 510–516.

Hess, R. D., & Shipman, V. (1967). Cognitive elements in maternal behavior. In *The craft of teaching and the schooling of teachers* (pp. 57–85). Denver, CO: U.S. Office of Education, Tri-University Project.

House, E. R., Glass, G. V., McLean, L. D., & Walker, D. F. (1978). No simple answer: Critique of the Follow Through evaluation. *Harvard Educational Review, 48,* 128–160.

Howard, V. F., Williams, B. F., Port, P. D., & Lepper, C. (2001). *Very young children with special needs.* Upper Saddle River, NJ: Merrill/Prentice Hall.

Hulit, L. M., & Howard, M. R. (2002). *Born to talk: An introduction to speech and language development* (3rd ed.). Boston: Allyn & Bacon.

Kearsley, R. B. (1979). Latrogenic retardation: A syndrome of learned incompetence. In R. B. Kearsley & I. E. Sigel (Eds.), *Infants at risk: Assessment of cognitive functioning.* Hillsdale, NJ: Lawrence Erlbaum Associates.

Krajicek, M. J., Hertzberg, D. L., Sandall, S. R., & Anastasiow, N. (2003). *First start program: Handbook for the care infants, toddlers, and young children with disabilities and chronic conditions.* Austin, TX: PRO-ED.

McDaniels, G. (1977). Successful programs for young handicapped children. *Educational Horizons, 56,* 26–33.

Nagera, H. (1975). Day-care centers: Red light, green light or amber light. *The International Review of Psycho-Analysis, 2*(1), 121–137.

National Advisory Committee on the Handicapped. (1976). *Annual report.* Washington, DC: U.S. Office of Education.

Owens, R. E. (2002). *Language development: An introduction.* Boston: Allyn & Bacon.

Payne, J. S., Mercer, C. D., Payne, R. A., & Davison, R. G. (1973). *Head Start: A tragicomedy with epilogue.* New York: Behavioral Publications.

Peterson, N. L. (1987). *Early intervention for handicapped and at-risk children: An introduction to early childhood special education.* Denver, CO: Love.

Polloway, E. A., Epstein, M. H., Polloway, C. H., Patton, J. R., & Ball, D. W. (1986). Corrective Reading Program: An analysis of effectiveness with learning disabled and mildly retarded students. *Remedial and Special Education, 7*(4), 41–47.

Sandler, A., Coren, A., & Thurman, S. K. (1983). A training program for parents of handicapped preschool children: Effects upon mother, father and child. *Exceptional Children, 49,* 355–358.

Schweinhart, L. J., Berrueta-Clement, J. R., Barnett, W. S., Epstein, A. S., & Weikart, D. P. (1985). The promise of early childhood education. *Phi Delta Kappan, 66,* 548–553.

Schweinhart, L. J., & Weikart, D. P. (1985). Evidence that good early childhood programs work. *Phi Delta Kappan, 66,* 545–551.

Shearer, M., & Shearer, D. (1972). The Portage project: A model for early childhood education. *Exceptional Children, 36,* 210–217.

Sherbenou, R. J., & Holub, S. (1982). The learning disabled adolescent: Ages 12 to 15. *Topics in Learning and Learning Disabilities, 2*(3), 40–54.

Skeels, H. M. (1966). Adult status of children with contrasting early life experiences: A follow-up study. *Monographs of the Society for Research in Child Development, 31*(3), (Whole No. 105), 1–68.

Smith, T. E. C., Polloway, E. A., Patton, J. R., & Dowdy, C. A. (2004). *Teaching learners with special needs in inclusive settings* (4th ed.). Upper Saddle River, NJ: Merrill/Prentice Hall.

Smith, T. E. C., Price, B. J., & Marsh, G. E. (1986). *Mildly handicapped children and adults.* St. Paul, MN: West.

Sontag, E. (1977). Introductory speech to 1977 BEH Project Directors' Conference, Arlington, VA.

Stebbins, L. B., St. Pierre, R. G., Proper, E. C., Anderson, R. B., & Cerva, T. R. (1977). *Education as experimentation: A planned variation model, Volume IV—A, An evaluation of Follow Through.* Cambridge, MA: Abt Associates.

Trupin, L., Sebesta, D., Yelin, E., & LaPlante, M. (1997). *Trends in labor force participation among persons with disabilities.* San Francisco: University of California Disabilities Statistics, Rehabilitation Research, and Training Center/Institute for Health and Aging.

Turnbull, A. P., Summers, J. A., & Brotherson, M. J. (1984). *Working with families with disabled members: A family systems approach.* Lawrence: University of Kansas, University Affiliated Facility.

Turnbull, A. P., & Turnbull, M. R. (1986). *Families, professionals, and exceptionality: A special partnership.* Upper Saddle River, NJ: Merrill/Prentice Hall.

U.S. Department of Education. (1984). *Fifth annual report to Congress on the implementation of the Education for All Handicapped Children Act,* Washington, DC: Author.

U.S. Department of Education. (2002). *Twenty-third annual report to Congress on the implementation of the Individuals With Disabilities Education Act.* Washington, DC: Author.

Vygotsky, L. S. (1978). *Mind in society: The development of higher psychological processes.* Cambridge, MA: Harvard University.

Wehmeyer, M. L., & Patton, J. R. (2000). *Mental retardation in the 21st century.* Austin, TX: PRO-ED.

White, B. L. (1975). *The first three years.* Upper Saddle River, NJ: Prentice Hall.

Will, M. C. (1984). *OSERS programming for the transition of youth with disabilities: Bridge from school to working life.* Washington, DC: U.S. Department of Education.

Winton, P. J., & Turnbull, A. P. (1981). Parent involvement as viewed by parents of preschool handicapped children. *Topics in Early Childhood Special Education, 1*(3), 11–19.

CHAPTER 15

Parent and Family Involvement

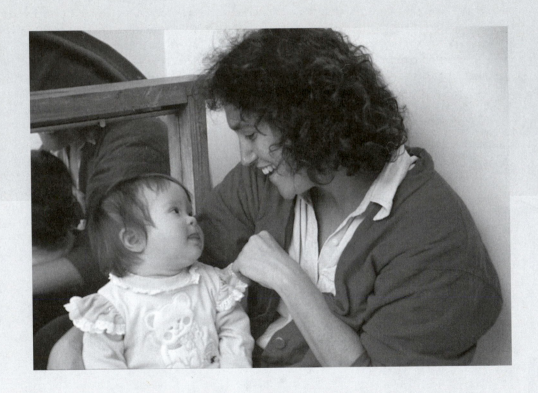

As Keasha and Tyrell looked through the window of the Neonatal Intensive Care Unit at their first-born son, they felt overwhelmed by waves of emotion. Feelings of joy, relief, anxiety, fear, grief, and confusion, to name only a few, swept over both parents. Their premature baby had made it through the night, but what lay ahead in both his immediate and distant futures? How would they care for their son, whose special needs they had only begun to learn about?

Since his birth, Lil' Ty, as he is affectionately called, and his family have utilized early intervention services to address his developmental disabilities. During his first 2 years of life, his parents worked with early interventionists to develop a routine that maximized Lil' Ty's ability to participate in family activities and become actively involved in family routines. They also worked with doctors and physical therapists to help their son develop gross and fine motor skills that were impaired as a result of his disabilities.

At age 3, Lil' Ty has just been referred to an early childhood program for 3 days a week. Keasha has rearranged her work schedule so that she will be home on the days Lil' Ty is not in school. As a result, she has agreed to work weekends. Tyrell is able to utilize flextime at his job, so for 3 days each week, he will meet Lil' Ty after school, and then return to work once Keasha arrives home in the early evening.

Tyrell and Keasha are also preparing for the birth of their next child, who is due in 2 months. Keasha's mother will have an extended stay with the family when the new baby comes home. Although both sets of grandparents have been actively involved in caregiving since Lil' Ty's birth and provide respite care whenever their schedules permit, accepting Lil' Ty's disability seems to have been particularly difficult for Tyrell's parents. They generally do not join the family on outings in public, and continue to ask questions about the nature of Lil' Ty's disabilities, as well as the opportunities for him to make developmental gains typical of "normal" toddlers.

Keasha and Tyrell have accepted the many challenges of parenting a child with disabilities. They are well informed about their son's disability and they are actively involved in implementing special services and advocating for his needs. While they acknowledge that these challenges have included financial difficulties and some marital stress, they believe that Lil' Ty was sent to them by God and that parenting him has been both inspiring and uplifting.

Parents of children with disabilities are required to fulfill a variety of roles throughout the lives of their children, including those of advocate, teacher, decision maker, collaborator, and expert (Turnbull & Turnbull, 2001). Although trying to fulfill multiple roles simultaneously can be exhausting and stressful, parents of children with special needs overwhelmingly agree that their children have impacted them in positive ways.

Great diversity in the American family has contributed to the highly variable needs, strengths, approaches, and strategies that can be described as parent and family involvement in special education. Relationships between educators and families have evolved since all children with disabilities were first entitled to a public education in 1975 with the passage of The Education of All Handicapped Children

Act (PL 94–142). Rather than consider teachers as experts who can "fix" or "treat" people with disabilities, and parents as passive "recipients" of advice and services, a more collaborative relationship between teachers and families is considered preferable and productive. Rather than separate children with disabilities by placing them in institutions away from their homes and families, inclusive and natural settings are considered healthier for families and their children. In this chapter we explore how family involvement in the special education system has evolved and what types of interventions are used to continue to move toward truly collaborative partnerships between families and school personnel.

BASIC CONCEPTS

Legal Mandates for Parent/Family Involvement

Although all parents have the right to be involved in the education of their children, the rights and responsibilities of parents of children with disabilities are more complex and demanding. Historically, parents of children with disabilities have been responsible for demanding that the education of people with disabilities be both equal to the education of children without disabilities and appropriate for the unique needs and strengths of exceptional children. Since the early 1900s, parents have created and joined organizations in support of their children with disabilities. In many cases, these organizations have become powerful political entities that have helped shape disability law and policy through lobbying, testifying as experts for congressional task forces, and grassroots organizing (Turnbull & Turnbull, 1990). Table 15.1 lists organizations in which parents of people with disabilities have historically been actively involved.

    Parent advocacy has made important contributions to the development of educational policy and practice. As a result, the Individuals with Disabilities Edu-

Table 15.1
Parent Advocacy Organizations

Organization Name	Year Founded	Focus
The Arc	1950	Educational rights, parent support
Autism Society of America	1965	Autism spectrum disorders, disability rights and legislation
The Beach Center on Families and Disabilities	1987	Research and policy related to families and disability
Closing the Gap	1983	Technology in special education, parent support
Federation of Families for Children's Mental Health		Emotional and behavioral disorders, educational rights, and family advocacy
Parent Advocacy Coalition for Educational Rights (PACER Center)	1977	Educational rights, parent support

cation Act (IDEA) of 1997, the key piece of disability and education legislation, contains numerous mandates for parent participation and parental rights. In fact, in the preface of the legislation, the importance of parent involvement in implementing effective special education programs is underscored:

> *Over 20 years of research and experience has demonstrated that the education of students with disabilities can be made more effective by . . . strengthening the role of parents and ensuring that families . . . have meaningful opportunities to participate in the education of their children at school and at home.* (p. 5)

Specifically, IDEA mandates the involvement of parents in every aspect of decision making during the special education process. Table 15.2 contains provisions stipulated in IDEA, which highlight parent participation during the special education process. The most common type of parent participation has been collaboration on individualized education plan (IEP) development (Smith, Polloway, Patton, & Dowdy, 2004).

Clearly, IDEA, the major guiding legislation for special education, is designed to facilitate the involvement of parents in the education of their children with dis-

Table 15.2
Provisions for Parent Involvement in IDEA 1997*

Special Education Process	Legislative Safeguard/Regulation
Referral for assessment and admittance into special education programs	School must inform parents (in their native languages) of any intent to conduct assessment or to admit a student to special education programs.
Development of the individualized education plan (IEP)	School must invite parents to participate and include parents in IEP meetings; school must consider parent input in plan development.
Sharing information	School must provide interpreters or translators as necessary; copies of paperwork must be in parents' native language whenever possible and must be supplied by school for parents.
Due process	Parents must be given written (in native language) information regarding their rights and the educational rights of their children; school must also include information about grievance procedures and mediation in cases of disputes.
Annual progress updates	School must provide parents with annual reports on the progress of individualized educational goals and present levels of functioning.
Access to special education records	Parents must be given access to all records including assessment results, educational placement decisions, and any special education paperwork.

*Full text of the IDEA 1997 law and regulations can be found at the U.S. Department of Education, Office of Special Education and Rehabilitative Services Web site, http://www.ideapractices.org/law/index.php

abilities. The law also acts as an important safeguard for parental rights. Embedded in this legislation, however, are culturally relative values and beliefs about disability and parental roles in the education system. For example, the idea that parents have the right to seek services for their children with disabilities and collaborate with educators to design an IEP is not a universally held belief. In particular, parents from culturally and linguistically diverse backgrounds may find this surprising and challenging (Kalyanpur & Harry, 1999). Parents are probably the greatest experts on the unique needs and strengths of their children, so including them as active decision makers is prudent; however, educators must realize that parent approaches to the roles of advocate and collaborator will likely vary as much as the parents themselves do.

Contemporary Definitions of Family

The composition of families served by the U.S. educational system can best be described as diverse. Families can no longer be described as traditional, two-parent households (Smith et al., 2001). According to data from the most recent census, single-parent households (headed by either a father or a mother, with the latter over three times as common) represent almost 15 percent of the number of total families. Additionally, grandparents and other extended family members continue to play key roles in child rearing, particularly in culturally and linguistically diverse families. In households in which grandparents were living with their grandchildren, 42 percent reported that they were the caregivers of those children (U.S. Census Bureau, 2000).

Other major changes in the structure of the American family involve women as members of the full-time workforce. Many children who do live with both parents experience daycare settings, care from siblings and other family members, and/or self-care and monitoring because both parents are employed outside the home. For children 6 years old and younger, 58 percent live in households where both parents are a part of the workforce (U.S. Census Bureau, 2000).

Another way the composite view of the American family has been changing is representative of the changing racial and ethnic diversity of the general population. The racial/ethnic identities of the school-aged population, as well as the linguistic backgrounds of students, continue to shift away from any homogeneous grouping. Whereas European American students have historically represented a majority of the school-aged population, this is rapidly changing. Figure 15.1 shows a breakdown of the U.S. school-aged population by race and ethnicity. In many urban areas, diverse students comprise the majority of the study body (Thorp, 1997). Some predict the national percentage of school-age population from racially/ethnically and linguistically diverse families will reach almost 50 percent by the first quarter of this century (Wolfe, Boone, & Barrera, 1997).

Diversity, whether defined in terms of race/ethnicity, family composition, or other variables that contribute to cultural identity such as economic status, native language, and/or religious beliefs, provides opportunities for educators to broaden

Figure 15.1
U.S. School-Aged Population by Race
and Ethnicity

Source: From *Racial/Ethnic Distribution of
Public School Students,* by National Center for
Education Statistics, 1999. Retrieved February
22, 2002, from http://nces.ed.gov/programs/
coe/2001/section1/tables/t03_1.html

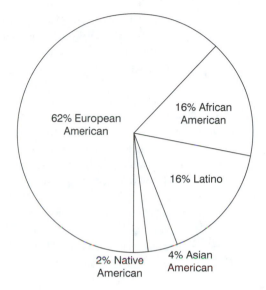

62% European American

16% African American

16% Latino

2% Native American

4% Asian American

their views of U.S. society and hone collaboration skills. Cross-cultural collaboration can be both challenging and rewarding for teachers.

For families, however, cross-cultural collaboration initiated by teachers can range from devastatingly negative to exuberantly successful, depending in part on the skill level of the professionals. Teachers, many of whom are European American (87 percent), are members of the dominant group in U.S. society and have enjoyed the power and privilege that often accompany membership in this group. Even for teachers of color, or teachers who have personally experienced life circumstances such as poverty or disability, the challenges of school have been met with success; otherwise they would not be in positions of leadership in the educational system (Kalyanpur & Harry, 1999). Therefore, teachers must accept and meet the challenges and rewards of cross-cultural collaboration if partnerships with parents are the most effective way to address the unique strengths and needs of children in special education.

Family Systems as a Conceptual Framework

Diversity of family structures and cultural characteristics are but two ways in which families may vary. Various sociological theories have been developed to explain both the functions and the interactions of families within a larger, societal context. Of these theories, one that has been merged with special education theory and is particularly useful when considering how disability can impact families is the family systems conceptual framework (Turnbull & Turnbull, 1990).

In this conceptual framework, four major components of family (characteristics, interaction, function, and life cycle) are constantly influencing one another, creating dynamic possibilities for family members' strengths and needs (Turnbull & Turnbull, 1990). Characteristics (e.g., details of disability, family structure, personal characteristics) are constantly influencing, and being influenced by, interactions among members (e.g., marital relationships, sibling relationships). These interactions are similarly interacting with functions (e.g., economic, affection, socialization). The life cycle of the family, then, is a force representative of change and the propensity for both characteristics and function to change over time.

The usefulness of this theory is to demonstrate that disability has tremendous potential (both positive and negative) to impact identifying characteristics of family, which will unavoidably impact family involvement in the educational system. To illustrate this concept, consider Keasha and Tyrell's family, described in the opening vignette. Their own family characteristics include having a son with developmental disabilities, maintaining a two-parent household, and having a strong religious orientation. Each of these characteristics (and many more) will influence and be influenced by their family interactions. For example, they are about to add a sibling to their family unit, which will influence their family structure.

Similarly, the family structure will influence the adaptability of the family to parent (family interaction) two children instead of one as the maternal grandmother joins the family. These interactions will impact and be impacted by the family's function to provide, among other necessities, economic support. Lil' Ty's care is expensive and likely influenced Keasha and Tyrell's decision to each maintain full-time employment. Of course, rearranging their work schedules to meet the function of economic support means that Keasha and Tyrell will not be able to spend much time together, which will likely impact their marital relationship. Over time, the family will develop and change according to the demands of different stages of life. As Lil' Ty becomes an adult, Keasha and Tyrell will have to adjust to meet the needs of an adolescent with disabilities. Additionally their life experiences as parents of a child with a disability may impact their family characteristics. Perhaps their experiences with Lil' Ty will prompt them to strengthen (or weaken) their religious identity.

The family systems conceptual framework illuminates the recursive nature of the four components of family. For teachers, it illustrates the idea that families have changing strengths, needs, and strategies. As these are identified, appropriate resources can be accessed to help the family meet its greatest challenges. Of course, teachers will have limited access to information on the four components, but a strong home–school partnership can contribute to teachers' knowledge of families' unique needs.

INTERVENTIONS

While collaborative relationships between families and special education professionals is mandated by law and considered sound practice, this has not always been the case. In fact, the transition from passive involvement to full partnership continues into the present. For several reasons, collaboration is considered ideal (Whemeyer, Morningstar, & Husted, 1999). First, parents and families have high stakes in the outcomes of their children with disabilities; interaction among family members will occur even after children with disabilities reach adulthood and exit the U.S. education system. Second, parent involvement has been associated with improvements in both student and school performance. Last, parents have important knowledge about their children and their own expectations of them, which serves to inform special educators regarding the appropriateness of selected interventions.

Early Parent–School Relationships

Early efforts to understand and treat disability resulted in attempts by experts (i.e., doctors and teachers) to determine the cause of the disability and the type of intervention that should be used to "treat" the person, following approaches similar to ones used in the field of medicine. In fact, special education is considered to be based, in part, on the medical model (Kalyanpur & Harry, 1999; Wehmeyer et al., 1990). Historically, parents have been blamed for the presence of disability in their children (Turnbull & Turnbull, 2001). Determinations by professionals that disabilities were caused by poor parenting or maladaptive behaviors have generally been unfounded and erroneous (Turnbull & Turnbull, 2001). For example, the cause of autism was first conceived as the result of cold and uncaring parenting styles of mothers who suffered from emotional problems. Dubbed "refrigerator mothers," women who had children diagnosed with autism in the 1940s and 1950s were squarely blamed for the disabilities of their children. Current research on autism has demonstrated that this is untrue (see chapter 7 for a full discussion of autism).

While it is true that the study of the etiologies of disabilities may lead to prevention and/or treatment, information of this nature provides only limited applicability in the development of interventions. For example, researchers have determined that consumption of alcohol during pregnancy can cause mental retardation and other disabilities associated with fetal alcohol syndrome. Yet, educators must devote much time and effort working with children with this and other disabilities to help them achieve academic success rather than focusing on the contributing factors that led to the disability.

This is not to say that the study of the causes of disabilities is not important. Certainly prevention of disabilities relies on etiological studies. The key point here is that knowing the cause of a disability, no matter how directly related to parental behavior or genetic predisposition, is not the most important knowledge for teachers in their implementation of interventions. Educators must learn to avoid blaming parents for the disabilities of their children. Even when parental behavior may have contributed to the disability, blaming parents will only inhibit a collaborative relationship, without which intervention is less likely to be successful (Turnbull & Turnbull, 2001).

Two Steps Forward, One Step Back

Many teachers do understand the importance of strong collaborative relationships with parents. In an effort to comply with federal legislation such as IDEA 1997, teachers must keep parents informed and encourage their participation in any decision-making activities. Utilizing a variety of home–school communication strategies (e.g., weekly reports and communication notebooks) is one way that teachers attempt to reach out and encourage parents to express their expectations, needs, and perspectives on the progress of their children with special needs. Adherence to procedural safeguards (some of which were listed earlier in Table 15.2) is another way special education teachers manage to uphold legislative requirements. Unfortunately, sometimes the letter of the law, rather than the spirit behind it, is upheld more carefully.

Parents and teachers may have misconceptions about one another that inhibit collaboration (Cutler, 1993). For example, parents may think of teachers as the experts, while teachers may think of parents as people who lack experience in the education system. Also, teachers may deem parents too emotionally attached to make good decisions, while parents may believe that teachers are unsympathetic.

Teachers have a professional duty to sharpen their own abilities to collaborate with families, as well as to provide opportunities for families to actively participate in the special education process. To do this, teachers must develop an understanding for the complex interactions between family characteristics and contextual variables of the larger society (Bauer, 2003; Turnbull & Turnbull, 2001). From a broad perspective, the experiences and contexts of the macroculture (e.g., societal mores, laws, and accepted practices) will influence familial responses to the education of their children. Additionally, family characteristics (e.g., composition of family members, language dominance, economic status) will interact with the larger, societal (i.e., macro) context to produce unique needs and strengths to which educators must respond. For example, teachers who work with children of migrant workers may need to access translations of special education paperwork in languages commonly spoken by these groups, but they also need to understand the literacy level of the individuals with whom they will be working, in case oral translations are required.

Moving Toward Truly Collaborative Partnerships

Building collaborative partnerships is neither easy nor simplistic. Yet, such relationships, once established, can be proactive and help limit misunderstandings and frustrations experienced by both parents and teachers. More importantly, such relationships can positively impact the educational experiences of students with disabilities.

An essential element of strong and productive collaborative relationships is effective communication. Both parents and teachers have to be effective listeners as well as speakers. Teachers can facilitate positive and effective communication by preparing essential information prior to any parent contact, using clear language that is jargon free, actively listening to parents, and offering realistic options rather than giving advice (Bauer, 2003). These guidelines can be applied to a variety of forms of communication, whether they are formal (e.g., IEP meeting) or informal (e.g., brief contact in the community). Providing good news and reports of accomplishments is equally important to providing progress reports in which challenges or difficulties are acknowledged (Smith et al., 2004).

While communication is important, collaboration involves much more than that. Turnbull and Turnbull (2001) have listed seven broad categories of opportunities in which teachers can and should collaborate with families. Both regular and special education teachers can maximize the opportunity for collaboration during each of these activities:

1. Communicating with families (includes general communication efforts directed at the entire class, e.g., parent newsletters; and specific communication addressing one family, e.g., telephone or face-to-face regarding unique situations)
2. Helping families meet basic needs (includes facilitating access to social supports and information)
3. Beginning the special education process (includes decision making during the referral and assessment process)
4. Delivering special education services (includes developing and implementing IEPs)
5. Linking school learning environments to home and community (includes involving family and community members in problem solving and extended learning opportunities for students)
6. Inviting parent involvement in school activities (includes encouraging parents and other family members to attend and actively participate in both academic and extracurricular activities)
7. Advocating for educational change (includes working together for school improvement and educational reform)

Considering the great diversity of family strengths, needs, and characteristics, the importance of participating in each of the above collaborative activities with the greatest attention to cross-cultural sensitivity cannot be overstated. Cultural identities of both teachers and students and their families are shaped by their affiliations with groups of people who share rules, traditions, beliefs, values, and goals (Kalyanpur & Harry, 1999). Because people rarely, if ever, belong to just one group, cross-cultural interactions can be exceedingly complex.

Teachers must learn to be *culturally responsive,* that is, they must be aware of their own values, the values of the families they serve, and the significant ways in which these are either consistent or conflicting. Kalyanpur and Harry (1999) outline four steps educators should follow in an effort to maintain what they call "a posture of cultural reciprocity":

1. *Values identification:*   What values are embedded in the professional perspective? In other words, why do teachers interpret the child's behavior as problematic? What, in the view of school personnel, has led to special education recommendations?
2. *Family perspective identification:*   Do the parents/family members agree with the perspectives of school personnel? Do both parties share the same underlying values? If not, what are the perspectives of the family?

Table 15.3
An Example of the Application of Cultural Reciprocity

Scenario: Daniel, a 16-year-old European American male, has autism. He is enrolled in all regular education classes except English and is expected to graduate with a standard diploma. His mother is a 59-year-old secretary with a high school education. His stepfather, 70, is retired from the U.S. military. During a transition planning meeting, the special education teacher plans to facilitate the development of a plan for Daniel's postsecondary living arrangements, in addition to other transition issues.

What beliefs and values do the teachers/school hold?	In preparation for the meeting, Daniel's teacher considers the following questions: *Is it preferable for Daniel to live independently? Why do I favor a group-home arrangement over his continued living at home with his parents? What values underlie the idea that individuals should live independently once they reach adulthood? Will Daniel actually benefit from one setting more than the other?*
What beliefs and values does the family hold?	Daniel's teacher reflects on what she knows about the family's perspectives of this issue, as well as what she needs to know: *Daniel's mother has stated that she and his stepfather expect their son to continue living at home after graduation. What are Daniel's parents' reasons for wanting their son to stay at home? What are Daniel's preferences? How will the family (including Daniel) likely react to the idea of a group-home living arrangement?*
How can the teacher directly communicate the beliefs and values?	The teacher prepares to provide information about alternatives and to explain her perspective on this subject: *Pamphlets on the group home and contact information for the manager of the home will be provided. The rationale will be explained: The benefits to such a setting include the independent living skills the home will address, the possibility that in the distant future Daniel may be on his own if and when his parents are unable to care for him, and the importance of Daniel to become self-determining.*
Where/what are the opportunities for discussion and collaboration?	During the meeting, the teacher makes efforts to involve the family in active participation in transition planning: *Ample opportunity and time for both Daniel and his parents to share their thoughts about postsecondary living arrangements is provided. The teacher then provides her own perspective, but presents it in the context of an additional option the family should consider. She offers to provide a personal contact to the manager of the group home, if the family chooses to investigate this option. In addition, she offers to help Daniel's family become connected with other families who have considered this same topic to gain the perspectives of people with similar experiences. She acknowledges that, ultimately, the decision is up to Daniel and his parents.*

Source: Questions used in example are adapted from *Building Cultural Reciprocity with Families,* by B. Harry, M. Kalyanpur, and M. Day, 1999, Baltimore: Paul H. Brookes.

3. *Explicit recognition:*   If differences exist, what cultural assumptions are embedded in the perspectives held by the school? These must be explicitly discussed with parents.
4. *Discussion and collaboration:*   What solutions can be reached that are acceptable to both parents and teachers? How can both belief systems be respected? Ultimately, how can the school support the belief system of the family and the most appropriate educational plan for the student?

Maintaining a posture of cultural reciprocity is complex and requires a keen sense of self-awareness, sharp communication skills, and practice. Many teachers may identify with the embedded values and assumptions pervasive throughout the educational system, and therefore have difficulty implementing cultural reciprocity. To help illustrate this process, an example of the implementation of cultural reciprocity is presented in Table 15.3.

Increasing teachers' collaborative skills is a current focus of special education research and practice. The two interventions mentioned herein are examples of the current direction of these efforts. Notice that these interventions are quite compatible. Each necessitates that teachers' think critically about decisions regarding the educational planning for students with disabilities and earnestly attempt to make decisions *with* families rather than *for* families.

FINAL THOUGHTS

While the mind-set regarding parents and families of children with disabilities has come a long way from the days in which blaming parents and separating families through institutionalization was acceptable, we are still trying to reach the goal of active collaboration. As teachers are trained to become better collaborators, the active involvement of parents as decision makers, interventionists, and advocates should increase. The realization that families are diverse and, as such, have unique strengths, needs, and strategies that contribute to their "brand" of collaboration, can only strengthen teachers' ability to work with families to achieve the most appropriate educational plan for each individual in special education.

PONDER THESE

1. In the opening vignette, Keasha and Tyrell are getting ready to enroll Lil' Ty in an early childhood classroom. If you were going to be Lil' Ty's teacher, how would you use the family systems framework to determine the family's current strengths and needs?

2. How can teachers balance their role as "expert" and their role as "collaborator"?
3. Think of one barrier to effective collaboration not mentioned in this chapter. Now brainstorm two possible solutions to this problem.

ONLINE RESOURCES

Each of the Web sites listed here provides a large variety of information resources about disability, support, education, legislation, and a variety of other topics related to parents and family involvement in special education.

The Beach Center on Families and Disabilities
http://www.beachcenter.org

Family Village
http://www.familyvillage.wisc.edu/index.htmlx

Loving Your Disabled Child
http://www.lydc.org

National Information Center for Children and Youth with Disabilities
http://www.nichy.org

Parent Advocacy Coalition for Educational Rights
http://www.pacer.org/index.htm

Parent to Parent
http://www.parenttoparent.com/wecounttoo.html

REFERENCES

Bauer, A. M. (2003). *Parents and schools: Creating a successful partnership for students with special needs.* Upper Saddle River, NJ: Merrill/Prentice Hall.

Cutler, B. C. (1993). *You, your child, and special education.* Baltimore: Paul H. Brookes.

Harry, B., Kalyanpur, M., & Day, M. (1999). *Building cultural reciprocity with families.* Baltimore: Paul H. Brookes.

Kalyanpur, M., & Harry, B. (1999). *Culture in special education.* Baltimore: Paul H. Brookes.

National Center for Education Statistics. (1999). Racial/ethnic distribution of public school students. Retrieved February 22, 2002, from http://nces.ed.gov/programs/coe/2001/section1/tables/t03_1.html

Smith, T. E. C., Polloway, E. A., Patton, J. R., & Dowdy, C. A. (2001). *Teaching students with special needs in inclusive settings* (3rd ed.). Boston: Allyn & Bacon.

Thorp, E. K. (1997). Increasing opportunities for partnership with culturally and linguistically diverse families. *Intervention in School and Clinic, 32,* 261–269.

Turnbull, A. P., & Turnbull, H. R. (1990). *Families, professionals and exceptionality: A special partnership* (2nd ed.). Upper Saddle River, NJ: Merrill/Prentice Hall.

Turnbull, A. R., & Turnbull, H. R. (2001). *Families, professionals and exceptionality: Collaborating for empowerment* (4th ed.). Upper Saddle River, NJ: Merrill/Prentice Hall.

U.S. Census Bureau. (2000). P34. Family type by presence and age of own children. Retrieved November 15, 2002, from http://factfinder.census.gov/servlet/DTTable?ds_name=D&geo_id=D&mt_name=DEC_2000_SF1_U_P034&_lang=en

Wehmeyer, M. L., Morningstar, M., & Husted, D. (1999). *Family involvement in transition planning and implementation.* Austin, TX: PRO-ED.

Wolfe, P. S., Boone, R. S., & Barrera, M. (1997). Developing culturally sensitive transition plans: A reflective process. *The Journal for Vocational Special Needs Education, 30*(1), 30–33.

Index